Planning the Unthinkable

A volume in the series

CORNELL STUDIES IN SECURITY AFFAIRS

edited by Robert J. Art, Robert Jervis, and Stephen M. Walt

A full list of titles in the series appears at the end of the book.

Planning the Unthinkable

HOW NEW POWERS WILL USE NUCLEAR, BIOLOGICAL, AND CHEMICAL WEAPONS

Peter R. Lavoy, Scott D. Sagan, *and* James J. Wirtz

Cornell University Press

ITHACA AND LONDON

BPF 8684 - 2/2

First published 2000 by Cornell University Press

Printed in the United States of America

Library of Congress Cataloging-in-Publication Data

Planning the unthinkable: how new powers will use nuclear, biological, and chemical
weapons / edited by Peter R. Lavoy, Scott D. Sagan, and James J. Wirtz.
     p. cm.—(Cornell studies in security affairs)
   Includes index.
   ISBN 0-8014-3776-8 (cloth)—ISBN 0-8014-8704-8 (pbk.)
   1. Weapons of mass destruction.   2. World politics—21st century.   I. Lavoy, Peter R.
(Peter René), 1961–   II. Sagan, Scott Douglas.   III. Wirtz, James J., 1958–
U793 .P53 2000
358'.3—dc21

                                   00-037678

Cloth printing   10 9 8 7 6 5 4 3 2 1

Paperback printing   10 9 8 7 6 5 4 3 2 1

Contents

Acknowledgments

This book could not have been written without the strong commitment of the individual case study authors. They wrote and then repeatedly revised their chapters with patience and grace. Our first word of thanks therefore goes to them for seeing this ambitious project to its completion.

We also thank the individuals, organizations, and foundations that provided financial support. The Carnegie Corporation of New York and the Smith Richardson Foundation supported the project through Stanford University's Center for International Security and Cooperation. Our work at the Naval Postgraduate School was kindly funded by a number of organizations and we thank Catherine Montie at the Defense Threat Reduction Agency, Thomas Skrobala at the Naval Treaty Implementation Program, Jim Smith, Peter Hays, and Jeffrey Larsen at the USAF Institute of National Security Studies, Kevin Farrell at the Naval Information Warfare Activity, Samuel Perez of the Navy Theater Air Defense Program, and William Potter and the Center for Nonproliferation Studies at the Monterey Institute of International Studies. Of course, this book does not reflect the institutional positions adopted by any of our sponsors or official U.S. policy.

Two conferences were key in the development of the project. The first was a large plenary session, "WMD Use Concepts and Command and Control Practices," held in Monterey in August 1997. We are grateful to those who contributed to the initial vetting of our ideas: Michael Altfeld, Kathleen Bailey, Ken Campbell, Seth Carus, Frank Dellermann, Vladimir Dvorkin, Peter Feaver, Benjamin Frankel, David Holloway, Harlan Jencks,

Acknowledgments

James Lamson, Alexander Leontenkov, John Lepingwell, Boris Mikhailov, James Clay Moltz, Maria Moyano-Rasmussen, Congressman John P. Murtha, Vladimir Petoukhov, Tariq Rauf, Tom Reed, Glenn Robinson, Boris Uchenik, Gleb Vasiliev, Valery Yarynich, and Zou Yunhua. The second event was an authors' workshop held at Stanford University in January 1998. We thank Barton Bernstein, Peter Hays, Neil Joeck, Zue Litai, Ashley Tellis, Andrew Terrill, and Dean Wilkening, for their comments on our work. We especially thank Marjorie Kiewit for a gift that supported this workshop. We also express our special gratitude to our friends Bates Gill of the Brookings Institution and Michael Wheeler of Science Application International Corporation for their participation in both of these meetings and for contributions to the development of our ideas.

We owe a special debt to Elizabeth Skinner, who helped to edit the manuscript by fixing all too frequent breakdowns in our prose, standardizing footnotes, and catching failures of logic and evidence that would have caused us much embarrassment. Libby also managed the large volume of correspondence produced by the effort to edit multiple drafts of manuscript and helped us run both conferences. Without Libby's efforts, this book would have taken much longer to complete.

All three of us thank our wives, Debra, Bao, and Janet, for tolerating home offices forever littered with manuscript pages. They accepted that we too often would be distracted from better pursuits by our efforts to get the book done. We dedicate this book, with love, to them.

Planning the Unthinka

Introduction

James J. Wirtz

The dawn of the twenty-first century has been accompanied by growing fears about the use of nuclear, chemical, and biological weapons. Numerous alarming events in the late 1990s fanned these fears. In May 1998, both India and Pakistan conducted a series of nuclear test explosions, and in the spring of 1999, armed forces from these nuclear powers battled in the mountains of Kashmir. In December 1998, the United Nations Special Commission on Iraq (UNSCOM) was forced to leave the country, abruptly ending its effort to monitor and destroy Saddam Hussein's chemical, biological, and nuclear weapons programs and prompting repeated American and British air strikes against Iraq. Serious concerns also emerged concerning whether North Korea would renege on its commitments under the 1994 *Agreed Framework* to stop its nuclear weapons program, concerns that were heightened when the North Koreans shot a space-launch rocket that passed directly over Japan in August 1998. The Aum Shinrikyo cult's 1995 sarin gas attack on a Tokyo subway, which killed twelve Japanese citizens and injured six thousand more, raised the specter of a new form of terrorism. In August 1998, the United States tried to ensure that such an attack would not be repeated by others and launched a cruise missile strike against a pharmaceutical plant in the Sudan that Washington officials alleged was producing chemical weapons materials for terrorist groups financed by Osama Bin Laden.

The new century thus began with a looming sense of danger. Proliferation of nuclear, chemical, and biological weapons has become a fixture on the strategic landscape. The crises of the late 1990s are warning signals of more dangerous crises brewing just over the horizon.

This book examines how new powers will use the chemical, biological, and nuclear weapons that they have developed or are trying to acquire. Many books and articles examine why states have developed nuclear, chemical, and biological weapons.[1] This volume, however, looks toward the future, examining the evolving military doctrines and command systems of the states and nonstate groups that have such weapons. It addresses how the leaders of new proliferators think about the use of this weaponry and how they ensure that the weapons will be used when, but only when, they decide they should be used.

Scholars who seek to explain why states acquire chemical, biological, or nuclear weapons and those who devise new nonproliferation policies often fail to address these fundamental questions because they are reluctant to recognize that new weapons programs may be faits accomplis. The normative objectives guiding their efforts would suffer a serious blow if they accepted that nuclear, chemical, or biological capabilities are integrated into military plans and organizations. The international community also has constructed global regimes such as the Non-Proliferation Treaty (NPT), the Biological Weapons Convention (BWC), the Chemical Weapons Convention (CWC), and the Missile Technology Control Regime (MTCR) to stem the proliferation of these weapons and associated hardware. Supporters of these institutions, too, are loath to draw attention to states or groups that possess weapons in violation of international norms and conventions. Recognizing cases of proliferation, they fear, might weaken the existing nonproliferation regimes.

The authors of this book understand these concerns. Yet we also believe that scholars and policymakers must base their analyses and decisions on the most accurate information available about what new proliferators actually think about the possible uses of the weapons they have developed. We therefore intend to lift the curtain that hangs in front of the states and terrorist groups that have developed or are seeking to acquire chemical, biological, and nuclear weapons. These leaders are "thinking the unthinkable": How should these new weapons be used in diplomacy and war? This book examines emerging evidence about this thinking and the resulting war plans and command and control systems that are being developed by new proliferators.

---

1. The causes of proliferation are discussed in Scott D. Sagan, "Why Do States Build Nuclear Weapons: Three Models in Search of a Bomb," *International Security* 21 (Winter 1996): 54–86; U.S. Congress, Office of Technology Assessment, *Proliferation of Weapons of Mass Destruction: Assessing the Risks*, OTA-ISC-559 (Washington, D.C.: U.S. Government Printing Office, 1993); Bradley A. Thayer, "The Causes of Nuclear Proliferation and the Utility of the Nuclear Nonproliferation Regime," *Security Studies* 4 (Spring 1995): 463–519; Jonathan Tucker, "Motivations for Biological Weapons Proliferation: Examining Proliferators and Nonproliferators in North Africa and the Middle East," in *Biological Warfare*, ed. Raymond Zilinskas, (Boulder: Lynne Rienner, 1999); and Mitchell Reiss, *Bridled Ambition: Why Countries Constrain Their Nuclear Capabilities* (Washington, D.C.: Woodrow Wilson Center Press, 1995).

Introduction

Our case study authors seek to answer a series of questions about new states and terrorist organizations that possess unconventional weapons. How do state and nonstate actors integrate these weapons into their military force structures, delivery systems, command and control procedures, and war plans? In other words, how do they transform dual-use technology or experimental devices into usable weapons integrated into operational forces and plans? What doctrines do they embrace to guide the use of unconventional weapons, and how do they maintain command and control over them? Additionally, what does the behavior of these states and groups say about the utility of theories developed to explain the evolution of military doctrine and command and control procedures? These questions must be answered if we are to understand the future impact of nuclear, chemical, and biological weapons on international politics.

UNCONVENTIONAL WEAPONS: A PRIMER

A thorough description of the production and lethality of biological, chemical, and nuclear weapons would involve chemistry, biology, human physiology, nuclear physics, metallurgy, and meteorology, not to mention mechanical, material, genetic, electrical, and chemical engineering. This brief analysis, however, focuses on the key factors that influence the ease with which these weapons can be produced and their potential for causing mass casualties.[2] The central point is that the three kinds of weapons differ in important ways with respect to both production and lethality. In general, chemical weapons are the easiest to make but are unlikely to produce the cataclysmic levels of destruction that could result from the use of biological or nuclear weapons. By contrast, nuclear weapons are the most difficult to produce but also the most destructive both in lethality and in the speed by which death and destruction could occur. Biological weapons share the most frightening aspects of each of the other two: biological weapons can be made almost as easily as chemical weapons, yet their destructive potential could approach that of nuclear weapons.

Chemical Weapons

Chemical weapons use toxic agents to incapacitate or kill people. The technology needed to make such weapons is widely spread throughout the

---

2. This section is based on *The Biological and Chemical Warfare Threat* (Washington, D.C.: U.S. Government Printing Office, 1999); *The Effects of Nuclear War* (Washington, D.C.: U.S. Congress, Office of Technology Assessment, 1979); Richard K. Betts, "The New Threat of Mass Destruction," *Foreign Affairs* 77 (January–February 1998): 26–41; and Chuck Hansen, *U.S. Nuclear Weapons: The Secret History* (New York: Orion Books, 1988).

world because it is used in basic pharmaceutical and industrial production. Chemical weapons can differ in lethality, mode of action (how they enter the body), speed of action (the period between exposure and observed effect), persistency (the amount of time an agent remains dangerous once released into the environment), and state (solid, liquid, or gas). Chemical weapons also vary greatly in their toxicity, the amount of substance needed to achieve a given effect against a target population. At one extreme, about 3000 milligrams of the choking agent phosgene per cubic meter of air will kill 50 percent of the people exposed. Only about 70 milligrams of the nerve agent sarin, however, are needed to generate the same fatality rate. At the other extreme, only 10 milligrams of the nerve agent VX are needed to kill the average adult.

Chlorine gas and mustard gas were widely used during World War I. Chlorine is one of the oldest chemical weapons, a *choking agent* that destroys the respiratory system of victims. *Blood agents* (such as hydrogen cyanide) harm their victims by preventing normal use of oxygen, thereby rapidly damaging body tissues. *Blistering agents* (such as mustard gas) are used to cause casualties by burning exposed eyes, lungs, and skin. On exposure, most blistering agents cause little pain, which in part explains why they can inflict large numbers of casualties among unsuspecting people or soldiers.

"G-series" *nerve agents* were discovered in the 1930s by German scientists experimenting with pesticides. Taubun, sarin, and soman inhibit the action of enzymes in the body that are critical to the function of the human nervous system. Nerve agents act rapidly, can be absorbed through the skin, and generally kill by causing paralysis of the respiratory system. More advanced "V-series" nerve agents (VE, VG, VS, and VX) were developed in the 1950s. They are more toxic and persistent than G-series agents and can be used to contaminate territory for extended periods.

The older chemical weapons are easy to produce and use ingredients that have widespread commercial application. Even the G and V series agents, however, are similar to pesticides that are commercially available. The Chemical Weapons Convention has been signed and ratified by 123 countries pledging not to develop, produce, acquire, retain, stockpile, transfer, or use chemical weapons. North Korea and Iraq, however, have not signed the CWC. Iran is known to have used chemical weapons in the 1980s against Iraqi troops and is suspected of having ignored its current commitment to the CWC by maintaining a significant chemical arsenal.

Biological Weapons

Biological weapons use pathogens (bacteria, viruses, and fungi) and toxins (poisonous compounds) to cause disease in humans. Because these

Introduction

weapons use living germs or proteins, rather than chemicals, they inherently possess more lethal potential: germs can self-amplify, spread throughout a population, and mutate to form even more virulent disease. Advances in biotechnology also raise the possibility that known pathogens and toxins might be altered to increase their utility as biological weapons. Antibiotic-resistant bacteria, vaccine-resistant viruses, and pathogens genetically engineered to facilitate human infection are all theoretically possible.

Primitive biological weapons have been used many times in the history of warfare. Tartar armies in the fourteenth century catapulted cadavers infected with the plague into enemy cities; British troops distributed smallpox-infected blankets to Native American tribes in the Ohio Valley in the eighteenth century; and the Japanese released millions of plague-infected fleas from aircraft over Chinese cities during World War II.[3] What is new about the problem today is the development of novel and more lethal pathogens and the ability of increasing numbers of states and nonstate groups to develop such weapons.

The way biological agents are disseminated is an important factor in determining their lethality. The manner in which agents enter the body also affects how much agent is needed and the size of the agent particle required to cause infection. Weather can affect the concentration of biological agents once they are dispersed into the atmosphere as aerosols, and exposure to the environment can degrade their ability to cause infection. The difficulty of controlling the spread of highly infectious diseases once they take hold in a population was traditionally believed to limit the military utility of biological weapons. If states or terrorists want to spread such diseases throughout a population, however, such problems of control could be seen as an attraction of, rather than a constraint on, use of biological weapons.

No specialized facilities are required for the production of many biological agents. Equipment associated with manufacturing legitimate vaccines and pharmaceuticals or even brewing beer at home can be used to make lethal agents. The scale of production efforts, not the presence of containment facilities or fermenters for growing microorganisms, probably provides the best indication that a country is accumulating biological weapons, although over time a laboratory or pilot-scale infrastructure could produce enough agent for use as a weapon. The materials and technical skills needed to start a biological weapons program also are readily available and inexpensive. Organisms ready for culture are commercially available. The Biological Weapons Convention was signed by 141 countries pledging not

3. See George W. Chistopher, Theodore J. Cieslak, Julie A. Pavlin, and Edward M. Eitzen, "Biological Warfare: A Historical Perspective," in *Biological Weapons: Limiting the Threat*, ed. Joshua Lederberg (Cambridge, Mass.: MIT Press, 1999), 17–35.

to develop, produce, stockpile, or acquire biological agents not intended for peaceful purposes. Iraq and Russia, however, have admitted that they developed biological weapons in the past despite having joined the treaty, and the U.S. government suspects that other states, including North Korea, have similar clandestine programs.

Nuclear Weapons

Nuclear explosions are caused by uncontrolled nuclear fusion or uncontrolled nuclear fission. Fission occurs when high-explosive "lenses" squeeze (implode) a subcritical mass of fissile material (e.g., plutonium), forcing the mass to become supercritical. Fat Man, the bomb that destroyed Nagasaki in August 1945, was a fission implosion device that used about 13 pounds of plutonium and had an explosive yield equal to about 15 thousand tons (15 kilotons) of TNT. Fusion occurs when a fission device is used to fuse nuclei of light elements with each other to form heavier elements. Both the United States and the Soviet Union deployed thousands of fusion (thermonuclear) warheads during the Cold War, some of which had the explosive yield of millions of tons (megatons) of TNT.

Although the physical principles behind the design and manufacture of nuclear weapons are well understood, new states encounter significant stumbling blocks in trying to build their own weapons. International safeguards protect against the diversion of nuclear materials from nuclear power plants. Transfer of specialized equipment to enrich commercial-grade nuclear fuels for weapons use also is closely monitored. Making a weapon small and light enough to be delivered by missiles or aircraft and yet able to produce a yield beyond a few kilotons remains a significant technical challenge.

The non-nuclear states that have ratified the Non-Proliferation Treaty have agreed "not to manufacture or otherwise acquire" nuclear weapons, whereas the five nuclear states recognized by the treaty (the United States, United Kingdom, Russia, France, and China) pledged to work in good faith toward the eventual elimination of nuclear weapons. India, Israel, and Pakistan, however, never joined the NPT. After the 1991 Gulf War, a large-scale nuclear program was discovered in Iraq, in clear violation of its NPT commitments. North Korea also was caught violating its NPT commitment by removing weapon-usable materials from a reactor in the 1990s. The U.S. government also suspects that Iran has a long-term plan to develop nuclear weapons or at least a nuclear option despite its membership in the NPT. These states, for understandable reasons, are the focus of great attention today.

Introduction

We are venturing into uncharted intellectual territory. No group of scholars has made a systematic comparison of the use doctrines embraced by the
states and groups that have recently acquired unconventional weapons.[4]
As we demonstrate in this book, however, such a comparison generates
empirically rich and theoretically original insights into the role these
weapons play in military organizations and in world politics. This is no
small claim. During the Cold War, those who tried to say something new
about either deterrence or the global nuclear predicament often acknowl-
edged that their efforts were yielding diminishing returns. But by exploring
how the leaders of Iran, Iraq, North Korea, Israel, India, Pakistan, and the
Aum Shinrikyo cult think about the use of nuclear, chemical, or biological
weapons, our authors address new subjects and discovered novel and disturbing facts. Readers, for example, will discover the following:

- The Islamic Revolutionary Guard Corps in Iran has its own chemical
  weapons and has conducted exercises suggesting that plans exist to attack U.S. naval forces with chemical weapons in future conflicts.
- Iraqi leader Saddam Hussein might have predelegated authority to use
  biological weapons to special Scud missile commanders during the
  1991 Gulf War.
- North Korean leaders claim that the United States used biological
  weapons against their forces and citizens during the Korean War, which
  justifies their use of unconventional weapons in future conflicts.
- For years, Israeli leaders refused to make basic doctrine decisions about
  how nuclear weapons would be used if necessary, even in severe crises
  and wars with their Arab neighbors.
- Indian officers developed special preventive military strike plans to destroy Pakistan's nuclear infrastructure in the absence of direct orders
  from political leaders.
- Pakistani military officers are engaged in a debate over whether they
  should target their nuclear arsenal to kill millions in New Delhi or to
  destroy Indian armor and infantry on the battlefield.
- Before the 1995 chemical weapons attack on the Tokyo subway, members
  of the Aum Shinrikyo cult used anthrax in an unsuccessful operation in

---

4. Other scholars, however, have called for such a study. See Robert D. Blackwill and Ashton
B. Carter, "The Role of Intelligence," in *New Nuclear Nations: Consequences for U.S. Policy*, ed.
Robert D. Blackwill and Albert Carnesale (New York: Council on Foreign Relations Press,
1993), 236–37.

Japan and visited the site of an Ebola outbreak in Africa in the hopes of collecting a sample of this deadly virus.

Our voyage into this uncharted territory was a collective enterprise, the product of a deliberate effort by many scholars to refine and then answer a specific set of questions about the behavior and policies of new military powers. Initially, we used the general term *weapons of mass destruction* as a kind of shorthand to describe chemical, biological, and nuclear weapons. But as the authors examined the evidence, they discovered that there was great diversity in the purposes behind the acquisition, the doctrines developed, and the command procedures associated with nuclear, biological, and chemical weapons in different states. We therefore decided to abandon the term weapons of mass destruction as an analytical construct in our book. Not only does the term overstate the destructive potential of chemical weapons but it also can lead analysts to ignore the important differences in the way new actors treat different weapons.

Identifying Policies for Using Chemical, Biological, and Nuclear Weapons

To identify how states and groups intend to use unconventional weapons, our authors use a common analytic framework. The following chapters describe the fundamentals of a specific actor's military policy, often referred to by the term *doctrine*. Doctrine reflects ex ante formal and informal plans or widely shared expectations about how organizations will use weapons or forces at their disposal to achieve political, military, or other objectives. It provides large military organizations with an approved set of principles and methods that foster a common outlook and a uniform basis for action. Doctrine is often divided into several facets for study: *procurement doctrine*, the weapons and delivery systems developed or acquired; *deployment doctrine*, where these weapons are stationed in peace or war; *employment doctrine*, plans for how they will be used in wartime; and *declaratory doctrine*, public statements about the doctrine.[5] Doctrine also can shape the command and control procedures that ensure that weapons will be employed only by specific individuals following orders from a legitimate authority.

Doctrine is critical to any consideration of how nuclear, chemical, or biological weapons will be used and how the presence of these weapons might affect international relations generally. Doctrine limits strategic deliberations: plans, weapons, or deployment options that do not reflect or advance

---

5. Daniel Moran, "Doctrine, Military," in *The Oxford Companion to Military History*, ed. Richard Rhodes (New York: Oxford University Press, forthcoming); Desmond Ball, "U.S. Strategic Forces: How Would They Be Used?" *International Security* 7 (Winter 1982–83): 31–60. Ball includes arms control policy as another facet of doctrine.

existing doctrine are likely to be rejected by military organizations. Because time constraints make crises a poor time to explore the first principles of strategy, doctrine guides organizations and constrains political leaders' freedom to maneuver as the threat of hostilities increases. Doctrine itself can shape the course and outcome of crises by designating events that will mobilize forces, launch preemptive strikes, or trigger retaliatory attacks. Doctrine does not determine the outcome of crises on its own, but by shaping war plans, doctrine can condition how states or groups respond to provocation or opportunities.

Crises also are an exceptionally bad time to begin to think about potential opponents' military doctrines. Intelligence officers and military leaders should always take into account rival states' military plans when developing their own. Diplomatic or military initiatives that are based simply on quantitative measures of military capability will likely yield unintended, if not disastrous, outcomes.

A challenge we face is that many traditional distinctions or "logical" linkages often associated with military doctrine might not apply to the behavior and policies of states and nonstate actors with divergent capabilities, governments, geographic and demographic settings, organizations, and strategic cultures. For example, if a state embraces an employment policy based on deterrence, one might expect that explicit threats of retaliation would be made, survivable weapons would be purchased and deployed, appropriate "countervalue" targets would be identified, and a command and control system would be constructed to resist decapitation attack. Yet our studies reveal that these expectations often are not met. The proximity of military installations to population centers combined with inaccurate delivery systems, for instance, could reduce the value of counterforce and countervalue targeting distinctions (which some believed were more rhetoric than reality even during the Cold War).[6] Poor civil-military relations or even outright fear that domestic political opponents might use nuclear, biological, or chemical weapons to seize power or to settle old scores might preclude the "logical" command and control arrangements dictated by external threats and employment or declaratory doctrine.[7] Some actors appear drawn to one type of weapon, integrating it into every element of their

6. William Daugherty, Barbara Levi, and Frank von Hippel, "The Consequences of 'Limited' Nuclear Attacks on the United States," *International Security* 10 (Spring 1986): 3–45; William Daugherty, Barbara Levi, and Frank von Hippel, "Civilian Casualties from 'Limited' Nuclear Attacks on the Soviet Union," *International Security* 12 (winter 1987–88): 168–89.

7. For explanations of why some states might find internal challenges so threatening that they directly influence military doctrine ostensibly aimed at external enemies, see Steven David, *Choosing Sides: Alignment and Realignment in the Third World* (Baltimore: John Hopkins University Press, 1991); Stephen M. Walt, *Revolution and War* (Ithaca: Cornell University Press, 1996).

armed forces, whereas others appear to produce strategically redundant weapons and delivery capabilities. In a sense, our case studies identify significant mutations of the species *terribilis imperium* that we grew to know so well during the Cold War. These actors are "new proliferators" not just in the sense that they have recently acquired nuclear, chemical, or biological weapons but also because they reflect new ways of integrating unconventional weapons into arsenals, of controlling the weapons, of "planning the unthinkable."

Our authors develop more than just an empirical description of the policies and behavior of these actors. By identifying the forces that shape the evolution of the doctrines in question, they provide insights into the process by which decisions about doctrine and command systems are made (or sometimes not made). This information is extraordinarily sensitive or secret because it can produce immediate and profound consequences on the battlefield. To overcome this hurdle, our contributors consider various categories of "indirect evidence" to gain insights into the policies of the states and nonstate groups under consideration. For example, employment doctrine can be scrutinized by identifying the specific organizations that are responsible for holding weapons, operating delivery systems, or conducting training exercises. Our authors also explore whether strategic concepts are widely debated and formally articulated or are more ad hoc, secretive, and intuitive. Insights can be found in identifying the relationships between civilian and military agencies—or in the case of nonstate actors, leaders, followers, and technicians—that have a role in planning for the eventual use of nuclear, chemical, or biological weapons. Thus our contributors answer fundamental questions posed by the possible use of nuclear, chemical, or biological weapons: What strategic purposes do the actors in question hope to achieve with their new arsenals? Is there a guiding principle—deterrence, coercion, aggression, revenge, prestige, or some unique idea embedded in a given strategic culture—that shapes their plans to use these highly lethal weapons systems?

Is the Cold War Legacy a Global Legacy?

At the dawn of the nuclear age, Bernard Brodie argued that given the potential for cataclysmic destruction, only one conclusion could be reached about nuclear weapons: "Thus far the chief purpose of our military establishment has been to win wars. From now on its chief purpose must be to avert them."[8] The leaders of nuclear states, however, were left to grapple

---

8. Bernard Brodie, ed., *The Absolute Weapon: Atomic Power and World Order* (New York: Harcourt, Brace, 1946), 76.

with the implications of this "nuclear revolution."[9] As more states acquire nuclear, chemical, and biological weapons and ballistic missiles, questions emerge about whether the superpowers' experiences during the Cold War can serve as a useful guide to understanding or predicting the behavior of new military powers. Unfortunately, no real consensus exists about the proper lessons to be drawn from the Cold War nuclear standoff. Indeed, as the Cold War ended, a lively debate was occurring about the role nuclear deterrence played in fostering the "long peace."[10] Some argued that the fact that there were only two superpowers (bipolarity) or that people on both sides of the Iron Curtain shared an aversion to bloodshed could better account for the absence of warfare between the United States and the Soviet Union than could nuclear deterrence.[11] Some suggested that despite the apparent stability of mutual assured destruction, nuclear war could be sparked by inadvertent escalation or an unexpected accident with a weapon, delivery system, or command and control network.[12] Some scholars argued that arms control agreements were essential to mitigate the risks and costs of the nuclear arms race, whereas others wondered if the whole arms control enterprise was worth the effort.[13]

Finally, several scholars point to an evolving tradition of "nuclear nonuse," a "taboo" against the detonation of nuclear weapons. These scholars argue that such a taboo is spreading throughout the world.[14] The possibility exists, however, that the nuclear taboo is simply an artifact of the

9. Scholars continue to offer conflicting opinions about when and if the "nuclear revolution" was ever embraced by U.S. policymakers. For differing opinions, see Steven Kull, *Minds at War: Nuclear Reality and the Inner Conflicts of Defense Policymakers* (New York: Basic Books, 1988); Steve Weber, *Cooperation and Discord in U.S.-Soviet Arms Control* (Princeton: Princeton University Press, 1991); and Eric Mlyn, "U.S. Nuclear Policy and the End of the Cold War," in *The Absolute Weapon Revisited,* ed. T. V. Paul, Richard J. Harknett, and James J. Wirtz (Ann Arbor: University of Michigan Press, 1998), 189–212.

10. John Lewis Gaddis, "The Long Peace: Elements of Stability in the Postwar International System," *International Security* 10 (Spring 1986): 99–142.

11. Kenneth Waltz, *Theory of International Politics* (Reading, Mass.: Addison-Wesley, 1979); John Mueller, *Retreat from Doomsday: The Obsolescence of Major War* (New York: Basic Books, 1989).

12. Bruce Blair, *The Logic of Accidental Nuclear War* (Washington, D.C.: Brookings Institution, 1987); Scott D. Sagan, *The Limits of Safety: Organizations, Accidents, and Nuclear Weapons* (Princeton: Princeton University Press, 1993); Barry Posen, *Inadvertent Escalation: Conventional War and Nuclear Risks* (Ithaca: Cornell University Press, 1991).

13. Colin S. Gray, *House of Cards: Why Arms Control Must Fail* (Ithaca: Cornell University Press, 1992).

14. Thomas C. Schelling, "The Conventional Status of Nuclear Weapons," Center for International Relations, UCLA, Working Paper 5 (February 1994), 8; Richard Price and Nina Tannenwald, "Norms and Deterrence: The Nuclear and Chemical Weapons Taboo," in *The Culture of National Security: Norms and Identity in World Politics,* ed. Peter J. Katzenstein (New York: Columbia University Press, 1996), 114–52; T. V. Paul, "Nuclear Taboo and War Initiation in Regional Conflicts," *Journal of Conflict Resolution* 39 (December 1995): 696–717.

Cold War or even a figment of scholarly imaginations.[15] Even if a nuclear taboo exists, similar normative constraints might not extend to the use of chemical or biological weapons or to the tactical use of nuclear weapons on the battlefield. Some states go to extreme lengths to honor the nuclear taboo, while others work frantically to equip their forces for the first use of nuclear, chemical, and biological weapons in battle. For many of the groups studied here, perceptions of threat, organizational interests of military and scientific communities, strategic cultures, and even dreams of glory and revenge—not some universally accepted norm against using unconventional weapons—appear to have the most influence on emerging use doctrines.

A related Cold War legacy is the sanctity of the idea of deterrence as the guiding principle of nuclear doctrine. Americans used deterrence to justify everything from placing bombers on airborne alert, to equipping infantry squads with nuclear weapons, to advocating sinking Soviet submarines equipped with nuclear-tipped ballistic missiles in the event of conventional war in Europe. But deterrence, the idea that retaliation against an opponent who first uses nuclear, chemical, or biological weapons is the only realistic employment and declaratory strategy available, is not always reflected in the doctrines of new military powers. Some appear willing to load unconventional weapons onto all types of delivery vehicles to gain maximum military advantage on the battlefield. Others treat them as a weapon of last resort but do little to strengthen their effectiveness as a deterrent by establishing operational readiness or making clear deterrent threats. Some actors appear willing simultaneously to embrace nuclear, chemical, or biological weapons for deterrence (retaliation in kind), potential battlefield use, first use against a neighbor's arsenals, or as a means to eliminate domestic opposition. Several of our cases also raise the possibility that some state leaders believe that unconventional weapons might deter outside intervention in regional conventional warfare intended to eliminate enduring rivals or nagging low-level security threats.

Whether officers and civilian policymakers treat their nuclear, chemical, or biological arms as weapons of last resort, a deterrent, a status symbol, or just another weapon to be used on the battlefield has enormous political and military implications. When powers embracing different doctrines and systems interact, the consequences are difficult to predict. For example, a military power might view its chemical arsenal as a tactical system, but its opponents might view any use of chemical weapons as a threat to their very national existence, requiring a massive response against population centers with nuclear, chemical, or biological weapons. Asymmetrical capabilities also can produce escalatory pressures: a state's leaders might recog-

15. Colin Gray, "Nuclear Weapons and the Revolution in Military Affairs," in *The Absolute Weapon Revisited*, ed. Paul, Harknett, and Wirtz, 119–20.

nize that they had just suffered a counterforce attack against their unconventional forces, but retaliation still might take the form of a countervalue attack because of limited intelligence and operational capabilities. Because regime survival or visions of national grandeur can be associated with newly acquired nuclear, chemical, or biological arsenals, international efforts to "roll back" these weapons programs might be viewed as evidence of a profound threat to national survival, prompting renewed efforts to acquire highly lethal and destructive weapons.

Certain military doctrines also can hamper attempts to limit the most damaging consequences of proliferation. For instance, international efforts to promote regional arms control might prove counterproductive if the parties involved view unconventional weapons as useful battlefield tools. The transparency that lies at the heart of arms control would simply provide targeting data to a leader convinced that nuclear, chemical, or biological weapons provide important battlefield advantages. Similarly, providing assistance to new military powers to increase the survivability and safety of their arsenals might be helpful if it strengthens policies of deterrence.[16] The same type of assistance provided to states planning for the offensive use of unconventional weapons would simply make nuclear, biological, or chemical war more likely because it would reduce concerns about safety or security that could limit field deployments.[17] The doctrines new military powers embrace might also affect whether ballistic missile defense strengthens or undermines regional security. Deterrence policies might be undermined by missile defenses that threaten to reduce the effectiveness of limited retaliatory capabilities. By contrast, stability might be enhanced by defenses that undermine confidence in arsenals intended to support conventional forces or preemptive attacks.

The Quest for Theoretical Insight

A rich literature offering competing explanations about how and why military organizations adopt weapons and doctrine has been produced by scholars who recognize that military plans and arsenals can influence the likelihood and outcome of war.[18] We have encouraged our contributors to

16. Lewis A. Dunn, *Containing Nuclear Proliferation*, Adelphi Paper 263 (London: International Institute for Strategic Studies, 1991), 23–25, 46–55.

17. For other potential downside risks to this kind of assistance, see Steven Miller, "Assistance to Newly Proliferating Nations," in *New Nuclear Nations*, ed. Blackwill and Carnesale, 101–2.

18. Barry Posen, *The Sources of Military Doctrine* (Ithaca: Cornell University Press, 1984); Jack Snyder, *The Ideology of the Offensive* (Ithaca: Cornell University Press, 1984); Alastair Iain Johnston, *Cultural Realism* (Princeton: Princeton University Press, 1995); Elizabeth Kier, *Imagining War: French and British Military Doctrine between the Wars* (Princeton: Princeton University Press, 1997).

use concepts or hypotheses drawn from this realist, organizational behavior, and strategic culture literature not only to facilitate their empirical efforts but also to lay the groundwork for an evaluation of the theories themselves. The conclusions therefore also examine how well these theories correspond to the events and preferences described in our case studies. In addition, we identify phenomena that shape doctrine and arsenals that are not recognized by existing theory.

Critics may argue that there are two reasons not to use traditional political science theories concerning the evolution of doctrine, military organizations, and weapons systems to explain the behavior of the new states and groups considered in this volume. First, the most influential literature on the evolution of doctrine is based on an intrawar European experience in integrating new conventional weapons into existing arsenals, and it is inappropriate, even Eurocentric or ethnocentric, to impose these models on developing world cases. Second, some would suggest that it is inappropriate to use experience gained with conventional arsenals as a guide to how actors will handle nuclear, chemical, or biological weapons. State and nonstate actors can be expected to treat unconventional weapons, especially nuclear weapons, differently from conventional weapons.

We have three responses. First, the Eurocentric criticism misunderstands the difference between theory development and testing. These theories were developed primarily through logical deduction; they were tested with historical observations from Europe. Testing them against new cases is therefore a useful and valid exercise. Second, realism and organizational theory are no more or less vulnerable to charges of ethnocentrism than most important theories embraced by political scientists. Each of these theories at least purports to have some wider validity across states and time in the presence of certain conditions. Third, theories emphasizing the importance of strategic culture are based on the notion that important differences do exist between people with different histories, outlooks, and preferences. In other words, because it identifies the importance of local factors, a strategic culture perspective calls our attention to the possibility that history and culture can have an enormous impact in shaping doctrines and command and control practices.

In the cases that follow, readers will discover how realism, organization theory, and strategic culture theory account for important aspects of our case studies. The cases also raise new questions about theorizing about the complex circumstances encountered by actors as they incorporate unconventional arms into their arsenals. Realists' focus on the nature and intensity of external threats as a guide to doctrine, for instance, offers little insight into what will happen if internal threats are generated by political rivals, counterrevolutionaries, or ethnic enemies. Organization theory suggests that officers' biases or poor civil-military relations will have a negative impact on doctrine. But what is the effect of organizational biases when the very idea of discussing "nuclear doctrine" is taboo or if the head of state is a military officer? Finally, the state and nonstate actors in question must deal with an international nonproliferation regime that constrains proliferation activities, but traditional theories leave little explanatory room for this important normative and practical restraint on behavior. Many of our authors also suggest that idiosyncratic factors, especially recent wartime experiences, can influence citizens, soldiers, and politicians alike, producing profound changes in attitudes toward nuclear, biological, and chemical weapons. In short, the seven cases of proliferation described here offer a varied test of the ability of realist, organizational, and strategic culture theories to explain the way leaders transform ideas into weapons.

THE WAY AHEAD

As Americans look to a new century, they would like to be able to consign chemical, biological, and nuclear weapons to the ash heap of history. Our studies of Iraq, Iran, Israel, India, Pakistan, North Korea, and the Aum Shinrikyo cult, however, demonstrate that this sentiment is not universal. States and nonstate groups are attracted to unconventional weapons as tools to achieve their political and military objectives. What was once considered a "lesser included threat" in the context of the Cold War now looms on the horizon as the major security challenge of the twenty-first century.

The following chapters outline the threats posed by the proliferation and possible use of nuclear, chemical and biological weapons by describing how the states and nonstate groups in question view their arsenals. We begin with an overview of the theories our authors use to guide their empirical inquiry. Our case studies follow this opening chapter, each seeking to explain the central doctrines and command systems developing in the state or nonstate groups in question. The concluding chapter unifies our effort, drawing a series of theoretical and empirical conclusions by revisiting the three questions posed at the outset of our analysis. How do states and nonstate groups integrate unconventional weapons into their military infrastructure, delivery systems, command and control procedures, and war plans? What will be the future impact of nuclear, chemical, and biological weapons on regional and international politics? And what does the behavior of new military powers indicate about the theories that explain military doctrines and command and control systems?

[1]

The Origins of Military Doctrine and Command and Control Systems

SCOTT D. SAGAN

States or nonstate groups that acquire nuclear, chemical, or biological weapons are confronted with two sets of critical questions. First, how and for what purposes should they plan to use such weapons? Second, how do they ensure that these weapons actually are used according to these plans and not under different circumstances or for other purposes? The first questions are the heart of military doctrine; the second set concerns strategic command and control.

How are the new possessors of nuclear, chemical, and biological weapons planning to use these weapons? This chapter presents three theoretical frameworks that can be used to make predictions and explain military doctrine and command systems: organization theory, realist theory, and strategic culture theory. The first section examines the underlying logic of each theory, presents alternative predictions derived from the theory about what doctrines will be developed by states, and then uses each theory as a lens to examine specific historical decisions. The second half of the chapter repeats this process for military command and control systems.

In this chapter I use evidence drawn primarily from one source, the early years of U.S. Cold War nuclear history, to illustrate and provide a preliminary test of these theories. I use the U.S. case for two reasons. First, more detailed, declassified information is available about U.S. nuclear history during this period than for any other nuclear state or for the U.S. policies undertaken later in the Cold War era. Second, the early U.S. experience with nuclear weapons may present especially relevant lessons for new states (or even nonstate groups) that acquire nuclear weapons today. We should not forget that the United States was a new proliferator in 1945 and U.S. officials were forced to grapple with profoundly new and difficult dilemmas in planning to use and control the atomic arsenal.

This focus, however, raises obvious questions about applicability of the theories to other states, to nonstate groups, and to other kinds of unconventional weaponry. This chapter and the subsequent individual case studies must therefore be sensitive to the following issues: To what degree are our current understandings about state behavior, organizational interests, or strategic culture colored by the Western and nuclear focus of earlier work? Do leaders and military organizations in new proliferators behave in similar ways, for similar reasons, as did their predecessors? Are plans and procedures governing the use and control of biological or chemical weapons developed in ways similar to those for nuclear forces?

Scholars using social science theory and historical case studies to predict the behavior of new proliferant states or nonstate groups must avoid two specific dangers. First, analysts must avoid the danger of *mirror-imaging*, the tendency to assume that all actors in the international system will act in the same way, for the same reasons, as did the United States during the early Cold War. Second, analysts also must avoid the *myth of uniqueness*, the tendency to assume that because each new state or nonstate group that acquires such weapons has different internal characteristics and faces different external challenges, no important patterns exist across proliferant states and even nonstate groups.

In their search for evidence, international scholars must look for both similarities and differences between the present and the past and between "us" and "them." The leaders of all states and terrorist groups that acquire nuclear, chemical, and biological weapons have to think about the unthinkable: how should these weapons be used and controlled? The subsequent chapters examine in detail how new proliferators in the developing world are answering such questions. These chapters therefore both use the three theories as guides to look for clues about doctrines and command and control procedures in new proliferators and use the facts thus uncovered as important new tests of the strength of these different theoretical perspectives.

EXPLAINING MILITARY DOCTRINE

Military doctrine consists of plans about how and when military force is to be used. Doctrines thus differ on many dimensions: whether they are basically offensive or defensive in character; whether they call for decisive use of force or whether they permit more limited operations; and how they define what kinds of targets—military forces, enemy leaders, or industrial capabilities—need to be destroyed in war. The three theoretical lenses focus on different possible explanations for why specific military doctrines are chosen.

Organization Theory: Doctrine Reflects Organizational Process and Interests

The first approach examines the decision-making processes of military organizations and the parochial interests of individual officers and services. Two common characteristics of organizations lead to patterns in the kinds of military doctrines that professional military officers are likely to prefer. First, military organizations, like other organizations, are only boundedly rational: by necessity they use many simplifying procedures to understand and respond to uncertainty in the external world. Professional militaries develop routines and standard operating procedures to simplify decisions and coordinate actions of diverse units in the field. They do not rely on each unit's independent rational judgment about appropriate behavior. Military organizations are myopic: instead of searching through the entire environment for information to make decisions, they often take shortcuts by relying on biased evidence from recent training or the last war in which they fought. Military planners, because of their responsibilities and training, also tend to concentrate primarily on purely military factors that influence combat. Officers thus often see the world through lenses that filter out important political considerations that can (and should) influence strategic decisions and military outcomes in war.

Second, military organizations, like all other organizations, have parochial interests. Their leaders and members are concerned not only with the security of the state they are employed to protect but also with protecting their own organizational strength, autonomy, and prestige. These parochial interests do not always conflict with the state's national security interests, but there is no reason to believe the two are always consistent.

These characteristics lead to a common set of military preferences with regard to military doctrines.[1] First, functional organization interests and widespread organizational routines lead military officers to hold strong biases in favor of offensive doctrines. Offensives reduce organizational uncertainty: since militaries must develop intricate war plans to coordinate their operations, they have a strong interest in taking the initiative to be able to implement their own war plans rather than having to react to the enemy's plans. Offensive operations usually require larger forces (recall the general 3:1 superiority rule for the success of an attack), and hence developing offensive doctrines can produce increases in the budgets and size of a military organization.

1. See Scott D. Sagan, "The Perils of Proliferation: Organization Theory, Deterrence Theory, and the Spread of Nuclear Weapons," *International Security* 18 (Spring 1994): 66–107; Barry R. Posen, *The Sources of Military Doctrine* (Ithaca: Cornell University Press, 1984); Jack Snyder, *The Ideology of the Offensive: Military Decision Making and the Disasters of 1914* (Ithaca: Cornell University Press, 1984); and Kimberly Martin Zisk, *Engaging the Enemy* (Princeton: Princeton University Press, 1993).

Organization theory also provides predictions about five more specific aspects of military doctrine. First, from an organizational perspective, there are strong reasons to predict that militaries will be biased in favor of *preventive* wars. (A preventive war is an attack deliberately initiated, or deliberately provoked, in peacetime because of the belief that long-term military trends favor an adversary and that it is therefore better to conduct war now rather than at a later date. A *preemptive* attack refers to a strike launch under the belief that an enemy's attack is imminent and unavoidable.) Military officers, by their self-selection into the profession and their professional training, tend to believe more strongly than do civilians that war is inevitable over the long run.[2] If one believes war is inevitable, however, then it is better to attack now with a preventive strike than to wait until a rival has gained military advantages. The military bias in favor of decisive operations also should be at play here: preventive wars rely on military power to defeat the adversary decisively rather relying on civilians to bargain with the enemy during or after limited war campaigns. Officers also are less likely to focus attention on the political factors that can argue against preventive wars. The opposition of domestic public opinion or allied governments to preventive war could be critical, for example, to civilian assessments of preventive attacks but are less likely to be considered inside military organizations because war planners are trained to focus on operational efficiency and the quest for military victory.

Evidence from U.S. nuclear history during the early Cold War supports these points. Although in April 1950 NSC-68 officially rejected preventive war against the Soviet Union, senior U.S. officers continued to recommend such a policy in the 1950s.[3] Perhaps the most dramatic example of such thinking was General Nathan Twining's August 1953 top secret memorandum to the Joint Chiefs of Staff in which he argued for preventive war against the "proven barbarians" in Moscow:

Prior to entering the second period of time [when the Soviet Union could destroy the United States] if our objectives have not been achieved by

2. Evidence for this view includes sociological survey research comparing views of civilian university undergraduates with those of military academy cadets. See John P. Lovell, "The Professional Socialization of the West Point Cadet," in *The New Military*, ed. Morris Janowitz (New York: Russell Sage, 1964), 129; Bengt Abrahamsson, "Military Professionalization and Estimates on the Probability of War," in *Military Profession and Military Regimes*, ed. Jacques van Doorn (The Hague: Mouton, 1969), 35–51.

3. NSC-68, in *Foreign Relations of the United States* (hereinafter *FRUS* followed by year and volume), *1950*, Vol. 1, *National Security Affairs*, 281–82. Soon after NSC-68 was adopted as administration policy, Major General Orvil Anderson was fired for publicly advocating preventive war. Anderson had stated: "Give me the order to do it and I can break up Russia's five A-bomb nests in a week. . . . And when I went up to Christ—I think I could explain to Him that I had saved civilization" (Austin Stevens, "General Removed over War Speech," *New York Times*, 2 September 1950, 8).

means short of general war, it will be necessary to adopt other measures. We must recognize this time of decision, or, we will continue blindly down a suicidal path and arrive at a situation in which we will have entrusted our survival to the whims of a small group of proven barbarians. If we believe it unsafe, unwise or immoral to gamble that the enemy will tolerate our existence under this circumstance, we must be militarily prepared to support such decisions as might involve general war.[4]

Second, military officers are skeptical about the ability to control escalation and have strong interests in keeping civilian authorities from interfering in operational planning. This view leads officers to maintain that force should be used decisively or not at all.[5] Although this bias for decisive operations is often attributed to the effects of the Vietnam War on the U.S. officer corps, it has a longer history. The transcripts of deliberations during the Cuban missile crisis, for example, dramatically illustrate such logic in action. After President John F. Kennedy stated his preference for a naval blockade of Cuba or a limited attack on the missile sites, General David Shoup, commandant of the Marine Corps, was secretly recorded telling the other Joint Chiefs of Staff why a decisive attack on Cuba was necessary:

Somebody has to keep them from doing the goddamn thing piecemeal. That's our problem. Go in there and friggin' round with the missiles. You're screwed. Go in there and friggin' round with the lift. You're screwed. You're screwed, screwed, screwed. Some goddamn thing, some way, that they either do the son of a bitch and do it right, and quit friggin' round. You got to go in and take out the goddamn thing that's going to stop you from doing your job.[6]

Third, the proclivity for decisive operations and taking the initiative is likely to encourage military officers to advocate large-scale *preemptive* strikes, if adequate warning is available and, at a minimum, the development of *launch-on-warning* options if technically feasible. Waiting for an attack to be completely executed before retaliating both relinquishes the initiative to the enemy and means that fewer forces would be available for one's own strike. From a military planner's perspective, "anticipatory retaliation" would be preferred to striking second. This desire for decisive operations also should lead military officers to oppose the development of limited-use options in

4. Memorandum by the Chief of Staff, U.S. Air Force, to the JCS, "The Coming National Crisis," 21 August 1953, Twining Papers, series 2, Topical Series, Nuclear Weapons 1952–61 folder, USAF Academy, Colorado Springs, Colorado.

5. The classic study is Richard K. Betts, *Soldiers, Statesmen, and Cold War Crises*, rev. ed. (New York: Columbia University Press, 1991). For further empirical evidence see Ole R. Holsti, "A Widening Gap between the U.S. Military and Civilian Society," *International Security*, 23 (Winter 1998): 20.

6. Ernest R. May and Philip D. Zelikow, eds., *The Kennedy Tapes: Inside the White House during the Cuban Missile Crisis* (Cambridge, Mass.: Harvard University Press, 1997), 106.

peacetime and the execution of such options in war. The remarkable inflexibility of the first U.S. integrated nuclear war plan—SIOP-62—is a stunning testament, for example, to the desire of the U.S. military for simple and decisive atomic operations. This nuclear war plan offered President Kennedy fourteen ostensible options. The first called for launching every U.S. nuclear weapon on alert against targets in every state in the Sino-Soviet bloc. The second option called for waiting one hour to place more U.S. nuclear forces on alert and then launch the entire ready force against targets in every state in the Sino-Soviet bloc. The third option called for waiting an additional hour, alerting more nuclear forces, and then attacking both military and industrial targets in every state in the Sino-Soviet bloc, and so on.[7]

Fourth, military officers are likely to favor countermilitary or "counter-force" targeting doctrines (those that target enemy military forces) over "countervalue" doctrines (those that target enemy populations). Officers have a strong interest in personal and organizational preservation, which leads to biases in favor of attacks on enemy military targets, especially offensive weapons, to destroy the forces that could kill them and their organization. Because officers seek to minimize uncertainty in war planning, they also will prefer weapons and targeting doctrines that produce easily measured outcomes.[8] Finally, since counterforce strategies require larger arsenals than do countercity strategies, military services or commands can gain budget and size if counterforce doctrines are chosen. It is not surprising, therefore, that the U.S. Air Force and the Strategic Air Command (SAC) were strong advocates of counterforce targeting during much of the Cold War.[9]

Fifth, although a key requirement of stable deterrence is the development of secure, second-strike retaliatory forces, military organizations are

7. See Scott D. Sagan, "SIOP-62: The Nuclear War Plan Briefing to President Kennedy," *International Security* 12 (Summer 1987): 22–51. The first SIOP did permit the president to "withhold" attacks on industrial targets in individual countries but military targets (especially air defenses) were planned to be destroyed in all "enemy" states regardless of which ostensible "withhold" option was chosen. For example, even though Albania had pulled out of all alliances with the USSR, it was to be attacked because there were Soviet air defenses on its borders. As SAC commander General Thomas Power reportedly told Secretary of Defense Robert McNamara, "Mr. Secretary, I hope you don't have any friends or relations in Albania, because we're just going to have to wipe it out" (Fred Kaplan, *The Wizards of Armageddon* [New York: Simon and Schuster, 1983], 272).

8. See Lynn Eden, *Constructing Destruction: Organizations, Knowledge, and the Effects of Nuclear Weapons* (Ithaca: Cornell University Press, forthcoming); and Robert Frank Futrell, *Ideas, Concepts, Doctrine: A History of Basic Thinking in the United States Air Force, 1907–1964* (Maxwell Air Force Base: Air University, 1971), 218.

9. It is not surprising that the U.S. Navy supported minimum deterrence and countercity targeting in the 1960s but later switched its preferences. Its submarine-launched ballistic missiles (SLBMs) were insufficiently accurate to attack Soviet missile silos in the 1960s but would permit counterforce targeting once more accurate SLBMs were developed in the 1980s. See Graham Spinardi, *From Polaris to Trident: The Development of U.S. Fleet Ballistic Missile Technology* (Cambridge, U.K.: Cambridge University Press, 1994).

unlikely to develop such forces of their own accord. Programs for making weapons invulnerable to attack are often expensive and take away resources that could be used to buy more military hardware or support more personnel in uniform, which are higher organizational priorities. Moreover, military organizations generally favor continuing their traditional missions, which discourages the use of innovative operations to reduce vulnerability. Finally, officers' preferences to preempt the enemy or to launch on warning of an enemy attack are further disincentives to build secure second-strike forces.[10]

The history of U.S. strategic nuclear missile forces confirms these predictions. The most invulnerable portion of the U.S. force is its nuclear-armed submarine-launched ballistic missile (SLBM) fleet, but the U.S. Navy was not initially supportive of this SLBM program and even argued that missile development funds should come out of the air force, not the navy, budget. Similarly, the U.S. Air Force was strongly in favor of building larger numbers and increasing the accuracy of missiles in the 1980s but did not support the costly and innovative basing schemes, such as the use of deep underground shelters or the placement of mobile missiles on concrete "race track" deployments.[11]

Organization theory not only identifies military biases and preferences but also points to three pathways by which such parochial interests influence state policy. First, military organizations will obviously directly determine doctrine in states that lack the rudiments of civilian control over the military. Second, even in states with official civilian control of the military, because military doctrine is such a complex and technical matter, civilian authorities are often poorly equipped to investigate and influence the details of war plans and procedures. Third, if civilians are informed of military plans, officers are likely to exert subtle or unsubtle pressures to maintain their doctrinal preferences. The most common form of such pressure is the claim that "military necessity" requires that current plans be implemented. Even in the United States, where strong civilian control of the military exists, senior officers were not averse to suggesting to the presi-

10. Organization theory also predicts that military routines will often create "signatures" in the operations of retaliatory forces that will make them vulnerable to a surprise attack. For examples, see Sagan, "More Will Be Worse," and "Sagan Responds to Waltz," in Scott D. Sagan and Kenneth N. Waltz, *The Spread of Nuclear Weapons: A Debate* (New York: Norton, 1995), 66–75, 126–28.

11. Harvey M. Sapolsky, *The Polaris System Development* (Cambridge, Mass.: Harvard University Press, 1972); Theo Farrel, *Weapons without a Cause* (New York: St. Martin's Press, 1997), 98–106.

dent that any changes in their nuclear war plans would result in national disaster.[12]

Organization theory thus predicts that militaries are likely to hold strong preferences in favor of offensive doctrines, preventive war, and decisive military options. They are likely to support counterforce targeting doctrines and may not build secure second-strike forces on their own accord. Most of the evidence in support of these arguments, however, comes from the U.S. Cold War experience with nuclear weapons. Subsequent chapters of this book therefore address two sets of questions. First, do all professional militaries exhibit these or similar propensities? How do the different roles that professional militaries play in different societies influence their interests and biases? Second, even if such common interests and biases do exist, do they have strong effects on the military doctrines of all state and nonstate groups?

Realism: Doctrine as Rational Response to Systemic Pressures

A second theoretical approach uses realist theory from international relations to deduce arguments about why different states are likely to construct different military doctrines. Realism posits that states are the principal actors in international politics and that relative power among states is the critical factor that determines differences in their behavior. Because the international system is anarchic, all states, regardless of their domestic regime type, are forced, by self-help logic, to do whatever they can to protect their security and other national interests. States thus engage in two forms of balancing behavior: "internal balancing" (increasing their own arms capabilities) and "external balancing" (gaining military strength through alliances with other states).[13]

Realists generally treat states as unitary actors and assume that state leaders behave with relatively high degrees of rationality. Realists disagree among themselves, however, over whether states' primary goal is to protect their own security (which encourages more defensive strategies to protect the status quo) or whether states seek to maximize their power (which encourages more offensive, revisionist policies). Neorealist writers often accept the first assumption; classical realist writers take the second

---

12. General Lyman Lemnitzer, for example, told President Kennedy that "withholding of a portion of the planned [nuclear] attack could degrade our plan and the forces committed to it to the point that the task essential to our national survival might not be fulfilled" (Sagan, "SIOP-62," 50).

13. The seminal text is Kenneth N. Waltz, *Theory of International Politics* (New York: Random House, 1979).

position.[14] Realists of different schools agree, however, that states must be both cognizant of their current power relative to others and constantly vigilant lest new threats from other states emerge. For all realists, the international condition of anarchy encourages statesmen, even if they are relatively satisfied with the status quo today, to be prepared to protect their future security interests. Realist state leaders will be ruthless in pursuit of their interests, but they always will act within the constraints of their current military power capabilities.

For realists, military doctrine, like war, is a continuation of policy by other means. Barry Posen, in his influential *Sources of Military Doctrine*, deduces a set of realist predictions about what kinds of general military doctrines different states will adopt.[15] First, states with strong incentives to change the status quo need offensive weapons and doctrines if they wish to pursue their war aims. Second, states that have strategically exposed allies, which they are unable to defend simultaneously on the ground, are likely to favor offensive doctrines because they permit them to concentrate limited forces and to take the fight to enemy territory. Third, states that face several adversaries at the same time might wish to pursue offensive doctrines so that they can take on enemies sequentially. In contrast, states that are more satisfied with (or are forced to accept) the status quo are more likely to adopt defensive doctrines for the simple reason that they have no territorial ambitions against their neighbors. In addition, a strong status quo power can encourage weaker allies to adopt defensive doctrines because the dependent ally may feel compelled to conform with the stronger power's preferences to maintain the alliance.

Posen tested these ideas against the history of the development of European military doctrines in the interwar period. Although he found much evidence that professional militaries held offensive biases in the 1930s, Posen argues that the military doctrines in place when war finally broke out in 1939 and 1940 more strongly supported realist predictions. Military biases were influential in peacetime, when military autonomy over plans and policies was greatest; in contrast, when war was on the horizon in the late 1930s, civilians intervened to produce military doctrines that better supported the state's grand strategy for coping with international threats.

---

14. See Kenneth Waltz, "Realist Thought and Neorealist Theory," *Journal of International Affairs* 44 (Spring 1990): 21–37; Randall Schweller, "Neorealism's Status Quo Bias: What Security Dilemma?" *Security Studies* 5 (Spring 1996): 90–121; Gideon Rose, "Neoclassical Realism and Theories of Foreign Policy," *World Politics* 51 (October 1998): 144–72; Jack Snyder, *Myths of Empire: Domestic Politics and International Ambition* (Ithaca: Cornell University Press, 1991); and Jeffrey W. Legro and Andrew Moravesik, "Is Anybody Still a Realist?" *International Security*, 24 (Fall 1999): 5–55.

15. Posen, *Sources of Military Doctrine*, 59–79.

Hence the French adopted defensive doctrines so as to ensure that their major status quo ally, Great Britain, would stand by them. The Germans developed a highly offensive doctrine because it was deemed necessary to support Hitler's expansionist war aims. The British developed a defensive, airpower doctrine, emphasizing fighter-interceptor aircraft, because civilians intervened to promote self-defense alternatives to the single-minded obsession of the Royal Air Force with offensive strategic bombing.

Applying these general realist predictions to specific doctrinal choices about nuclear, chemical, or biological weapons, however, is complicated by the interactions that exist between balances or imbalances in conventional forces, chemical and biological weapons, and nuclear forces. Nevertheless, four specific predictions can be made. First, realism suggests that leaders of stronger military powers, when they confront a weaker potential adversary who is developing a nuclear, chemical, or biological capability that will threaten them, will consider preventive war as an option to stop that weapon's development.[16] Military transition periods, just before potential enemies have the full capability to retaliate in kind, are therefore particularly dangerous moments. If the leader of a stronger power nevertheless rejects preventive war, according to realist logic, it should be because of the expected costs of war, not because of moral qualms or domestic political constraints.

Second, the maintenance of a secure retaliatory capability is a requirement of deterrence, and realism provides predictions about why and when states will develop doctrines that emphasize secure retaliatory forces and second-strike deterrence. If a stronger state faces extremely weak rivals—especially rivals that lack strong nuclear, chemical, or biological weapons—it may be possible to rely on first-strike plans and preventive war options. But once its rivals have developed sufficient military forces to make preventive war and successful first strikes implausible, the development of invulnerable second-strike forces will be a leader's highest priority. States may still pursue weapons programs that could provide for future military advantages, but they will be forced to accept a condition of mutual deterrence in the immediate term.

Third, while realists agree that all states must focus on the military power of rivals, they disagree about whether a military balance with one weapons system increases or decreases the likelihood of the use of other weapons systems. If, for example, two states develop secure second-strike nuclear

---

16. See Robert Gilpin, *War and Change in World Politics* (Cambridge, U.K.: Cambridge University Press, 1981); and Jack S. Levy, "Declining Power and the Preventive Motivation for War," *World Politics* 40 (October 1987): 82–107.

forces and hence maintain a form of deterrence stability, does this increase the likelihood of conventional aggression since the fear of escalation would be reduced? Or does the ever-present fear of nuclear escalation minimize the dangers of conventional war as well? There is no simple, logical answer to these questions, which is why Glenn Snyder coined the phrase "the stability/instability paradox" to describe the phenomenon.[17] Some realists have been concerned that states with conventional and unconventional weapons and facing a similarly armed enemy could adopt "counterdeterrent doctrines" using nuclear, chemical, or biological weapons as a shield behind which to launch conventional attacks with less fear of enemy escalation.[18] This should be an especially attractive doctrine for states that have strong revisionist ambitions. Other scholars, like the neorealist Kenneth Waltz, have argued that all states will be cautious in any effort to exploit their chemical, biological, or nuclear weapons for purposes other than basic deterrence once the risks of costly retaliation become grave.[19]

Both realist camps would agree, however, that statesmen contemplating the stability/instability paradox must take into account both the relative balance of military capabilities between their state and their adversaries and the enemy's specific reactions to military probes. Thus, even if revisionist leaders attempt to use nuclear, chemical, or biological weapons in a coercive manner—as a shield to permit conventional aggression to alter the status quo—they will likely adopt more defensive or deterrent postures if they are met with strong resistance. "Probe with bayonets," Lenin's adage went. "If one meets mush, continue; if one meets steel, withdraw." If states continue to be aggressive despite meeting firm resistance, their behavior will be better explained by theories other than realism.

Fourth, realism suggests that even status quo states are likely to maintain threats to use their unconventional weapons first if they have exposed allies who cannot be protected in other ways or if they find it necessary to offset an adversary's conventional military superiority. States in such a strategic condition will adopt a doctrine emphasizing limited-strike options, threatening to raise the stakes in a conflict but not escalating immediately to a full-scale retaliation. As Thomas Schelling argued, such a military doctrine would turn limited wars, including wars in which limited uses of unconventional weapons occurred, into a "competition in risk-taking, characterized not so much by tests of force as by tests of nerve."[20]

17. Glenn Snyder, "The Balance of Power and the Balance of Terror," in *The Balance of Power,* ed. Paul Seabury (San Francisco: Chandler, 1965), 184–201.

18. The classic article that spread this concern was Paul Nitze, "Deterring Our Deterrent," *Foreign Policy,* No. 25 (Winter 1976–77): 196.

19. See Waltz, "More May Be Better," in Sagan and Waltz, *The Spread of Nuclear Weapons,* 1–45.

20. See Thomas C. Schelling, *Arms and Influence* (New Haven: Yale University Press, 1966), 94.

These realist predictions about unconventional weapons doctrines have been tested primarily in historical studies of the United States during the Cold War. Why did the United States maintain a nuclear first-use policy and counterforce targeting doctrines throughout the Cold War? A realist interpretation is that these strategies and the nuclear forces needed to support them were developed primarily to protect Japan, South Korea, and the NATO allies in Europe against the conventional threats from China, North Korea, and the Warsaw Pact powers. Thus the Soviet Union and the People's Republic of China could maintain, or at least profess to hold, no-first-use doctrines in the Cold War, but the United States steadfastly refused to accept such a doctrine. Similarly, even after the growth of the Soviet arsenal in the 1960s and 1970s provided Moscow with a secure second-strike retaliatory capability—and thus reduced the possibility of U.S. first-strike attacks producing "damage limitation" in a war—the United States pursued counterforce weaponry and developed "limited nuclear options" to enhance the credibility of the U.S. first-use threats. As Secretary of Defense James Schlesinger argued when explaining U.S. targeting policy innovations in the 1970s: "The recognition that a high level of conventional conflict may elicit a nuclear response, be it tactical, or be it strategic, is, I think, a major contributor to the deterrent. . . . That is the major reason behind the change in our targeting doctrine during this past year."[21]

U.S. Cold War history also provides an important example of a political leader—President Dwight Eisenhower—who seriously considered and then rejected the notion of preventive nuclear war. Eisenhower confided to Secretary of State John Foster Dulles in September 1953 that he believed that a preventive war attack on the USSR might be necessary. In a future arms race with the Soviets, he argued:

> [The United States] would have to be constantly ready, on an instantaneous basis, to inflict greater loss upon the enemy than he could reasonably hope to inflict upon us. This would be a deterrent—but if the contest to maintain this relative position should have to continue indefinitely, the cost would either drive us to war—or into some form of dictatorial government. In such circumstances, we would be forced to consider whether or not our duty to future generations did not require us to *initiate* war at the most propitious time that we could designate.[22]

---

21. BBC Radio 4, "Analysis," 24 October 1974, as quoted in Lynn E. Davis, *Limited Nuclear Options: Deterrence and the New American Doctrine,* Adelphi Paper 121 (London: Institute of International Security Studies [IISS], 1975–76), 5 n. 17, 6 n. 18.

22. Memorandum by the President to the Secretary of State, 8 September 1953, *FRUS, 1952–1954,* Vol. 2, *National Security Affairs* p. 1, 461 (emphasis in original).

Despite these considerations, and despite strong military advice in favor of preventive war, Eisenhower rejected the idea in 1954. There are a number of possible explanations for this decision, of course: Eisenhower could have been influenced primarily by normative constraints, by fears of domestic electoral consequences, or by more realist concerns about the costs of any preventive war. The available evidence supports realism, however, because Eisenhower's primary concern was the estimated costs of such a preventive war, though it is important to note that his view of the costs of war included the consequences of war on the nature of the American domestic system. After receiving a briefing on nuclear war objectives in a March 1954 meeting of the National Security Council (NSC), for example, "the President pointed out that we could anticipate in the aftermath of a third world war a tremendous swing toward isolationism in the United States. Moreover, the colossal job of occupying the territories of the defeated enemy would be far beyond the resources of the United States at the conclusion of this war."[23]

At another NSC meeting that month, Eisenhower stressed that the domestic costs of victory in such a war were unacceptable: "Every single nation, including the United States, that entered into this war as a free nation would come out of it as a dictatorship. That would be the price of survival."[24] Domestic political constraints were a factor because Eisenhower believed that the U.S. public would object to an unprovoked war; yet it was concern about the costs of even a successful preventive war that seems to have driven his decision. On 3 December 1954, Eisenhower secretly told his advisers that he had concluded that the United States would use nuclear weapons promptly and massively in any war with the USSR but that it would not initiate such a conflict: "We are *not* going to provoke the war, and that is why we have got to be patient. If war comes, the other fellow must have started it. Otherwise we would not be in a position to use the nuclear weapon. And we have got to be in a position to use that weapon if we are to preserve our institutions in peace and win the victory in war."[25] Throughout the rest of the 1950s, U.S. nuclear doctrine therefore explicitly rejected preventive war, although it continued to emphasize the desirability of a preemptive strike if a Soviet attack was deemed imminent and unavoidable.[26]

The realist perspective also explains why the Eisenhower and Kennedy administrations forced the U.S. armed services to develop secure second-

---

23. Ibid., 636.
24. Ibid., 641–42.
25. Ibid., 804–6.
26. See Marc Trachtenberg, *A Constructed Peace* (Princeton: Princeton University Press, 1999), 156–78.

strike nuclear forces in the late 1950s and early 1960s. Once the Soviet Union developed sufficient nuclear weapons and delivery systems to make a successful first strike impossible, reliance on deterrence through the threat of unacceptable retaliation became necessary. By the mid-1960s, the period of mutual assured destruction emerged, as both superpowers maintained invulnerable nuclear forces in submarines at sea and in hardened intercontinental ballistic missile (ICBM) silos.[27]

Finally, Cold War history provides some evidence supporting the realist stability/instability paradox argument that revisionist powers would use their new unconventional weapons as a shield behind which to attempt conventional aggression. The best example is Soviet policy toward Berlin. As the Soviet Union developed a larger nuclear force in the late 1950s, Premier Nikita Khrushchev practiced "rocket rattling," threatening nuclear retaliation if the United States tried to defend Berlin with conventional forces: "Your generals talk of maintaining your position in Berlin with force. That is a bluff. If you send in tanks, they will burn and make no mistake about it. If you want war, you can have it, but remember, it will be your war. Our rockets will fly automatically."[28] Fortunately, after the United States displayed its resolve to fight over Berlin in 1958 and 1961, the Soviet government ceased using nuclear threats to support potential conventional aggression. As realism predicts, Russian leaders confronted steel rather than mush and adjusted their doctrine accordingly.

While organization theorists and realists agree that the nature of civil-military relations in a state is one of the most significant factors influencing which of the two theories should be expected to hold, they disagree about the degree to which civilian control of the military shapes doctrine. Organizational theories suggest that states lacking strong institutions of civilian control, especially states whose governments are dominated by military officers, are more likely to have doctrinal decisions determined by military biases. In contrast, realism suggests that military officers who take over the reins of government are forced by their new responsibilities to make rational assessments of their country's interests based on its position in international politics. Similarly, organization theorists can accept that military influence over doctrines and strategy is greatest in peacetime, when incentives for civilian oversight are reduced. But they also argue that civilian oversight is inherently limited by the complexity of military planning, and civilian intervention can be highly constrained in crises and wartime because there is little time to change plans or retrain forces. Realists counter,

27. See Lawrence Freedman, *The Evolution of Nuclear Strategy* (New York: St. Martin's Press, 1982).

28. Quoted in Paul Bracken, *The Command and Control of Nuclear Forces* (New Haven: Yale University Press, 1983), 42.

however, that nuclear, chemical, and biological weapons create such fears of war that civilians will intervene in peacetime, with a depth of involvement that occurred only during serious crises in the prenuclear era.

Strategic Culture Theory: Doctrines Reflect Domestic Politics and Culture

A third theoretical lens draws attention to the influence of domestic politics and culture on military doctrine. For these theorists, strategic choice is determined by different cultural influences on decision makers and not by the rational pursuit of similar national security or functional organizational interests. Individual leaders act according to what they believe is appropriate behavior, not according to clear and objective interests shared by all leaders. This cultural perspective finds the roots of military doctrine in historical experiences and resulting myths, religious beliefs, and norms, and it suggests that different states in similar strategic conditions (or different organizations in similar conditions) would likely develop different military doctrines.

During the 1970s, the idea of strategic culture was adopted by scholars as a way to understand the seemingly profound differences between Soviet and American nuclear strategy. While the United States government was seen to ascribe to countercity targeting and the principle of mutual assured destruction in its nuclear doctrine, the Soviet Union was believed to maintain counterforce targeting and to seek to limit damage to itself in any nuclear conflict. "The principal differences between American and Soviet strategies are traceable to different conceptions of the role of conflict and its inevitable concomitant, violence, in human relations," argued Richard Pipes in a highly influential 1977 article.[29] Pipes and other scholars traced the Soviet "nuclear war fighting" strategy and development of large-scale civil defense programs to deeply held cultural beliefs. These included the traditional Russian peasant belief that "cunning and coercion alone ensured survival," the Communist Party elites' view that war between communist and capitalist states was as natural and inevitable as was class conflict, and beliefs—underscored by the enormous casualties in World War II—that even a highly destructive war could bring ultimate victory.[30]

This Cold War perspective on strategic culture, however, was as problematic as it was influential. The first problem was that scholars were insufficiently rigorous in their efforts to differentiate cultural explanations

---

29. Richard Pipes, "Why the Soviet Union Thinks It Can Fight and Win a Nuclear War," *Commentary* 64 (1977): 25.

30. Ibid., 25–26. Also see Colin S. Gray, *Nuclear Strategy and National Style* (Lanham, Md.: Hamilton Press, 1986); and Jack Snyder, *The Soviet Strategic Culture: Implications for Limited Nuclear Operations*, RAND Report R-2154-AF (Santa Monica, Calif.: RAND, 1977).

from other explanations for military doctrines. Pipes, for example, emphasized the deeper cultural factors that might have influenced Soviet strategy,
but he also maintained that American doctrine would have been very similar if it had been determined by the professional military rather than by
civilian scientists.[31] (If this were the case, however, then factors suggested
by organization theory, such as military biases and civil-military relations,
rather than deeper cultural beliefs were the most important determinants
of doctrine.) Second, as Cold War documents from the United States were
declassified, assumptions about the fundamental differences between U.S.
and Soviet doctrine were called into question. The declassified evidence
clearly demonstrates that the United States, too, had a large-scale counterforce targeting doctrine, developed forces, and command systems for a pro-
longed nuclear war, and hoped to limit damage even in the event of a major
nuclear exchange.[32]

A new wave of cultural studies in international relations—what can be
called neoculturalism—emerged in the 1990s, leading to two improved
conceptualizations of strategic culture.[33] First, neoculturalists trace the
causal relationship between domestic politics and strategic culture by exploring the domestic constraints placed on military organizations as they
develop doctrine. Second, neoculturalists focus more attention on moral
norms or cultural taboos that can influence state leaders' nuclear decisions.

The link between domestic politics and strategic culture is best seen in
Elizabeth Kier's *Imagining War*. In contrast to realism and organizational
theory, Kier presents a different perspective on both civilian and military
leaders. Civilian leaders are not seen as statesmen; they are politicians and
thus they seek to influence military policy, not to maximize national security
but to advance their own domestic political interests. This kind of civilian intervention does not focus directly on influencing military doctrine per se;
instead, its purpose is to influence those military structures (for example,
conscription policies or budgetary allocations) that can influence domestic

---

31. Pipes, "Why the Soviet Union Thinks It Can Fight," 29.

32. See Scott D. Sagan, *Moving Targets* (Princeton: Princeton University Press, 1989); and
Desmond Ball and Jeffrey Richaldson, eds., *Strategic Nuclear Targeting* (Ithaca: Cornell University Press, 1986). For an excellent critique of the early strategic culture literature, see Alastair
Iain Johnston, *Cultural Realism: Strategic Culture and Grand Strategy in Chinese History* (Princeton: Princeton University Press, 1995).

33. Important contributions to neoculturalism in international politics include Johnston, *Cul-
tural Realism*; Peter J. Katzenstein, ed., *The Culture of National Security* (New York: Columbia
University Press, 1996); Katzenstein, *Cultural Norms and National Security: Police and Military in
Postwar Japan* (Ithaca: Cornell University Press, 1996); Elizabeth Kier, *Imagining War: French and
British Military Doctrine between the Wars* (Princeton: Princeton University Press, 1997); Jeffrey
Legro, *Cooperation under Fire: Anglo-American Restraint during World War II* (Ithaca: Cornell Uni-
versity Press, 1995); and Richard M. Price, *The Chemical Weapons Taboo* (Ithaca: Cornell Univer-
sity Press, 1997).

political interests. Kier also argues that senior military officers and the institutions they lead are not uniformly wedded to offensive doctrines. Even though military officers might believe that offenses offer advantages for both national security and organizational interests, they also hold strong cultural beliefs about what military forces are best suited for specific military missions. These beliefs are the product of the organization's recent history and the indoctrination of officers through military training. Since different military organizations have different historical experiences and training regimes, they should hold different cultural beliefs about what military doctrines are appropriate for different tasks.

Kier tested her theory using a case study of France in the 1930s. She argues that French politicians on the Left insisted on staffing the military through short-term conscription because they feared that a professional army would instill passive obedience rather than democratic values in its soldiers and thus could be used for domestic repression as it had in 1870. French right-wing politicians, in contrast, supported a professional army precisely because of such a possibility. Domestic political interests, not national security concerns, drove French military conscription policy. Once the Left took over the reins of government, a conscript army was set in place. This change had a profound effect on doctrine, however, because the French military leadership held strong beliefs that only an elite, professionalized army could have the necessary morale and discipline to conduct complex offensive operations on the technological battlefield. This view was not universally held: the Germans, for example, planned to use reservists and short-term conscripts for offensive operations. But French officers believed that training conscripts for technologically demanding offenses was absolutely impossible and thus could not be done even though the offense was otherwise the preferred doctrine for senior officers in Paris. These two factors—domestic political preferences and organizational culture—thus interacted to produce military doctrine.

Although there are no thorough case studies that apply neocultural theories to the development of military doctrine for the use of nuclear, chemical, or biological weapons, several predictions can be deduced from the approach. First, political authorities will apply constraints on military budgets and arsenals that serve their domestic political interests. These constraints will have an indirect impact on military doctrine. For example, political authorities could decide to place severe budgetary restrictions on the number of weapons or related delivery systems in a state's strategic arsenal. Conversely, politicians could push for spending on specific weapons systems (e.g., aircraft rather than ballistic missile submarines) because the budgetary increases benefit domestic constituents or bureaucratic supporters. Political authorities could build a specific arsenal because some delivery systems, such as fighter-bomber aircraft, might be difficult to keep under direct political control and could therefore be used in a coup attempt against them. Ballistic missiles, not aircraft, might be the delivery system of choice for leaders who see their militaries as a threat to their own political and personal survival.

In these cases, political authorities would not directly be making doctrinal decisions, but their procurement choices could nevertheless be influential. If military officers believe that specific doctrines depend on the numbers of weapons available, for example, then budgetary constraints could indirectly constrain doctrinal choice. Professional officers would prefer offensive counterforce doctrines if sufficient weaponry exists, but if only minimal numbers of weapons were available, they might reluctantly accept countercity targeting. Similarly, even if the specific delivery systems were developed for parochial political reasons, their existence could nevertheless strongly influence doctrinal choices: for example, a force of submarine-launched ballistic missiles would encourage the development of second-strike options and countercity targeting because such missiles are less vulnerable to attack and are generally less accurate than are land-based missiles or bomber aircraft; conversely, development of a fixed-based missile force, rather than a bomber force, would encourage preemptive options because it would make prompt counterforce attacks possible.

A second innovation in the neoculturalist literature is to focus attention on the development and consequences of cultural norms concerning unconventional weapons. Cultural norms are seen as widely held views, within a specific community, of what behavior is appropriate and legitimate. These norms can be, but are not necessarily, universally held: different states, or different groups in a state, may hold quite different views about what behavior is legitimate.

This norms perspective has been used to explain why some states devote enormous economic and human resources to develop advanced high-technology military weapons, whereas others that could easily produce them choose not to do so.[34] Both in France in the 1960s and in India in the 1990s, for example, nuclear weapons were seen by many leaders and the public as a symbol of sovereignty, modernity and scientific prowess. In other countries, most notably Germany and Japan, nuclear weapons do not symbolize modernity but precisely the opposite. In these states, neoculturalists argue, a strong nuclear allergy—based in large part on the states' experiences in World War II—has emerged that strongly constrains a leader's

---

34. See Scott D. Sagan, "Why Do States Build Nuclear Weapons? Three Models in Search of a Bomb," *International Security*, 21 (Winter 1996): 73–85.

ability to develop any form of chemical, biological, or nuclear weapons.[35] In short, national culture—in the form of the symbolic meaning of weapons acquisition, not the degree of threat experienced by the state—is seen by neoculturalists as determining whether the state becomes a nuclear power.

The strongest application of neoculturalism to doctrines governing the use of unconventional weapons concerns the so-called chemical weapons taboo. Chemical weapons, which were widely used during World War I, were conspicuous in their absence during the World War II campaigns in Europe. A traditional realist explanation for the nonuse of chemicals focuses on the fear of retaliation on the part of all the major World War II powers and would note that the states did use chemical weapons when they did not fear retaliation in kind: Italy against Ethiopia, Japan against China, and Germany inside the concentration camps.[36] Neocultural theorists have challenged this view, however, by calling attention to incidents in which chemical weapons were inadvertently used in a limited fashion in Europe but that did not lead to further escalation. The cultural taboo against use of chemical weapons influenced the outcome of these incidents in an important but indirect way: had military leaders been fully prepared and willing to launch retaliatory strikes, it is argued, escalation to large-scale chemical warfare would have occurred.[37]

Several scholars maintain that this historical experience with chemical weapons both reflects and has contributed to the emergence of a global cultural taboo against the use of nuclear, chemical, and biological weapons.[38] The use of both chemical and biological weapons is now deemed illegal by the international community, and any state that violates this norm is likely to face significant international opprobrium. Although there is not as comprehensive a prohibition against the use of nuclear weapons under interna-

35. See Katzenstein, *Cultural Norms*, 128–29; and Harald Mueller, "The Internalization of Principles, Norms and Rules by Governments: The Case of Security Regimes," in *Regime Theory and International Relations*, ed. Volker Rittberger (Oxford: Clarendon Press, 1993), 361–88. Realists would, of course, emphasize the existence of U.S. nuclear guarantees to Japan and Germany as the most important factor permitting them to maintain their non-nuclear status.

36. Frederic J. Brown, *Chemical Warfare: A Study in Restraints* (Princeton: Princeton University Press, 1968); John Ellis van Courtland Moon, "Chemical Weapons and Deterrence: The World War II Experience," *International Security* 8 (Spring 1984): 3–35.

37. See Jeffrey W. Legro, "Military Culture and Inadvertent Escalation in World War II," *International Security* 18 (Spring 1994): 131–38.

38. See Richard Price and Nina Tannenwald, "Norms and Deterrence: The Nuclear and Chemical Weapons Taboos," in *Culture of National Security*, ed. Katzenstein, 114–52; Price, *Chemical Weapons Taboo*, 164–76; and, Nina Tannenwald, "The Nuclear Taboo: The United States and the Normative Basis of Nuclear Non-Use," *International Organization* 53 (Summer 1999): 433–68.

tional law, many leaders have internalized moral norms against nuclear use in ways that constrain peacetime doctrine and wartime use.

Although there is relatively little evidence that cultural taboos significantly influenced U.S. nuclear weapons doctrine during the Cold War, historians cite evidence in at least two important cases suggesting that moral concerns influenced U.S. decisions regarding use of nuclear weapons. First, when Eisenhower was briefed on plans to use nuclear weapons against Viet Minh troops at Dienbienphu in 1954, he replied that "you boys must be crazy. We can't use those awful things against Asians for the second time in less than ten years. My God."[39] Second, in March 1955 Eisenhower ruled that the primary military option for U.S. intervention in the event of a Chinese attack on Quemoy and Matsu would be with conventional forces only, in part because he knew that the early use of tactical or strategic nuclear weapons would produce significant moral repulsion and hence very negative political repercussions among U.S. allies in Europe and Japan.[40] This was an important, albeit reluctant, acceptance that moral norms would affect U.S. nuclear behavior.[41]

It is important to note, however, that U.S. war plans and nuclear doctrine did not change after these crises. U.S. classified war plans continued to emphasize large-scale preemption, if possible, and massive retaliation, if necessary. Eisenhower insisted that he would use nuclear weapons first in the event that the United States or countries vital to its interests were attacked.[42] This points to an additional observation about the effects of cultural norms or "taboos" on military doctrine. Moral norms can more easily influence state behavior in the absence of military "necessity." Realists can accept that moral norms influence behavior but only when the security of the state is not gravely threatened. Neoculturalists can also accept that conditions of severe necessity might make statesmen reluctantly break even a strong taboo. The key difference between these views therefore concerns whether norms actually influence statesmen's perceptions of necessity and hence their behavior. Norms that are always broken are not significant. Yet norms that redefine or limit the realm of necessity, making it less likely that unconventional weapons would be used in less than absolute conditions, can be meaningful.

---

39. Quoted in John Lewis Gaddis, "The Origins of Self-Deterrence," in Gaddis, *The Long Peace: Inquiries into the History of the Cold War* (New York: Oxford University Press, 1987), 142.
40. Ibid., 133–40.
41. Indeed, Dulles told Eisenhower on 26 December 1955 that "our whole international security structure is in jeopardy. The basic thesis [is] local defensive strength with the backing up of United States atomic striking power. However, that striking power [is] apt to be immobilized by moral repugnance" (quoted ibid., 142).
42. Ibid., 140.

Scott D. Sagan

Explaining Command and Control

Command and control systems are developed by governments to ensure that unconventional weapons are used when and only when state leaders decide they should be used.[43] Peter Feaver has described the central challenge of any strategic command and control system as an "always/never dilemma": "Leaders want a high assurance that the weapons will *always* work when directed and a similar assurance that they will *never* be used in the absence of authorized direction."[44] Achieving these twin objectives presents leaders with a severe trade-off problem because actions taken to meet one objective often reduce the likelihood of achieving the other goal. At one extreme, state leaders could maintain a highly "assertive" or centralized system, with weapons under strict civilian custody, maintained in a nonalert state of readiness, and with only the central leadership holding the capability and authority to order their use. This would maximize the goal of ensuring that weapons would never be used by accident or in an unauthorized manner but would also reduce the likelihood that the weapons could be used, even in retaliation against a major attack. Indeed, if a single weapon destroyed the state capital—in what has been called a "decapitation attack"—such a highly assertive command system could be paralyzed and the arsenal rendered unusable. At the other extreme, a state could adopt a highly "delegative" command system, in which weapons were kept on high states of alert, under the physical custody of military officers in the field, and with the authority to use the weapons delegated in advance to many lower-ranking military commanders. This system would virtually eliminate the danger of a successful decapitation attack but at the cost of increasing the risk that unconventional weapons would be used by accident, through false warnings, or in an unauthorized manner.

How to resolve this dilemma is a critical question faced by all states. Who should be able and authorized to order the use of unconventional weapons?

---

43. See Bruce Blair, *The Logic of Accidental Nuclear War* (Washington, D.C.: Brookings Institution, 1993); Paul Bracken, *The Command and Control of Nuclear Forces* (New Haven: Yale University Press, 1983); Ashton B. Carter, John D. Steinbruner, and Charles A. Zraket, eds., *Managing Nuclear Operations* (Washington, D.C.: Brookings Institution, 1987); Peter D. Feaver, *Guarding the Guardians: Civilian Control of Nuclear Weapons in the United States* (Ithaca: Cornell University Press, 1992); and Scott D. Sagan, *The Limits of Safety: Organizations, Accidents and Nuclear Weapons* (Princeton: Princeton University Press, 1993). For rare studies of the command and control systems of new nuclear states, see Peter D. Feaver, "Command and Control in Emerging Nuclear States," *International Security* 17 (Winter 1992–93): 160–87; and Jordan Seng, "Command and Control Advantages for Minor Nuclear States," *Security Studies* 6 (Summer 1997): 50–92.
44. Feaver, "Command and Control," 163 (emphasis added).

On what basis should first-use or retaliatory launches be ordered? Each of the three theoretical lenses provides a different set of possible answers.

Organization Theory: Command Systems Protect Autonomy

Organization theorists predict that most organizational leaders value "autonomy" or "turf" as much as, if not more than, having extra resources at their disposal.[45] Leaders of organizations usually have multiple goals, and at times these goals can be in conflict with one another. Autonomy, however, is especially important to ensure that organizational members—and not outsiders—determine how important missions are accomplished and how any trade-offs between competing organizational goals are resolved. With respect to unconventional weapons command and control, this priority should lead officers to seek both an independent *capability* and the *authority* to use any and all weapons in the state's arsenal. Officers should lobby hard to maximize their autonomy and oppose any technical or procedural innovations that take operational decision-making power out of their hands.

Numerous cases of such behavior can be seen in the history of U.S. nuclear command and control procedures during the Cold War. Until the Korean War, a civilian bureaucracy, the Atomic Energy Commission (AEC), maintained physical custody of all U.S. nuclear weapons and the president had sole authority to order their use. This condition was unacceptable, however, from the perspective of U.S. military leaders. "It is a prerequisite to national security that all possible means of defense be available to the Armed Forces for instant use," Lieutenant General Lewis Brereton insisted in a 1947 letter, adding that "divided responsibility in fields affecting national defense was one of the major problems examined as a result of the Pearl Harbor disaster."[46] General Curtis LeMay also complained about civilian interference in nuclear operations years later: "There were so many hurdles to negotiate before you could get to a target that it was ridiculous."[47]

Even after military units were granted custody over large portions of the U.S. nuclear stockpile in the mid-1950s, senior officers continued to push for more direct military authority over decisions concerning their use. In

---

45. See Morton H. Halperin, *Bureaucratic Politics and Foreign Policy* (Washington, D.C.: Brookings Institution, 1974), 51–54; James Q. Wilson, *Bureaucracy* (New York: Basic Books, 1989), 179–95.

46. Quoted in Feaver, *Guarding the Guardians*, 114.

47. "U.S. Strategic Air Power, 1948–1962: Excerpts from an Interview with Generals Curtis E. LeMay, Leon W. Johnson, David A. Burchinal, and Jack J. Catton," ed. Richard H. Kohn and Joseph P. Harahan, *International Security* 12 (Spring 1988): 83–84.

1956, for example, the Joint Chiefs of Staff requested that senior commanders be granted the authority to order the use of nuclear weapons in response to any major conventional or nuclear attack from a member of the Sino-Soviet bloc.[48] In 1956, President Eisenhower was willing only to predelegate nuclear use authority to military commanders for the defensive surface-to-air or air-to-air missiles used to attack enemy bombers.[49] Still, the U.S. military continued to press for increased autonomy over nuclear use decisions. During the 1958 Taiwan Strait crisis, for example, the Joint Chiefs of Staff lobbied President Eisenhower to grant local commanders the freedom to use nuclear weapons on their own authority, going so far as to warn the president that U.S. forces could not defend the Quemoy and Matsu islands unless such predelegated authority was given.[50] This authority was not granted during the crisis, but in December 1959, Eisenhower did authorize senior military commanders "to expend nuclear weapons in defense of the United States, its Territories, possessions and forces when the urgency of time and circumstances does not permit a specific decision by the President, or other persons empowered to act in his stead."[51] As President John F. Kennedy was informed when he took office, the widespread deployment of nuclear weapons and this delegation of authority to order their use "have created a situation today in which a subordinate commander faced with a substantial Russian military action could start the thermonuclear holocaust on his own initiative if he could not reach you (by failure of communication at either end of the line)."[52] Senior officials of the Kennedy administration believed that the Eisenhower administration had tipped the balance too far toward direct military control and initiated efforts to reassert more direct civilian control over the nuclear arsenal. As predicted by organization theory, however, these efforts were opposed by senior U.S. officers, who claimed that they were a slur on military professionalism. PAL (permissive action link) coded-locking devices were devel-

48. "Atomic weapons will be expended under this authorization," the JCS insisted, "only in cases wherein the circumstances, in the judgment of the operational commander concerned, will not permit the normal Presidential consideration and decision regarding their use" ("Draft Implementing Instructions," Appendix B to Radford to Secretary of Defense, memorandum, 14 November 1956, as quoted in Peter J. Roman, "Ike's Hair-Trigger: United States Nuclear Predelegation, 1953–1960," *Security Studies* 7 [Summer 1998]: 121–64).

49. Ibid.

50. Halperin, *Bureaucratic Politics*, 54.

51. JCS Memorandum for the Commander in Chief, Strategic Air Command, December 1959, "Instructions for Expenditure of Nuclear Weapons in Emergency Conditions," 1, Office of the Special Assistant for National Security Affairs, NSC Series, Subject subseries, Box 1, Atomic Weapons, Correspondence and Background for Presidential Approval, Dwight D. Eisenhower Library, Abilene, Kansas.

52. Memorandum from the President's Special Assistant for National Security Affairs (Bundy) to President Kennedy, 30 January 1961, *FRUS, 1961–1963*, 8: 18.

oped in the early 1960s, for example, but—in significant part because of the strong U.S. military objections against their widespread use—PALs initially were placed only on U.S. and NATO "dual key" nuclear weapons in Europe, not on a larger portion of the U.S. arsenal. Moreover, PALs and similar locking devices only reduced the likelihood that low-level weapons control officers (or terrorists who got access to the weapons) could use them in an unauthorized manner. As long as more senior commanding officers possessed the PAL codes, which was likely given the concerns about a decapitation strike on Washington, there would continue to be both some deterrent benefit from the knowledge that senior officers could retaliate on their own authority and some enduring risk of unauthorized use or "legal" accidental use (use following predelegation rules but under a false warning that an attack has occurred) by these same senior commanders.

This historical evidence thus suggests that organizational interests lead military officers to seek both direct custody over nuclear, chemical, and biological weapons and the predelegated authority to use them if necessary. In short, militaries prefer delegative command and control systems. To the degree that such organizational preferences determine state policy in new proliferant states—either because military officers are in power and thus make key decisions on their own or because they exert strong influence through political and bureaucratic maneuvering—a more decentralized command system is to be expected.

Realism: Command and Control Reflects the Demands of Military Doctrine

Just as realist theory suggests that military doctrine ought to be well integrated with a state's grand strategy, it also predicts that command and control systems ought to be well integrated with its military doctrine. Realists believe that the central factor that determines whether a state will develop delegative or assertive command and control systems is the nature of the military doctrine the state has chosen, which is in turn determined by the nature of the threat posed by the state's enemies. Therefore, different command and control systems are likely because states find themselves in different security environments.

Under realist logic, state leaders are likely to develop a highly assertive national command and control system under three conditions. First, if a proliferant state faces only conventionally armed adversaries, its leaders can more easily afford to maintain extremely tight control over its arsenal. Second, a state that confronts other nuclear, chemical, or biologically armed rivals but does not fear a decapitation strike because its capital city is located too far away from enemy forces to be targeted by them is also likely to develop assertive command structures. Third, assertive command systems are more likely if a state's adversaries lack sufficient numbers of weapons, accuracy of delivery, or intelligence-gathering capabilities to threaten its retaliatory forces or its leadership command posts. In short, state leaders who face adversaries that cannot threaten their command and control infrastructure can afford the luxury of a highly assertive command and control system.

If a state develops a military doctrine that requires the prompt use of unconventional weapons, it is likely to develop a more delegative command system. This arrangement would be the case under a variety of conditions. If state leaders feared that their entire arsenal was vulnerable to attack, they would have strong incentives to preempt enemy attacks if possible or, at a minimum, to launch forces on warning of an attack. To shorten response time in such scenarios, leaders would need to eliminate links in the chains of command and would have strong incentives to delegate authority. Similarly, state leaders facing much weaker enemies (and who believed that they might be able to win a war against them or at least significantly limit damage through counterforce strikes against enemy forces) would have strong incentives to develop prompt-use doctrines. Such doctrines would be more effective if weapons were placed on a high state of alert and if authority to order their use were dispersed to field commanders. Finally, even if civilian authorities develop a delayed-retaliation strategy, fears that leadership command bunkers are vulnerable to a prompt enemy first strike would create strong incentives to predelegate authority to retaliate to surviving military commanders in the field. Publicizing the existence of such predelegation orders presumably would enhance deterrence. If deterrence nevertheless failed, such delegation of authority would permit retribution. In short, realism suggests that the nature of international security threats determines doctrines. Different strategic doctrines produce different command systems.

This basic realist perspective can be used to explain the major shift in the U.S. nuclear command and control system that took place during the 1950s. During the first years of the Cold War, the Truman administration developed an extremely assertive national command and control system for nuclear weapons. President Harry Truman strongly supported the legislation that established the AEC in 1946. The legislation gave full responsibility for the custody of the atomic stockpile to the civilian AEC and made the president the sole authority able to "direct the Commission to deliver such quantities of weapons to the armed forces for such use as he deems necessary in the interests of national defense."[53] In July 1948, in the midst of the

---

53. Richard G. Hewlett and Oscar E. Anderson Jr., *The New World: A History of the Atomic Energy Commission*, Vol. 1, *1939–1946* (Berkeley: University of California Press, 1990), 512.

Berlin Crisis, Truman repeatedly underscored this desire for tight presidential control over atomic weapons. After a meeting on 15 July, for example, Secretary of Defense James Forrestal recorded in his diary that Truman said he "proposed to keep, in his own hands, the decision as to the use of the bomb, and did not propose 'to have some dashing lieutenant colonel decide when would be the proper time to drop one.'"[54] On 21 July, Truman rejected a request to pass custody of atomic weapons to military commanders, telling his senior advisers that "we have got to treat this [the atomic bomb] differently from rifles and cannon and ordinary things like that. . . . You have got to understand that I have got to think about the effect of such a thing on international relations. This is no time to be juggling an atom bomb around."[55]

From a realist perspective, however, Harry Truman's decisions must be seen in the context of U.S. nuclear weapons doctrine and war plans in the late 1940s. Truman had been briefed on the HALFMOON war plan in May 1948. HALFMOON called for American B-29 bombers to be loaded with atomic munitions in the United States, flown to bases in England, Okinawa, and Egypt, and from there to commence attacks on Russian industrial centers fifteen days after the war had begun.[56] This delayed timing of the strategic bombing campaign was certainly not desirable from a military perspective, but because the Soviets had not yet developed their own nuclear weapons and more prompt counterforce attacks were not required to limit damage to the United States and its forces, Truman had little incentive to loosen presidential control over the atomic arsenal.

By the end of the Eisenhower administration, in contrast, U.S. nuclear command and control had evolved into a highly delegative system, and most of the arsenal was under the physical control of commanders in the field and delegated use authority was dispersed widely throughout the command structure. A realist interpretation of this development would emphasize that this new command structure was the logical offshoot of the New Look and the resulting massive retaliation nuclear doctrine adopted by the Eisenhower administration. The authority given to the SAC commander in 1959 "to expend nuclear weapons in defense of the United States, its territories, possessions and forces, when the urgency of time and circumstances clearly does not permit a specific decision by the president" was, as the top secret orders put it, "necessitated by the recognition of the

---

54. Walter Millis, ed., *The Forrestal Diaries* (New York: Viking, 1951).

55. *The Journals of David E. Lilienthal*, Vol. 2, *The Atomic Energy Years, 1945–1950* (New York: Harper & Row, 1964), 389–90.

56. On HALFMOON, see Stephen T. Ross, *American War Plans, 1945–1950* (New York: Garland, 1988), 79–101.

fact that communications may be disrupted by an attack."[57] From a realist perspective, the emerging Soviet nuclear threat in the 1950s produced Eisenhower's command and control system. As early as 1954 Eisenhower told his advisers, "that our only chance of victory in a third world war against the Soviet Union would be to paralyze the enemy at the outset of the war."[58] The details of doctrine and command and control—from SIOP options and delegation orders to the name of the new ICBM coming into the force when Eisenhower left office, the Minuteman missile—were a product of that basic decision.

In summary, realists should predict that any state possessing nuclear, chemical, or biological weapons that confronts one or more potential enemies with prompt delivery systems for their own unconventional weapons will be pressed to develop a delegative command and control system. Highly assertive command systems, however, might be maintained in rare cases—such as South Africa in the 1980s—in which a state built unconventional weapons when it did not face a similarly armed rival. Similarly, if emergent proliferant rivals—such as India and Pakistan—remain in a mutual state of "weaponless deterrence" (maintaining nuclear capabilities but not deploying them into the field), more assertive command systems are likely.[59] Yet, once potential enemy capabilities begin to threaten a decapitation strike against central leadership targets, some form of delegation of command authority is likely to be deemed necessary.

Strategic Culture Theory: Command Systems Reflect Traditions and Fears

According to strategic culture theory, a state's command and control system could be strongly influenced by domestic political interests and decision-making traditions and by specific historical experiences and myths concerning initiation of war. With respect to domestic politics, two cultural factors are likely to be most relevant. First, different states hold different cultural norms concerning whether political authority should be highly centralized or more widely shared through some form of a checks-and-balances system. Such cultural traditions, and the institutions built around them, could have a strong impact on state leaders when they acquire nuclear,

57. Memorandum for Commander in Chief, Strategic Air Command, December 1959, Office of the Special Assistant for National Security Affairs, NSC Series, Subject subseries, Box 1, Atomic Weapons, Correspondence, and Background for Presidential Approval, Eisenhower Library.

58. Memorandum of Discussion of NSC meeting, 3 December 1954, *FRUS, 1952–1954*, Vol. 2, *National Security Affairs*, p. 1, 805–6.

59. On these points, see David J. Karl, "Proliferation, Pessimism and Emerging Nuclear Powers," *International Security* 21 (Winter 1996–97): 110.

chemical, or biological weapons and have to think through how best to design a command and control system. Second, just as domestic political interests in different conscription policies or budget assignments were seen to shape military doctrine, neoculturalists also would predict that command systems can reflect internal political struggles and the state's mechanisms for political succession. For example, political leaders who hold strong fears concerning the possibility of a military coup will have strong incentives to maintain tight, centralized control over all military forces and especially tight control over nuclear, chemical, and biological capabilities and the authority to use such weapons.[60] (An important exception to this generalization would be weak civilian government during a transition after a period of direct military rule. Such civilian leaders could fear that efforts to exert tighter control over military responsibility for war plans and command operations would jeopardize their tenuous hold on the reins of state power.[61]) A state leader also could be concerned that issuing predelegated use authority to a military commander or another civilian authority would serve to identify his or her successor. If control over a state's unconventional weapons arsenal symbolizes the highest political authority in a state, then predelegation of weapons release authority would signal who was next in the line of succession.

These cultural arguments have been used to explain important details of the Soviet Union's nuclear command and control system during the Cold War. According to Bruce Blair, "The procedures for authorizing the use of nuclear weapons embodied a core value of Russian political culture, collective centralized decision-making. No individual, regardless of rank or position, could alone issue the authorization to employ nuclear weapons. This power was less concentrated than it is in the United States, where the president is entitled to authorize the use of nuclear weapons."[62] This cultural argument suggests that the tradition of collective decision making meant that senior General Staff officers, each possessing a portion of the critical nuclear weapons release code, served as an important check on the power of individual political leaders in the Politburo. At the same time, the desire for centralization inhibited the willingness to disperse release codes or delegate authorization to military commanders outside of Moscow. In addition, the lack of an institutional mechanism to deal with political succession in the USSR may have inhibited nuclear weapons delegation policies. As

---

60. For an excellent analysis of how such coup d'état concerns influence conventional force operations, see Stephen Biddle and Robert Zirkle, "Technology, Civil-Military Relations, and Warfare in the Developing World," *Journal of Strategic Studies* 19 (June 1996): 171–212.

61. On this issue, see Hasan-Askari Rizvi, "Civil-Military Relations in Contemporary Pakistan," *Survival* 40 (Summer 1998): 96–113.

62. Blair, *Logic of Accidental Nuclear War*, 71.

Stephen Meyer noted during the Cold War, "Many Western students of Soviet politics believe that the Soviets may have avoided predelegation of highest authority precisely because it could imply political succession rights during regular political transitions."[63]

The second major strategic cultural factor that could exert a strong influence on the evolution of command and control systems is leaders' beliefs about the likelihood of surprise attacks in warfare. Strategic culture theory would suggest that such beliefs would not be based on objective technical characteristics of specific weapons systems or the strategic balance but rather on leaders' memories and interpretations of military history. Thus leaders of states that were victimized by a surprise attack in a recent war would be extremely sensitive to, and perhaps even obsessed with, concerns about surprise counterforce or decapitation attacks. This phenomenon could be called "strategic hormephobia": a collective form of the "fear of shock" phobia that some individuals experience. Such fears could lead state leaders to maintain high military alert levels in peacetime and would encourage the delegation of launch authority for unconventional weapons.

This strategic culture perspective raises important questions about the degree to which American and Soviet civilian and military planners during the Cold War focused on the risks of surprise attack. Throughout the Cold War, Soviet and American officials viewed the ability to retaliate even after receiving a "bolt out of the blue" surprise attack as a natural, if conservative, criterion for effective deterrence.[64] A cultural lens, however, suggests that such concerns were the lingering effects of the December 1941 Pearl Harbor attack and the June 1941 Barbarossa attack. From this perspective, it is revealing to note how often senior U.S. military officers complained in the 1950s that failure to predelegate nuclear weapons release authority to the military would "make scapegoats of the operational commanders in the event of a modern Pearl Harbor."[65] Similarly, Soviet military writers in this period—once they were free to criticize Stalin's official line that the Soviet retreat in June 1941 had been a preplanned strategy of "active defense"—

63. Steven M. Meyer, "Soviet Nuclear Operations," in *Managing Nuclear Operations*, ed. Carter, Steinbruner, and Zraket, 485–86.

64. See Richard K. Betts, *Surprise Attack: Lessons for Defense Planning* (Washington, D.C.: Brookings Institution, 1982).

65. Letter, October 21, 1957, General Thomas Power to General Thomas D. White, 2, Top Secret–General File, Thomas D. White Papers, Library of Congress. Curtis LeMay also argued that "the military believes it can be trusted with nuclear weapons, that it can exercise prudence and follow orders, but that it must be permitted to use its own judgment when all contact is lost with higher authority. Otherwise we ask for a nuclear Pearl Harbor" (Curtis E. LeMay with Dale O. Smith, *America Is in Danger* [New York: Funk and Wagnalls, 1968], 279).

argued that the Barbarossa surprise attack demonstrated the need for the Soviet Union to have civil defense preparations and preemptive nuclear attack options.[66]

In contrast, this cultural perspective also would suggest that political and military leaders of states that were not victimized by surprise attacks in recent wars would be far less worried about bolts out of the blue. Such leaders might be more willing to accept the vulnerability of their forces and command structure in peacetime, relying on the ability to alert forces and command structures in crises when strategic warning of possible attack is available. In short, the dominant beliefs in a society about whether successful surprise attacks are likely could have a strong effect on national command and control structures.

Strategic culture arguments predict that different state leaders are likely to develop different types of command systems depending on their domestic decision-making cultures, domestic interests and procedures for succession, and their state's military experiences and dominant interpretations concerning whether or not wars often begin with surprise attacks. Such arguments provide a new, and demanding, set of questions for research concerning new nuclear, chemical, or biological weapons states. Subsequent chapters sift through the empirical evidence for signs that such cultural factors may have influenced the leaders of the states in question.

This chapter presents a set of alternative theoretical lenses that can be used as tools to help understand the origins of military doctrine and command and control systems. These theories sometimes provide conflicting predictions about how and why different states plan to use and control unconventional weapons. Sometimes the theories are complementary, focusing attention on and explaining different dimensions of doctrine and command and control. These theoretical perspectives present a severe challenge to analysts seeking to understand current and predict future doctrines and command systems. In each case, analysts must both identify the *outcome* (what kind of doctrine or command system exists) and the *reasons* it was adopted. Because the theories often predict similar outcomes, albeit produced by very different causes, researchers must lift the veil of official announcements about military doctrine or command procedures and look at the underlying causal processes hidden beneath.

Scholars, statesmen, soldiers, and intelligence officers have similarly strong interests in understanding the determinants of doctrines and

---

66. See David Holloway, *The Soviet Union and the Arms Race* (New Haven: Yale University Press, 1983), 36–37.

command systems of their own states and their potential rivals. Theories are necessary—for scholars and policymakers alike—to make sense of a very complex reality. The difference between scholars and policymakers in this regard is not that one group uses theory and the other does not but rather that scholars try to be more explicit about their theories and their assumptions and the causal predictions derived from them. Our understandings of how states plan the unthinkable will be improved, however, if scholars and policymakers are more open to alternative explanations, more explicit in their efforts to link theory with practice, and more thorough in their search for evidence.

[2]

Saddam's Toxic Arsenal: Chemical and Biological Weapons in the Gulf Wars

TIMOTHY V. MCCARTHY

AND JONATHAN B. TUCKER

By the time of the 1991 Persian Gulf War, Iraq had amassed the most exten-sive arsenal of chemical and biological weapons in the developing world, together with a ballistic missile force capable of delivering conventional and nonconventional payloads to theaterwide targets. Baghdad also main-tained an ambitious nuclear research and development program, and by 1990 the Iraqis were perhaps one year away from deploying a nuclear de-vice. Saddam Hussein thus sought a robust capability in all categories of unconventional weapons and was prepared to invest enormous financial and human resources to achieve this goal. The value he placed on uncon-ventional weapons is indicated by one telling fact: Baghdad's determina-tion to retain these capabilities in defiance of the UN disarmament regime is the chief reason for continuation of international sanctions, which have cost Iraq more than $130 billion in lost oil sales.[1]

Iraq's huge nonconventional warfare capability and its repeated or threatened use of some of these weapons raise profound questions for those concerned with proliferation. This chapter addresses three questions about Iraqi weapons and strategy. Why was this nonconventional arsenal acquired? What were the military doctrines governing its use? And finally, what was the nature of Iraq's unconventional weapons command and con-trol arrangements?

This chapter offers four key arguments: First, Iraq conceived of its noncon-ventional weapons as serving a spectrum of military and political missions, ranging from tactical war-fighting to strategic deterrence; second, these

---

1. Christopher Marquis, "Sanctions on Iraq Likely to be Eased," *San Jose Mercury News,* 4 De-cember 1999, 4A.

missions were integrally linked with Saddam Hussein's personal and strategic ambitions; third, Iraqi doctrine evolved in response to crises; and finally, command and control arrangements for strategic and tactical use of chemical and biological weapons were largely distinct. Although the analysis focuses on Iraq's unconventional arsenal (chemical and biological weapons and missile delivery systems) during the 1991 Gulf War, many of the patterns evident in this case are likely to reappear in future conflicts if the Iraqi regime has chemical, biological, or nuclear weapons.

The chapter also provides some theoretical insights into the factors that shape military doctrine and command and control systems. Realist theory would predict that Iraq would seek to acquire and use nuclear, chemical, and biological weapons to support its national security objectives and that Iraq would develop an offensive doctrine to support expansionist ambitions against its neighbors because a larger and stronger Iraqi state would be more secure. At the same time, realists would predict that if the Baghdad government were thwarted by stronger military powers, it would modify its offensive ambitions and develop strategies of deterrence. Realist theory also suggests that Iraq would develop a decentralized command structure to deter decapitation attacks and to ensure retaliation. Organizational theory, in contrast, would predict an offensively oriented military doctrine and a highly delegative command and control system because both would promote the interests of the professional military.

Cultural theories offer a third set of predictions: Iraq should develop doctrines that support the domestic interests of key actors and reflect the unique historical experience of the Iraqi state. Saddam's personal vision of Iraq's destiny and his own legacy should be paramount. With respect to command and control, this model would suggest that Iraq's domestic politics (especially civil-military relations) are the prime constraint on the level of decentralization implemented in Iraq. Given his fear of a military coup, Saddam would never delegate the authority for strategic use of chemical and biological weapons to lower-level officers.

This chapter suggests that there is some explanatory value in realist theory, which would ascribe the maximization of power as a key determinant of Iraq's behavior. Organizational theory also can explain some initiatives in the Iraqi weapon development programs. Taken together, however, these two approaches do not provide a full account of Iraq's choices. A common thread running through this history is that Saddam Hussein is a leader who has near total power to make and implement decisions. Saddam's vision of Iraq and his own place in history, as well as the state security apparatus he created to realize that vision, provide the unique domestic and strategic milieu in which Iraq's behavior must be understood. This is *Saddam's* arsenal. Iraq's strategic doctrine and command and control structures are shaped by his idiosyncrasies.

SADDAM'S VISION: OBJECTIVES AND IMPLEMENTATION

Given Iraq's population size and composition, location, and oil resources, Baghdad has certain foreign policy and defense concerns that would exist whatever regime was in power. Iraq borders on six different countries, and it has little secure access to the Persian Gulf. A bitter civil conflict with the Kurdish minority in the northern part of the country and historical enmities with Iran to the east and Israel to the west help to make heavy investment in national defense a state priority. Iraq's near total reliance on oil exports as a source of revenue and the consequent need to secure this resource and protect its export outlets also influence the country's geostrategic calculus.

These legitimate security interests, however, are overshadowed by Saddam Hussein's immense personal ambitions, belief systems, and vision of his place in history.[2] Saddam's Weltanschauung has several components. His calculations are conditioned by his desire to remain in power and to ensure the continued dominance of his Ba'athist regime. In keeping with Ba'athist ideology, however, Saddam promotes the popular dream of the rebirth (ba'ath) of a united Arab-Muslim empire.[3] This dream remains a rallying cry for the Ba'athist revolution and a legitimizing force for Saddam's policy initiatives. Saddam Hussein also views himself as a great military leader and strategist, supreme leader of a reborn Arab-Muslim empire, and heir to the legacy of great Arab and Middle Eastern rulers such Salah al-Din and the 'Abbasid caliphs.[4] He seeks to dominate the entire Arab world economically, politically, and militarily. This near boundless ambition provides a rationale to seek the most powerful weapons available.

Saddam Hussein has two central political and security objectives: to retain uncontested power in Baghdad and to promote Iraq as the leading state in the Arab world. Remaining in control is no easy task, given the instability of the Iraqi polity, but Saddam has proven equal to the task. Seasoned by years of intrigue preceding the 1968 Ba'ath Party triumph, Saddam came equipped to consolidate the regime's power in a decades-long process.[5] To do so, he neutralized the Iraqi army as a threat to his regime, gave decision-making authority to his relatives and close associates, and started to develop an arsenal of unconventional weapons.

2. See Kanan Makiya's classic interpretation of Ba'athist rule in Iraq, *Republic of Fear: The Politics of Modern Iraq*, originally published under the pseudonym Samir al-Khalil (Berkeley: University of California Press, updated edition with new introduction, 1988); Amatzia Baram, "U.S. Foreign Policy and Iraq," presentation at the United States Institute of Peace, C-SPAN, 20 November 1997.

3. Adel Darwish and Gregory Alexander, *Unholy Babylon: The Secret History of Saddam's War* (New York: St. Martin's Press, 1991), 211.

4. Baram, "U.S. Foreign Policy and Iraq."

5. See Simon Henderson, *Instant Empire: Saddam Hussein's Ambitions for Iraq* (San Francisco: Mercury House, 1991), 51–71.

The army and its officer corps have figured decisively in numerous Iraqi domestic power struggles since the 1930s, either by backing a particular civilian faction or by seizing power themselves.[6] Recognizing the inherent political threat posed by the army, Saddam and the Ba'ath Party moved quickly to infiltrate and control it.[7] They created alternative command relationships and allegiances by suffusing the ranks and officer corps with Ba'athist cadres. The so-called Military Bureau, led by Saddam Hussein, is responsible for party organization in the army and is considered the highest authority in the armed forces.[8] Purges of "suspect" officers and centralization of command through the president are used to neutralize potential challenges to the regime. As a result, army officers largely have been removed from key positions of authority in the Revolutionary Command Council (RCC) and the government.[9] This situation has left the armed forces without an effective voice in the highest-level security decisions.[10]

In addition, Saddam created parallel military, intelligence, and security structures to contain the army's domestic ambitions and to consolidate and expand the regime's control. The Republican Guard (RG) and its offshoot, the Special Republican Guard (SRG), stand outside the authority of the Ministry of Defense and Army General Staff and report directly to the president, normally through one of Saddam's relatives. Among the tasks of these units are the protection of senior officials and service as a praetorian guard in the event of domestic insurrection. Security and intelligence institutions—including the Mukhabarat al-'Amma (General Intelligence Service) for foreign intelligence; the Amn al-Amm (General Intelligence) for domestic intelligence and repression; and the supra-intelligence organ, the Amn al-Khas (Special Security Organization, or SSO), which oversees the other state security institutions—are also controlled directly by the president through one of Saddam's relatives or close associates. Recruits for these organizations are thoroughly vetted for their party allegiance and, especially in the SSO and SRG, for kinship, tribal, or geographic ties to Sad-

---

6. See Mark A. Heller, "Iraq's Army: Military Weakness, Political Utility," in *Iraq's Road to War*, ed. Amatzia Baram and Barry Rubin (New York: St. Martin's Press, 1993), 37–50.

7. *Political Report of the Eighth Congress of the Arab Ba'ath Socialist Party in Iraq, January 1974* (London: Ithaca Press, 1979), 103.

8. See the report "Military Bureau," Iraqi National Congress. http://www.inc.org.uk.

9. See Heller, "Iraq's Army," 44–46; Amatzia Baram, "The Ruling Political Elite in Ba'athi Iraq, 1968–1986: The Changing Features of a Collective Profile," *International Journal of Middle East Studies*, no. 21 (1989): 447–93; and Amatzia Baram, "Saddam's Iraq, 1968–1998: The Interplay between Domestic Affairs and Foreign Policy" (Washington, D.C.: United States Institute of Peace, 1998), draft manuscript.

10. The minister of defense and the chief of the General Staff, for example, were the last senior officials to become aware that Iraqi forces intended to capture all of Kuwait in 1990 rather than undertaking a more limited invasion. See Baram, *Saddam's Iraq*, 38.

dam Hussein.[11] Saddam consistently turns to these units to implement his most important policies.

At the same time, Saddam Hussein has eliminated anyone suspected of disloyalty from the RCC and the Regional Command of the Ba'ath Party.[12] Over the years, the circle of highest level advisers has narrowed to members of Saddam's immediate family and to his long-term associates in political struggle and intrigue. Meeting in an informal "family council," these advisers deal with the most important security questions facing the regime. Participants during the Persian Gulf War probably included Saddam, his sons Qusay and Uday, sons-in-law Hussein and Saddam Kamel, and his cousin Ali Hassan al-Majid.[13] These advisers supervised or held senior posts in key security and governmental organs such as the SSO, SRG, and RG. Meanwhile, Saddam's continued survival requires a delicate political balancing act. He must demonstrate to his power base—close associates, security services, and allied tribes—that he deserves their loyalty.[14] It is for this reason, according to a critic, that Saddam "is more afraid of losing face before his enemies . . . than he is of the entire military arsenal of the United States."[15]

What insights does this information give us into Iraq's weapons policies and actions? Obviously, Saddam's views on unconventional weapons are crucial, and the Iraqi military has little say in setting national policy. Only a few individuals close to the Iraqi president have any real chance to influence Saddam's policies. They do so primarily by implementing presidential decisions through the security institutions they control such as the SSO, SRG, and RG. It is to these institutions that Saddam has turned to control his strategic arsenal.

BUILDING THE ARSENAL

Iraq's extensive weapons acquisition efforts show similarities across weapons programs.[16] In both the chemical and biological weapons and missile fields, Iraqi technicians explored nearly every conceivable develop-

---

11. With respect to SRG recruitment, see Amatzia Baram, "Neo-Tribalism in Iraq: Saddam Hussein's Tribal Policies, 1991–1996," *International Journal of Middle East Studies*, no. 29 (1997): 5.

12. Baram, "Ruling Political Elite," and "Saddam's Iraq."

13. These high-level meetings reportedly were known as the Special Bureau. See Latif Yahia and Karl Wendl, *I Was Saddam's Son* (New York: Arcade, 1997), 85, 238. Uday reportedly left for Geneva in the midst of the 1990–91 Gulf crisis.

14. Baram, "U.S. Foreign Policy and Iraq."

15. Makiya, *Republic of Fear*, xx.

16. For a more in-depth discussion of these issues with a special focus on foreign technology procurement, see Kenneth R. Timmerman, *The Death Lobby: How the West Armed Iraq* (Boston: Houghton Mifflin, 1991).

ment path and weapon type, often because the Iraqi leadership created a competition between rival research groups. All of the Iraqi special weapons programs received impetus from the war with Iran and the crisis atmosphere preceding the Gulf War. By the late 1980s, most of the weapons projects were controlled by Hussein Kamel, both in his formal role as head of the Ministry of Industry and Military Industrialization (MIMI) and through his informal relationships with chemical and biological weapons and missile scientists.

Weaponization and Delivery of Chemical Weapon Agents

Iraq produced several chemical weapon agents, including mustard gas and the nerve agents tabun (GA), sarin (GB), cyclosarin (GF), and VX. These agents were placed in a variety of delivery systems, including artillery and mortar shells, 250- and 500-kilogram aerial bombs, 122mm surface-to-surface rockets, and 90mm air-to-surface rockets (mounted on helicopters). From 1991 to 1994 the United Nations Special Commission on Iraq (UNSCOM) destroyed a total of 28,049 Iraqi chemical munitions and more than 481,000 liters of chemical warfare agents and precursors.[17] Even so, UNSCOM was unable to find or eliminate Iraq's suspected VX stockpile. Iraq also pursued a strategic chemical weapons capability by developing and deploying chemical warheads for the long-range Al-Hussein missile. Iraq has declared that fifty chemical warheads were produced for the Al-Hussein missile. Nevertheless, Iraq's unilateral destruction practices after the Gulf War and the lack of independent documentation make it impossible to verify the total number of chemical warheads produced.

Biological Weapons Program

Iraq appears to have decided in late 1972 to acquire biological weapons.[18] The chief aim of this initial effort, reportedly on behalf of the intelligence services, was to develop botulinum toxin for covert "dirty tricks" against the regime's enemies, but the effort was unsuccessful and the program was closed down. In 1983, during the Iran-Iraq War, the Iraqi microbiologist Abdul Nassir al-Hindawi wrote a secret paper for the Iraqi leadership outlining how large-scale production of biological agents could provide an an-

17. "Seventh Report of the Executive Chairman of UNSCOM," UNSC Document No. S/1994/750, 24 June 1994.
18. This section draws extensively on the chronology in UNSCOM, UNSC Document No. S/1995/864, 11 October 1995; and the updated chronology in R. Jeffrey Smith, "Iraq's Drive for a Biological Arsenal," *Washington Post*, 21 November 1997, 1.

tipersonnel weapon for tactical use against Iran. Iraqi leaders soon ordered the directors of the chemical weapons program to create a separate complex for making germ weapons. The project was designated a "presidential priority" and was exempted from usual spending and personnel constraints. After beginning with literature studies in 1986, the Iraqi scientists ordered seed cultures of various pathogens from commercial laboratories in France and the United States.[19] The research effort covered a wide array of biological agents, including pathogenic bacteria (anthrax, plague, and *Clostridium perfringens*, the causative agent of gas gangrene), potent toxins (botulinum toxin, aflatoxin, ricin, and trichothecene mycotoxins), an anti-crop agent (wheat cover smut), and three incapacitating viruses (hemorrhagic conjunctivitis, rota-virus, and camel pox).[20]

In 1987, the program was placed administratively under the Technical Research Center, an entity controlled by the SSO. Hussein Kamel—who at the time was director of the MIMI and the SSO—ordered the construction of new biological weapons research facilities, including an aerosol test chamber where the effects of biological agents were studied on sheep, donkeys, monkeys, and dogs. The Iraqis also initiated field trials of munitions containing anthrax simulant and botulinum toxin. After Iraq's invasion of Kuwait on 2 August 1990, Baghdad initiated a "crash" program of large-scale production and weaponization. The Iraqis maintain that this effort was undertaken as a "personal initiative" by Hussein Kamel. Most biological weapons agent production occurred in a three-month period between the invasion of Kuwait and the onset of Operation Desert Storm. Iraq has admitted production of at least 19,000 liters of concentrated botulinum toxin, 8,500 liters of a concentrated slurry of anthrax spores (10^{10} spores per milliliter), and 2,200 liters of concentrated aflatoxin. Although Iraq claims that it produced anthrax only in slurry form, UNSCOM suspects that Iraq was capable of producing dry anthrax spores, which have a much longer shelf life and can be disseminated as an aerosol cloud over greater distances.[21] UNSCOM has been unable to find any documentary evidence to corroborate Iraq's claimed aflatoxin production.[22] At the same time, UNSCOM has found new indications that *Clostridium perfringens* (gas gangrene) bacteria were

19. Smith, "Iraq's Drive." See also U.S. Senate, Committee on Banking, Housing, and Urban Affairs, Hearing, *United States Dual-Use Exports to Iraq and Their Impact on the Health of Persian Gulf War Veterans*, 103d Cong., 2d sess., 25 May 1994, 264–75.

20. Lois Ember, "Iraq Was Poised to Use Biological Arms in 1991," *Chemical and Engineering News*, 4 September 1995, 7–8.

21. Lecture by Rolf Ekeus at the Monterey Institute of International Studies, 17 March 1997.

22. Iraqi accounts of aflatoxin production are implausible. The claimed production methodology for aflatoxin could not provide for the quality and quantity stated in their declaration to UNSCOM.

cultivated on a large scale under the control of Staff 7 of the SSO.[23] In late 1990, the Iraqis also worked around the clock to harvest castor beans, from which to extract a large quantity of ricin, a potent toxin.

Iraq claims to have filled 157 aerial bombs and 25 Al-Hussein missile warheads with biological agents. Additionally, the Iraqi Agricultural Research Institute modified a "belly" drop tank for the Mirage F-1 aircraft as a spray tank (with a liquid fill capacity of 2,000 liters) for aerosol dissemination of biological agents. Although Iraqi officials claim the spray tank failed in testing, Iraq produced and stored three additional tanks, all of which were reportedly destroyed on the last day of the Gulf War.[24] Finally, Iraq experimented with a remote-controlled MiG-21 jet fighter and other remotely piloted vehicles that could be used to disseminate biological weapon agents on targets in Israel.[25]

Ballistic Missiles and Chemical and Biological Weapons

In 1973, Iraq signed an initial five-year contract with the Soviet Union for the purchase of Scud-B missiles, including transporter-erector-launchers (TELs), propellants, transport trailers, test vehicles, propellant vehicles, and spare parts.[26] Soon thereafter, Iraq formed a missile brigade known as Unit 224. At the end of the five-year contract, Iraq had an operational missile infrastructure with the capability to repair and maintain its Scud systems. Ultimately, some 819 Scuds, 15 training missiles, 11 TELs (including one training launcher), and associated vehicles, spare parts and propellants were imported from the Soviet Union. Missile deliveries continued until at least the spring of 1988.

The driving force behind the development of the longer-range Scud derivative known as the Al-Hussein was Iran's repeated ballistic-missile attacks against Baghdad during the Iran-Iraq War. Iraq was unable to retaliate in kind against the Iranian capital because Tehran was 580 kilometers away from the Iraqi border. The unanswered Iranian attacks became politically intolerable during the summer of 1986.[27] Unable to procure longer-range missiles from Moscow, the Iraqis sought to develop this capability indigenously.

23. Author (Tucker) interview with UNSCOM staff member, 20 April 1998.
24. UNSCOM, UNSC Document No. S/1995/864, 11 October 1995, 22–28.
25. R. Jeffrey Smith, "UN Pursuing 25 Germ Warheads It Believes Are Still Loaded with Deadly Toxin," *Washington Post*, 21 November 1997, 1.
26. Unless otherwise noted, the following section is based on discussions with UNSCOM staff and interviews with relevant Iraqi authorities by one of the authors (McCarthy).
27. The Iraqis had been able to launch some 330 unmodified Scuds at Iranian cities and other targets. These launches, however, lacked the political and strategic impact of a strike against the enemy capital.

Late in the winter of 1986, the armed forces' Scientific Research and Technical Development Organization (SRTDO), the Military Research and Development Commission, Unit 224's Technical Battalion, and the Research and Development Group from the State Organization for Technical Industries (SOTI) began to assess the possibility of extending the Scud-B's range. The project was supervised by the director of SOTI but was under the administrative control of SRTDO.[28] The initial flight test for the Al-Hussein took place in February 1987. By the 1988 battle of opposing missile forces known as the War of the Cities, the Iraqis were able to produce three Al-Husseins per day. Iraq's missile development efforts did not end with the Al-Hussein. Design work on the approximately 950-kilometer-range Al-Abbas missile began late in 1987, and an initial flight test was made in late April 1988. Although Iraqi officials claim that MIMI ordered this work to begin, the relationship between a specific combat requirement and the Al-Abbas is unclear. In any event, the onset of the 1991 Gulf War ended work on the Al-Abbas. The Iraqi army also pressured Project 144 (the unit charged with Al-Hussein production) to develop a more accurate version of the Al-Hussein, which had been salvo-fired during the War of the Cities to compensate for its poor accuracy. In response, Iraqi engineers developed the so-called short Al-Hussein, which was designed to solve flight instability problems and thereby increase accuracy. Flight tests began in January 1990, but the Iraqi army was displeased with operational difficulties inherent in the new design.

Project 144 was also called upon to design and construct a "kinetic energy" warhead and "special warheads" for chemical and biological payloads. For the kinetic-energy version, three steel-reinforcement rods were cast inside a concrete-filled warhead, which was thought capable of penetrating the Israeli underground nuclear reactor at Dimona. Iraqi officials claim that the idea for this type of warhead came from within Project 144, but it seems likely that some higher authority was involved at least in authorizing work on the weapon.

Iraqi officials state that shortly after the invasion of Kuwait, Hussein Kamel ordered a crash program to develop seventy-five chemical and biological warheads. The director of Project 144 claims that he believed all of the special warheads were intended for chemical fill and that he shipped

---

28. At the time, SOTI was a "technical appendage of the Ministry of Defense" under the direction of General Amer Rashid al-Ubeidi. See Timmerman, *Death Lobby,* 257–59. General Rashid was a key figure in the history of Iraq's military-industrial infrastructure and is currently minister of oil. Hussein Kamel took over SOTI in January 1987, and General Rashid continued his close supervision of the range-extension project. In the context of this essay, it is useful to note that the beginnings and ultimate success of the range-extension program coincided with the rise to power of Hussein Kamel.

the finished products to the Muthanna State Establishment, Iraq's main chemical weapon production facility, from late September through November 1990. Since a ballistic missile warhead of this type has a terminal velocity of about Mach 3, triggering it to disseminate chemical and biological agents before impact is a challenging task. The Iraqis say that the special warheads contained impact fuses. If the warheads simply detonated on impact, however, the agent would not be disseminated efficiently. According to one analyst, had Iraq's biological warheads actually been used, "their effect would have been limited to contaminating a relatively small area of ground surrounding the point of impact and exposing nearby individuals to aerosolized pathogens or toxins."[29]

As an apparent alternative to proximity fusing, Iraq launched a program to use parachutes to retard the speed of its ballistic-missile warheads to help disperse agent payload before impact. In 1988, the Iraqis imported a parachute device with the capability to decelerate a supersonic missile payload. The Iraqis claim, however, that this parachute system was not designed for special warheads but was intended for recovery of photographic equipment used to record missile airframe performance during flight.

RATIONALE FOR ACQUIRING UNCONVENTIONAL WEAPONS

In a series of speeches and in meetings with foreign officials, Saddam Hussein articulated some of the policies associated with Iraq's unconventional weapons programs. These statements reflect the difficulties of understanding the motivations behind Iraqi unconventional weapons and the doctrines guiding their use. On the one hand, Saddam's speeches include reasoned analyses of deterrence; on the other, they are indicative of his intense concerns over internal and external threats and his abiding pursuit of hegemony and self-aggrandizement. For example, a key reason offered for new Iraqi weapons programs is the need to deter Israel. This justification, however, often entails deterring not just physical attack but also conspiratorial Israeli plots to dominate the Arabs. Additionally, it is not known whether Saddam's words reflected or were translated into a formal military planning process. One is left with the impression that Iraq's nonconventional weaponry evolved from both rational strategic calculation and the idiosyncrasies of Saddam Hussein.

---

29. Raymond A. Zilinskas, "Iraq's Biological Weapons: The Past as Future?" *Journal of the American Medical Association* 278 (6 August 1997): 421.

Deterrence and Beyond

Two key speeches, delivered nearly ten years apart, provide the basis for assessing Saddam's concept of deterrence. The first speech came just two weeks after the June 1981 Israeli surprise attack on the Osirak nuclear reactor.[30] Addressing his cabinet, Saddam argued that Israel's aim was to prevent "the Arab nation's progress and development and its realization of a suitable living standard." Consequently, the future of the Arab-Israeli conflict would be defined by a "struggle for civilization between the Arab nation and its enemies, headed by the Zionists." The key to victory in this struggle was the development of Iraq's scientific potential, economy, and self-confidence within a Ba'athist political framework. Accordingly, Saddam claimed that Israel had attacked Iraq because it was a front-line Arab state working to develop its technology base, *not* because it was allegedly developing nuclear weapons.[31] Tel Aviv sought not only to destroy high-technology Arab facilities like Osirak but also to dictate the terms of the Arab-Israeli relationship. Saddam also raised the specter of Israeli nuclear blackmail, which would allow Israel to force changes in Arab governments, rewrite Arab history, and ban Arab scientific education.

To end the Israeli nuclear monopoly, Saddam called upon "any state in the world . . . which does not want [Arabs] subjugated to foreign forces to help the Arabs in one way or another to acquire atomic bombs." A nuclear capability, he argued, would "prevent the Zionist entity from using atomic bombs against the Arabs, thus saving the world from the dangers of using atomic bombs in wars." Saddam went on to describe this future nuclear balance as analogous to the balance of terror between the superpowers, since "I do not believe either the Americans or the Soviets will use the atomic bomb against each other." Thus, in his view, Iraq's acquisition of unconventional (specifically nuclear) weapons would lead to a state of mutual deterrence that would dissuade Israel from repeating a preventive attack and preclude Israeli nuclear compellance.

Iraq's theory of deterrence was further defined in Saddam's 1 April 1990 speech to his senior military commanders. At that time, the furor caused by Baghdad's execution of the British journalist Farzod Bazoft as an alleged

---

30. Baghdad Domestic Service, 23 June 1981, "Text of Saddam Husan [*sic*] 23 June Cabinet Statement," FBIS-NES, 24 June 1981, E1–E7. The authors thank Amatzia Baram for pointing out this statement. The following section draws heavily on Professor Baram's "Iraqi Imagery of Non-Conventional Deterrence vis-à-vis Israel," manuscript, 1992.

31. See also Gabriel Ben Dor, "Arab Rationality and Deterrence," in *Deterrence in the Middle East: Where Theory and Practice Converge,* ed. Aharon Klieman and Ariel Levite (Tel Aviv: Jaffee Center for Strategic Studies, 1993), 89–91.

spy and the interception in the United Kingdom of equipment bound for the Iraqi nuclear program led Iraqi officials to believe that another Osirak-like attack was imminent.[32] Saddam criticized the West's outraged response to the Bazoft affair, saying: "They will be deluded if they imagine that they can give Israel a cover in order to come and strike at some industrial metalworks. By God, we will make fire eat up half of Israel if it [attacks] Iraq." In the same speech, Saddam boasted that Iraq had developed a "binary" chemical weapon, adding that, "according to our information, only the United States and the Soviet Union have it."[33] The speech was interpreted in the West as an Iraqi threat to attack Israel with chemical weapons.

Meeting eleven days later with a delegation of U.S. senators, Saddam stated that he had predelegated authority to launch a retaliatory chemical attack in the event of an Israeli nuclear strike on Baghdad.

> I repeat now, in your presence, that if Israel strikes, we will strike back. I believe this is a fair stand. *A stand known in advance is what helps peace. . . . For if Israel realizes it will be struck, it might refrain from striking.* . . . If Israel uses atomic bombs, we will strike at it with the binary chemical weapon. . . . We have given instructions to the commanders of the air bases and the missile formations that once they hear Israel has hit any place in Iraq with the atomic bomb, they will load the chemical weapon with as much as will reach Israel and direct it at its territory. For we might be in Baghdad holding a meeting with the command when the atomic bomb falls on us. So, to make the military order clear to the air and missile base commanders, *we have told them that if they do not receive an order from higher authority and a city is struck with an atomic bomb, they will point toward Israel any weapons capable of reaching it.* [emphasis added][34]

Iraq's deterrent threats toward Israel made no direct reference to biological weapons, whose very existence remained a closely guarded secret. While denying that Iraq was pursuing biological weapons, Saddam did emphasize to the visiting U.S. delegation that Iraq had the right to obtain any weapon already in the Israeli arsenal.[35]

---

32. Describing a 13 February 1990 meeting with Hussein Kamel, Richard Murphy recounts: "The Iraqis were worried that the Israelis were planning another attack against them, and Hussein Kamel said they had solid evidence to back up their suspicions. What evidence? I asked. 'Never mind,' he said. 'It's just a given. Israel is going to repeat its 1981 attack on us, and soon.' " (Timmerman, *Death Lobby*, 372).

33. Speech by Saddam Hussein on 1 April 1990, translated from Arabic in Baghdad Domestic Service, "President Warns Israel, Criticizes U.S.," FBIS-NES-90-064, 3 April 1990, 32-36.

34. The transcript from the meeting is in FBIS-NES-90-076, 17 April 1990, 7.

35. Iraqi News Agency, 7 April 1990, in FBIS-NES-90-072, 13 April 1990, 6-7.

The Iraqi media reiterated the deterrence theme but, unlike Saddam, hinted at Baghdad's apparent possession of biological weapons.[36] The *Al-Jumhuriyah* newspaper noted that Iraqi missiles and chemical weapons could inflict "terrible losses on the enemy if it dares attack Iraq. This is *in addition to* its ability to mount decisive retaliation to inflict perhaps further losses on the enemy, *something Iraq lacked in the past*" (emphasis added). The paper concluded that Iraq's possession of nonconventional weapons, Israel's awareness of those capabilities, and the Iraqi leadership's proven record of "doing what it says" and "making the most serious decisions" provided for an effective deterrent.

The statements coming out of Baghdad in April 1990 revealed a clear understanding of the logic of deterrence. It is impossible to know if this understanding was the result of extensive studies undertaken by others and then communicated to Saddam. Nevertheless, the Iraqis were aware of several key prerequisites for a viable deterrent policy: acquiring the capability itself, communicating to the enemy the nature of the capability, and signaling resolve to use the weapon if certain conditions were violated.

The failure to mention a weaponized biological capability in various official Iraqi pronouncements raises the question of how an unknown weapon can deter an adversary. Iraqi officials probably knew that Israeli and Western intelligence believed that they possessed biological weapons, enabling Baghdad to make veiled threats. The Iraqis may have lacked suitable means to deliver biological agents and were waiting for more sophisticated delivery systems (such as proximity fuses and submunition warheads). Finally, having learned a bitter lesson from the preventive Israeli strike against the Osirak reactor in 1981, Saddam probably feared provoking an attack against Iraq's biological facilities or deployed weapons.

Once Saddam believed he had established a mutual deterrent relationship with Israel, however, he quickly moved to offer Iraqi protection to the rest of the Arab world. In an 18 April 1990 speech to the members of his General Command and the Revolutionary Command Council, Saddam boasted, "If any party . . . tries to attack any Arab that accepts our assistance, we will respond to the aggressor to the best of our ability. . . . If we can strike him with all our missiles, bombs and resources, then we will strike him [with these weapons]."[37] Two months later, Saddam made his offer of extended deterrence more specific, stating, "We will strike at them [Israel] with all the arms

---

36. The government and the Ba'ath Party own all print and broadcast media and operate them as propaganda outlets. Thus any published account must be considered to reflect official Iraqi government desires. See U.S. Department of State, "Iraq: Report on Human Rights Practices for 1996," Bureau of Democracy, Human Rights, and Labor, January 1997 (Internet version).

37. Iraqi News Agency, 17 April 1990, in FBIS-NES-90-075, 18 April 1990, 14–15.

in our possession if they attack Iraq or the Arabs. . . . Whoever strikes at the Arabs we will strike back from Iraq."[38] Saddam and other Iraqi officials made similar pledges throughout the summer.

The speeches on extended deterrence did not refer to symmetrical responses. Instead, Saddam threatened to use "all the arms in our possession" against "whoever strikes the Arabs." Saddam's wording may have been a function of his audience, but it does indicate that asymmetrical chemical or biological weapons responses to conventional attack were being contemplated. It is not at all clear, however, that there was any specific Iraqi policy—aside from a rhetorical flourish—actually to *implement* extended deterrence. Saddam received glowing Arab reviews of his April 1990 speech threatening massive retaliation to an Israeli attack; he probably believed there was additional glory, and little cost, in extending the deterrent umbrella more widely.

Saddam probably recognized the positive impact that an unconventional weapons arsenal would have on the popularity of his regime at home. For example, he emphasized to the visiting U.S. Senate delegation that the people of Iraq demanded that he defend the country's dignity and sovereignty in the face of Israeli threats and that he had to respond. Otherwise, "In our country, when the people change their view of their leaders, the entire system falls."[39]

The perception of Iraq as the one Arab state capable of breaking the Israeli nuclear monopoly also served Saddam's aspirations to become a regional hegemon. Iraq's offers of "extended deterrence" placed Saddam at the forefront of the defense of the pan-Arab nation. To benefit from Iraqi extended deterrence, other Arab states would have to accept Iraqi leadership. Saddam even went so far as to distribute, rhetorically, ownership of Iraq's chemical weapons to other Arab states. In his 18 April 1990 speech, Saddam claimed that Western leaders had reacted harshly to his announcement about Iraq's advanced chemical weapons because they had discovered "that the Arabs, too, can deal with modern arms to an excellent degree and that they actually have managed this technology and given it a national and pan-Arab identity."[40]

DOCTRINE, OPERATIONS, AND COMMAND AND CONTROL

This section traces the evolution of Iraq's chemical and biological weapons doctrines, operations, and command and control systems from the Iran-Iraq War through the interwar period, culminating in the Persian Gulf War. As

38. Baghdad Radio, 18 June 1990, in FBIS-NES-90-135, 19 June 1990.
39. FBIS-NES-90-076, 17 April 1990, 8.
40. Iraqi News Agency, "Saddam Comments on Binary Chemicals, Missiles," 19 April 1990, translated from Arabic in FBIS-NES-90-076, 19 April 1990, 23–25.

with Iraq's rationale for acquiring these weapons, two themes emerge. First, the Iraqi army, when left to its own devices, developed doctrine and operations that were responsive to its combat environment in what appears to be a rational fashion, particularly with respect to tactical chemical weapons use and conventional missile operations. Second, important aspects of Iraqi strategic doctrine and the related command and control structures cannot be understood outside the specific context of Saddam Hussein's political ambitions at home and abroad. The Iraqi leader was unable to trust the army with his most important chemical and biological weapons missions and was determined to respond to developing circumstances in a manner consistent with his primary objective of staying in power.

Iraqi Operational Doctrine for Use of Chemical and Biological Weapons

Developing and formulating chemical weapons operational doctrine, defensive tactics, and training is the responsibility of the Iraqi Army's Chemical Weapons Branch (CWB). The CWB commander also serves as commander of the Iraqi Chemical Corps, a unit founded in 1964 with responsibilities for chemical weapons planning, transport, use, and defensive operations. Chemical Corps officers are present at each level of military command from General Headquarters to brigade.[41] While this chain of command and unit organization appears coherent, the Ba'ath Party's Military Bureau stands atop the entire military structure, and it is almost certain that bureau personnel review all chemical and biological weapon operations and plans.

Heavily influenced by Soviet thinking and training, Iraqi chemical warfare doctrine stresses that the use of chemical weapons to demoralize and provoke fear in an enemy is as important as inflicting battlefield casualties. Chemical weapons planning is an integral part of all Iraqi military operations, but the weapons themselves are not forward-deployed with the units until their actual use has been ordered. According to an Iraqi infantry officer, "Iraqi doctrine states that if a chemical round is received, it must be fired that same day." [42] The doctrine does not clearly define the circumstances

41. The following source documents are available on a Department of Defense Web site called GulfLINK (www.gulflink.osd.mil). Defense Intelligence Agency (DIA), "Iraqi Chemical Employment Doctrine," 3 October 1991, GulfLINK file no. 950727_27640053_92r.txt; Army Central Command, VII Corps, "Iraqi Chemical Warfare, Tactics, Policy and Doctrine," (undated), GulfLINK file no. 123096_jung6_decls3_0001.txt; Central Intelligence Agency (CIA) "Iraqi Chemical Warfare," February 1991, GulfLINK file no. cia_65142_65142_01.txt; author (McCarthy) interview with UNSCOM staff member, 25 November 1997.

42. DIA, "Desert Shield—Iraqi Command and Control," December 1990, GulfLINK file no. 950727_27640078_91rtxt; DIA, "Iraqi Air Force Issues," undated, GulfLINK file no. 123096_15170137_91r_0001.txt; CIA, "Use of Chemical Weapons," 1990, GulfLINK file no. 970613_23400258_90d_txt_0001.txt; CIA, "Extract from VII Corps Report," undated, GulfLINK file no. 970613_7_corps_ext_txt_0001_txt.; author (McCarthy) interview with UNSCOM staff members, 1 November 1997.

under which chemical weapons would be employed in defensive or offensive operations but focuses instead on how to deliver weapons on target and how to operate in a contaminated environment.[43]

In addition to its responsibilities for chemical weapons, the Iraqi CWB was in charge of formulating doctrine for biological weapons.[44] Two Iraqi military manuals published during the Iran-Iraq War offer insight into Iraqi doctrine for biological weapons. They describe the offensive use of biological agents and suggest that Iraq viewed such agents as a "force-multiplier" for countering a numerically superior foe. The first manual, *Chemical, Biological and Nuclear Operations*, published by the Iraqi Chemical Corps in 1984, discusses the use of biological agents to inflict nonfatal casualties so as to overburden the enemy and damage troop morale: "It is possible to select antipersonnel biological agents in order to cause lethal or incapacitating casualties in the battle area or in the enemy's rear areas. . . . Incapacitating agents are used to inflict casualties which require a large amount of medical supplies and treating facilities, and many people to treat them. Thus it is possible to hinder the opposing military operations."[45] Iraqi military strategists understood that it is more debilitating to the adversary to injure rather than kill troops, because dead soldiers require far less attention than wounded ones.

A second Iraqi manual, *Principles of Using Chemical and Biological Agents in Warfare*, was published by the Iraqi Ministry of Defense in 1987. In the section on military use of biological agents, the manual states: "It is possible to undertake small attacks and sabotage operations through the use of vehicles or small boats in coastal areas. The use of these quick attacks before beginning the general offensive requires its protection and secrecy."[46] This statement suggests that the Iraqi military considered covert biological weapons operations behind enemy lines. Iraqi special forces probably received training in unconventional warfare from Soviet, East German and Yugoslav military advisers.

Iraqi doctrine for conventional ballistic missile operations was similar to Soviet Scud doctrine, with modifications to fit Iraqi conditions. This Iraqi doctrine considered missiles "national strategic assets" and called for massed volleys against strategic targets such as civilian population centers.

43. CIA, "Iraqi Chemical Weapons Doctrine; Iranian Use of Chemical Weapons against Iraqi Troops," December 1994, GulfLINK file no. 110296_cia_61884_61884_01.txt.

44. Author (McCarthy) interview with UNSCOM staff members, 1 November 1997.

45. Armed Forces Medical Intelligence Center (AFMIC) *Manual: Chemical, Biological and Nuclear Operations*, by Col. Sameem Jalal Abdul Latif, Training Department, Iraqi Chemical Corps, 1984, Foreign Armies Studies Series, No. 21, AFMIC-HT-101–92, (Fort Detrick, Md., 1992), 6.

46. AFMIC, *Manual No. 469: Mobilization Use of Arms of Mass Destruction*, Vol. 2, pt 1: *Principles of Using Chemical and Biological Agents in Warfare*, by the Iraqi Army General Staff, 1987, AFMIC-HT-099–92, (Fort Detrick, Md., 1992), 14.

These attacks were designed to produce panic, a goal also reflected in Iraqi chemical weapons doctrine.[47] Saddam's reliance on ballistic missiles rather than aircraft for this mission probably was based on his political fear of a capable, motivated air force and that service's relatively poor combat performance.[48]

Command and Control during the Iran-Iraq War, 1980–1988

At the beginning of the Iran-Iraq War, Iraq relied on a rigid, highly assertive command and control system for chemical weapons and missile operations. Pressed by battlefield setbacks, however, the Iraqis modified these procedures, especially release authority, to improve the performance of available weapon systems. Similarly, Iraq gradually revised its plans for delivery methods, target selection, and agents used for chemical warfare.

From the initial use of chemical weapons in August 1983 through late 1986, chemical release authority was held exclusively by Saddam Hussein. The General Staff could request chemical fires—as could corps and division commanders in the event they were in imminent danger of being overrun or defeated—but Saddam would approve or deny the request. This highly centralized procedure preserved what was then a limited chemical weapons stockpile and guaranteed adequate supplies of chemical munitions in the event of a large Iranian offensive. Once the decision to release these weapons had been made, the order was passed through the operational chain of command: from the president to the minister of Defense, the chief of staff, the army general headquarters, and finally reaching the Chemical Corps commanders.[49] Operational security was maximized: attack orders were issued by courier or through secure land lines. Air force chemical attacks followed similar procedures, including specially cleared pilots and coded "go/no go" signals.[50]

Once an order for a chemical attack had been received and validated, Chemical Corps units were responsible for transporting and employing the weapons.[51] Ten company-sized detachments under the control of Chemical Corps headquarters in Baghdad were assigned this task. Although the Chemical Corps chose the numbers and types of munitions to be used, the

47. This paragraph is based on author (McCarthy) discussions with Iraqi officials and with UNSCOM staff members.

48. See Lt. Matthew M. Hurley (USAF), "Saddam Hussein and Iraqi Air Power: Just Having an Air Force Isn't Good Enough," *Airpower Journal*, Winter 1992 <www.airpower.maxwell.af .mil/airchronicles/apje.html>.

49. DIA, "Iraqi Chemical Employment Doctrine."

50. DIA, "Desert Shield—Iraqi Command and Control."

51. Author (McCarthy) discussion with UNSCOM staff member, 1 November 1997.

field commander normally would decide which of his own units would fire the mission (based on its position along the front and other factors). Some field units may have specialized in firing chemical rounds, but none was assigned that task to the exclusion of firing conventional munitions. Once mission planning was complete, Chemical Corps troops would travel to the front, deliver the weapons, take wind speed and direction measurements, and supervise the fire mission. Attacking units were required to wait for approval from the chemical detachments before advancing.[52] These procedures were followed throughout the Iran-Iraq War.

In the war's initial phase, Iraqi employment of chemical weapons was militarily ineffective because of poor agent quality and supply and inferior tactics. Iraqi tabun and sarin nerve agents, for example, contained impurities that gave them a shelf life of only four to six weeks. Chemical weapons operations were flawed because pilots dropped their bombs from too high or too low an altitude, while ground troops employed the weapons in unfavorable weather conditions or failed to concentrate enough agent at the point of attack. During some battles, Iraqi helicopters simply dropped 55-gallon drums of mustard agent on Iranian positions.[53] Inadvertent exposure of friendly troops was not uncommon. When Iraq first used chemical weapons in February and March 1984 during operations in the Majnoon Marshes, for example, the wind shifted and blew back mustard gas against the Iraqi forces, causing casualties.

As the war went on, Iraqi forces learned to tailor the delivery of chemical agents to the specific tactical situation. For example, the Iraqis learned to launch chemical strikes to maintain the momentum of ground engagements or to deny terrain to the enemy. Nonpersistent, volatile agents such as sarin (GB) were used to attack targets that would be overrun quickly by advancing forces, while more persistent agents such as mustard gas or cyclosarin (GF) were used for missile or aerial-bomb attacks against supply depots, assembly areas, and command-control nodes in the Iranian rear, causing poorly protected rear-echelon soldiers and volunteers to flee.[54]

During the final offensives of 1988, Iraqi commanders integrated chemical weapons into their offensive battlefield operations. The Iraqis first laid down persistent mustard agent in the Iranian force's rear area and then bombarded the front with the nonpersistent nerve agent sarin, so that Iranian troops retreating from the sarin-contaminated area would be exposed to the mustard

52. CIA, "Iraqi Army Chemical Weapons Doctrine."

53. DIA, "Iraqi Air Force Capability to Deliver Chemical Weapons," 1 December 1990, GulfLink file no. 961031_950925_0422pgf_90.txt.

54. DIA, "Iraqi Chemical Weapon Trends," 8 August 1990, GulfLINK file no. 961031_950925_007bk_90p.txt.

agent as well.[55] According to General Wafiq al-Sammarai, Iraq also employed
VX nerve agent during the battle of Al Fao in long-range artillery shells and
bombs dropped from aircraft, causing panic among the Iranian Revolutionary Guards.[56] Iraq's most devastating use of chemical weapons took place on
Majnoon Island in June 1988, when front-line Iranian defensive positions
were subjected to an artillery barrage delivering a mixture of hydrogen
cyanide, nerve agent, and high explosives. Iraqi helicopters and fighter aircraft joined the attack, dropping mustard and nerve agent on command centers, logistics sites and reserve forces in the Iranian rear.[57]

Apart from tactical improvements, Iraqi use of chemical weapons became more effective when release authority was delegated to corps commanders in late 1986. At a meeting before Iran's December 1986 offensive,
Saddam gave permission to the Third and Seventh Army Corps commanders and the air force and missile defense commanders to use chemical
weapons and long-range missiles without prior presidential approval.
After field commanders balked at the unexpected change in policy, Saddam
traveled to the front in January 1987 to confirm these orders.[58] This change
in command and control procedures arose out of serious Iraqi losses during
the Al Fao and Mebran campaigns and the military's ability to convince
Saddam that delegation of use authority would allow improved chemical
weapons planning and response to changing tactical situations.[59] Once Saddam had personally approved the new procedures, Iraqi field commanders
took full advantage of their new authority to conduct chemical warfare
operations.[60]

Between the Wars: The Thunderstrike Option

As the long war with Iran drew to a close, Iraq's military, intelligence,
and security services began to address other regional threats, particularly
Israel.[61] The Iraqi army reoriented and upgraded its conventional forces for
a future confrontation with the Jewish state. The key questions that arose
were how to counter the Israeli nonconventional arsenal and how to deter

55. DIA, "Iraq: Potential for Chemical Weapon Use," 1 February 1991, GulfLINK file no.
970613_dim37_91d_txt_0001.txt.
56. Reuters, "Iraq Reportedly Used VX Nerve Gas in Iran-Iraq War," 3 July 1998, 05:10 GST.
57. Lee Waters, "Chemical Weapons in the Iran/Iraq War," *Military Review* 70 (October 1990):
57–63.
58. CIA, "Authorization for Use of CW," January 1987, GulfLINK document no. 071496/
76426_cia_76426_76426_01.txt.
59. CIA, "CW Use in Iran-Iraq War," GulfLINK file no. 070296_cia_72566_72566_01.txt.
60. DIA, "Iraq: Potential for Chemical Weapon Use."
61. This section is based on author (McCarthy) discussions with relevant Iraqi officials, along
with interviews with UNSCOM staff members, 17 and 26 July, 17 August, and 1 November 1997.

another preventive strike against Baghdad's nuclear, chemical, and biological weapons facilities.

In early 1988, the SSO produced an intelligence estimate of Israel's non-conventional weapon capabilities. Included in the SSO report were recommendations that Iraq undertake civil defense measures and acquire the capability to retaliate, notably with biological weapons. This recommendation led to the establishment of Iraq's biological weapons arsenal as a strategic deterrent and prompted the so-called Thunderstrike option, calling for a massive retaliatory blow against Israeli cities using long-range ballistic missiles armed with chemical and biological warheads.

To operationalize this strategy, the Iraqis began in 1988 to construct a series of fixed-arm launch positions in the western desert. The Thunderstrike project envisioned a total of sixty fixed launchers, configured in groups that took into account the circular error probable of the Al-Hussein's guidance system. Six to eight launchers grouped together and fired simultaneously would ensure that the missiles would land on a city-size target. The plan also called for Unit 224 to establish forward missile storage and support centers at Qaim and Rutbah, which are located 400 kilometers west of Baghdad along main east-west highways.

The Iraqi army did not like the fixed-arm concept because its valuable missiles would be tied down in vulnerable launch positions. But the army was overruled: twenty-eight of the sixty planned fixed sites were constructed by the summer of 1990. As the Kuwait crisis deepened, however, a debate took place within the Iraqi government over how to implement the massive blow against Israel inherent in the Thunderstrike option.

The political and intelligence organizations supported fixed missile launchers, while the military opposed them.[62] These debates centered on tactical efficacy rather than on the broader concept of strategic retaliation. At some point during the Kuwait crisis, the military position against fixed launchers prevailed. One reason may have been Project 144's belief that all of the fixed launchers would not be completed by the January 1991 UN deadline for Iraqi withdrawal from Kuwait. Having fewer launchers than planned would render the fixed-position concept inoperative because the numbers were dictated by the limited accuracy of the Al-Hussein. The missile unit also may have won the debate by stressing the relative security of mobile launchers from enemy attack. As a result of this outcome, key parts from the fixed-arm launchers were cannibalized to complete production of the indigenous Al-Nida mobile launchers, rendering the static launch positions incapable of being used in combat.

---

62. Author (McCarthy) interview with UNSCOM staff member, 17 July 1997.

The legacy of the fixed-arm concept and the Thunderstrike option was reflected in Iraqi military strategy during the Gulf War, including the deployment of mobile missiles to forward storage positions along the western launch axis, such as Qaim and Rutbah, and the opening salvo of conventionally armed missiles against Israel.

The Gulf War

Saddam Hussein almost certainly did not anticipate the U.S. response to his 1990 invasion of Kuwait, much less that fellow Arabs would join with Washington to evict him from the emirate. It follows that a military strategy designed to deal with this contingency did not exist before August 1990. Yet it appears that by modifying existing strategies and adapting some novel concepts, Saddam incorporated chemical and biological weapons into his plans in hope of emerging victorious from his difficult predicament. This crisis-inspired gambit included deterrence with nonconventional weapons, war winning through escalation dominance, and strategic provocation.

Shortly after the invasion and the subsequent U.S. military buildup in Saudi Arabia (Operation Desert Shield), the Iraqi government alleged that Israel was the guiding hand behind the Coalition. Thus any attack against Iraq by Coalition forces would be interpreted as an attack by the Jewish state, and Baghdad would retaliate accordingly. For example, Iraqi Foreign Ministry under secretary Nizar Hamdoon declared that Iraq would hold "jointly responsible" the United States, its allies, and Israel, "which ignited conspiracies and aggression in the region. . . . On this basis, Iraq reserves the right of legitimate defense, *reciprocal treatment*, and a firm response to these parties if it is exposed to any aggression" (emphasis added).[63] Iraq's leaders apparently calculated that because of the high value Washington placed on protecting Israel, Iraq would be able to deter a U.S. conventional attack by holding Israel hostage.[64]

The deterrent threat against Israel had both conventional and unconventional components. One week after Iraq's invasion of Kuwait, the Iraqi ambassador to Greece announced that Baghdad would use chemical weapons if it was attacked by the United States or Israel. The ambassador also noted that Iraq expected an attack from Israel with planes bearing U.S. insignia.[65]

63. Baghdad Domestic Service, 13 September 1990, in FBIS-NES-90-179, 14 September 1990, 18.

64. See Communique No. 4 issued by the Armed Forces General Command, carried on Baghdad Domestic Service, 18 January 1990, in FBIS-NES-91-013, 18 January 1991, 26.

65. "Ambassador in Athens Warns of Chemical Warfare," Athens Domestic Service in Greek, 1500 GMT, 9 August 1990, in FBIS-NES-90-155, 10 August 1990, 28.

A September 1990 statement issued jointly by the Revolutionary Command Council and the Ba'ath Party Regional Command declared that, in the event of hostilities, "Israel will be transformed into something different from what [it is] now," adding that this could happen "by mistake or deliberately and afterward cause a huge conflagration."[66] In January 1991, the Iraqi military command threatened to use a "secret weapon" and, just before the Coalition ground campaign, Saddam implied the first use of chemical weapons by asking "the people of justice" to "forgive Iraq for any action they will initiate."[67]

Whether Saddam believed that such threats would deter Coalition forces from attacking is unclear. Once the battle had been joined, however, Saddam's new arsenal still played a role in Iraqi military strategy. Mindful of the American public's aversion to casualties and drawing lessons from the U.S. experience in Vietnam, Saddam apparently believed he could destroy enemy morale by inflicting high casualties. The Iraqi leader apparently calculated that large numbers of dead and injured troops would generate strong domestic political pressures for the United States to end the war, forcing the Bush administration to settle the conflict on terms favorable to Iraq.[68] Saddam warned that there would be no "lighting strike": a land campaign would be long and costly.[69] This strategy could work only as long as Washington did not resort to using nuclear weapons. Thus Saddam had to deny the Coalition an escalatory option by using his own unconventional arsenal as an countervailing escalatory threat.

Finally, Iraq's arsenal of conventionally armed ballistic missiles became weapons of intentional provocation once they were launched against Israel on 18 January 1991. Iraqi strategy rested largely on the attempt to break up the Coalition by forcing an Israeli response, thereby changing the dynamics of the entire conflict. Saddam attacked Israel, as one analyst put it, "not despite but rather because he thought he could count on Israel to respond."[70]

66. Baghdad Domestic Service, 23 September 1990, in FBIS-NES-90–185, 19–21. Iraq also threatened to destroy Saudi and Kuwaiti oil fields in the event of an attack: the oil fields "will be rendered incapable of responding to needs of those who came to us as occupiers."
67. As cited in Baram, "Iraqi Imagery," 29–30.
68. In his meeting with U.S. envoy April Glaspie, Saddam characterized the United States as a "society that cannot accept 10,000 dead in one battle." See Transcript of meeting, cited in Ofra Bengio, ed., *Saddam Speaks on the Gulf Crisis: A Collection of Documents* (Tel Aviv: Moshe Dayan Center, 1992), 103. See also CNN interview with Saddam, conducted in the midst of Desert Storm, ibid., 180; and an interview with retired General Bernard Trainor of Harvard University, PBS Frontline Special "The Gulf War, Part I," 9 January 1996.
69. FBIS-NES-90–185, 19–21. See also Saddam's "Message to Bush," Bengio, ed., *Saddam Speaks*, 169.
70. Shai Feldman, "Israeli Deterrence and the Gulf War," in *Deterrence in the Middle East*, ed. Klieman and Levite, 128.

The Iraqis have since declared that their unconventional forces were intended only for a retaliatory response in the event of a Coalition nuclear strike. According to Iraq's deputy foreign minister Tariq Aziz, "Shortly before the Gulf War our leadership reached the following decision: as long as the enemy used conventional weapons, we would do the same. But if nuclear weapons were used against us, then our military had the following order: to utilize all weapons at our disposal, including chemical and biological agents."[71] In October 1995, Iraqi oil minister Amer Rashid also insisted that Iraq would have launched its biological missiles only in retaliation: "Iraq had no intention of using biological weapons unless the allies or Israel attacked Baghdad with nuclear weapons."[72]

Senior Iraqi officials also have stated that they were deterred from using unconventional weapons by fears that the United States or Israel would retaliate with nuclear weapons. U.S. secretary of state James Baker told Tariq Aziz on 9 January 1991, "If there is any use of [chemical and biological weapons], our objectives won't just be the liberation of Kuwait, *but the elimination of the current Iraqi regime*, and anyone responsible for using those weapons would be held accountable" (emphasis added).[73] In August 1995 Aziz told UNSCOM executive director Chairman Rolf Ekeus that he interpreted this position to mean that the United States intended to retaliate for Iraqi use of chemical and biological weapons with nuclear weapons.[74]

A consensus now exists that there was no widespread Iraqi use of chemical and biological weapons during the Gulf War.[75] Nevertheless, the forward deployment of chemical munitions and decontamination sites indicates that the Iraqis followed doctrinal and command and control practices for tactical employment of chemical weapons established before the Gulf crisis. UNSCOM has collected data on the production and deployment of chemical munitions

71. "Zum Narren gehalten," *Der Spiegel*, no. 43 (10 October 1995): 164.

72. Farouk Choukri, "Interview with Iraqi Oil Minister Amer Rashid," Agence France Presse, 18 October 1995.

73. The U.S. threat was meant to hold hostage that which Saddam valued most: his regime and his maintenance of power. The specific targeting of the Ba'ath under these circumstances was decided in December 1990. Baker writes that the "calculated ambiguity on our part has to be part of the reason" that Iraq did not use CBW (James A. Baker, *The Politics of Diplomacy: Revolution, War and Peace, 1989–1992* [New York: G. P. Putnam's Sons, 1995], 359).

74. "Iraq Provides IAEA with Significant New Information," *Arms Control Today* 25 (September 1995): 27.

75. Although Iraq made no large-scale use of chemical weapons, some indirect evidence suggests that Iraqi forces may have launched sporadic, uncoordinated chemical attacks during the ground war. If so, it is unclear whether the weapons were launched deliberately or accidentally. See Jonathan B. Tucker, "Evidence Iraq Used Chemical Weapons during the 1991 Persian Gulf War," *Nonproliferation Review* 4 (Spring–Summer 1997): 114–22; and Chapter 11 of the MITRE report on CW detections during the Gulf War, http://www.gulflink.osd.mil/mitre_report/1997254-0000139_0000001.html.

before the outbreak of hostilities.[76] At Muthanna, Iraq filled 13,500 artillery shells (155mm) with mustard agent before 15 October 1990 and stockpiled them at Muthanna and at the nearby Muhammadiyat storage facility. Between December 1990 and January 1991, Iraq also filled 8,320 122mm rockets with a sarin/cyclosarin (GB/GF) mixture at Muthanna. In January 1991, Hussein Kamel (presumably at Saddam's request) asked the Ministry of Defense to provide thirty-one trailers to forward-deploy these munitions to the Ikhaidar and Nasiriyah depots in southern Iraq. UNSCOM has no evidence that chemical weapons were moved further south into Kuwait or that they were deployed to the front lines early in the crisis and then returned to their storage locations in Iraq.

Despite the purported predelegation of launch authority for missiles with chemical and biological warheads in the event of a nuclear strike on Baghdad, Saddam Hussein probably retained release authority for the tactical use of these weapons during the Gulf War. He was well aware, after the Aziz-Baker meeting, of the American attitude toward even the tactical use of nonconventional weapons. Even so, the fact that chemical munitions were deployed into southeastern Iraq indicates that there were plans for use against Coalition forces. One explanation is that the Iraqi army wanted to be prepared for any contingency. Furthermore, since chemical weapons use was integrated into Iraqi military planning, the deployment of chemical munitions during this particular crisis may have reflected standard operating procedures.

Missile Operations and Tactics in the Gulf War

Immediately before the initiation of hostilities in January 1991, the Iraqi missile force consisted of some 220 Al-Husseins and 11 standard Scud-B missiles, along with 10 MAZ-543 launchers and four indigenously produced Al-Nida mobile erector-launchers (MELs).[77] Target lists had been drawn up earlier for attacks against Israel, including several in Tel Aviv, two in Haifa, and one each at the Dimona nuclear reactor in the Negev and a suspected missile base. It is difficult to determine, however, if Iraq's target selection implied a counterforce or a countervalue strategy, at least as these terms are understood in Western strategic thinking. Given the doctrine of volley launch, both sets of targets were likely to be struck at roughly the same time. The Iraqi missile attack against the Israeli nuclear facility at Dimona (counterforce) in February 1991 came *after* an attack on Israeli population centers (countervalue). Thus at least one aspect of a counterforce

76. Testimony of Charles Duelfer and Igor Mitrokhin (UNSCOM) before a public meeting of the Presidential Advisory Committee on Gulf War Veterans' Illnesses, Buffalo, New York, 29–30 July 1997. The transcript is available on GulfLINK.
77. The following is based on author (McCarthy) discussions with UNSCOM staff members.

strategy—restraint in targeting civilians—was not present. Iraqi military planners, missile officers and engineers understood the limitations on the Al-Hussein's accuracy. They probably realized that any plan of operations based purely on counterforce targeting would be impossible to implement.

The answer to the targeting question lies not with strictly military factors, however, but rather with political considerations. Nizar Hamdoon had stated that Iraq demanded the "right of legitimate defense, reciprocal treatment, and a firm response" to any aggression committed against Baghdad. Saddam Hussein probably believed that the targeting of Dimona was a means to settle the score ("reciprocal treatment") for Israel's 1981 attack on the Osirak reactor and that Dimona was a legitimate target given the precedent set by Israel. The Osirak attack had caused severe disquiet in Baghdad because it had demonstrated that Iraq—and hence Saddam—was vulnerable.

The U.S.-led response to the invasion of Kuwait forced Iraq to modify its operational missile plan to address the new threat from the south. The new plan called for mobile operations along the western and southern firing axes, directed against Israel and Saudi Arabia. Before the initiation of hostilities, conventional combat loads and reloads were predeployed to sites in western and southern Iraq.

The final plan of operations for conventional missile strikes was not finalized and briefed to field units until just before the air war started. The entire Iraqi TEL/MEL force, fourteen launchers in all, moved to the western zone just before the initiation of hostilities. In the early hours of 18 January, Unit 224 launched its first missiles. Because of fueling and other problems, only eight Al-Husseins were fired successfully. Following the launch, eight launchers left for southern Iraq, traveling along the main Qaim or Rutbah-Ramadi-Baghdad roads and then along the main Baghdad-Kut-Amarah highway. Two other Al-Nida launchers left the following day. These movements continued throughout the war, with TELs firing in one location and then traveling across the country, a distance of some 725 kilometers. The Al-Nida launchers, however, remained in the south. As in the Iran-Iraq War, the Iraqis state that the operational chain of command for the conventional missile force ran through the General Staff Headquarters in Baghdad. No operational mobile launchers were destroyed by Coalition air- or ground-based forces. Iraqi tactics of camouflage, concealment, and deception, combined with mobile forces and strict communications security, ensured the survival of the launcher force.

Effecting Deterrence: Problems of Predelegation

During the Gulf War, Iraq had the capability to carry out chemical and biological weapon strikes against Israeli and Coalition targets. Iraq had two delivery options: aircraft and ballistic missiles. According to a report from an Iraqi defector, in the fall of 1990 Saddam Hussein personally ordered that plans be drawn up for airborne delivery of a biological agent using an SU-22 ground-attack aircraft equipped with an onboard spray tank.[78] Key aspects of this account are, however, unconfirmable or inconsistent with what is known about Iraqi military operations. Moreover, Saddam Hussein had ample reason to believe his air force would perform poorly even *before* the war began, given its disappointing performance in the Iran-Iraq War, the vastly superior capabilities of Coalition air forces, and the quality of Israeli air defenses. Saddam—highly skilled at the game of internal Iraqi politics—was also unlikely to entrust his most important weapons and missions to the air force, which he viewed as a potential threat to his regime. Indeed, because Saddam feared the political ambitions of certain senior air force officers, he had deliberately and systematically undermined the capabilities of that service.[79] During the Gulf War, Coalition forces rapidly established air supremacy over the battlefield, grounding aerial biological weapons delivery systems for the duration of the conflict. For all these reasons, the choice of strategic delivery system devolved to the use of ballistic missiles armed with chemical and biological warheads.

Iraq officials maintain that the chemical and biological missile force had four characteristics: warheads were stored separately from the delivery systems; nonconventional, strategic operations were executed by the same units that controlled conventionally armed Al-Husseins; launch of the missiles was conditionally predelegated; and there was no first-use strike option.

Iraq has declared that seventy-five "special" chemical and biological missile warheads were produced and filled late in 1990. The Iraqis now claim that of the fifty chemical warheads, sixteen were filled with live agent (GB or GB/GF mix) and thirty-four were Iraqi-type binary (precursors mixed manually shortly before launch). The special chemical warheads were filled in June and July 1990. After the invasion of Kuwait on 2 August, the Iraqis dispersed the sixteen chemical warheads with live-agent fill to the Kubisa forest. The binary warheads were sent to the Fallujah forest and then to Tel Zagoreed, near the Tigris canal, some 30 kilometers west of Baghdad.

Of the twenty-five biological warheads, those with anthrax fill were dispersed to abandoned railroad tunnels north of Mansuriya, 40 kilometers northeast of Baghdad, while the others, containing botulinum toxin and aflatoxin, were concealed underground in a berm next to the Tigris canal (in

78. CIA, "Iraqi BW Mission Planning," 1992, GulfLINK file no. 062596_cia_74624_74624_01.txt.

79. Hurley, "Sadddam Hussein and Iraqi Air Power."

the same general location as the chemical warheads). The Iraqis state that there were additional "interim" storage sites for the warheads, including one located at the Tharthar storage site in the southeast corner of Lake Tharthar, 75 kilometers northeast of Baghdad. All the warheads purportedly were kept within a 100-kilometer radius of the capital. The Iraqis claim that the First Missile Maintenance battalion (Technical Battalion) from Unit 224 retained physical control over the warheads at the various dispersal sites. Every two or three days, a senior engineer from either Al-Hakam (for biological weapons) or Muthanna (for chemical weapons) would travel to the site and check on the condition of the warheads, looking for problems with structural integrity and leakage.

The Iraqis have claimed that no special procedures were instituted to fire missiles armed with chemical and biological warheads and that launch operations mirrored those of a standard Surface-to-Surface Missile Group operation. The Unit 224 commander would receive an order and a target and then communicate this information to field units. A warhead or warheads would be moved to one of the mating sites, uploaded onto a missile by Unit 224 troops, driven to a surveyed site onboard a TEL, and launched.

According to Iraqi officials, authority to launch the missiles was predelegated to field commanders "in the event that Baghdad was hit by nuclear weapons during the Gulf War."[80] The Iraqis have repeatedly emphasized the conditional, second-strike nature of the chemical and biological weapons missile force.[81] Of course, predelegation does not exclude the possibility of a launch executed through the chain of command from President Saddam Hussein down through the General Staff. Indeed, one Iraqi official stated that a launch could be executed by a valid order through either military or political channels.[82]

Nevertheless, the Iraqi explanation of its command and control network and operational doctrine presents a number of puzzles. First, deterrence is strengthened only when an adversary is aware that predelegation has occurred. In theory, fear of unavoidable retaliation should deter an opponent from using unconventional weapons first or launching a decapitation attack. Yet Saddam spoke about predelegation only in April 1990, during a period of high tension with Israel; no similar statements followed in the months leading to, or during, the Gulf War. This silence is particularly telling because in the last days of the war, it was clear that Saddam's forces were crumbling and that Coalition aircraft were targeting him directly with

---

80. UN Secretary General, *Eighth Report on the Status of the OMV*, S/1995/864, 11 October 1995.

81. For example, see Tariq Aziz's statement cited above, note 72.

82. Author (McCarthy) interview with UNSCOM analyst, 4 November 1997.

conventional weapons. Given this tenuous situation, it would have been in Saddam's personal interest to make the Coalition unambiguously aware of the predelegation posture. This did not happen. Instead, the statements claiming that Iraq had a predelegation posture during the Gulf War were made four years later, in October 1995.

Second, the Iraqi claim of predelegation for immediate retaliation is questionable because biological warheads were not colocated with delivery vehicles. The Iraqi system would therefore have been unable to retaliate promptly in response to a "bolt from the blue" attack, although it might have been able to launch on warning once it had been placed on generated alert.

Another puzzle involves the existence of seven fully fueled Al-Hussein missiles and their peculiar movement patterns in western Iraq during the Gulf War.[83] Soviet technical manuals state that a Scud can remain fueled for sixty days; after that, the kerosene fuel and oxidizer must be replenished. Each missile has a "passport," or log, that accompanies it and records the time and nature of maintenance activities. The passport therefore provides a unique record of the life history of the missile. The passports associated with the seven Al-Hussein missiles indicate that they were deployed in September 1990 to the western zone, in secure hide sites within the Qaim-Ramadi launch area.[84] In November, the missiles returned to Baghdad to have their propellants replenished. Sixty days later, in late January–early February 1991, they were brought to Baghdad again for refurbishment.

The key point is that the missiles returned to Baghdad *during* combat operations, when Iraqi strategy called for massive strikes against Israeli targets to provoke a response. If the seven missiles had been designated as conventional weapons, they would have been viewed as precious assets and almost certainly would have been launched while deployed in western Iraq. Any prudent military commander would not risk exposing the missiles to attack during the long drive back to Baghdad simply to replenish the propellants in weapons that just as easily could have been launched. No similar pattern of missile movements occurred along the southern (Saudi) firing axis. The seven missiles probably were deployed in the western desert to execute unconventional (chemical and biological weapons) missions or, though much less likely, they constituted a "conventional strategic reserve" that was not included in the standard firing plan.

---

83. Reference is made to these missiles in CIA, "Review of NESA Files," 21 February 1996, GulfLINK file no. 062596_cia_68357_01.txt.

84. This and the following paragraphs are based on author (McCarthy) interviews with an UNSCOM staff member, 10, 26 July 1997.

The notion that Iraq maintained a nonconventional strategic missile reserve during the Gulf War is strengthened by notes found in a command log maintained by General Hazim Ayubi, who led Unit 224 forces. In these "diaries," Ayubi writes that fifteen Al-Hussein missiles were not under his operational control during the war. Five of those missiles were not combat-operational (undergoing repairs and the like), but the log notes regarding the movement of the remaining ten missiles correspond with the known movements of the seven systems mentioned above. The reason behind the three-missile discrepancy is not clear. It is very likely, however, that some missiles were kept as a strategic reserve force and that the seven missiles that were refurbished were not under Unit 224's control.

Who controlled the warheads for these strategic reserve/deterrent missiles? Soviet doctrine called for one military branch to control delivery systems while the KGB controlled the warheads. The Iraqis may have adapted this doctrinal precept, given their close relationship with Soviet security and intelligence services. When asked to whom he reported (i.e., his chain of command), General Aybubi responded, "to military *and* political command staff" (emphasis added). UNSCOM analysts concluded that for conventional missile operations, Unit 224's command link ran through General Staff Headquarters, but for nonconventional operations, it ran through the SSO. Ultimately, Saddam Hussein stood atop both chains of command. It makes sense that the SSO, Saddam's most trusted instrument of internal power, would safeguard his most important means of wielding external power. Based on these considerations, UNSCOM analysts concluded that the SSO controlled the chemical and biological missile warheads, rather than Unit 224 security troops as the Iraqis had claimed.[85]

The SRG also was involved in protecting the chemical and biological warheads and may have had control over a few launchers. After his defection, Hussein Kamel revealed that the SRG had retained two launchers (it is not clear if they were TELs or MELs) and was hiding them from UNSCOM.[86] If this statement is true, then the SRG—with this capability—could also physically have performed the biological weapons mission.

If, in fact, a small strategic reserve force existed during the Gulf War, it might be explained as a compromise between the twin fears of strategic decapitation and unauthorized use. Saddam understood that keeping all authority for use of chemical and biological weapons in his own hands

85. Author (McCarthy) interview with UNSCOM staff members, 4 November 1997.

86. CIA, "Comments on Iraqi Weapons of Mass Destruction," August 1995, GulfLINK file no. 070396_cia_75849_75849_01.txt.; author (McCarthy) interview with UNSCOM staff member, 26 July 1997. It appears that in late 1986, ten to fifteen Soviet biological warfare specialists were in Baghdad teaching BW tactics to SRG commanders. See DIA, "Use of Biological Warfare by IZ [Iraq]," 26 November 1987, GulfLINK file no. 960525_27620018.88.txt.

Timothy V. McCarthy and Jonathan B. Tucker

would risk a decapitation strike, yet he did not trust giving the small number of biological warheads to General Ayubi, who might launch them without permission or even use his control over them as a political tool in a domestic power struggle. In addition, Saddam could have reason to worry that Ayubi might not fire the chemical and biological weapons missiles in response to an Israeli or U.S. nuclear strike, undermining Saddam's revenge. Thus he created an entirely separate unit to control just the chemical and biological weapons missiles, under the auspices of the SSO, his most trusted security organization (and possibly under the SRG as well).

Senior Iraqi officers apparently did not delegate the authority to launch missiles armed with chemical or biological warheads to all officers, as Saddam Hussein claimed. The available evidence, however, does support the hypothesis that Saddam delegated launch authority in a more limited way. The most likely explanation is that Saddam gave the capability and authority to a special unit commander to carry out a "revenge" strike in the event of a decapitation attack. Use of a separate and more reliable command structure for missiles carrying chemical or biological warheads also may have existed to fire first in a crisis or war. Iraqi command and control thus mirrors realist theory, but with an important modification made necessary by Saddam's fear of domestic enemies. Saddam permitted limited delegation as a solution to the dual threats of decapitation and domestic opposition.

Iraq's unconventional weapons doctrine and command and control system were influenced, in complex and often contradictory directions, by two goals other than the imperatives of national security. First, Saddam's vision of his leadership role in the Arab world led him to offer extended deterrence to other Arab states. Second, his fear of coups and constant need to reinforce his domestic power base encouraged him to rely on regime security organizations rather than the armed forces to control his strategic biological and chemical capabilities. At the same time, Saddam's internal concerns affected Iraqi strategic doctrine by requiring complex procedures to decrease the risk of unauthorized use.

Iraq's unconventional weapons served a spectrum of military and political purposes. Chemical weapons and conventionally armed ballistic missiles were employed tactically during the Iran-Iraq War, and captured military manuals suggest that Iraq had an operational doctrine for the use of incapacitating and lethal biological agents. Saddam also viewed CBW warheads delivered by missiles as strategic assets that could deter or offset the nuclear capabilities of Israel and, during the 1991 Gulf War, the United States and its allies.

Iraq's military doctrine and command and control arrangements for the use of chemical and biological weapons were integrally linked with Saddam Hussein's ambitions and political agenda. Realist theory would suggest that to the extent that Saddam's ambitions reflected Iraqi security interests, others would adopt similar policies. But Saddam pursued expansionist goals for personal glory. He sought to use chemical and biological weapons to deter others from interfering with his aggressive objectives. By offering other Arab states "extended deterrence" against Israel, Saddam sought to further his ambition of leading the pan-Arab nation and achieving Iraqi hegemony over the Persian Gulf. The acquisition of chemical, biological, and nuclear weapons capabilities also reinforced Saddam's position with the Iraqi public, the military, and the security services, whose support he ultimately relied on to remain in power.

Iraqi operational doctrine for unconventional weapons evolved in response to crisis. Iraq's use of chemical weapons during the Iran-Iraq War followed a steep learning curve, to the point that Iraqi chemical warfare played a significant role in some of the final battles. Similarly, Iraq's strategic chemical and biological weapons capabilities, originally directed against Israel, were adapted during the Gulf War to threaten Saudi Arabia and the Coalition forces.

The command and control arrangements for tactical and strategic chemical and biological weapons missile use were distinct and addressed in different ways the trade-offs between positive and negative control. During the final years of the Iran-Iraq War, Saddam delegated tactical use of chemical weapons and conventionally armed ballistic missiles to field commanders to make the most effective use of these capabilities. This change in policy was so unexpected that the army leadership was initially unwilling to accept it, and Saddam had to deliver the order in person.

In contrast, strategic chemical and biological capabilities developed to deter Israel were tightly controlled by a political chain of command involving Saddam, the Ba'ath Party leadership, and the Special Security Organization. Saddam's claim to have predelegated launch authority for missiles armed with chemical and biological weapons to military commanders in the event of a decapitating strike on Baghdad would have been inconsistent with the way strategic decisions are implemented in Iraq. Instead, Saddam apparently delegated launch authority in a tightly controlled way to his most trusted security organization because of his fears of a coup d'état. Future leaders of Iraq may adopt different command and control procedures.

More generally, the evidence suggests that realist explanations for Iraq's doctrine and command and control procedures are inadequate. These behaviors emerged instead from a complex interaction between geostrategic calculations and the particular strategic milieu—political objectives, ways of thinking, and regime structures—of Saddam Hussein's Iraq. Analysts should therefore examine internal factors as closely as they assess a country's geostrategic calculus in seeking to explain unconventional weapons doctrine and command and control arrangements.

[3]

The Islamic Republic of Iran and Nuclear, Biological, and Chemical Weapons

GREGORY F. GILES

The Iranian Revolution of 1979 brought to power an Islamic fundamental-ist regime, one without experience in national governance or international security affairs. Initially, Iran's clerical leaders demonstrated no interest in nuclear, biological, and chemical weapons, going so far as to cancel the Shah's ambitious nuclear program, which included weapons-related re-search. Saddam Hussein's invasion of Iran in 1980 and his subsequent use of chemical weapons and ballistic missiles throughout the conflict, how-ever, forced Iran's mullahs to reconsider nuclear, biological, and chemical weaponry. Today, the United States holds that Iran not only has developed and used chemical weapons but probably has created biological agents for use as weapons and is seeking to build nuclear weapons.[1] This chapter ad-dresses four key questions that have confronted the Iranian leadership: What are Iran's nuclear, chemical, and biological weapons requirements? How are its capabilities organized? Under what circumstances would it use such weapons? Under whose orders?

In seeking to answer these questions, this chapter focuses on Iran's chem-ical weapons capability, since it is the most mature of Iran's nuclear, biolog-ical, and chemical weapons programs and information about it is more readily available. Moreover, some of the doctrinal and control problems raised by chemical weapons are likely to be similar to future problems Iran will face with other unconventional weapons. The Iranian chemical

---

1. U.S. Department of Defense, *Proliferation: Threat and Response* (Washington D.C.: U.S. Gov-ernment Printing Office, 1997), 24–29.

weapons program can be used with caution to draw inferences about Iranian approaches to biological and nuclear weapons.

The chapter employs three prominent social science theories to help explain Iranian nuclear, biological, and chemical activities: realism, organizational theory, and strategic culture. None of the theories successfully predicts specific details of past Iranian decisions. Realists, for example, would expect the fledgling Islamic Republic immediately to embrace nuclear, biological, and chemical weaponry to protect itself against its numerous adversaries. Yet this was not the original course taken by Iran's new leaders because nuclear, biological, and chemical weaponry ran counter to overarching cultural, religious, and ideological concerns. Organizational theorists would predict that Iranian military organizations would want to acquire nuclear, biological, and chemical weaponry to expand their resources and missions. While this interest is evident to a certain degree, the mullahs' mistrust of the regular armed forces puts limits on this process. Neoculturalists would anticipate that Islamic strictures against inhumane warfare would rule out Iranian development or use of nuclear, biological, and chemical weaponry. But the mullahs responded otherwise to the reality of war with Iraq.

From a broader viewpoint, however, the Iranian government ultimately behaved as realists would expect, developing and using chemical weapons in retaliation against Iraq, and its efforts to control the Iranian military had imperfect results, as organization theory would predict. Finding the international community unwilling to force Baghdad to stop its chemical weapon attacks during the Iran-Iraq War, Tehran eventually adopted a strategy of self-help. In accordance with realist expectations, Iran acquired its own chemical weapons and used them against Iraq in the latter stages of the war. Embittered by their wartime experience, Iran's mullahs have striven to build a completely self-sufficient chemical weapons capability ever since, despite their official advocacy of the Chemical Weapons Convention. Having created the Islamic Revolutionary Guard Corps (IRGC) as a more politically reliable counterweight to the regular military, the mullahs must now contend with the IRGC's enthusiasm and active training for offensive chemical and biological warfare. In part, the IRGC's interest in offensive chemical and biological weapons doctrine reflects an attempt to offset the conventional superiority of U.S. forces in the Persian Gulf. As organizational theory predicts, it also stems from the relative degree of institutional autonomy enjoyed by the IRGC and the organization's custodial role over chemical and biological agents. The ability of Iran's clerical leaders to moderate IRGC biases toward the use of nuclear, biological, and chemical weaponry and to ensure that such weapons are used only with their prior approval remains an open question.

Iran's Nuclear, Biological, and Chemical Requirements

When Iran's religious leaders took power, they also assumed responsibility for national security policy. Among the issues they confronted was whether the Islamic Republic needed to acquire nuclear, biological, and chemical weaponry. In 1979, Iran had no offensive or defensive chemical warfare program to speak of and no biological warfare program.[2] As a part of the civilian nuclear program, however, the Shah had undertaken nuclear weapons–related research, including paper and computer studies.[3] The mullahs made no effort to continue the Shah's work or to initiate chemical and biological weapons programs. By closing down the country's nuclear program altogether, the Islamic Republic promptly foreclosed its nuclear, biological, and chemical weapons options. Of greater importance to the mullahs was a complete disavowal of the monarchy and its Western influences. This meant a purging of the regular armed forces and an infusion of Islamic military values, or *Maktabi*.[4]

Iran's clerical leadership was thus ill prepared to deal with Iraqi chemical attacks, even though Baghdad made public in July 1982 its intention to use chemical weapons if Tehran carried the war back into Iraq.[5] Reflecting a cultural belief that chemical weapons were illegitimate and provided no match for the high morale of its revolutionary soldiers, Iran disregarded Baghdad's warning and crossed into Iraqi territory later that month.[6] Iraqi chemical attacks on Iranian troops soon followed.

Iran's initial response to Iraqi chemical attacks was diplomatic rather than military. Tehran resorted to public allegations that Iraq was using chemical weapons in the hope that international condemnation would press Baghdad, a signatory of the Geneva Protocols of 1925 prohibiting their use, to discontinue such attacks. The charges failed to ignite world opinion, however, and Iraqi chemical attacks continued into late 1983. In reply, Iran stepped up its diplomatic campaign by seeking independent confirmation of Iraqi chemical weapons use. It not only brought United Nations investigators to the "scene of the crime" but also dispatched a handful of victims to European and Asian capitals. Although these efforts made

2. Specialized chemical and biological warfare training under the Shah appears to have been limited to a handful of Iranian officers who attended U.S. Army training courses from 1955 to 1960. See Gordon M. Burck and Charles C. Floweree, *International Handbook on Chemical Weapons Proliferation* (New York: Greenwood Press, 1991), 252.

3. Leonard S. Spector, *Going Nuclear* (Cambridge, Mass.: Ballinger, 1987), 50.

4. Sepher Zabih, *The Iranian Military in Revolution and War* (London: Routledge, 1988), 136–42.

5. Anthony H. Cordesman, *Weapons of Mass Destruction in the Middle East* (London: Brassey's, 1991), 85.

6. Dilip Hiro, *The Longest War* (New York: Routledge, 1991), 86.

it harder for the international community to ignore the mounting evidence—the United States formally censured Iraq for using chemical weapons in March 1984—they had little real effect on Baghdad. Western powers were more concerned about the potential spread of Tehran's Islamic fundamentalism to key oil-producing Arab states than about the use of chemical weapons against Iran.

The weak international response to Iraqi violations of the Geneva Protocols greatly disappointed Iran's leaders and encouraged Tehran to consider military responses. In 1983 Iran launched a crash effort to acquire chemical defensive gear, and in 1984 it set out to acquire offensive chemical agents.[7] The mullahs even reversed themselves and began to resurrect Iran's nuclear program. In response to Iraq's use of Scud missiles against Iranian cities in 1984, Iran acquired its own Scud missiles from Libya and began using them against Baghdad in 1985. By the late 1980s, Iran was engaged in biological weapons research.[8] As the war dragged on, Iran increasingly fulfilled realist expectations by developing its own nuclear, biological, and chemical weaponry capabilities to offset those of Iraq.

According to the realist view, even if Iraq had not invaded in 1980 or used chemical weapons in the years that followed, the sheer scale of Baghdad's investment in nuclear, biological, and chemical weaponry throughout the 1980s would have required a response from Tehran. Yet had the war with Iraq not occurred, we cannot assume that Iran would have decided to build its own nuclear, biological, and chemical weaponry. The Islamic regime had higher domestic priorities at the time; increasing defense spending to counter a theoretical threat would have been difficult to justify. Purely defensive options, such as investment in chemical protective gear, might have been preferred. The use of chemical weapons by Iraq, as well as the ineffective international response to that use, however, forced Iran's leaders to confront the issue. Because Iranian chemical defenses were so poor, Tehran could not deny Iraq the benefits of chemical weapons use. Short of strategic retreat from Iraqi territory, which was politically unacceptable, Tehran's only remaining hope of stopping the chemical attacks was to raise their cost to Iraq by seeking to retaliate in kind.

Cultural factors made the decision to acquire and use chemical weapons difficult for the Iranian regime. Ayatollah Khomeini, Iran's spiritual leader and overall commander in chief, opposed the use of chemical weapons because of the Islamic prohibition on polluting the atmosphere, even in the course of a holy war.[9] Khomeini might even have gone so far as to issue a

7. Cordesman, *Weapons of Mass Destruction*, 82–83.

8. Michael Eisenstadt, *Iranian Military Power: Capabilities and Intentions* (Washington, D.C.: Washington Institute for Near East Policy, 1996), 27.

9. Hiro, *Longest War*, 201–2.

binding religious edict, or *fatwa*, against such weapons.[10] In more secular terms, since Iran itself had signed the Geneva Protocols—without reserving the right to retaliate in kind—matching Iraq's chemical attacks would put Tehran in technical violation of the accord and undermine the diplomatic campaign to castigate Saddam Hussein. [11] Debate within Iran over the legitimacy of chemical weapons use continued until the latter stages of the war, when Khomeini is reported to have come under increasing pressure from elements in the regular military, as well as the IRGC, to authorize the use of chemical weapons.[12] At the time, Iran was experiencing major reversals on the battlefield, more frequent and effective use of chemical weapons by Iraq, and public threats by Baghdad that Iranian cities would be the next target for chemical attack.[13] By 1987 Ayatollah Khomeini relented and secretly authorized the use of chemical weapons.[14]

Iran's use of chemical weapons came "too little, too late" to affect the outcome of the war. Having derived no military benefit from their own chemical weapons use, Iranian leaders preferred to ignore that it had occurred, enabling Tehran to retain the moral high ground on chemical weapons use during the war. The disappointing results of their own chemical weapons use did not devalue chemical weapons in the eyes of Iran's leaders. Rather, it convinced them to strive for industrial-scale production of chemical weapons so that militarily significant quantities of agent would be on hand in the future.

By war's end, Iran appears to have suffered as many as fifty thousand chemical warfare casualties, of whom perhaps five thousand died.[15] This is a small percentage of the over one million civilian and military casualties

10. Con Coughlin, "Iranian Ayatollahs Building Chemical Arsenal," *Electronic Telegraph*, 13 October 1996. In the mid-1980s, several prominent clerics, including Ayatollahs Hassan Qomi, Golpayegani, Morteza Haeri, Meshkini, Azeri Qomi, and Tabatabai, voiced their opposition to the conduct of the war, in some cases calling it religiously unlawful. See Shahram Chubin and Charles Tripp, *Iran and Iraq at War* (Boulder: Westview, 1988), 82–83. While Khomeini dismissed such charges, similar criticism would be aimed at his approval of CW use.

11. Gordon M. Burck and Charles C. Floweree, *International Handbook on Chemical Weapons Proliferation*, (New York: Greenwood Press, 1991) 238. Iran became a party to the Geneva Protocol in 1929. Iraq ratified the protocol in 1931 but stated that it would cease to "be bound by the Protocol towards any State at enmity with Iraq whose armed forces, or the forces of whose allies, do not respect the provisions of the Protocol." See *Geneva Protocol Reservations*, projects .sipri.se/cbw/docs/cbw-hist-geneva-res.html. Iran entered no reservations and remains bound by the protocol pending a formal withdrawal.

12. Youssef M. Ibrahim, "Iran Reports New Iraqi Gas Raids; And Says Cities May Be Hit Next," *New York Times*, 2 April 1988, A1.

13. Ibid.

14. Patrick E. Tyler, "Both Iraq and Iran Gassed Kurds in War, U.S. Analysis Finds," *Washington Post*, 3 May 1990, A37.

15. Iranian claims in this regard vary considerably. According to recent state-run media broadcasts, the total number of casualties from Iraqi CW attacks is fifty thousand, with between nine and ten thousand killed. See "Radio Views Chemical Weapons Convention in

caused by the war. Iraqi use of chemical weapons, however, appears to have had disproportionate psychological effects, which by 1987–88 compounded Iran's growing sense of war weariness and contributed to Tehran's acceptance of a cease-fire.[16] Speaking in October 1988, Speaker of the Parliament Hashemi Rafsanjani drew the following lessons for Iran:

> With regard to chemical, bacteriological and radiological weapons training, it was made very clear during the war that these weapons are very decisive. It was also made very clear that the moral teachings of the world are not very effective when war reaches a serious stage; the world does not respect its own resolutions, and closes its eyes to the violations and all the aggressions which are committed on the battlefield. . . . We should fully equip ourselves in the defensive and offensive use of chemical, bacteriological and radiological weapons.[17]

Iranian leaders apparently have concluded that Islamic fervor is no substitute for modern weaponry. Instead, self-sufficiency in armaments, a high state of readiness and the ability to retaliate are now recognized as requirements for deterring future aggression against Iran.[18] This thinking extends to Iran's approach to nuclear, biological, and chemical weaponry.[19]

Iran has two policies on nuclear, biological, and chemical weaponry: a declared policy advocating global abolition of such weapons and a secret policy to build and sustain offensive nuclear, biological, and chemical capabilities. Under the former, for example, Tehran has acceded to the CWC but admits only to developing a limited chemical weapons capability during the war and promptly dismantling it following the cease-fire.[20] Iran continues to deny ever having used chemical weapons or having chemical weapons on

---

Tehran," FBIS-NES-95-233, 5 December 1995, 81, and "Iran: Seminar on Chemical Weapons Opens in Tehran," FBIS-NES-96-080, 24 April 1996, 69. Iran's Center for the Victims of Chemical Warfare, which is operated by the Bonyad-e Mostazafan, estimates that one hundred thousand Iranians were victims of Iraqi chemical attacks ("CW Victims Demonstrate, IRI to Sue," *Inside Iran,* 5 May 1997, 3). In 1989, Iranian foreign minister Akbar Velayati put the number of CW casualties at forty-five thousand with five thousand fatalities. See Shahram Chubin, *Iran's National Security Policy* (Washington, D.C.: Carnegie Endowment for International Peace, 1994), 24. Anthony Cordesman accepts that Iranian CW casualties in the war were in excess of forty-five thousand, though he does not estimate the number of resulting fatalities (*Weapons of Mass Destruction,* 90).

16. Thomas L. McNaugher, "Ballistic Missiles and Chemical Weapons: The Legacy of the Gulf War," *International Security* 15 (Fall 1990): 22.

17. Quoted in Cordesman, *Weapons of Mass Destruction,* 93.

18. Chubin, *Iran's National Security Policy,* 18–28.

19. "Iran's Chemical and Biological Warfare Programs," *Jane's Intelligence Review,* Special Report no. 6, June 1995, 17.

20. Statement by His Excellency Ambassador Mohammad R. Alborzi, director general of the Ministry of Foreign Affairs and head of delegation of the Islamic Republic of Iran to the Third Session of the Conference of the States Parties of the Chemical Weapons Convention, the Hague, the Netherlands, 16–20 November 1998.

its territory. These claims are inconsistent with public reporting that Tehran not only continues to produce and stockpile chemical weapons but that it is expanding its chemical weapons production capacity.[21]

That Iran would accede to nonproliferation regimes with the intention to cheat is less surprising in light of the recent behavior of Iraq and North Korea with respect to the Non-Proliferation Treaty and Russian violations of the Biological Weapons Convention. These countries have demonstrated that accession to nonproliferation regimes does not preclude the development of nuclear, biological, and chemical weaponry. On the contrary, it provides a veneer of international respectability, thereby facilitating access to the materials and technologies needed to develop such weapons. Getting to the bottom of Iran's chemical weapons program will be a major task for the body overseeing CWC compliance, the Organization for the Prohibition of Chemical Weapons (OPCW) and other CWC States Parties, especially in light of Iran's efforts to curry favor with the OPCW.[22]

By adopting a secret nuclear, biological, and chemical weapons policy, Tehran hopes to deter future unconventional attacks against Iranian troops and rear areas by developing the means to threaten retaliation in kind.[23] The prospect that Iraq might one day reconstitute its nuclear, biological, and chemical weaponry programs weighs heavily on Iranian defense planning.[24] Concerns about a possible Osirak-type strike by Israel also factor into Iranian thinking. In recent years, Tehran has tried to deter possible Israeli conventional strikes by implicitly warning of its ability to retaliate with unconventional means. According to then commander of the IRGC Major General Mohsen Reza'i, "Iran possesses excellent facilities for delivering an appropriate response to any possible aggression by Israel. These types of facilities may not be present in the entire region. We also have some practical possibilities insofar as all the countries of the Islamic world. If the situation were to arise, we would deliver an appropriate response."[25]

21. Greg Seigle, "Iran Is Accelerating NBC Weaponry, Claims Opposition," *Jane's Defense Weekly*, 10 February 1999, 16.
22. In May 1999, Tehran hosted a course on medical defense against CW for the OPCW and has offered both to establish an international center for the medical treatment of chemical weapons victims and to provide medical assistance to other OPCW members in the event of chemical attack. Speaking at the Tehran course, the deputy director general of the OPCW stated that "the Islamic Republic of Iran holds a special position in our organization" (*Course on Medical Defense against Chemical Weapons*, Statement by John Gee, Deputy Director General of the OPCW, 15 May 1999).
23. Shahram Chubin, *Eliminating Weapons of Mass Destruction: The Persian Gulf Case*, Henry L. Stimson Center Occasional Paper 33 (Washington, D.C.: Henry L. Stimson Center, 1997), 25.
24. Saideh Lotfian, "Threat Perception and Military Planning in Iran: Credible Scenarios of Conflict and Opportunities for Confidence Building," in *Military Capacity and the Risk of War: China, India, Pakistan, and Iran*, ed. Eric Arnett (Oxford: Oxford University Press, 1997), 227.
25. "Revolutionary Guard Commander Interviewed," FBIS-NES-92–134, 13 July 1992, 63. Additional warnings were issued to Israel in early 1995.

In an apparent effort to back up such a threat, Iran flight-tested the 1,300-kilometer-range Shehab-3 ballistic missile on 21 July 1998. The missile is capable of delivering nuclear, biological, and chemical payloads throughout Israel.

Some Iranian defense planners also see nuclear, biological, and chemical weaponry as a means to deter conventional attacks by the United States. Commenting on Iranian military exercises in April 1997, a Tehran newspaper underscored Iran's interest in asymmetrical military responses: "The present circumstances required Iran to send a message to Washington that any military adventurism against Iran may have unpredictable repercussions because, as [Commander in Chief Ayatollah Khamene'i, Khomeini's successor] put it recently, the U.S. can start a war against Iran but the end of such a war will not be in America's hands."[26]

Iranian policy, or at least IRGC policy, does not appear to have come fully to grips with the possible riposte from Washington should Tehran resort to chemical and biological weapons use. This is not surprising from an organizational perspective, since the Iranian element most actively engaged in developing nuclear, biological, and chemical weapons doctrine—the IRGC—historically has not been attuned to the broader diplomatic results of its undertakings. During the war against Iraq, for example, the IRGC attacked Kuwait with Silkworm missiles and declared that the overthrow of the Kuwaiti regime was an additional Iranian war objective. Later in the war, IRGC naval forces threatened an attack against Saudi offshore oil facilities. These moves contradicted official Iranian efforts to improve relations with both countries to lessen their support for Baghdad. Alternatively, Iran might understand fully the potential consequences of chemical and biological weapons use against the United States or Israel and is seeking nuclear weapons to deny its adversaries an escalatory advantage. Iran's wartime experience and current threat perceptions together underscore why the Islamic Republic has concluded that nuclear, biological, and chemical weaponry is essential to its national security.

THE ORGANIZATION OF IRANIAN NUCLEAR, BIOLOGICAL, AND CHEMICAL CAPABILITIES

The structure of Iran's nuclear, biological, and chemical weapons programs reflects the interplay of wartime exigencies, organizational dynamics, and cultural influences. Prominent among the latter is the mullahs' attempt to reduce the prospects for a military coup by encouraging bureau-

26. "Iran: Daily on Success of Tariq Ol-Qods Maneuvers," FBIS-NES-97-120, 30 April 1997.

cratic friction and competition, a practice first adopted by the monarchy.[27] To counterbalance the regular armed forces, the mullahs encouraged the development of a parallel IRGC structure with its own naval, air, and ground forces. As the officially designated "defender of the Islamic revolution," the IRGC was entrusted with the new regime's special projects, such as the acquisition of nuclear, biological, and chemical weaponry.

Because the IRGC initially lacked the technical and industrial base to develop nuclear, biological, and chemical weaponry, it had to rely on other organizations for help. Assistance with chemical weapons came from the Defense Industries Organization and commercial firms in the National Industries Organization.[28] Revolutionary bodies created on an ad hoc basis to meet wartime production needs, such as the Construction Jihad and the Jahad-e-Daneshgahi, or University Crusade, also undertook chemical weapons–related work.[29] Following the war, another chemical weapons entity, the Special Industries Organization, was created in the Office of the President.[30] By the early 1990s, there were nearly a dozen different organizations in Iran with chemical weapon production–related responsibilities of one sort or another, each representing a key constituency (see Figure 1). Similar redundant arrangements probably exist in Iran's BW and nuclear weapons programs.

This system of multiple actors playing roles in a key strategic program ensures that there will be continued bureaucratic competition for resources, missions, and influence. With so many entities involved in the chemical weapon complex, a "production push" rather than "consumer demand" may be contributing to the proliferation of chemical weapons systems in Iran.

Iran's military is capable of employing chemical weapons on the battlefield, at sea, and against strategic targets deep in the rear. It can do so using a variety of delivery systems, from mines, tube, and rocket artillery to rotary- and fixed-wing aircraft, naval vessels, and long-range ballistic missiles. Iran has adapted virtually every major type of weapon system to deliver chemical agents. The modification of delivery systems also may apply to biological and nuclear weaponization efforts.

27. Nikola B. Schahgaldian, *The Iranian Military under the Islamic Republic* (Santa Monica: RAND, 1987), 32.

28. "Secret German Documents on Iran," *Economist Foreign Report*, 17 November 1994, 2; "Iran: Armed Forces News, Events," FBIS-NES-97–103, 1 February 1997 (electronic version); Burck et al., *Chemical Weapons Proliferation*, 252; Terry J. Gander, ed., *Jane's NBC Protection Equipment, 1997–1998* (Alexandria, Va.: Jane's Information Group, 1997), 22.

29. Robert Karniol, "China Supplied Iran with Decontamination Agent," *Jane's Defense Weekly*, 30 April 1997, 17; Burck et al., *Chemical Weapons Proliferation*, 244.

30. "Iran's Chemical Build-Up," *Intelligence Newsletter*, 9 November 1995, 7.

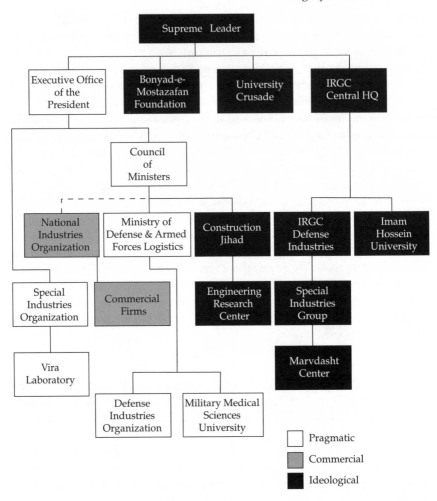

Figure 1. Chemical weapons procurement, R&D, and production in Iran.

The IRGC is ahead of the regular armed forces in adopting chemical weapons. The IRGC controls Iran's nuclear, biological, and chemical programs, dominates its naval forces, controls its long-range ballistic missiles, and embraces a more offensive doctrine than the regular military. IRGC ground force units possess their own protective chemical gear.[31] Independent nuclear, biological, and radiological, or Shin-Mim-Re, brigades also

31. Anthony H. Cordesman, *Iran and Iraq: Threat from the Northern Gulf* (Boulder: Westview, 1994), 49.

exist within the IRGC order of battle, possibly at the corps level.[32] These units presumably possess extensive decontamination gear and were reported to include heliborne teams.[33] Custody of chemical munitions probably resides with Shin-Mim-Re brigades until they are turned over to delivery units.

The principal chemical weapon delivery units in the IRGC ground forces are the artillery brigades, which are equipped with chemical weapon–capable tube and rocket artillery.[34] When the IRGC deployed 155mm guns to Abu Musa as part of its buildup on that island beginning in late 1994, it reportedly brought along chemical weapons.[35] The precise nature of these munitions has not been divulged, but it is possible that they were chemical rounds for 155mm guns. It also is not clear if the IRGC routinely deploys with chemical munitions or if this was a specially authorized operation.

Little is known about the IRGC's ability to deliver chemical weapons by air. Its main aircraft is the Chinese-built F-7M. The F-7M can carry up to 1,300 kilograms of ordnance, but its ability to penetrate modern air defenses is questionable.[36] IRGC pilots operating these aircraft have been trained for suicide attacks, raising the possibility of one-way missions to help offset the aircraft's limitations.[37] Alternatively, if the IRGC has managed to integrate more advanced aircraft, such as the Iraqi MiG-29s that sought shelter in Iran during the Gulf War and were subsequently seized by Tehran, it may be able to pose a greater chemical threat from the air. Given the IRGC's broad-based approach to integrating chemical weapons, it would be surprising if its air element were not equipped to deliver chemical munitions.

The IRGC air force may be able to compensate for any weakness in fixed-wing delivery of chemical weapons by using Iran's long-range ballistic missiles. This includes the Scud, for which crude chemical warheads are believed to exist. A 1995 report names the Seventh Brigade of the IRGC air

32. Kenneth Katzman, *The Warriors of Islam: Iran's Revolutionary Guard* (Boulder: Westview, 1993), 86.

33. Burck et al., *Chemical Weapons Proliferation*, 252.

34. Data on the IRGC ground forces' chemical weapons capability are derived from "Iran's Chemical Build-Up," 7; W. Seth Carus and Joseph S. Bermudez, "Iran's Growing Missile Forces," *Jane's Defense Weekly*, 23 July 1988, 126–31; Anthony H. Cordesman and Ahmed S. Hashim, *Iran: Dilemmas of Dual Containment* (Boulder: Westview, 1997), 208–9, 214; and Katzman, *Warriors of Islam*, 86.

35. Douglas Jehl, "U.S. Says It's Worried about Iranian Military Buildup in Gulf," *New York Times*, 23 March 1995, A9. See also Barbara Starr, "CW Stockpile 'A Threat to Straits of Hormuz,' " *Jane's Defense Weekly*, 1 April 1995, 3.

36. John W. Taylor, ed., *Jane's All the World's Aircraft, 1989–1990* (Surrey: Jane's Information Group, 1989), 34–35.

37. "Iranian Suicide Brigades," *Iran Brief*, 5 August 1996, 3–4. See also Katzman, *Warriors of Islam*, 90.

force as a Scud missile unit.[38] The IRGC air force is also gearing up to induct the longer-range Shehab-3 ballistic missile.

For years, the IRGC naval command also has exercised control over Iran's regular naval forces.[39] Some Iranian naval vessels are equipped with chemical weapons.[40] In 1991, Major General Hoseyn Firuzabadi, chief of Iran's Armed Forces Command Headquarters, falsely asserted that "the U.S. naval fleets in the Persian Gulf are equipped with chemical arms," evidently to justify Iran's own chemical weapons arming of naval vessels.[41] Similarly, the use of helicopters equipped with spray tanks during maritime exercises suggests that Iran's naval air arm may be preparing to take on a chemical weapons delivery role.

The IRGC's widespread interest in chemical weapons is perhaps surprising since the organization in general was slow to adapt to chemical warfare during the war with Iraq. For instance, it lagged behind the regular military in outfitting itself with protective gear such as gas masks and antidote injectors, a reflection of the IRGC's belief at the time in the supremacy of Islamic zeal over technology.[42] The IRGC's current stake in chemical warfare, however, may stem from bureaucratic competition with the regular military over roles and missions, with the Guard trying to stave off demobilization by recasting itself as a specialized nuclear, biological, and chemical force.[43]

The regular military's ability to integrate chemical weapons into its force structure is constrained by the IRGC's exclusive control over long-range missiles and chemical weapons storage. The regular army itself has Shin-Mim-Re units at the brigade level. These are small units responsible for detecting the presence of chemical weapons, taking samples, and demarcating the boundaries of contaminated areas.[44] In all likelihood, these Shin-Mim-Re troops are responsible for coordinating offensive chemical operations once chemical weapons are turned over to them by the IRGC. The

38. "Iran," *Nonproliferation Review,* 2 (Spring–Summer 1995): 175.

39. Paula A. DeSutter, *Denial and Jeopardy: Deterring Iranian Use of NBC Weapons* (Washington, D.C.: National Defense University Press, 1997), 24.

40. Anthony H. Cordesman, "Weapons of Mass Destruction in Iran: Delivery Systems and Chemical, Biological, and Nuclear Programs," Center for Strategic and International Studies, 28 April 1998, 35.

41. "Spokesman Affirms 'Right' to Chemical Weapons," FBIS-NES-91–051, 15 March 1991, 44–45.

42. Burck et al., *Chemical Weapons Proliferation,* 251.

43. In 1995, for example, allegations that half of the IRGC was to be demobilized and the other half subordinated to the regular military coincided with attempts by IRGC commander Mohsen Reza'i to recast the Guards as a "rapid deployment force."

44. Adel Hamid-panah, "History of Chemical Warfare and Techniques to Combat It," *SAFF,* no. 62 (1985): 27–29, 33, translation from Farsi provided by Ahmed Hashim.

regular army can deliver chemical attacks using both artillery and battle-field rockets.[45] Regular air force units also are capable of delivering chemical bombs.[46]

IRAN'S UNCONVENTIONAL WEAPONS USE DOCTRINE

Anticipating how Iran might use nuclear, biological, and chemical weaponry requires an examination of wartime experiences, broader cultural norms, and current training patterns. Different constituencies within Iran also hold different views on this issue. For example, while civilian leaders tend to have a defensive orientation, the IRGC is investigating an asymmetrical war-fighting posture.

Iran has only limited experience in the actual use of chemical weapons. Like Iraq, Iran first used nonlethal CS (tear gas) agents but quickly learned that such agents had limited battlefield utility. Iran then turned to lethal chemical weapons during 1984–85. The chemical artillery rounds fired by Iranian troops at this time were captured Iraqi stocks. Since it was Iraqi practice not to mark chemical rounds in any special fashion, it is possible that the Iranian troops involved were not even aware that they were firing chemical munitions.[47] Regardless of the source, the limited chemical weapons employed by Iran appear to have had no appreciable military impact.

Iran may have used chemical weapons sporadically again in early 1987 in conjunction with Tehran's Karbala-5 offensive.[48] This conjecture is consistent with reports that Iran was filling its own chemical munitions at the time and that Ayatollah Khomeini had authorized the use of chemical weapons. There also are indications that Iran used chemical weapons against the Kurdish village of Halabja in March 1988. Initially, Iraq was believed to have been the sole culprit, but apparently Iran used about fifty artillery shells or aerial bombs loaded with cyanide against the village. Some one hundred to two hundred civilians succumbed to the Iranian chemical attacks and the Iraqi use of mustard gas that followed.[49] This incident may

45. Cordesman and Hashim, *Iran*, 208–9, 214.

46. Tyler, "Both Iraq and Iran Gassed Kurds," A37. During the war, IRGC air capabilities were extremely limited. Any aircraft-delivered chemical attacks thus would have been carried out by the regular air force.

47. Terry J. Gander, "Iraq—The Chemical Arsenal," *Jane's Intelligence Review,* September 1992, 415. There are other reports that the weapons in question were provided by Syria. See "Iran's Chemical and Biological Warfare Programs," 16. It was during this time also that Iran first produced its own CW.

48. David B. Ottaway, "In Mideast, Warfare with a New Nature," *Washington Post,* 5 April 1988, A1.

49. Cordesman, *Weapons of Mass Destruction,* 91.

be attributed to the failure of Iranian intelligence to detect the withdrawal of Iraqi troops from the village, rather than an explicit Iranian policy to target civilians.

Iranian chemical weapons use against Iraq during the war suggests that Tehran would not be the first to use nuclear, biological, and chemical weaponry, instead adopting a second-strike posture to deter follow-on nuclear, biological, and chemical attacks by an adversary. Iran's behavior in the war is thus consistent with realist predictions that a status quo power (i.e., Tehran did not launch the war) will prefer defensive doctrines. Iran's use of chemical weapons primarily against Iraqi troop concentrations conforms to organizational theory expectations that the armed forces will prefer counterforce doctrines that blunt or remove the threat to themselves.[50]

A preference for counterforce targeting also reflects Iranian cultural dispositions not to attack civilians. Islamic scholarship is divided on the issues of retaliation against cities and the use of chemical weapons. In some situations attacks against cities may be considered permissible under Islam, for example when the target is distant and it is not possible to distinguish combatants from noncombatants. Some Islamic teachings seem to allow the use of "poisons" against an enemy, whereas others deem it forbidden.[51] Throughout the war, however, the Islamic leaders generally decided a course of action and then sought a suitable Koranic injunction to justify it.[52] This process of rationalization could be adopted in future nuclear, biological, and chemical crises or conflicts.

Iran's leaders were particularly unnerved by the prospect of Iraqi chemical weapons attacks against Tehran and other major cities. The mere threat of such attacks triggered massive disruptions, and millions of people evacuated Tehran.[53] For a regime whose support is drawn from poor urban dwellers, the protection of Iranian cities from unconventional weapon attacks is of utmost importance. Reports during the war indicate that Iranian leaders were trying desperately to fashion a chemical warhead for their re-

50. "Use of Chemical Weapons during the Iran-Iraq War," 4 September 1990, Central Intelligence Agency report declassified and released electronically via GulfLINK, www.gulflink.osd.mil, document no. cia_62690_62671_01.txt, released 17 April 1996.

51. See Hamid Algar, "The Problem of Retaliation in Modern Warfare from the Point of View of Fiqh," in *The Iran-Iraq War: The Politics of Aggression*, ed. Farhang Rajee (Gainesville: University Press of Florida, 1993), 191–97.

52. At the outset of the war with Iraq, for example, Khomeini instructed the Iranian military to "do nothing to harm the cities which have no defense.... Our hands are tied, because we do not wish ordinary people, the innocent people, to be hurt" (quoted in Chubin and Tripp, *Iran and Iraq*, 50). In part, this policy was calculated to encourage Iraqi Shiite Muslims to rebel. In 1984, after the hoped-for rebellion failed to materialize, Iran loosened its restraint on attacking civilian targets.

53. I am grateful to Patrick Clawson, Washington Institute for Near East Policy, for pointing this out.

maining Scuds to deter the Iraqi countervalue threat.[54] Whether Iran would resort intentionally to nuclear, biological, and chemical attacks against civilian populations thus would depend largely on the adversary's behavior. For example, if Iraq were to conduct chemical and biological weapons missile strikes against Iranian cities in a future conflict, Tehran could be expected to retaliate in kind until Baghdad ceased such attacks, Islamic prohibitions against inhumane warfare notwithstanding. A failure to deal effectively and swiftly with such attacks against its domestic power base could amount to political suicide for the mullahs.

Current training patterns provide other clues about Iranian attitudes toward the use of nuclear, biological, and chemical weapons. During the war, the widespread disarray in Iranian military organization severely hampered Tehran's ability to mount an effective chemical defense. Numerous soldiers panicked and injected themselves with atropine, even though they were not under chemical attack, and were poisoned as a result. Soldiers who did not shave, either out of Islamic fervor or lack of discipline, could not achieve tight seals on their gas masks, and suffered predictable consequences. Formal chemical defensive training was limited before 1986.[55]

Since the war's end, the Iranian military has made a more concerted effort to improve its ability to operate in a nuclear, biological, or chemical environment. Only two months after the cease-fire with Baghdad, Iran announced that its Shin-Mim-Re troops were participating in ground forces maneuvers.[56] An exercise in 1990 similarly featured Shin-Mim-Re units.[57] Following Iraq's defeat by the U.S.-led coalition in early 1991, the frequency of Iranian chemical exercises picked up dramatically. As Table 1 indicates, since 1992, most major Iranian exercises have incorporated nuclear, biological, and chemical operations.

The exercises indicate that the Iranian military expects nuclear, biological, and chemical weaponry to be likely in future warfare. The upswing in the number of exercises after Operation Desert Storm suggests that the Iranian armed forces are looking to nuclear, biological, and chemical weapons to offset the U.S. advantage in high-technology conventional weapons. Of the twenty-one chemical exercises identified in Figure 2, two-thirds were held in and along the waters of the Persian Gulf where Iranian and U.S. forces operate in proximity to one another. The remainder of Iran's chemical exercises tend to occur inland near the border with Iraq.

---

54. See Joseph S. Bermudez, "Ballistic Missiles in the Third World—Iran's Medium-Range Missiles," *Jane's Intelligence Review,* April 1992, 149; and Cordesman and Hashim, *Iran,* 291.

55. Burck et al., *Chemical Weapons Proliferation,* 251.

56. "Ground Forces Stage Maneuvers 14 Oct," FBIS-NES-89–198, 16 October 1989, 63.

57. "Sahand Combined Maneuvers: A Show of Force in the North of the Persian Gulf," *SAFF,* no. 127, 1990, translation from Farsi provided by Ahmed Hashim.

Table 1: Chemical operations in Iranian military exercises, 1992–97

Date	Code name	Location	Service(s)	Iranian media references
October 1992[a]	Kheybar-3	Persian Gulf	Regular army and navy; IRGC navy and air force	Involved "operations to neutralize enemy chemical attacks."
November 1992[b]	—	Yazd	IRGC	"First comprehensive exercises to counter chemical weapons . . . units broke through enemy lines in face of chemical bombing by hypothetical enemy."
April 1993[c]	Piruzi-4	Northern Persian Gulf	Regular navy, army, and air force; IRGC navy, ground forces, and air force	Involved "chemical, biological, and radioactive operations."
May 1993[d]	Arvand-6	Shiraz	Regular army and air force	Participating forces carried out "antichemical activities."
September 1993[e]	Sahand-1	Marand	Regular army and air force	Patricipation of "antichemical forces."
November 1993[f]	Wa al-Fajr-1	Pursian Gulf and Strait of Hormuz	IRGC and regular army	Participation of "chemical, biological, and nuclear units."
July 1994[g]	Fajr-7	Northern Persian Gulf	Regular navy and air force; IRGC navy	Participation of "nuclear, chemical, and biological units."
September 1994[h]	Kheybar-73	Persian Gulf	Regular navy and air force; IRGC navy	Troops "carried out special operations to neutralize enemy chemical attacks."
September 1994[i]	Falaq-2	Persian Gulf	IRGC navy	Maneuvers concluded with "the implementation of a chemical offensive and counteroffensive."
February 1995[j]	Shahamat-73	Persian Gulf	Regular navy; IRGC navy	Involved "defense operations against chemical and micro-biological attacks."
May 1995[k]	Nasr-3	Northern Persian Gulf	IRGC navy	Troops "repulsed the enemy's chemical attack."
May 1995[l]	Fajr-4	Beyt ol-Moqaddas	Regular army; IRGC army; Basij	Involved "units responsible for countering chemical attacks."
July 1995[m]	Piruzi-6	Northern Persian Gulf	Regular navy and air force; IRGC navy; Basij.	Activities included "dealing with injuries from chemical, biological, and nuclear attacks."
August 1995[n]	Beyt ol-Moqaddas	Kermanshah Province	Regular army and air force	Participation of "Shin-Mim-Re defense units."
March 1996[o]	Zafar	Sistan-Baluchestan Province	Regular army and air force	Involved "defensive operations including repelling chemical attacks."
April 1996[p]	Fateh	Persian Gulf and Strait of Hormuz	Naval forces	Exercise "participants completed systematic and nonsystematic air defense of chemical, microbic, and nuclear exercise."

(continued)

Table 1: (continued)

Date	Code name	Location	Service(s)	Iranian media references
June 1996[q]	Velayat	Qom	Regular army and air force	Involved "utilization of tactics to combat the use of chemical weapons."
July 1996[r]	Falaqh-5	Persian Gulf	Regular navy and IRGC navy	"Performed operation to thwart hypothetical enemy's chemical attacks."
November 1996[s]	Piruzi-7	Persian Gulf	Regular navy and IRGC Navy	"Among the programs carried out . . . were . . . chemical attack and detoxification."
May 1997[t]	Salman Fateh	Persian Gulf	Naval forces	Included "operations against possible attacks with . . . chemical weapons . . . containing the impacts of such agents."
September 1997[u]	Zolfaqar	Qom	Regular army and air force; IRGC	Featured "defense operations against chemical warfare." Used "powerful chemical defensive weapons."

[a] "Kheybar-3 Exercises in Gulf End Successfully," FBIS-NES-92-203, 20 October 1992, 44.

[b] "Anti-Chemical Warfare Maneuvers Held in Yazd," FBIS-NES-92-225, 20 November 1992, 55.

[c] "Victory-4 Maneuvers Continue," FBIS-NES-93-079, 27 April 1993, 64.

[d] "Arvand-6 Maneuvers Conclude in Shiraz," FBIS-NES-93-099, 25 May 1993, 64.

[e] "Military Maneuvers Held in Marand Border Region," FBIS-NES-93-168, 1 September 1993, 54.

[f] "Further on Nasr-1 Military Exercises in Persian Gulf," FBIS-NES-93-219, 16 November 1993, 79.

[g] "Nuclear, Chemical Units Participate," FBIS-NES-94-132, 11 July 1994, 85.

[h] "Naval Maneuvers Continue in Northern Gulf Waters," FBIS-NES-94-134, 13 July 1994, 58.

[i] Tehran Voice of the Islamic Republic quoted in News on Iran, no. 44, 3 July 1995 (a publication of the National Council of Resistance of Iran, Foreign Affairs Committee, Auvers-sur-Oise, France).

[j] "Gulf Military Exercise Begins," FBIS-NES-95-021, 1 February 1995, 60.

[k] "Maneuvers End, Called 'Total Success,'" FBIS-NES-95-093, 15 May 1995, 46.

[l] "Second Phase Begins," FBIS-NES-95-100, 24 May 1995, 50.

[m] "Victory-6 Naval Maneuvers Begin in Persian Gulf," FBIS-NES-95-127, 3 July 1995, 65.

[n] "Military Exercise under Way in Kaseh Kabud Region," FBIS-NES-95-167, 29 August 1995, 73.

[o] "Iran: Troops Start 'Zafar' Maneuver," FBIS-NES-96-047, 8 March 1996, 79.

[p] "Iran: Naval Maneuvers Continue in Persian Gulf," FBIS-NES-96-074, 16 April 1996, 85.

[q] "Iran: Army Chief on Maneuvers, Programs," FBIS-NES-96-110, 6 June 1996, 55.

[r] Quoted in Sharam Chubin, Eliminating Weapons of Mass Destruction: The Persian Gulf Case, Henry L. Stimson Center Occasional Paper 33 (Washington, D.C.: Henry L. Stimson Center, 1997).

[s] "Iran: Report on Victory-7 Maneuver," FBIS-NES-97-030, 1 January 1997, electronic version.

[t] "Iran: Military Concludes Second Stage of Gulf Maneuvers," FBIS-NES-97-133, 13 May 1997, electronic version.

[u] "Iran: Shahbazi Details Zolfaqar Maneuver Activities," FBIS-NES-97-343, 9 December 1997, electronic version; "Iran: Zolfaqar Maneuver Commanders Interviewed," FBIS-NES-97-343, 9 December 1997, electronic version.

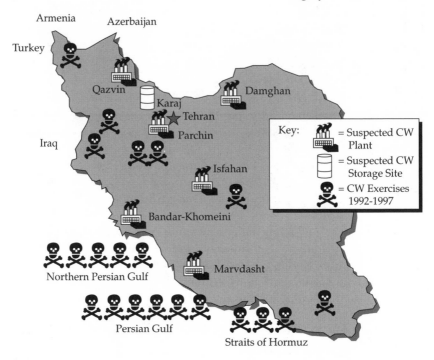

Figure 2. Iranian chemical weapons (CW) facilities and exercises, 1992–97.

It generally is not possible to determine from Iranian press releases which military units were engaged in unconventional weapons training. The data in Table 1, however, indicate that the IRGC, which commands all Iranian naval forces, participated in 75 percent of the nuclear, biological, and chemical exercises, whereas the regular military (i.e., army or air force) participated in 60 percent of these operations. Because Tehran is typically ambiguous about whether its forces are training to use chemical and biological weapons or merely defending against it—a practice observed by other countries of proliferation concern—conclusions about organizational bias toward offensive unconventional weapons doctrines are difficult to draw. Nonetheless, IRGC naval forces are apparently involved in offensive chemical and biological weapons training. In addition to the IRGC's Falaq-2 maneuvers in September 1994 that included an Iranian chemical offensive, IRGC helicopters equipped with spray tanks overflew Iranian naval vessels in both the Piruzi-6 exercise in July 1995 and the Piruzi-8 maneuvers in October 1997, evidently simulating a chemical or biological weapons attack against ships at sea.[58]

Tactical use of chemical and biological weapons at sea generally is underrated in Western military circles, which is precisely why it may be appealing

58. Transcript of background briefing on "CENTCOM Theater Update," 16 October 1995, www.defenselink.mil/news/Oct1995/x101695_xback-a1.html.

to the IRGC. In describing the organization's strengths, IRGC commander Mohsen Reza'i once observed: "Our innovative forces . . . identify the weak spots of the Americans, the weak spots of the world . . . and attack them exactly at the weakest point . . . By the time they have overcome one of their weaknesses, we have developed weapons against another two of their weaknesses and will attack them from other directions. This is one of the secrets of our success."[59] In light of Tehran's investment in fast-attack boats, antiship cruise missiles, mines, and naval frogmen, chemical and biological weapons may constitute yet another dimension of the naval guerrilla war that Iran is preparing to wage in the Gulf.[60] Indeed, since collateral civilian casualties would be minimized and traces of the attack could be reduced by wind and water, chemical and biological weapons use at sea would be easy to deny. Tehran, after all, denied sowing the Persian Gulf with mines during the Iran-Iraq War even after the naval vessel *Iran Ajr* was caught in the act by U.S. forces. Given the numerous false alarms reported by U.S. chemical detection gear during the Gulf War and lingering uncertainties about Gulf War Syndrome, officials in Washington might face a tough battle convincing the international community that Iran used chemical or biological weapons against U.S. naval forces. Rogue IRGC elements also could find this enhanced deniability particularly attractive for concealing covert chemical and biological weapons operations from political authorities in Tehran.

In contrast to the civilian leadership, which tends to view nuclear, biological, and chemical weaponry as a deterrent against the use of unconventional weapons by Iran's adversaries, IRGC naval doctrine does not call for a response in kind. Other naval forces in the Persian Gulf, particularly those of the United States, simply are not equipped with chemical and biological weapons, despite Iranian charges to the contrary. The IRGC's emerging maritime doctrine for chemical and biological weapons apparently is intended as an asymmetrical escalation option, either to preempt or to respond to a high-technology conventional attack. The prospect that the IRGC might use chemical and biological weapons at sea before the actual onset of hostilities with the United States cannot be dismissed, since that is when Iranian vessels and aircraft presumably would have the greatest chance of closing on U.S. naval forces, a maneuver they have practiced in peacetime. Alternatively, hard-to-detect fast-patrol boats may be able to penetrate U.S. defenses at later stages in a conflict,[61] or IRGC forces could opt to disperse chemical and biological weapons from safe standoff distances.

---

59. "Guard Corps Commander Marks War Week," FBIS-NES, 25 September 1987, 49.
60. On Iran's unconventional naval threat, see Cordesman and Hashim, *Iran*, 244–62.
61. Michael Eisenstadt of the Washington Institute for Near East Policy notes that reports of CW-armed Iranian vessels could refer to fast-attack boats that have been equipped with 130mm rocket launchers.

Gregory F. Giles

The contrast between Iranian civilian leaders' preference for defensive nuclear, biological, and chemical weapons doctrine and the IRGC's preference for an offensive posture is anticipated by organizational theory. In the case of the IRGC, offensive biases may be increased by the organization's desire to "settle the score" following the 1988 rout of Iranian naval forces by their American counterparts. A key question in future crises will be whether Iran's civilian leaders can rein in the IRGC's offensive chemical and biological weapons doctrine and subordinate it to the regime's overall defensive posture.

The Islamic Republic may use chemical and biological weapons in acts of terrorism. Iran's extensive support of terrorism is yet another facet of its military weakness. By masking its involvement in terrorist attacks, Tehran has been able to strike U.S. and Israeli interests, for example, without military reprisals. At the same time, Iran's sense of grievance makes any means of retaliation, even targeting noncombatants, appear legitimate.[62] For these same reasons, Tehran may consider chemical and biological agents as useful terrorist weapons. Press reports claim that Iran has developed a biological weapons aerosol for terrorist use and that Iranian leaders used a poison to assassinate three opponents of the regime in 1996.[63] Tehran would have to weigh its own terrorist use of chemical and biological weapons, however, against the possibility that opponents of the regime who remain active in Iran, might then feel similarly unconstrained in their use.[64]

COMMAND AND CONTROL OF IRANIAN NUCLEAR, BIOLOGICAL, AND CHEMICAL WEAPONS

Just as Iran has two policies on the acquisition of unconventional weapons and at least two doctrines on use of chemical weapons, it also has a dual approach to the command and control of chemical weapons. This dual approach stems, in part, from a history of volatile civil-military relations, as well differing perceptions of time-urgency.[65] Iranian civil-military relations have had a troubled history since the 1920s. The Pahlavi dynasty itself was founded by a military coup. The Iranian armed forces continued to play a pivotal role in Iranian politics, whether by acts of omission or commission, right up to the failed 1980 coup attempt against the fledgling

62. See Michael Eisenstadt, *Iranian Military Power*, 65–78.
63. See "Iran: Israelis Warn of Tehran's Biological Arsenal," FBIS-NES-96–156, 11 August 1996, 11; and "Regime Poisons Kurds," *Iran Brief*, no. 27 (1 October 1996): 1.
64. Lotfian, "Threat Perception and Military Planning in Iran," 199.
65. Peter D. Feaver, "Command and Control in Emerging Nuclear Nations," *International Security* 17 (Winter 1992–93): 160–87.

Islamic Republic. To counter the coup threat, the mullahs not only constituted the IRGC but also created multiple and overlapping organizations to
ensure tight political control over the regular armed forces.[66] The Political-
Ideological Directorate (PID), for example, is composed of clerics who
monitor military behavior from the Joint Staff level down to individual
platoons. Another religious organization, the Imam's Representatives (IR),
similarly permeates the armed forces. Reportedly, the permission of an
Imam's Representative must be given before regular military units can undertake certain actions.

Mullahs also have implemented an assertive system of control over the
regular military's access to and use of nuclear, biological and chemical
weapons. Chemical weapons are under the custody of the more politically
reliable IRGC. In practice, these arrangements ensure that the regular military would be able to initiate chemical attacks only after the civilian leadership authorized the IRGC to turn over the weapons and parallel PID and IR
oversight chains of command added their consent. During the war with
Iraq, for example, chemical weapons use required the consent of Iran's
supreme leader. This policy reflected the supreme leader's constitutional
status as commander in chief of all Iranian forces, as well as the controver-
sial nature of unconventional weapons under Islam. In the event the national leadership was incapacitated, the regular military's ability to access
and use chemical weapons in a timely fashion would be significantly, if not
drastically, constrained, that is, the command and control system would
"fail safe."

Iraq's surprise invasion in 1980 could have encouraged Tehran to delegate more authority over nuclear, biological, and chemical weapons to the
regular military. Yet two factors argue against a more delegative command
and control system. The first is overriding concern about internal security.
The second has to do with Iran's sense of urgency. With a land mass
roughly the size of Alaska, Iran has considerable strategic depth. In addition, the regular army is forward deployed to meet threats at the border.
Iran has dispersed its chemical weapons infrastructure widely within this
territory. Iran therefore can expect its army to slow an enemy advance and
has sufficient industrial redundancy to compensate for air attacks against
individual chemical weapons plants. Tehran does not face a likely "use it or
lose it threat" to its chemical and biological weapons capabilities on the
Iranian mainland, nor has there been public discussion in Iran about enemy
decapitating attacks. Together, these factors help to dampen pressures for
delegating nuclear, biological, and chemical weapons control to the regular
military.

---

66. Information on political-ideological control is drawn from Schahgaldian, *Iranian Military*,
28–32.

Iranian leaders may have adopted a more delegative stance over nuclear, biological, and chemical weapons control with respect to the IRGC. The IRGC has staunchly defended its autonomy, and in contrast to the regular military, the assignment of clerical overseers to major IRGC formations has taken years to accomplish. There has been frequent turnover in the post of the Imam's Representative to the IRGC because various clerics found it difficult to establish control over this radical organization. Again in contrast to the regular military, there is no evidence that Iran's "clerical commissars" have ever held veto authority over IRGC operations.[67] Iran's clerical leaders presumably have been willing to tolerate a relatively greater degree of IRGC autonomy for two reasons. First, the organization is more politically reliable than the regular military. Second, the IRGC is very influential and has powerful protectors among radical clerics. Thus the IRGC has acquired physical custody over chemical weapons, and the organization probably has tried to increase its autonomy over the use of such weapons.

In this context, the deployment of chemical weapons with IRGC forces on the island of Abu Musa assumes great significance. Because the weapons are forward deployed in close proximity to U.S. forces and communication links with the island are tenuous, command and control takes on a greater time urgency. In contrast to the Iranian mainland, IRGC forces on Abu Musa could face a "use them or lose them" dilemma with respect to chemical weapons. Anticipating this possibility, the IRGC is likely to have moved, either with or without civilian sanction, to ensure that its units on the island could use all the weapons at their disposal in self-defense. With the Abu Musa precedent, the IRGC might well have extended such rules of engagement to other units such as its chemical weapons–armed ships. The IRGC's determined pursuit of organizational autonomy and its disregard for wider national policy could lead it to stretch authorization to use chemical weapons in self-defense to their use in *preemptive* self-defense.

As biological and nuclear weapons enter the Iranian arsenal, command and control arrangements deemed adequate for chemical weapons could be significantly altered, though for different reasons and in different directions. In particular, the relatively greater lethality of biological agents compared to chemical agents could lead the mullahs to adopt tighter controls over their handling and use, even by the IRGC. Here the primary motivation might be to prevent an accidental release that could affect Iranian troops or civilians. For this reason, biological weapons probably would not be forward deployed and would fall under a more assertive command and control system.

67. Information in this paragraph is taken from Katzman, *Warriors of Islam*, 120–23. Katzman attributes the IRGC's autonomy to the fact that the Guard is not the creation of the clerical leadership but rather a partner that fought alongside it to depose the Shah.

Barring a diversion from a foreign source, nuclear weapons initially would become available to Iran only in small numbers over a protracted period. Despite its significant strategic depth, Tehran may deem it necessary to adopt a higher degree of readiness for a nascent nuclear force, particularly since fears of a preventive attack by Israel or the United States undoubtedly will grow the closer Iran comes to possessing the bomb. This raises the possibility of a more delegative command and control system for Iranian nuclear weapons. It also raises the risk of inadvertent escalation resulting from false warnings or unauthorized action—that is, the system could "fail deadly." To mitigate this risk, Iran's clerical leadership might create a new organization for nuclear weapons, one that was more professional and reliable than either the regular military or the IRGC. Such bureaucratic differentiation and counterbalancing would be consistent with past Iranian behavior.

It is also conceivable that since chemical, biological, and nuclear weapons pose different control challenges for Iran's civilian leaders, distinct rules of engagement and control mechanisms might be developed for each type of weapon. The wide array of institutional actors in Iran's chemical weapons program poses enormous challenges for centralized control. The picture becomes more complicated still as specialized and competing biotechnology and nuclear energy constituencies enter the field. Having intentionally pitted the IRGC against the regular military, Iran has faced an uphill battle trying to get the two to act in a coordinated fashion. Nuclear, biological, and chemical weapons command and control arrangements might not be able to overcome these production and organizational hurdles. The end result could be a delegative command system for chemical weapons with significant IRGC autonomy, an assertive system for biological weapons that keeps the IRGC on a shorter leash, and a delegative system for some nuclear force other than the IRGC, each chain tied in some fashion to the civilian authorities.

The safety culture governing the Iranian chemical weapons program is another important aspect of Iranian chemical weapons command and control. Iraq's battlefield use of chemical weapons made Iranian leaders aware of how lethal chemical agents can be. Iran's leaders also understand the hazards posed by the production of these weapons. An explosion apparently occurred in 1984 at the Marvdasht complex, killing a dozen technicians involved in chemical and biological weapons experiments.[68] Four years later, the Iranian parliament debated the wisdom of constructing

---

68. Burck et al., *Chemical Weapons Proliferation*, 245.

chemical weapons facilities close to population centers.[69] Commercial satellite imagery also indicates that Iran has taken some safety precautions, such as locating the suspected chemical weapons plant at Damghan downwind of the nearby town and leaving the surrounding fields fallow.[70]

Reported use of binary chemical weapon designs also may reflect Iranian concern over safety. Such designs, which stop just short of mixing relatively nontoxic precursors into lethal agents, provide for more stable storage.[71] This safety advantage could be negated, however, if Iranian technicians do not observe proper precautions when the time comes to mix the agents. Since this is likely to take place in the field and under crisis conditions, there could be significant potential for a chemical weapons accident.

Recent reports of accidents at Iran's chemical weapons facilities indicate that safety remains poor. Iranian opposition elements reported that in July 1995 a fire broke out at the Chemical National Koshavarz factory near Qazvin. These elements claimed that the facility was a chemical weapons production site and that some twenty-five hundred people were poisoned from the fire's emissions.[72] Later in the year, it was reported that lax safety at Iran's chemical weapons facilities had resulted in numerous workers becoming ill and, in some cases, dying.[73] There is every reason to expect that Iran's safety record in chemical weapons production and handling will be comparable to that of Iraq, which has experienced about one hundred chemical weapons mishaps a year, ten of which were considered serious.[74]

Lessons learned during the war with Iraq, lingering regional insecurities, cultural attitudes toward inhumane warfare, a history of volatile civil-military relations, and Islamic militancy influence Iranian nuclear, biological, and chemical weapons behavior. These factors have yielded a chemical weapons program that is in many respects dysfunctional. Multiple organizations overlap and compete at every stage of the proliferation cycle, from research and development and production, to weapons delivery and doctrinal development, to command and control. Cognitive inconsistencies also are apparent as Iran continues to invest in weapons deemed largely il-

69. Anthony H. Cordesman and Abraham R. Wagner, *The Lesson of Modern War*, vol. 2, *The Iran-Iraq War* (Boulder: Westview, 1990), 513. See also Burck et al., *Chemical Weapons Proliferation*, 262, n. 101.

70. "Iran's Chemical and Biological Warfare Programs," 16.

71. On Iraq's approach to binary chemical munitions and the model it might provide to countries like Iran, see U.S. Congress, Office of Technology Assessment, *Technologies Underlying Weapons of Mass Destruction*, OTA-BP-ISC-115 (Washington, D.C.: U.S. Government Printing Office, 1993), 35.

72. "CW Plant Burns," *Iran Brief*, 1 August 1995, 6. The fire was also reported in the Iranian press but with a much lower casualty figure and no mention of CW.

73. "Iran's Chemical Build-Up," 7.

74. "Accidents," *Arms Control Reporter*, December 1991, 704.E-2.49.

legitimate under Islam. The system is sustained by a production push and growing institutional demand. Iran now turns out chemical weapons munitions for every major type of delivery system, including mines, tube and rocket artillery, fixed- and rotary-wing aircraft, ships, and long-range missiles. The regular military and the IRGC routinely train in nuclear, biological, and chemical warfare.

The Iranian chemical weapons program poses enormous challenges for coordination and control. Already a gap exists between civilian leaders, who largely see nuclear, biological, and chemical weaponry as a deterrent, and the IRGC, which is preparing to use chemical and possibly biological weapons offensively against U.S. naval forces in the Persian Gulf. Subordinating such organizational biases to the Islamic Republic's overall defense strategy is an urgent task for Iran's civilian leaders if they are to control when and how the projected arsenal of chemical, biological, and possibly nuclear weapons will be used in the future.

[4]

Nuclear Arms in Crisis under Secrecy: Israel and the Lessons of the 1967 and 1973 Wars

AVNER COHEN

Since the late 1980s, security analysts have presumed that Israel's nuclear arsenal is both sophisticated and large. Estimates now suggest that Israel has the world's sixth largest nuclear arsenal, lagging behind China but ahead of India and Pakistan.[1] For over thirty years, however, Israel's declaratory policy on nuclear weapons has been restricted to one sentence: "Israel will not be the first to introduce nuclear weapons to the Middle East." Without elaborating what that "nonintroduction" pledge means, Israel has maintained an opaque policy of "neither confirming, nor denying" its nuclear status and activities. It is nevertheless widely believed that Israel crossed the nuclear threshold in the 1960s and developed a nuclear posture referred to as the "bomb in the basement." This "opaque" nuclear posture allows Israel to project an image of nuclear deterrence without explicitly declaring a nuclear doctrine.

How have Israeli political and military leaders planned to use this nuclear weapons capability?[2] Since Israel faced a superior Arab conventional threat through the 1950s and 1960s, realists would not be surprised by a decision to build the bomb and to use it to deter massive conventional attacks. Realists also would predict that Israeli leaders would contemplate preventive nuclear attacks to ensure that no Arab states could successfully counter the Israeli bomb. Finally, realists would expect the Israelis to adopt a highly centralized command system until Arab adversaries developed a nuclear decapitation capability. Organization theorists would expect Israel to de-

---

1. David Albright, Frans Berkout, and William Walker, *Plutonium and Highly Enriched Uranium 1996: World Inventories, Capabilities and Policies* (Stockholm: SIPRI/Oxford University Press, 1997), 258–59.

2. Some of the historical evidence presented here is further elaborated in Avner Cohen, *Israel and the Bomb* (New York: Columbia University Press, 1998).

velop offensive nuclear doctrines and decentralized command systems. Military biases in favor of such doctrine and command structures should be strong and influential there, as they have been elsewhere. Strategic culture explanations would stress that Israel's historical experience and cultural beliefs—the Holocaust, the repeated Arab threats to Israel's survival, and normative concerns about moral behavior in wartime—would cast a long shadow on Israel's nuclear doctrine. These cultural constraints on strategy might encourage Israel to develop the bomb yet simultaneously would discourage Israeli leaders from planning to use nuclear weapons in offensive ways or defensively in anything other than situations of "last resort."

There is now some historical evidence with which to reconstruct Israel's early nuclear thinking and behavior. Not unlike the early American nuclear experience, Israeli thinking and planning about the use of nuclear weapons evolved more slowly than its nuclear infrastructure. Abstract use concepts emerged in the mid-1960s, yet Israel's actual nuclear doctrine was born and shaped only in the two crises surrounding the 1967 and 1973 wars.

This chapter traces the origin of Israeli nuclear thinking and examines how it was conditioned by the 1967 and 1973 wars. Important caveats must be raised, however, at the outset. First, the available historical evidence is meager and obscure, so any effort to address these questions is at best tentative. Second, the chapter examines only Israel's nuclear doctrine, because despite some claims that Israel has a large chemical and biological weapons program, no compelling evidence exists to confirm these reports, much less to analyze the country's potential chemical or biological weapons systems. Third, the chapter focuses on doctrine more than command systems, again because of the paucity of evidence available on this issue.

New evidence about the history of the Israeli nuclear program reveals that Israel had nuclear weapons in 1973 and nuclear devices in 1967 but that policymakers were highly constrained from using them or even from thinking thoroughly through possible deterrent and limited use scenarios. The very apocalyptic nature of "planning the unthinkable," particularly under conditions of opacity, generated cognitive and cultural obstacles to articulating nuclear doctrines and command and control procedures. Israeli leaders remain reluctant to think, let alone to plan, the unthinkable. Indeed, over time, a strategic culture has developed in Israel that nuclear weapons are near taboo and should not be used, short of situations that threaten the country's existence.

THE ROOTS OF OPACITY

Israel's early decisions to acquire a nuclear infrastructure and the modus operandi under which it was made shaped Israel's nuclear thinking. David Ben Gurion, Israel's first prime minister, initiated the nuclear project in the late 1950s without making long-term commitments on the strategic-military objectives of the program. Under Ben Gurion's leadership, decisions were made about the immediate issues related to building the infrastructure, leaving all political, strategic, doctrinal, and financial issues for later consideration. Keeping those issues unresolved was a great advantage for Ben Gurion both at home and abroad. It shielded the super-secret project from domestic controversy, permitting Ben Gurion to present nuclear weapons development as a way to create options for future decision makers. Ambiguity also allowed Ben Gurion to claim that Israel's nuclear program was oriented toward "peaceful purposes" (at least "for the time being," as he told President Kennedy in May 1961).[3]

By 1962–63, the situation was different. In July 1962, as the Dimona reactor was nearing completion, Egypt introduced ballistic missiles, presenting Israeli decision makers with a new set of political, strategic, and financial issues. What strategic posture and doctrine should Israel be seeking, and how quickly should they be attained? How much of its limited resources should Israel invest in advanced future weaponry, including strategic missiles and nuclear weapons? What should be the proper balance between long-term investment in research and development (R&D) in the area of advanced weaponry (e.g., missiles and nuclear weapons) and short-term investment in a strong conventional army?

The issues were sensitive and complex. By the early 1960s, Ben Gurion no longer had either the authority or the political will to make those fateful decisions alone. Such decisions now required more than an act of leadership and intuition; they required consultations at the highest levels. This was the only time that Israel had the semblance of a national debate about its nuclear dilemma, although only the tip of the iceberg was revealed to the public.

Only sketchy information is available about the intense discussions held inside the halls of government. No public records exist, and the testimony of eyewitnesses is veiled and fragmentary.[4] Two schools of thought concerning the future of R&D, force structure, and Israeli Defense Force (IDF) doctrine apparently emerged among senior officials. One school advanced the notion of reorganizing the IDF "as an army of deterrence and decisive victory by relying on the anticipated achievements in science and technology of the 1970s," a veiled reference to nuclear weapons and ballistic missiles.[5] The chief political advocates of this technological-nuclear school were Ben Gurion's two protégés: Deputy Minister of Defense Shimon Peres

3. Ibid., 108–13.

4. Moshe A. Gilboa, *Six Years, Six Days: Origins and History of the Six Day War* (in Hebrew) (Tel Aviv: Am Oved, 1968), 29–30; Yigal Allon, *Contriving Warfare* (in Hebrew) (Tel Aviv: Ha'kibbutz Ha'meuchad, 1990), 200, 205, 207, 305; Yair Evron, *Israel's Nuclear Dilemma* (Ithaca: Cornell University Press, 1994), 6–7.

5. Gilboa, *Six Years, Six Days*, 30.

and Minister of Agriculture (and former chief of staff), Moshe Dayan. They argued that only decisive, unconventional weaponry could provide Israel with the stable deterrence it needed in the long run. The continuation of an unconstrained conventional arms race would drain Israel's economy and would tempt the Arabs to prolong conflict. They publicly urged that Israel should "equip the army for tomorrow."[6]

Members of the technological-nuclear school suggested that the bomb was the most effective deterrent weapon and eventually would convince the Arabs to come to political terms with the reality of Israel. In the absence of a superpower security assurance, the bomb would be Israel's only viable independent security guarantee. Peres called this view "the doctrine of self-reliance"—in effect, an Israeli version of the French *force de frappe*.[7] Advocates of this position also argued that nuclear weapons and ballistic missiles were bound to spread and Israel must follow this trend.

The second school advocated strengthening the IDF and its war-fighting doctrine as a modern *conventional* army based on modern armor and a strong tactical air force. The chief political protagonists of the "conventionalist" school were the leaders of Achdut Ha'avodah: Yigal Allon, minister of labor and former Palmach commander, who was regarded as a hero of the War of Independence; and Israel Galili, former chief of staff of the Haganah. They rejected the three fundamental assumptions of the Dayan-Peres analysis, questioning the inevitability of the spread of nuclear weapons, challenging the view that the bomb was the only solution for Israel's long-term security, and, more important, raising grave doubts about the applicability of the nuclear balance of terror in the Middle East. They believed that conventional military doctrine, built on modern, highly mobilized armor and a strong tactical air force, would keep Israel safe for years to come.

The conventionalist school maintained that if Israel developed nuclear weapons its nuclear monopoly would be brief and soon would be replaced by a mutually nuclearized Middle East. Even if Egypt were not able to keep up with Israel, they argued that the Soviets would not allow Israel to remain the sole nuclear power in the region. Given the fundamental geopolitical and demographic asymmetries, Israel could not tolerate the nuclearization of the Arab-Israeli conflict; investment in a dedicated nuclear weapons program therefore would only weaken the IDF and might even encourage the Arabs to wage another war.[8]

6. Ibid.

7. Peres never argued publicly in Israel for the bomb but always used code phrases such as "technological edge" or "independent deterrent." Outside Israel, however, he allowed his views to be echoed by others close to him; see, for example, "An Independent Deterrent to Israel," *Jewish Observer*, 28 December 1962.

8. Yigal Allon, *Curtain of Sand* (in Hebrew) (Tel Aviv: Ha'kibbutz Ha'meuchad, 1968), 400–402; also Allon, *Contriving Warfare*, 195–209.

The debate between these two groups took place in various governmental forums. It involved strategic issues, domestic politics, and other rivalries. Although information is still sketchy, it appears that the advocates of a nuclear-oriented posture avoided articulating the doctrinal implications, such as emphasis on first use and early employment of nuclear weapons, and were not forced to do so. It is not even clear to what extent the antagonists were fully informed of the complex doctrinal issues concerning nuclear weapons and strategy. The debate was generally about the extent to which Israel should develop its infrastructure and capability, not a doctrinal debate about use. Indeed, doctrinal and organizational decisions were postponed, pending the completion of the missile program in the late 1960s. Moreover, Ben Gurion did not accelerate the nuclear project at the expense of the needs of the conventional army.[9] An Israeli nuclear weapons capability continued to be developed but was discussed only as an option. In retrospect, this ambiguity suited Ben Gurion because it permitted the development of a nuclear capability to proceed without controversy.

1966: Early Doctrinal Formulations

By 1965–66, under Prime Minister Levi Eshkol, a new set of decisions had to be made. Israel was approaching the point when it would have all the critical components of a basic nuclear capability. According to French sources, plutonium was being separated at Dimona in 1966, theoretical and experimental design work on the first Israeli nuclear device was completed around that time, and the French-Israeli missile was in its testing stage.[10]

The convergence of these timetables made it necessary to transform Ben Gurion's nuclear option from an intuition to a national strategic concept. The issue at stake was no longer purely political but was now operational. The long-term strategic implications of the project had to be considered.

Since political leaders were reluctant to provide clear guidance for the project, the R&D establishment itself, sometimes with limited interagency consultations with individuals from the outside, had to decide on its own how to translate complex strategic concepts into technical specifications for the products it was authorized to develop.[11] The R&D establishment could only assume that it understood the national strategic intentions, but the scientists' grasp of national security objectives might have been incomplete. As Prime Minister Eshkol and his deputy Zvi Dinstein made organizational changes in the R&D system in 1966, concepts and strategy at the national

9. Allon, *Contriving Warfare*, 305; Gilboa, *Six Years, Six Days*, 30.
10. John W. Finney, "Israel Said to Buy French Missiles," *New York Times*, 7 January 1966, 1, 8; Hedrick Smith, "U.S. Assumes the Israelis Have A-Bomb or Its Parts," *New York Times*, 18 July 1970, 1, 8.
11. Former senior defense official, interview by author, Tel Aviv, 8 September 1992.

level took form. In 1966, Prime Minister Eshkol, Deputy Prime Minister Dinstein, and Yitzhak Rabin asked a few individuals, among them Professor (and Colonel) Yuval Ne'eman and then-colonel Avraham Tamir, to develop explicit Israeli strategic doctrine in this area. What Eshkol intuitively called the "Samson Option" became the early foundation of an original and well-thought-out concept about the rationale and mission of the nuclear option.[12]

In those early discussions the images and metaphors of the Israeli nuclear option as a "national insurance policy" and a "national safety valve" were articulated.[13] These were two distinct uses of the nuclear option. In the first sense, the specter of the Israeli bomb assures a strong political incentive for the United States to keep Israel conventionally armed in the hope that a strong Israel would never have to use its nuclear option. As far as one can determine, this was not among the primary reasons that initially had led Ben Gurion to the nuclear project, but under Eshkol the insurance component became a crucial aspect of Israel's overall national security strategy. This component proved to be highly successful. It probably is the single most important cause for the change in the U.S. security commitment to Israel in the 1960s.[14]

As a national safety valve, nuclear weapons represent an option of last resort for extreme military and political contingencies. For example, if an Arab state were to produce or purchase a nuclear bomb, Israel could deploy weapons to counter this threat under rapidly deteriorating political circumstances. Soon after Eshkol came up with the formula "Israel will not be the first" to introduce nuclear weapons into the region, Allon added the caveat that Israel would not be the second either.[15] Allon's statement reflected his view that Israel should be prepared both to destroy Arab nuclear programs through preventive conventional attacks, if possible, and to "introduce" Israeli nuclear weapons into the region rapidly, if necessary. Unlike the United States, which feared that Germany was developing the bomb during World War II, fear of an Arab nuclear capability was not among the original reasons that Ben Gurion embarked on the nuclear project. But for the Eshkol government, the possibility of Arab nuclearization served as a double reminder: that nuclearization of the region is against Israeli national interest and that Israel must prudently prepare itself to meet the threat of rapid nuclearization of conflicts.

Another "last resort" contingency that always haunted those responsible for Israeli security, particularly Ben Gurion, was the possible formation of a

12. Yuval Ne'eman, interviews by author, 16–19 February 1994, 25 May 1995.

13. General (Ret.) Avraham (Abrasha) Tamir, interviews by author, Tel Aviv, 16 September 1992, July 1993.

14. Cohen, *Israel and the Bomb*, 219–42.

15. Allon, *Curtain of Sand*, 400–402; also Allon, *Contriving Warfare*, 195–209.

pan-Arabic military coalition against a quantitatively inferior Israel. Given Arab rhetoric about the "destruction of the Zionist entity" or "pushing Israel into the sea," this possibility represented Israel's worst-case scenario. This was the original rationale that attracted Ben Gurion to the bomb, and it continues as the strongest incentive for Israel to retain its nuclear capability. Although most Israeli officials did not share Ben Gurion's political and military pessimism in the late 1950s and early 1960s or Dayan's gloomy conclusions that in the long run Israel could not keep pace in a regional conventional arms race, they did not dispute the notion that, as a matter of national prudence, Israel must prepare itself for worst-case scenarios. This rationale for the nuclear option as a safety valve for cases of last resort has always been backed by a strong national political consensus. Eshkol never questioned the notion that Israel must keep the option readily achievable as a weapon of last resort. Under Eshkol, the option became a reality.

Around 1966, the Israeli defense establishment began developing five-year force-structure plans and a ten-year R&D plan. During these strategic discussions, the original Ben Gurion rationale for going nuclear was defined in terms of having an option of last resort. These strategic discussions produced the early articulation of "red lines," whose crossing could trigger the use of nuclear weapons. There were four scenarios that could lead to nuclear use: a successful Arab military penetration into populated areas within Israel's post-1949 borders; the destruction of the Israeli Air Force (IAF); the exposure of Israeli cities to massive and devastating air attacks or to possible chemical or biological attacks; and the use of nuclear weapons against Israeli territory. Each of these scenarios was defined as a threat to the existence of the state of Israel against which the nation could defend itself by no other means than the use of atomic weapons. Furthermore, some emphasize that if Israel were to develop a nuclear capability, it must develop a weapon for use over its own territory.[16]

A strategic counterargument was that any attempt to conceptualize a last resort use in the context of what were then Israel's (pre-1967) borders runs into a fundamental dilemma. Use of a nuclear bomb as a true last resort, say when a massive Arab invasion already had penetrated Israel's borders, might be too late. Conversely, the use of nuclear weapons to preempt Arab armies might appear premature and therefore politically unacceptable.

These discussions led to the realization that it would be inconceivable for Israel to resort to atomic use in the heat of battle without warning. Furthermore, it was recognized that nuclear deterrence can work only if the deterrent capability is known to one's enemies. But Israel had committed itself not to be the first to introduce nuclear weapons into the region, leaving its

16. Former senior defense official, interview by author, Tel Aviv, 8 September 1992.

capability ambiguous. How can a state create deterrent effects with such nuclear ambiguity?

The answer, it was agreed, was that rumors of an Israeli nuclear capability, as long as they were not attributed to identifiable sources, would be in Israel's best interest. In case of emergency, Israel also had to be ready to increase an adversary's certainty about its nuclear capability. To reinforce nuclear deterrence during a crisis or even at the outbreak of hostilities, Israel would need to develop the technical means to demonstrate its nuclear capability on very short notice. These strategic ideas emerged as the project's developers tried to make sense of the notion of an ambiguous and uncertain nuclear option. Political leaders at the cabinet level provided little guidance to the strategists and weapons developers for such discussions.

It also was understood that Israeli efforts to establish a posture of deterrence through ambiguity was a double-edged sword. If the Egyptians were convinced that Israel was building nuclear weapons, they might have responded violently, possibly even initiating a preventive war. In February 1966, following speculations in the international press, Egyptian President Gamal Abdul Nasser publicly threatened that Egypt would have to wage "preventive war" to stop Israel from developing nuclear weapons.[17] His warnings made an impact in both Israel and the United States.

On the issue of testing, however, the political guidance was clear and straightforward. Despite persuasive pleas from the project's top leaders that a full test was needed to complete the program, Eshkol categorically refused to consider even a "peaceful nuclear explosion."[18] No matter how much the project's executives wanted it, Israel's leaders overruled them decisively. Testing is the most decisive and clear manner of introducing nuclear weapons; it was obvious to Eshkol that to maintain its nonintroduction pledge, Israel must not test a nuclear device.

To the extent that a handful of senior Israeli military officers in the mid-1960s knew about this debate, they apparently viewed it as both theoretical and irrelevant to their own military mission. Rabin's generals did not believe in these doom and gloom scenarios. To them, these national contingency plans of last resort seemed militarily unrealistic, and they were barely informed about the issues.[19] They were committed to the notion that the IDF mission was to prevent these scenarios from ever coming to pass. Allon's idea of a "preventive counterattack," which meant that the IDF denied that the Arabs could ever force Israel to a point of last resort, was

17. Hedrick Smith, "Warning on Bomb Given by Nasser," *New York Times,* 21 February 1966.
18. Zvi Dinstein, interview by author, Tel Aviv, 19 July 1992. Dinstein recalls that Eshkol used to tell Ernst Bergmann, who always pushed for a way to conduct a test, "Do you think that the world would sit and applaud us for our achievement?"
19. Former Israeli defense officials, interview by author, Tel Aviv, 9, 16 July 1992.

ingrained in military thinking. To accomplish this mission, Israel needed a strong tactical air force and a massive armored force. These last resort scenarios planned for the contingency that the IDF had failed in defending Israel; senior Israeli military officers believed that they were irrelevant for all practical purposes.

The 1967 Crisis and War

New information about the status of Israel's nuclear program and the doctrinal discussions outlined above lead to a new interpretation of the 1967 crisis and war in the Middle East. Almost without exception, previous Israeli and Arab interpretations of the 1967 war ignored the nuclear dimension. While varying in assessments and judgments, both traditional Israeli and Arab narratives agree that the 1967 crisis was a case of inadvertent war caused by the failure of conventional deterrence.[20] The fact that Israel had a rudimentary nuclear weapons capability on the eve of the war, however, had a real effect on the handful of Israelis who were aware of it. To what extent did these nuclear-related considerations shape the Israeli response to, and understanding of, the crisis?

Perhaps the most striking feature of the 1967 crisis is that all those nuclear-related considerations were made under extreme secrecy. Neither the political leadership in the United States nor the Egyptian leadership was aware in May 1967 that Israel had a rudimentary nuclear weapons capability that could become operational during a crisis. In a U.S. National Security Council meeting on the Middle East crisis, held on 24 May 1967, CIA director Richard Helms reported that he "was quite positive in stating there were no nuclear weapons in the area."[21]

Helms was wrong. In his autobiography, Munya M. Mardor, the director of Israel's Armament Development Authority (RAFAEL), cites the following dramatic entry from his diary on 28 May 1967:

20. Donald Neff, *Warriors for Jerusalem: The Six Days That Changed the Middle East* (New York: Simon and Schuster, 1984); Avner Yaniv, *Deterrence without the Bomb: The Politics of Israeli Strategy* (Lexington, Mass.: Lexington Books, 1987), 109–25; Michael Brecher with Benjamin Geist, *Decisions in Crisis: Israel, 1967–1973* (Berkeley: University of California Press, 1981); Janis Gross Stein and Raymond Tanter, *Rational Decision-Making: Israel's Security Choices, 1967* (Columbus: Ohio State University Press, 1980); Michael Bar Zohar, *Embassies in Crisis* (Englewood Cliffs: Prentice-Hall, 1970); Richard B. Parker, *The Politics of Miscalculation in the Middle East* (Bloomington: Indiana University Press, 1993); Eitan Haber, *Today War Will Break Out* (in Hebrew) (Tel Aviv: Edanim, 1987); Gilboa, *Six Years, Six Days;* Yitzhak Rabin, *The Rabin Memoirs* (Boston: Little, Brown, 1979), 67–99; Indar Jit Rikhye, *The Sinai Blunder* (London: Frank Cass, 1980).

21. Memorandum for the Record, "Record of National Security Council Meeting Held on 24 May 1967 at 12 noon—Discussion of Middle East Crisis," NSF, NSC History, Box 17, Lyndon B. Johnson Library, Austin, Texas.

I went to the assembly hall. I met Jenka . . . as he monitored the working teams in the project under his supervision. The teams were assembling and testing the weapon system, the development and production of which was completed prior to the war. The time was after midnight. Engineers and technicians, mostly young, were concentrating on their actions. Their facial expression was solemn, inward, as if they fully recognized the enormous, perhaps fateful, value of the weapons system that they brought to operational alert. It was evident that the people of the project were under tension, the utmost tension, physical and spiritual alike.[22]

Mardor does not explain what that unique "fateful weapons system" was or why it was "fateful," but new testimonies shed more light on Mardor's veiled remarks.[23] By the eve of the 1967 war Israel had taken emergency measures to weaponize its rudimentary nuclear capability. As part of these preparations Israel assembled its first nuclear device—not yet a full-blown bomb—made it operational for a test, and made contingency plans to move it to a test site behind enemy lines, in a desolate area of the eastern Sinai.

Israel did think the unthinkable, yet it did so in a most prudent and cautious manner. Although contingency planning for a demonstration test did occur, those who participated in it understood clearly that only a truly "existential threat" could provoke the leadership to consider such a step. And this was deemed unlikely. It was further understood that the purpose of such a test would be demonstrative—a stark warning to the enemy (and the superpowers) to freeze the situation and prevent a scenario of last resort from developing—not an actual military use.

Details still are not available concerning the decision making and the authorization process that led to readying this fateful weapons system and placing it on operational alert, but it is possible to outline what transpired. The crisis reached its climax during the last week of May, as external and domestic crises converged. The external threat was the collapse of Israeli conventional deterrence. It included all the ingredients of Ben Gurion's nightmare: Israel was confronting a grand Arab coalition on three frontiers and was facing it alone. The American failure to take prompt action after the closing of the Straits of Tiran and the Johnson administration's 27 May

22. Munya M. Mardor, RAFAEL (in Hebrew) (Tel Aviv: Misrad Habitachon, 1981), 499.

23. The following paragraphs are based on a series of interviews I conducted in 1999 with former senior Israeli officials. The interviewees asked to remain anonymous. Myer Feldman, deputy counsel in the Kennedy and Johnson White Houses (until 1965) and a liaison with the Jewish community, also recalls that "early on" some elements in the U.S. government knew (or estimated) that before the war the Israelis had two nuclear devices: "I remember the number two" (Feldman, interview by author, Washington, D.C., 22 June 1992). This information was confirmed by credible Israeli sources.

warning to Israel against unilateral action were seen as violations of the public pledges given by Presidents John Kennedy and Lyndon Johnson to guarantee the security of Israel and the written commitment given to Abba Eban by U.S. secretary of state John Foster Dulles in 1956. Israel viewed these pledges as a commitment by the United States to use military force, if necessary, to keep the straits open. In Israel's short history, there has never been a time of greater anxiety over the state's survival.

On 26 May war appeared inevitable; the only question was when it would break out and who would start it. That morning, Egyptian jets flew their second high-altitude reconnaissance flight over Dimona; Israeli forces were unable to intercept them.[24] There were some intelligence indications that the Egyptian air force was ready to attack the next dawn. Two days later, in the wake of President Johnson's warning not to attack, the Eshkol cabinet decided, against military advice, to wait two or three additional weeks before taking military action. It was evident that Israel was strategically vulnerable. There were growing concerns that Nasser might be tempted to take the initiative, as his military leaders were suggesting, and to strike first against Israel's sensitive targets: air bases and the nuclear complex at Dimona. It also was known that Egypt possessed substantial quantities of chemical weapons, which it had used in the war in Yemen two years earlier. There were new fears that Nasser might use these weapons against Israel, perhaps in response to an Israeli attack. Because of these fears, Israel ordered gas masks from Germany while at the same time preparing temporary burial sites for tens of thousands of potential victims.

If Israel did not attack first, it could find itself in dire circumstances. Even if Israel did move preemptively, the IAF could not rule out the possibility that it would fail to execute its Moked plan to destroy the entire Egyptian air force on the ground. The success of the Moked plan relied on complete secrecy, total surprise, and some luck (i.e., the Egyptians had to maintain their standard operating procedures). Given these uncertainties and pressures, it is not surprising that Israeli leaders placed the nation's most "fateful weapon system" on some form of operational alert. In a crisis that for so many Israelis invoked memories of the Holocaust, prudence required making the nation's nuclear capability operational.

While these emergency preparations were made under extreme secrecy, Israel made no nuclear deterrent threat against Egypt and made no attempt to coerce the United States. There were those in Israel who suggested the

24. Haber, *Today War Will Break Out*, 161–63, 187–86, 208; Aluf Benn, "The First Nuclear War" (in Hebrew), *Ha'aretz*, 11 June 1993.

country should make a demonstrative use of its nuclear capability for coercive or deterrent purposes.[25] But apparently such proposals were never seriously entertained by the Eshkol government.

Lessons and Insights

Israel could have revealed to the United States that it had a nuclear capability, possibly making an oblique declaration or even conducting a nuclear test for coercive purposes. Notwithstanding the emergency planning of last resort, there was little, if any, discussion of nuclear use for coercive purposes among the prime minister and his inner cabinet (defense ministerial committee). This was not merely because most political leaders had no knowledge of the state of the nuclear project and the contingency preparations that were under way but also because nuclear weapons and their use were alien to mainstream Israeli political and military thinking. With the possible exception of Shimon Peres—then an opposition leader—Israeli political and military leaders simply did not think in nuclear terms. To entertain the possibility of using nuclear weapons either in demonstration or on the battlefield, short of the need to survive, was simply foreign to Israeli thinking. In this respect, Israel was truthful in its public commitment not to introduce nuclear weapons into the Middle East.

If physical possession of a nuclear device is the criterion for nuclear status, then by May 1967 Israel became a nuclear weapons state. In a political and strategic sense, however, Israel was not a nuclear weapons state. It did not directly or indirectly make any political use of its nuclear capability. Eshkol did not renege on his pledge not to be the first to introduce nuclear weapons. Why?

It certainly is possible to present a set of post-hoc realistic rationales for the lack of enthusiasm to test a nuclear device. Strategically, an Israeli nuclear demonstration or declaration during the crisis could have been interpreted as a sign of panic and despair that might have invited Nasser to call Israel's hand. It could even have triggered further Egyptian defiance of Israeli deterrence, likely leading to a Soviet nuclear guarantee to the Arab

25. Apparently the most prominent among them was Shimon Peres, the former deputy minister of defense and the man who made the nuclear program a reality. In his 1995 memoirs, Peres writes: "My contribution during that dramatic period was something that I still cannot write about openly for reasons of state security. After Dayan was appointed Defense Minister I submitted to him a certain proposal which . . . would have deterred the Arabs and prevented the war." This obscure remark was widely interpreted as a suggestion that a nuclear test might have deterred war. See Shimon Peres, *Battling for Peace: Memoirs* (London: Weidefeld and Nicolson, 1995), 166–67; and Dan Margalit, *I Saw Them* (in Hebrew) (Tel Aviv: Zmora Bitan, 1997), 60–61.

states.[26] If Israel disclosed the existence of its nuclear weapons to induce the United States to act promptly out of fear of nuclear escalation, such disclosure also might have been interpreted as blackmail and would have had a long-term negative impact on U.S.-Israeli relations. Finally, disclosure would have eliminated Israel's moral advantage when facing an existential threat from Nasser's aggression.

There were other inhibitions against contemplating the use of nuclear weapons. The very notion of developing a nuclear doctrine was at odds with the IDF's offensive military doctrine. Before 1967 the IDF philosophy was based on the idea of a conventional preventive war: if and when Israel faced a conventional military threat it must wage a war to destroy that threat, and better early than later. The use of nuclear weapons, even in the form of a demonstration test, undermined this commitment to a preventive war. The tiny size of the arsenal—no more than two "devices" were ready—would logically also counsel against an emergency test, encouraging officials to keep the "weapons" to be used later in military contingencies, if necessary. While a realist analyst can construct such a post-hoc cost-benefit calculation to support the Israeli decision, it is critical to realize that there never was a high-level cabinet discussion of the issue in 1967, much less a formal decision. The prime minister had pledged not to introduce nuclear weapons to the Middle East, only a handful of officials was privy to the details of Israel's operational capability, and, despite the hostility of the Arab states, unilateral escalation of the crisis to the nuclear level through nuclear testing was unprecedented and unpalatable. In short, Israeli use of the nuclear option may not have been unthinkable, but it presented so many normative inhibitions that it could not even be discussed at the cabinet level.

The first signs of a taboo against nuclear weapons thus emerged in the 1967 crisis. It cannot be known, however, whether these inhibitions would have remained as powerful if Israel had not been so successful in its conventional military response to Nasser's threat of war. Although some contingency plans for a test demonstration were drawn, almost no one believed that it would become necessary. Israel launched a preemptive attack, most of the Egyptian air force was quickly destroyed on the ground, and the war was over within a week. In retrospect, however, the failure to use nuclear weapons, whether by testing or in war, strengthened a tradition of nuclear opacity and restraint. Israeli leaders understood the inherent limitations on the use of nuclear weapons.

26. There are allegations that the Soviet Union did provide Egypt with an operational nuclear guarantee during the war and that Soviet submarines were instructed to target Israel with nuclear-armed missiles if Israel used nuclear weapons against Egypt or Syria. See Yehudit Yechezkelli, "We Were to Order the Launch of a Nuclear Missile on Israel" (in Hebrew), *Yediot Achronot Magazine—Shivah Yamim*, 8 May 1992.

Israel had developed its nuclear option as a weapon of last resort, and it could not use it in circumstances short of last resort. The silence of Israeli decision makers on this issue for so long indicates that they understood this point.

THE YOM KIPPUR WAR

Israel had to consider the unthinkable once again in the October 1973 war. Unlike the situation in 1967, this time Israel's nuclear arsenal was recognized and robust. During the 1973 war Israel also activated its nuclear capability, but it is not clear exactly what this entailed.

The most colorful account of October 1973 appears in Seymour Hersh's *Samson Option*.[27] Hersh tells a dramatic story of how Golda Meir's war cabinet, under pressure from Minister of Defense Dayan, "agreed that the nuclear missile launchers . . . would be made operational, along with eight specially marked F-4s [Phantoms] that were on twenty-four hour alert. . . . The initial target list included the Egyptian and Syrian military headquarters near Cairo and Damascus."[28] Some Israelis, however, publicly took issue with Hersh's account. In his 1994 book, *Israel's Nuclear Dilemma*, Yair Evron referred to unidentified "reliable accounts" that asserted that while Dayan "did indeed raise . . . some ideas connected with Israel's nuclear capability," Golda Meir followed the advice of Ministers Allon and Galili and "ruled against Dayan's tentative proposals."[29]

If Hersh's story is largely inaccurate, Evron's comment is obscure. Evron denies Hersh's account but does not state what Dayan actually proposed. Another obscure comment came from Shimon Peres, who confirmed that sometime after the beginning of the Egyptian-Syrian assault, Dayan ordered an "operational check" of the Israeli Jericho missiles but "categorically denied that the missiles were made ready, much less armed."[30] Peres noted that the operational check was not cleared by the cabinet, implying that whatever happened was still short of a cabinet-level decision.[31]

27. Seymour M. Hersh, *The Samson Option: Israel's Nuclear Arsenal and American Foreign Policy* (New York: Random House, 1991), 225–40.

28. Ibid.

29. Yair Evron, *Israel's Nuclear Dilemma* (Ithaca: Cornell University Press, 1994), 71–72.

30. Richard Ned Lebow and Janice Gross Stein, *We All Lost the Cold War* (Princeton: Princeton University Press, 1993), 189, 463 n 46.

31. Peres's emphasis that the matter never reached cabinet discussion is consistent with other testimonies. Meir Pail, an Israeli historian who had access to the minutes of Golda Meir's war cabinet, confirmed that the nuclear option was never formally discussed in this forum. There was one point, he noted, at which the commander of the air force, General Benjamin Peled, used a code word that may have been a reference to unconventional weapons; nevertheless, the issue was ignored (Meir Pail, interview by author, Tel Aviv, October 1993). This also is the view of Azariahu Arnan, Galili's close aide, who is convinced that the nuclear issue never

Professor Yuval Ne'eman, who served as Minister Dayan's liaison with the Pentagon during the war, also denied Hersh's story about Meir's war cabinet making a decision to deploy the "nuclear arsenal."[32] Notwithstanding his denial, Ne'eman cautiously confirmed that some sort of strategic alert ("operational check") involving the "nuclear infrastructure" did take place:

> Note that it would be normal, for whoever is responsible for anything relating to strategic missiles—even if their warheads are just filled with ordinary explosives—to advance their state of preparedness, in time of war. . . . Similarly, for whoever might be responsible for the nuclear infrastructure and the processing of further nuclear steps—whether it be development, production or the enhancement of the level of preparedness—to come to the Prime Minister in the beginning of a war and inquire whether such circumstances might indeed be expected, etc. Such a consultation should have taken place between 6 and 8 October. As I explained above, the Prime Minister's answer could not have implied a deployment. It might (and should) have indicated a need for some degree of preparedness for the strategic missiles, whatever their actual warheads, and some protective steps in the nuclear domain, such as stopping the activities of the reactors throughout the war, to minimize risks from bombardments.[33]

Ne'eman's comments, veiled as they are, may provide some insight into Israeli leaders' idea of strategic command and control. As was the case in 1967, the war cabinet did not issue a formal nuclear decision. Issuing certain measures of preparedness—a state of strategic alert—was not something to be discussed in the cabinet. Although Ne'eman is vague about who authorized what action, seeming to distinguish between those responsible for the missile system and those in charge of the nuclear infrastructure, he made it clear that all decisions about nuclear preparedness must be authorized personally by the prime minister of Israel.

American signal intelligence picked up some of this urgent activity. By the afternoon of 7 October, U.S. intelligence was aware of ground preparations associated with activation of the Jericho surface-to-surface missiles. That activity was interpreted in Washington to be nuclear-related. Furthermore, it was thought that the preparations were conducted in a manner

---

came before the cabinet at the time. To the extent that Dayan did take certain preparatory measures, what Peres calls an "operational check," it was probably prudence (just in case) as well as a possible political message to the United States (Azariahu Arnan, interview by author, Tel Aviv, October 1993).

32. Yuval Ne'eman, "The USA-Israel Connection in the Yom Kippur War (6–24 October 1973)," in *Nuclear Weapons and the 1973 Middle East War*, ed. Michael Wheeler and Kemper V. Gay, Center for National Security Negotiations, Occasional Paper, Nuclear Lessons and Legacies Project, Monograph no. 3, (1996), 5.

33. Ibid., 5–6.

aimed to be detected. William Quandt, at the time a member of the National Security Council (NSC) and of the Washington Special Action Group on the Middle East crisis, recalls the profound impact these reports made on National Security Adviser Henry Kissinger. Quandt maintains that those reports heightened tensions among the NSC staff, even though there was a reluctance to discuss the issue formally. Whatever activity was picked up by the U.S. intelligence community was only a partial picture. It did not shed light on what Israeli intentions were or how far the issue moved up the Israeli decision-making ladder.[34]

Ne'eman also recounts another "true nuclear episode" relating to Israel that took place during the war. This state of alert was initiated on 17 October and lasted until 20 October. Ne'eman provides a compelling description of this important episode:

> The Israeli alarms built up gradually. In his victory speech on the 16th [October], with Kosygin next to him, Sadat mentioned the presence in Egypt of strategic missiles which would retaliate against Tel Aviv, should the Israelis dare to bomb Egyptian cities. The missiles were mentioned as "Zafir," the name of the defunct missile project developed by Nasser, with the help of German technicians in 1961–67, not as Soviet Scud missiles. The next day, American satellite photographs showed a deployment of two brigades of Scud missiles, positioned in the Delta area, apparently with uncamouflaged nuclear warheads, manned by Soviet troops. This information (see *Aviation Week and Space Technology*, November 5, 1973, p. 13), relayed to Israeli Defense Intelligence, made General Elazar order the deployment of a Jericho missile battery. General Elazar's instructions were not to camouflage the site, assuming that the message of a counter-deployment would be read by the Soviet satellites and relayed to Sadat. It was left to them to guess the nature of the Israeli warheads. [35]

This second Israeli nuclear-related alert was probably the result of an error or misunderstanding. It appears that when the United States gave Israel information about the Scuds it referred to them simply as nuclear-capable missiles; there were no indications that they were armed with nuclear warheads. The Israelis, however, interpreted the U.S. message as a warning that the missiles might actually have nuclear warheads.[36] It is difficult to know whether this was a misunderstanding or preparation for a worst-case scenario.

34. William Quandt, interview by author, Washington D.C., 10 January 1994; also Stephen Green, *Living by the Sword: America and Israel in the Middle East* (Brattleboro: Amana Books, 1988), 90–92; Hersh, *Samson Option*, 225–40.

35. Ne'eman, "The USA-Israel Connection in the Yom Kippur War," 15.

36. This consensus emerged in discussion during the workshop "Nuclear Weapons and the 1973 Middle East War," Washington, D.C., 12 February 1996.

Avner Cohen

Lessons and Insights

From the outset, Israeli thinking about the unthinkable has been linked with the concept of last resort. That is, the defense of Israel must not rely on the threat or use of nuclear weapons as long as its enemies have no nuclear weapons, except in cases of extreme national emergency when the survival of the state as a political entity is threatened. But what constitutes a true case of last resort?

The 1973 war provided Israel a great lesson in what constituted a last resort, and the extent to which Israeli leaders were committed to the principle of nonuse and were aware of the nuclear taboo. Israel was traumatized by the ferocity of the Egyptian-Syrian surprise attack on the afternoon of 6 October. Within less than a day, Israel lost its hold over the Suez Canal and much of the Golan Heights. By the next morning most of the combat units of the regular army had suffered heavy losses and were no longer an organized fighting force. There was a real danger that the Syrian army would cross the Jordan bridges into Israel proper. On 7 October, the military position was approaching a last resort situation in which Israel's survival was in danger. By the morning of the seventh it was evident that the burden of defending Israel had fallen on the reserves. The reserves, however, were still in the process of a disorganized mobilization.

It is only logical, as Ne'eman pointed out, that "those responsible" for the strategic systems should order an "operational check" of those systems and place them on alert, but what is more impressive is that the prime minister, the ultimate custodian of all nuclear systems in Israel, did *not*, Peres and Ne'eman maintain, bring the nuclear issue up for a formal cabinet discussion. This reluctance to discuss nuclear weapons in the war cabinet—the only forum that can decide on these matters—is a measure of the depth of the nuclear taboo. Despite Dayan's pessimistic mood, the prime minister did not believe that the military situation in the first two days of the war demanded immediate consideration of the use of nuclear weapons.

The next day, while the situation on the Golan Heights stabilized, Israel made its first counterattack on the Suez front. This divisional attack failed miserably, however, because it lacked sufficient preparation, coordination, and tactical intelligence. On the morning of 9 October the overall Israeli military situation looked bleak. Even though the Egyptian-Syrian assault was stopped, it was evident that the war would stretch out. Concerns were raised about how long Israel could sustain such a high level of attrition, especially among the IAF.[37] This was the military situation when Ambassador Simcha Dinitz submitted to Secretary of State Henry Kissinger Israel's ini-

37. Arie Braun, *Moshe Dayan and the Yom Kippur War* (in Hebrew) (Tel Aviv: Edanim, 1993), 105.

tial request for immediate resupply on the morning of 9 October. Dayan was preoccupied with Israel's material limitations should the war last beyond two or three weeks. The IAF was losing planes at a high rate (eighty or so in the first week), the army lost over five hundred tanks in the first four days, and the supply of ammunition was falling fast. The United States had to be made to understand Israel's plight and the need to resupply it with military equipment. Without resupply of conventional weaponry, Israeli leaders would have to think the unthinkable.

Given Israel's policy of nuclear opacity, which did not allow an American-Israeli dialogue on strategic matters, the only way for Israel to signal its distress to the United States, its closest ally, was to display its strategic systems. This evidently was the meaning behind the missile activity that U.S. intelligence services reportedly detected in the early days of the war. Since the mid-1960s, one strategic objective of the Israeli nuclear program was directed at the United States: to remind the Americans that Israeli needs for conventional weaponry must be met.

Different theoretical perspectives would offer different interpretations of Israel's nuclear restraint during the 1973 war. A normative interpretation would make the claim that even during the bleak hours of the 1973 war, there was still reluctance among Israeli leaders, notably Prime Minister Golda Meir and her chief nuclear executive, Shalheveth Freier, to consider those hours as a real moment of last resort.[38] In retrospect, Meir's reluctance to consider use of nuclear weapons raised the bar of what constitutes a true dire moment in which the use of nuclear weapons is justified.

According to this reading, the nuclear experience of the Yom Kippur War highlights the prevalence of the taboo on Israeli thinking about nuclear weapons. The posture of nuclear opacity was shown to be more robust than could have been predicted before the war, able to endure even at a time of utmost military crisis.

There was, however, a more realist interpretation of the 1973 war as well. According to this view, nuclear restraint was the legacy of the 1973 war, not because of some taboo against the use of nuclear weapons among Israeli political leaders but rather because in 1973 the Israel nuclear arsenal lacked tactical nuclear weapons that could be used on the battlefield. Israel did not have the "right" nuclear weapons, hence it had no choice but restraint. Had such weapons existed, the argument went, the prime minister might have thought differently about using them.

---

38. Shalheveth Freier, director general of the Israel Atomic Energy Commission during the 1973 war, reports that when he got word that war was about to break out, he ordered his senior staff not to distribute any document outside their office without his personal approval, effectively banning written communication between his office and the external world. Such an order can be interpreted as more than simple concern over security; this is a testimony to the strength of the nuclear taboo in Israel.

As is the case with all counterfactual arguments, one cannot be certain how Israeli leaders would have behaved in 1973 had the nation had different nuclear weapons in its arsenal. I believe that Prime Minister Meir would have maintained nuclear restraint under the same circumstances, even if the arsenal had been different.

The evolution of Israeli nuclear thinking after the 1973 war remains generally unknown, but hints of change and continuity surface. On the one hand, the reported development of smaller-yield weapons for Israel's arsenal in the decades after the 1973 war suggests that realist concerns about the need for improved military utility in nuclear weapons design were not historically insignificant.[39] Nevertheless, the near taboo status of nuclear weapons continued to constrain Israeli leaders in peacetime and in war. Prime Minister Yitzhak Shamir refused to make direct nuclear threats against Iraq in the 1991 Persian Gulf War, for example, and Defense Minister Moshe Arens would state only that "Saddam has reasons to worry" if Iraq used chemical or biological weapons on the Scud missiles being launched on Israel.[40] During the January–February 1998 crisis in the Persian Gulf, to give another example, when it was hinted that Prime Minister Benjamin Netanyahu was considering using nuclear weapons in response to an Iraqi chemical or biological attack, leading Israeli commentators proposed a law that would place institutional checks and balances on the prime minister's ability to determine Israeli nuclear doctrine.[41]

Israel's behavior and lessons in the 1967 and 1973 wars shaped the development of the Israeli nuclear doctrine of existential deterrence, including the recognition of profound constraints concerning the use, or even threat of use, of nuclear weapons. This history highlights the reluctance of Israeli political leaders to consider the nuclear path, or to "think the unthinkable."

This does not mean, of course, that Israeli leaders lacked powerful realist incentives not to use nuclear weapons. On the contrary, my analysis of the nuclear situation in 1967 and in 1973 demonstrates the strength of these in-

39. Harold Hough, "Israel's Nuclear Infrastructure," *Jane's Intelligence Review* 6 (November 1994): 508–12, and "Could Israel's Nuclear Assets Survive Preemptive Strike?" *Jane's Intelligence Review* 9 (September 1997); Hersh, *Samson Option*, 271–83; Frank Barnaby, *The Invisible Bomb: The Nuclear Arms Race in the Middle East* (London: I. B. Tauris, 1989), 24–46.

40. Shai Feldman, "Israeli Deterrence and the Gulf War," in *War in the Gulf*, ed. Joseph Alpher (Boulder: Westview Press, 1992); Avner Cohen, "The Israeli Press Covers, and Then Covers Up, the Bomb," *Deadline* 6 (Summer 1991): 17–19.

41. Ze'ev Schiff, "The Red Button Law," *Ha'aretz*, 13 March 1988 (English translation on the *Ha'aretz* English Web site, www.haaretz.co.il/eng/1.1.html). Other Israeli commentators expressed similar concerns: Nahum Barnea and Shimon Shipper, "The Button and the Finger," *Yediot Ahronot* (in Hebrew), 27 February 1998. Ron Ben Yishai also raised questions about Israel's nuclear decision-making process in his two-article series on Israel's nuclear policy in *Yediot Ahronot*, 15 and 22 May 1998.

centives. Nevertheless, I cannot escape the conclusion that the reluctance of Eshkol in 1967 and Meir in 1973 to consider the use, or even the testing, of nuclear weapons was more than a matter of prudent calculations alone. This reluctance had strong instinctive and normative components that cannot be reduced to any specific cost-benefit calculations. Meir's profound sense of nuclear taboo has become, over time, an integral part of Israel's nuclear legacy: nuclear weapons, unlike all other weapons, are virtually unusable except in the extreme conditions of last resort.

Nina Tannenwald has argued that "the non-use of nuclear weapons since 1945" is not simply a matter of sheer luck or successful deterrence but rather a manifestation of "normative prohibition," a taboo that has evolved by way of learning throughout the nuclear age. Tannewald maintains that "although not (yet) a fully robust norm, [this taboo] has stigmatized nuclear weapons as unacceptable weapons of mass destruction."[42]

I think that a similar, perhaps even stronger, sense of normative constraint has prevailed in Israeli nuclear behavior as well. The instinctive reluctance of Israeli leaders to consider seriously the use of nuclear weapons in these two crises is rooted in a *double* sense of prohibition: the evolving global normative prohibition against the use of nuclear weapons and Israel's own code and culture of nuclear opacity. When Israeli leaders embarked on their nuclear path in the 1950s, many considered nuclear weapons to be usable weapons of war; but as Israel's nuclear program matured in the late 1960s, there emerged a general reluctance to think about nuclear weapons as usable weapons, except in dire situations of last resort. The emergence of nuclear opacity as part of Israel's culture of national security, built on secrecy, compartmentalization, and lack of explicit doctrine, provided an institutional reinforcement for this psychological sense of taboo.

This analysis does not exclude the fact that matters of prudence and necessity have played an important role in the formation of opacity and its associated inhibitions. Indeed, there is no clear line separating the realm of necessity and prudence from the realm of norms, values, and prohibitions. As ethicists and anthropologists have long maintained, virtually all norms and prohibitions have their origins in the realm of prudence and necessity.

Some realists may reverse my argument by claiming that the strength of the Israeli taboo was never fully tested because Israel never faced a true situation of last resort—that is, a real threat of extinction. In one sense, this is true. In a more important sense, however, the emergence of a taboo against nuclear use determined the very limited scope of situations that Israeli leaders could consider to be last resort. In short, the definition of "last re-

42. Nina Tannenwald, "The Nuclear Taboo: The Normative Basis of Nuclear Non-Use," *International Organization* 53 (Summer 1999), 443–68.

sort" is not objectively established but is rather a construct of a strategic community at a certain time.

It also is important to recognize that no normative prohibition is an absolute. Cultures and religions treat prohibitions as normative-based rather than as derived from prudence and necessity, yet they leave room for overriding matters of prudence and necessity in some extraordinary cases. For example, the Sabbath prohibitions in Judaism are normative but do not always override prudence and necessity. After all, "saving life overrides the Sabbath."

This point applies equally to strategic cultures and the claim that Israeli reluctance to use nuclear weapons has the force of a taboo-like prohibition. To assert this opinion does not mean, of course, that Israeli political leaders would never consider using the bomb. There may arise dire emergencies in which the state's existence is in danger, what Michael Walzer calls situations of "supreme emergency."[43] But the nuclear taboo has developed to the point at which uses of nuclear weapons that were once considered plausible by at least some Israeli decision makers—tests to coerce allies, direct threats to deter enemies from conventional attack, tactical battlefield uses in limited wars—have become virtually unthinkable. The realm of necessity has become increasingly smaller over time, and this decrease is a tribute to the emerging nuclear taboo.

43. Michael Walzer, *Just and Unjust Wars* (New York: Basic Books, 1977), 251–68.

[5]

India's Nuclear Use Doctrine

WAHEGURU PAL SINGH SIDHU

*India is now a nuclear weapon state. This is a reality that cannot be denied.
It is not a conferment that we seek; nor is it a status for others to grant. It
is an endowment to the nation by our scientists and engineers. It is India's
due, the right of one-sixth of humankind.*
        —Prime Minister Atal Behari Vajpayee, "XII Lok Sabha
        (Parliment) Debates," 1988

In May 1998 India conducted five nuclear tests and declared itself a nuclear
weapon state. The tests are the result of India's quest to acquire a wide-
ranging arsenal of low-yield, subkiloton nuclear munitions for artillery
shells, boosted fission weapons, and city-busting thermonuclear fusion
weapons.[1] In August 1999, New Delhi released the "Draft Report of the National Security Advisory Board on Indian Nuclear Doctrine," which stated
that India's future nuclear forces "will be based on a triad of aircraft, mobile
land-based missiles and sea-based assets."[2] Estimates of the numbers and
types of nuclear weapons that India has or could soon deploy, however,
vary considerably.[3]

How and under what circumstances would India use its nuclear weapons?
Prime Minister Vajpayee, the head of the Bharatiya Janata Party (BJP)–led

---

1. T. S. Gopi Rethinaraj, "Indian Blasts Surprise the World, but Leave Fresh Doubts," *Jane's
Intelligence Review* 10 (July 1998): 19–22; David Albright, "The Shots Heard 'Round the World,"
Bulletin of the Atomic Scientists 54 (July–August 1998): 20–25.

2. See "Draft Report of the National Security Advisory Board on Indian Nuclear Doctrine,"
paragraph 3.1 at http://www.meadev.gov.in/govt/indnucld.htm.

3. For different estimates, see Raj Chengappa and Manoj Joshi, "Future Fire," *India Today,* 25
May 1998, 22–24; Mark Hibbs, "India Made 'About 25 Bomb Cores' since First Tests in 1974,"
Nucleonics Week, 17 June 1998; and Waheguru Pal Singh Sidhu, "India Seeks Safety in Nuclear
Triad and Second Strike Capability," *Jane's Intelligence Review* 10 (July 1998): 23.

coalition government, declared that India does "not intend to use these weapons for aggression or for mounting threats against any country; these are weapons of self-defense, to ensure that India is not subjected to nuclear threats or coercion."[4] On 4 August 1998, Vajpayee announced in the parliament that India would follow a policy of "minimum deterrence" and "will not be the first to use nuclear weapons."[5] He reasoned that the "fact that we've become a nuclear weapons state should be a deterrent itself." When asked by opposition leaders what India would do if it were attacked, Vajpayee declared: "The thought should be discarded, that other countries use these weapons and we cannot retaliate. Our arsenal is a credible deterrent." [6] In an interview in November 1999, India's foreign minister Jaswant Singh elaborated that "the principal role of [India's] nuclear weapons is to deter their use by an adversary" and insisted that to maintain this "policy of 'retaliation only,' survivability becomes critical to ensure credibility."[7]

Vajpayee's statements reveal his desire to create a "credible minimum" nuclear deterrent, to avoid issuing nuclear threats, and to adopt a no-first-use doctrine. They also indicate a desire to create a second-strike capability that would be used only if deterrence were to fail. Yet India's practice may be at variance with its declaratory policy. On 18 May, five days after the final Indian tests, Home Minister Lal Krishna Advani warned Pakistan to "roll back its anti-India policy with regards to Kashmir" on the grounds that India's "decisive step to become a nuclear weapon state has brought about a qualitatively new stage in Indo-Pak relations."[8] Advani then suggested that the nuclear tests permitted Indian forces to follow a policy of "hot pursuit," chasing insurgents in Kashmir across the Line of Control (LOC) into Pakistan, a warning which officials in Pakistan perceived as a threat.[9] There is little evidence to suggest, however, that India's nuclear capability has been integrated into existing conventional forces to carry out Advani's threat. In fact, it is uncertain that the nuclear arsenal will be used even if deterrence fails. According to George Perkovich, this is because Indian strategists believe "that it was adequate to make an adversary *uncertain* that nuclear threats or attacks on India would *not* be met with nuclear reprisals" (italics in original).[10]

---

4. Prime Minister Atal Behari Vajpayee, "XII Lok Sabha (Parliament) Debates," Session II (Budget), 27 May 1998.

5. "PM Declares No-First Strike," *Indian Express*, 5 August 1998.

6. "CTBT Only after Parliament's Nod: PM," *Hindustan Times*, 5 August 1998.

7. "India not to engage in n-arms race: Jaswant," *Hindu*, 29 November 1999.

8. Harish Khare, "Roll Back Proxy War, Pak. Told," *Hindu*, 19 May 1998.

9. See Amit Baruah, "Pak. Reacts Sharply to Advani's Statement," *Hindu*, 20 May 1998; and remarks made by Pakistan foreign secretary Shamshad Ahmed at an Asia Society meeting on 7 July 1998.

10. George Perkovich, *India's Nuclear Bomb: The Impact on Global Proliferation*, (Berkeley: University of California Press, 1999), 3.

The August 1999 "Draft Doctrine" report is an effort to integrate Indian future nuclear policy with its grand strategy and military plans, but it is unusual in three respects. First, no other nuclear power has expounded its nuclear doctrine *before* all the actual nuclear weapons were in place. Most of the existing nuclear powers first accumulated nuclear weapons and then developed doctrines based on their arsenals (for instance, the United States, which used and possessed nuclear weapons from 1945, did not have any doctrine until 1948). Second, most nuclear doctrines (unlike the Indian one) are not known for their wordiness; they outline broad principles of use and nonuse of nuclear weapons but do not deal with a wide range of policy questions. Third, nuclear doctrines normally deal with employment of nuclear arsenals; they never advocate abolition. In contrast, the draft Indian nuclear doctrine calls not only for complete nuclear disarmament at one end but also for nuclear war-fighting capabilities at the other extreme.

This approach was necessary to accommodate the divergent views (ranging from disarmament doves at one end to nuclear war-fighting hawks at the other) of the members of the National Security Advisory Board (NSAB), which includes former diplomats, bureaucrats, and chiefs of the three services. Although two of the three legs of the triad are at least a decade away from being fielded, the document may have insisted on a triad-based minimum deterrent to preempt any interservices rivalry. While the cornerstone of the doctrine is to create a credible minimum deterrent, it does not advocate putting the nuclear arsenal on high alert. Instead it "envisages assured capability to shift from peacetime deployment to fully employable forces in the shortest possible time."[11] This statement indicates a reluctance to hand over the nuclear weapons to the armed forces.

Two other sections of the draft doctrine are significant in operational terms. First, the document insists that "effective conventional military capabilities shall be maintained to raise the threshold of outbreak both of conventional military conflict as well as that of threat or use of nuclear weapons." At the same time, it notes that the "Indian defence forces shall be in a position to execute operations in an NBC [Nuclear, Biological and Chemical] environment with minimal degradation."[12] The document thus reflects the military's desire both to maintain large and effective conventional forces and to adapt them for use in a nuclear, chemical, or biological war scenario. Second, the draft document backed away from Prime Minister Vajpayee's clear-cut no-first-use declaration by adding the important caveat that India could use or threaten to use nuclear weapons against nonnuclear states that are aligned with nuclear weapons states.

11. "Draft Report," paragraph 3.2.
12. *Ibid*, paragraphs 2.7, 5.5, 2.5.

Within months of the release of the draft nuclear doctrine, however, India's foreign minister, Jaswant Singh, publicly distanced the government's position from the NSAB document, particularly in terms of its call for a nuclear triad. Instead, he suggested that the Indian nuclear "triad" should be considered a "deterrent that is minimum but credible because it is survivable and backed by effective civilian command and control to ensure retaliation." While asserting that "India needs only that strategic minimum which is credible," he refused to define the "minimum" on the grounds that "it is a dynamic concept but firmly rooted in the strategic environment, technological imperatives and national security needs." While insisting that the Indian deterrent would be credible, and that "mobility and dispersal" would ensure survivability, he argued that "retaliation does not have to be instantaneous; it has to be effective and assured."[13]

In the wake of the 1999 Kargil conflict, Indian Defense Minister George Fernandes seemed to back away from this concept of a minimal nuclear deterrent for India. In speeches delivered in January 2000, he confirmed that India still maintained a "retaliation only" posture but cautioned that "war remains a possibility among nuclear states below the nuclear threshold."[14] He also promoted the concept of limited war and reaffirmed the need for India to maintain a conventional forces sufficient to "ensure that conventional war . . . is kept below the nuclear threshold."[15]

Jaswant Singh's rejoinder to the August 1999 draft nuclear doctrine and Advani's May 1998 veiled threat are signs of how difficult it will be for the Indian government to develop an integrated nuclear doctrine given its persistently hesitant attitude toward the deployment of nuclear weapons. The Indian armed forces, however, had begun planning for the unthinkable as early as the 1980s. One indication of this was that, on taking over as army chief on 1 February 1987, General Krishnaswami Sundarji stated: "We in the armed forces are gearing our organization, training and equipment in such a manner that in the unlikely event of the use of nuclear weapons by the adversary in the combat zone, we will limit the damage, both psychological and physical." [16]

This chapter traces how the Indian deterrence doctrine grew incrementally from one based purely on conventional forces in the early 1980s to one buttressed by nuclear weapons in the late 1980s. The resulting doctrine

13. "India not to engage in n-arms race: Jaswant," *Hindu,* 29 November 1999.
14. Inaugural address by Raksha Mantri [George Fernandes], 24 January, 2000, at *Second International Conference on Asian Security in the Twenty-First Century,* organized by the Institute for Defense Studies and Analyses (IDSA) in New Delhi, 24–25 January 2000.
15. Inaugural address by Raksha Mantri [George Fernandes], 5 January at *National Seminar on The Challenges of Limited War: Parameters and Options,* organized by the IDSA in New Delhi, 5–6 January 2000.
16. Interview with General K. Sundarji, "The Indian Army," *Times of India,* 1 February 1986.

called for India to counter a military threat from either China or Pakistan first by using conventional weapons, including conventional strikes against the nuclear arsenals of these countries. If, and only if, these countries threatened or actually used nuclear weapons against India, India would strike back with its own nuclear forces. The conventional war doctrine was one of "offensive defense" (an Indian military euphemism for preventive war rather than preemptive attack), which implied a preemptive strategy and was integrated with the military's operational plans.[17] This marked a shift from the earlier "defensive-defense" posture. Nuclear deterrence, however, was based on a no-first-use doctrine and a second-strike posture calling for deterrence by punishment. This strategy, however, was not fully integrated with operational plans.

In the absence of any clear instruction from the political leadership, the Indian military began to develop plans and options in the early 1980s to deal with a nuclear scenario. This planning for the unthinkable was not well coordinated, integrated, or supported by nuclear and defense technocrats or by civilian leaders, who had their own biases against involving the armed forces in nuclear planning and decision making. India's political leaders seek to use their nuclear weapons capability to bolster domestic political support and to play a dominant role in the region and a more important role globally. This was the rationale behind Advani's threat to Pakistan.[18] These political objectives do not require elaborate military preparations or use plans or command and control arrangements, and Indian political leaders are unlikely to spend time on these issues unless compelled by external nuclear threats or attacks.

For the nuclear and defense technocrats, prestige and the drive to acquire technology are the primary motives behind the push for nuclear weapons and missile delivery systems. Validating the technology is an end in itself; technocrats are unwilling to get involved with the complex business of command and control, except to the extent of wanting to retain control of the weapons themselves. They mistrust the military and fear the inadvertent use of nuclear weapons. They also believe that control of these weapons elevates their own position in the bureaucratic hierarchy. Technocrats believe the best way to achieve their goals is not to delegate authority or provide an elaborate nuclear use doctrine, which would justify handing nuclear weapons to the military.

17. For an explanation of preventive versus preemptive war, see Jack S. Levy, "Declining Power and the Preventive Motivation for War," *World Politics* 40 (October 1987): 83.

18. Also see Jaswant Singh, "What Constitutes National Security in a Changing World Order? India's Strategic Thought," Center for the Advanced Study of India, *Occasional Paper Number 6* (June 1998), 6–7; and "Against Nuclear Apartheid," *Foreign Affairs* 77 (September–October 1998): 41–52.

In contrast, two practical concerns have preoccupied Indian military strategists since 1964.[19] First, they have been concerned about countering a nuclear threat—initially from China and then from Pakistan—by conventional means, given the government's position of not exercising the nuclear option. Indian strategists also have thought about the possible role that nuclear weapons would play in the Indian military if the nuclear option were exercised. These concerns were compounded because the Indian military was kept out of the nuclear decision-making process: the different branches of the Indian armed forces were left to conduct nuclear planning on their own. In the 1980s their thinking was dictated by the perception of a clear and present nuclear threat from Pakistan's evolving nuclear weapon capability. This is not to say that the threats from China and nonregional nuclear weapons states were discounted but simply that the emerging Pakistani nuclear threat took precedence. During this period, the military's planning also appears to have had the tacit approval of the political leadership. Although the military did argue in favor of going nuclear, it is not clear whether this demand was taken into consideration by policymakers. There is some evidence, however, that the technocrats may have embraced the military's requirements to advance their own programs.

These different elements of India's nuclear doctrine evolved in reaction to Indo-Pakistani "nuclear" crises in 1983–84, 1986–87, and 1990. India's military doctrine moved from that of conventional deterrence (in 1983–84) to that of a no-first-use nuclear deterrence (in 1990), with the 1987 Exercise Brasstacks crisis marking the transition between these two positions. The Kargil crisis in the summer of 1999 marked the latest "nuclear" confrontation between India and Pakistan. Many Indians saw the crisis as proof that Pakistanis believed their nuclear umbrella would allow them to take Kashmir without risking Indian punishment.[20] Thus Kargil highlighted the need to develop an Indian limited-war doctrine. The Indian armed forces intended to use only conventional weapons in a future conflict with Pakistan, but they now prepared to operate against a nuclear-armed adversary.

In one sense, this doctrinal shift is consistent with realist expectations. Change in the security environment—especially the emergence of a Pakistani nuclear capability—caused a significant change in India's defense strategy. But this interpretation of Indian policy is insufficient. Without an appreciation of how the three different organizations viewed the nuclear program and interacted with one another, one cannot explain the inconsistencies evident in Indian nuclear policy from the Chinese nuclear test in

19. The earliest military writings appeared soon after the first Chinese nuclear test in 1964. See Major General D. Som Dutt, "The Defence of India's Northern Borders," *Adelphi Paper* 25, International Institute for Strategic Studies (London: IISS, 1966); Dutt, "India and the Bomb," *Adelphi Paper* 30, (London: IISS, 1966); and Colonel R. D. Palsokar, *Minimum Deterrent: India's Nuclear Answer to China* (Bombay, Thacker, 1969).

20. Raksha Mantri, inaugural address, *National Seminar on The Challenges of Limited War.*

1964 to the present. This chapter first describes the evolution of India's "weapon option" and notes how it was developed in a doctrinal vacuum until 1980. Then it relates how a series of "nuclear" crises between India and Pakistan in the 1980s and 1990s, coupled with technological and organizational factors, stimulated the development of doctrine that reflected consensus among political leaders, technocrats, and the armed forces. Despite the failure to integrate India's nuclear capability into conventional war plans, a rudimentary second-strike doctrine and related command and control system were established. This system is one of "divided control" in which the civilian authority has absolute control over the nuclear arsenal, while the military possesses the nuclear delivery systems. The chapter concludes by showing how the current divided control system could yield to one in which control of nuclear weapons is delegated to the military.

ORIGINS OF THE "WEAPON OPTION"

The option to make weapons was built into the Indian nuclear program from its inception in the early 1950s.[21] India has had an explicit policy of keeping open the "weapon option" since 1965, when India had completed construction of the CIRUS plutonium production reactor and the Trombay plutonium reprocessing plant. It was reinforced by the "peaceful nuclear explosion" in 1974, when India tested but did not weaponize its nuclear capability. Since 1974, however, India has developed an aircraft and missile-based delivery system for its nuclear weapons and started to adopt a deterrence policy, *without* actually deploying nuclear weapons.[22]

This state of weaponless deterrence did not necessarily reflect an "Indian" way of deterrence, although strategic culture theorists often use this explanation. India's latent nuclear capability was not immediately translated into a weaponized deterrent because of the slow development of India's technological capability to build nuclear weapons and missiles, the

21. See George Perkovich, *India's Nuclear Bomb* (Berkeley: University of California Press, 1999); Itty Abraham, *The Making of the Indian Atomic Bomb: Science, Secrecy and the Postcolonial State* (London: Zed Books, 1999); Peter R. Lavoy, "Learning to Live with the Bomb: India and Nuclear Weapons, 1947–1974" (Ph.D. dissertation, University of California, Berkeley, 1997); Waheguru Pal Singh Sidhu, "The Development of an Indian Nuclear Doctrine since 1980" (Ph.D. dissertation, University of Cambridge, 1997); and Zafar Iqbal Cheema, "Indian Nuclear Strategy, 1947–1991" (Ph.D. dissertation, University of London, 1991).

22. Scholars have called this doctrine "recessed deterrence," "nonweaponized deterrence," or "existential deterrence." See Devin T. Hagerty, "Nuclear Deterrence in South Asia," *International Security*, 20 (Winter 1995): 87; George Perkovich, "A Nuclear Third Way in South Asia: The 1990 Indo-Pakistani Crisis," *Foreign Policy*, no. 91 (Summer 1993): 86; and Air Commodore Jasjit Singh, "Prospects for Nuclear Proliferation," in *Nuclear Deterrence: Problems and Perspectives in the 1990s*, ed. Serge Sur (New York: United Nations Institute for Disarmament Research, 1993), 66.

exclusion of the military from the nuclear weapon program, and the absence of a clear and present nuclear danger to India's security until the 1980s. The basic nuclear policy laid down by India's first prime minister, Jawaharlal Nehru, remained keeping the weapon option open, yet nuclear capabilities were developed in a doctrinal vacuum until 1974.

The three nuclear crises in the 1980s challenged the weapon option policy and led to the emergence of a rudimentary nuclear doctrine. Pakistan's evolving nuclear weapon capability and the growing evidence of a Pakistan-China nuclear nexus, coupled with a series of military crises that India experienced with both China and Pakistan, lent new urgency to the notion that India had to respond to an increasingly dangerous strategic environment. The armed forces were still excluded from the nuclear decision-making process and were not formally tasked to develop explicit nuclear doctrine and targeting plans for China and Pakistan, but they were allowed to develop plans and options, particularly conventional options, for a possible nuclear conflict. The armed forces also considered nuclear options in the event that they should be given nuclear weapons. For instance, the Indian Air Force (IAF) began practicing "toss-bombing" from the late 1970s onward. Although this maneuver can be used to deliver both conventional and nuclear ordnance, the IAF may have introduced it to prepare for a future nuclear mission.

"NUCLEAR" CRISES AND THE DEVELOPMENT OF DOCTRINE

Although none of the Indo-Pak crises involved deployed nuclear weapons, they were *about* nuclear weapons: the threat to build them; the threat to prevent their construction; and the threat of future use. While nuclear threats may not have been explicitly conveyed to the other side, they loomed in the background and affected decisions made on both sides of the border. To that extent these crises were nuclear, even without overt deployment of nuclear weapons. This is particularly true of the Kargil crisis, which occurred after both sides had declared their nuclear capability and Pakistan issued a nuclear threat at the height of the confrontation.

South Asia's First Nuclear Crisis, 1983–1984

The 1983–84 crisis was the first time that Indian leaders discussed a military solution to deal with Pakistan's nuclear weapon program. This crisis had a direct bearing on the subsequent development of Indian nuclear doctrine and subjected the Indian nuclear option to its severest test. Decision makers debated whether the time had come to go overtly nuclear or whether it would be possible to deal with the Pakistani nuclear threat by using only conventional means. By the end of the crisis, Indian officials endorsed the doctrine of a conventional response to counter Pakistan's nuclear weapon capability.

Three considerations governed India's approach to the growing revelations of Pakistan's nuclear weapon capability in the early 1980s: India's inability to curtail this capability by diplomatic means, India's desire to maintain its conventional military edge over Pakistan, and its wish to maintain political-military supremacy in South Asia without exercising its own nuclear option. Consequently, the logical military strategy would be to curb Pakistan's nuclear capability by conventional means.[23] This strategy required a preventive war doctrine and the requisite military capabilities and political will to undertake preventive war.

In the early 1980s, two key elements for a preventive war strategy emerged. First, there was a shift in the strategy of the three services from "defensive defense" to "offensive defense." Second, with the purchase of the Jaguar fighter-bomber, India could carry out preventive strikes. As Air Chief Marshal Dilbagh Singh explained, "The time has come for us to shift our stance from one of retrospection and reaction to anticipation and action. We cannot perpetually forego our option to pre-empt our likely adversaries in the induction of high-technology military hardware with an emphasis on the building up of a demonstrable capability superior to that of our likely adversaries. The deterrent value of such a stance should be one of the main planks of our defence policy during this decade and for those to come."[24]

IAF officials considered plans to strike Pakistan's nuclear facility at Kahuta in a preventive raid.[25] Prime Minister Indira Gandhi ultimately decided against the attack, however, because she was advised that any operation against a Pakistani nuclear installation was bound to lead to a retaliatory strike and possibly to full-fledged war.[26] This may explain why Indian

23. See Air Commodore Jasjit Singh, "Air Strategy and Force Levels Required for the Nineties," *Trishul,* January 1990, 79.

24. Speech of Air Chief Marshal Dilbagh Singh at the Second Annual Session of the Congress for Defence Studies and the National Seminar on India's Defence Policy and Doctrines for 1980s, Poona University, reprinted in the *Poona University Bulletin,* 15 July 1982. For an indication of army and navy thinking on preemptive strategy, see Commander K. R. Menon, "The Pre-Emptive Naval Strike in Limited Wars," *USI Journal* 108 (January–March 1978): 46–54; Lieutenant Colonel J. K. Dutt, "Deep Thrust," *USI Journal* 108 (January–March 1978): 69–74.

25. Proponents of preventive war in the Indian military in the 1980s, like their U.S. counterparts, were "unlikely to present their arguments openly in unclassified forums" and thus used euphemisms. See Scott D. Sagan, "Correspondence," *International Security* 22 (Fall 1997): 195–96.

26. This was admitted by Air Commodore S. Javed, the Pakistani air attaché in Washington, who said, "We had threatened them [India] 10 years back when they threatened to attack our nuclear installations, that we would retaliate and they would probably lose their Bombay facilities in retaliation" (*Transcript of NBC Nightly News* report, 30 August 1994). See also M. Benjamin, "India Said to Eye Raid on Pakistan A-Plants," *Washington Post,* 20 December 1982, A1.

leaders consistently denied reports that they were planning a raid on Pakistani nuclear installations and yet cautioned that the supply of sophisticated weapons by the United States to Pakistan could precipitate a war. As early as April 1981, Prime Minister Gandhi warned that "such arms sales are creating a situation where everybody is drifting towards a war."[27] The danger of war was a recurring theme in her speeches and was most often voiced in late 1984. Although these references were to conventional war, the military considered Pakistan's nuclear facilities as legitimate targets. In April 1983, for example, Defense Minister R. Venkataraman mentioned the Pakistani military nuclear capability at the annual Indian army commanders' conference.[28] By raising the issue in this venue, the minister might have tried to signal India's right to target Pakistan's nuclear capability.

Coinciding with the 1983–84 crisis, three significant political decisions were taken that affected the development of doctrine. The first was Gandhi's decision to resume nuclear testing in 1983–84 to validate an operational device.[29] The second was Gandhi's creation of a high-powered committee between 1983 and 1984 to reconsider the nuclear option and discuss the possibility of weaponization.[30] The third was the 1983 decision to launch the Integrated Guided Missile Development Program, which would lead to the creation of the nuclear-capable Prithvi and Agni missiles in the late 1980s.[31] The first two decisions ultimately were reversed, but the missile program continued, probably because there was no immediate external pressure against it. The momentous decision to weaponize was deferred, as indeed was the decision to attack Pakistan's nascent nuclear weapon capability. Although the lack of information makes it difficult to say conclusively why these decisions were reversed, the realist explanation is the most compelling. According to this argument, India realized that any attack on Pakistan might not successfully deny Pakistan access to nuclear weapons. It was also bound to lead to a retaliatory strike, which might have compromised India's own nuclear weapons capability. Assembling weapons and moving them out of nuclear facilities was one solution to the threat of Pakistani retaliation, but the decision appears to have been postponed.

27. "Mrs. Gandhi Warns of War," *New York Times*, 28 April 1981, A9.
28. FBIS-SA 20.4.83, cited in *Arms Control Reporter*, 21 April 1983.
29. Raj Chengappa, "The Bomb Makers," *India Today*, 22 June 1998, 30. The then defense minister, Ramaswamy Venkataraman, who revealed that "I myself went down to the shaft to see things for myself," has also confirmed this. See "R. Venkataraman Praises Vajpayee for N-tests," *United News of India*, 26 May 1998, from http://www.redifindia.com/news/1998/may/26bomb2.htm.
30. Sidhu, "Development of an Indian Nuclear Doctrine," 282–83.
31. Indranil Banerjie, "The Integrated Guided Missile Development Program," *Indian Defence Review* (July 1990), 99–109.

Exercise Brasstacks: Accidental Crisis or Preventive War?

Exercise Brasstacks was a year-long military exercise, the objective of which, according to Army Chief General Sundarji, was to "validate some of the doctrines developed and check them out in the field."[32] The exercise was not explicitly designed around a nuclear scenario, but some of the tactics were appropriate for a nuclear battlefield.[33] Prime Minister Rajiv Gandhi and Defense Minister Arun Singh supported General Sundarji's initiative.[34] In November 1986, the size and location of the forces participating in the exercise in Rajasthan would have made it possible to cut Pakistan in half had they raced across Sindh to reach the Sukkur Barrage. In December 1986 Pakistan reacted by launching Operation Sledgehammer and moving its armed forces to their jump-off positions across from the troubled state of Punjab.[35] On or around 15 January, India launched Operation Trident, moving the army to its forward position to counter the Pakistani disposition. On 18 January 1987, Arun Singh and General Sundarji briefed the editors of some leading newspapers and hinted that war might be imminent. The crisis dissipated, however, after direct contact between Pakistan's general Zia-Ul-Haq and Prime Minister Mohammed Khan Junejo and India's prime minister Rajiv Gandhi.[36] Even as the deescalation began in February 1987, Pakistani nuclear scientist Abdul Qadeer Khan hinted in an interview that if pressed, Pakistan would develop nuclear weapons.[37]

Although Brasstacks was not planned around use of nuclear weapons, it was played out against a nuclear backdrop. General Sundarji's order of the day on 1 February 1986 conceded that the armed forces were "gearing" to "limit the damage, both psychological and physical," from "the use of nuclear weapons by the adversary in the combat zone."[38] On 4 March 1986, Arun Singh appeared on Doordarshan (India's government-run television

32. Author's interview with the former chief of army staff General K. Sundarji, Wellington, Tamil Nadu, March 1995.

33. Author's interview with former commander in chief, Northern Command, Noida, Uttar Pradesh, India, April 1995.

34. See Kanti Bajpai, P. R. Chari, Pervaiz Iqbal Cheema, Stephen P. Cohen, and Sumit Ganguly, *Brasstacks and Beyond: Perception and Management of Crisis in South Asia* (New Delhi: Manohar, 1995), 27.

35. The destruction of the Golden Temple during Operation Blue Star and the riots that followed the assassination of Indira Gandhi in 1984 led to deep resentment among Sikhs and made Punjab a soft spot for Pakistan to hit.

36. Bajpai et al., *Brasstacks and Beyond*, 2.

37. Kuldip Nayar, "We Have the A-Bomb, Says Pakistan's Dr. Strangelove," *Observer* (London), 1 March 1987. The interview with Khan actually took place in Pakistan on 28 January 1987.

38. Sundarji, "Indian Army."

station) and stated that the armed forces were overhauling their strategy and technology and that the nuclear option was being reconsidered at the highest level. On 1 January 1987, Indian foreign secretary A. P. Venkateswaran, who was visiting Islamabad, announced that an Indo-Pakistani agreement had been reached to sign a pact not to attack each other's nuclear installations.[39] Finally, Khan's interview appeared in the *Observer* on 28 February 1987.[40]

Arun Singh's interview on Doordarshan coincided with the commencement of Brasstacks I and indicated that the nuclear question was being reevaluated by the armed forces. Then an article written by a retired senior army officer in January 1987 war-gamed a fictitious nuclear scenario in 1987 under the same title, "Brasstacks," and assumed that Pakistan had made a preemptive nuclear strike on Punjab, which would not only help to isolate Kashmir from the rest of India but also help to eliminate the possibility of a Sikh state being established on Pakistan's frontier. In this scenario, India retaliated with a delayed nuclear strike against Islamabad. Another indication that India conducted nuclear training during the exercise was an air drill code-named Falcon-I, in which the IAF practiced passive defensive measures against a nuclear strike.[41]

There were three nuclear aspects to Brasstacks. First, it suggested that the Indian army was preparing for a preventive war and that Exercise Brasstacks was designed to provoke a Pakistani military response.[42] This response would set the stage for India to launch a counteroffensive and use the plans (probably developed in the time leading up to the 1983–84 crisis) to eliminate the Pakistani nuclear facilities in a preventive strike. Interest in the preventive war option was evident in General Sundarji's assertion that the Brasstacks crisis was the last all-conventional crisis in which India could have used its conventional superiority to destroy Pakistan's conventional and nuclear weapons capabilities.[43]

Second, even if Pakistan used nuclear weapons, it might not have been able to contain India's superior conventional power, which increasingly relied on mobility and mechanization to survive a nuclear war. Mobility created the possibility of quick dispersal and concentration, which could help the Indian military survive a nuclear strike. Mechanization provided a modicum of protection against radiation, especially while traversing areas contaminated by nuclear fallout. Once the Indian forces were able to achieve their objectives, Pakistan's leaders might hesitate to use a nuclear

39. Reuters, 1 January 1987.
40. Nayar, "We Have the A-Bomb."
41. See Major General Satinder Singh, "Nuclear War in South Asia—the Worst Case," *Indian Defence Review* 2 (January 1987): 65.
42. Sagan, "Correspondence," 195–96.
43. Interview with General Sundarji.

strike on their own territory. Brasstacks probably was an attempt to convince Pakistani leaders that their belief that nuclear weapons would be a great equalizer was unfounded and would not counter India's conventional superiority.

Third, Brasstacks demonstrated that even if Pakistan were to use the nuclear option for a first strike, not only would India still retain adequate conventional forces to threaten Pakistan, but it would have the ability to strike at the heart of Sindh, threatening Pakistan's very existence. In fact, a nuclear first strike from Pakistan inevitably would lead to a conventional Indian counteroffensive aimed at dismembering Pakistan.[44]

Indian strategists believed that the Brasstacks crisis was the last confrontation in which India would face a conventionally armed Pakistan, They were convinced that in subsequent crises they would have to contend with a Pakistani nuclear capability.[45] After the Brasstacks crisis ended, two significant developments influenced India's nuclear doctrine. First, in 1988, Rajiv Gandhi ordered nuclear scientists to develop weapons.[46] Various components for the devices were built and assembled to provide off-the-shelf air-deliverable weapons. There is no indication, however, that the military was tasked to develop explicit nuclear doctrines and targeting plans.

Indian policy statements indicated a possible shift from reliance on purely conventional deterrence to one that also accepted deterrence based on nuclear weapons. In his address at the Massachusetts Institute of Technology on 1 July 1989, Indian defense minister K. C. Pant stated that "India just cannot afford to overlook the fact that three major nuclear powers operate in its neighborhood and Pakistan is engaged in a nuclear weapon program. If we are to influence these major powers, then it becomes inescapably necessary for us to reckon with their nuclear deterrence belief concepts."[47] This statement was made about a year after the decision to weaponize had been taken and just a few months after the first test flight of the Agni "technology demonstrator," which effectively validated India's intermediate-range ballistic missile capability. In August 1989 Rajiv Gandhi referred specifically to the possibility of a Pakistani bomb and warned that

44. There was, however, a contrary opinion that argued that the Exercise Brasstacks strategy might be rendered ineffective because Pakistan's nuclear weapon capability makes the Thar desert terrain a "lucrative nuclear battlefield. Pakistan will not hesitate to use nuclear weapons in this area, least of all on its own side of the border if it feels threatened." See Colonel R. M. Sewal, "Organisational Philosophy for Indian Army," *Combat Journal* (August 1988): 1–9.

45. After the crisis, General Sundarji opined to Defense Minister V. P. Singh that the next Indo-Pakistani confrontation would be a nuclear one (author's interview with General Sundarji).

46. Chengappa, "Bomb Makers," 29. This opinion was also confirmed by one of the bomb makers in an interview with the author, New Delhi, March 1998.

47. K. C. Pant, "Philosophy of Indian Defence," *Strategic Analysis* 13 (August 1989): 482.

"our whole security will be in danger and we will have to think of various deterrents or preventive measures."[48]

These statements by Pant and Gandhi conveyed not only the existence of a high-level debate on the nuclear option but also the growing acceptance that a conventional preventive strike doctrine was being supplemented with a nuclear strike capability, although it still is not known what India did to improve its operational capability to use nuclear weapons at this time (apart from validating an air-deliverable capability).

Zarb-i-Momin, Kashmir, and the 1990 Nuclear Crisis

The 1990 crisis also began with a military exercise: Pakistan's Zarb-i-Momin. Although it did not create as much tension as Brasstacks, Zarb-i-Momin signaled that Pakistan, too, had adopted a strategy of "offensive defense" and "strategic depth" to counter India's doctrine developed during Brasstacks.[49] In the wake of the largest Pakistani exercise ever held, the insurgency movement in Kashmir suddenly intensified. India accused Pakistan of training the militants and rushed reinforcements to the Kashmir Valley. Tensions rose as the Indians threatened to carry out "hot pursuits" and to take the battle for Kashmir across the border into Pakistan by targeting alleged training camps. This danger led both Pakistan's prime minister Benazir Bhutto and Indian's prime minister Vishwanath Pratap Singh to talk of war. At the height of this confrontation, Pakistan is reported to have threatened India with nuclear retaliation in response to the hot pursuit doctrine.[50]

While India and Pakistan made precautionary preparations for war, they also took unilateral measures to avoid misperception and practiced restraint to ensure that the crisis did not escalate. Even as troops were being rushed to the border on both sides in early 1990, both India and Pakistan took the unusual step of giving U.S. military attachés in Islamabad and New Delhi permission to observe troop deployments. The movement of military attachés is generally viewed with suspicion, but in 1990 not only was permission to monitor troop movements forthcoming, it was also ex-

48. "Interview with El Pais of Spain," New Delhi, 6 July 1988, in *Rajiv Gandhi: Selected Speeches and Writings*, Vol. 4, Ministry of Information and Broadcasting (MIB), Government of India (GOI) (New Delhi: GOI, 1989), 470.

49. Details of Exercise Zarb-i-Momin can be found in Ross M. Husain, "Indian Combat Doctrine: Some Pertinent Aspects," *Strategic Studies* 9 (Summer 1989): 93, and "Zarb-i-Momin: A Preview and Appreciation," *Defence Journal* 16, nos.1–2 (1990): 3.

50. On the 1990 crisis, see B. G. Deshmukh, "Spring 1990 Crisis," *World Affairs* 3 (December 1994): 36–37; General V. N. Sharma's interview, "It's All Bluff and Bluster," *Economic Times*, 18 May 1990; Dilip Bobb and Raj Chengappa, "War Games," *India Today*, 28 February 1990, 22; "Conflict Prevention and Confidence Building Measures in South Asia: The 1990 Crisis," in Michal Krepon and Misha Faruqee, eds., *Occasional Paper* 17, (Washington, D.C.: Henry L. Stimson Center, 1994).

pedited.[51] This episode suggests that Indians and Pakistanis wanted to signal their nonaggressive intentions to each other. U.S. observers reported no deployments that would suggest that an offensive strike was imminent.[52]

Despite military and parliamentary pressure, the Indian government shelved the hot-pursuit policy and restricted deployment of its armor for fear that the other side might misread it.[53] The military, which favored the hot-pursuit policy, viewed these moves as a failure of political will. In spite of this criticism, military commanders did not cross the LOC in Kashmir and restricted their use of weapons. Similar restraint was evident on the Pakistani side, which made it a point to keep the I and II Strike Corps in their garrisons. Thus New Delhi and Islamabad sent clear messages that they were not willing to escalate the situation, provided the other side was equally circumspect.

Incidents did occur during the confrontation, however, that might have prompted escalation. In the course of the crisis the IAF launched a MiG-25 reconnaissance sortie over Pakistan to verify whether the Pakistan Air Force was preparing for a nuclear strike.[54] Normally, the prime minister authorizes a MiG-25 sortie. In this case, however, the IAF appears to have launched one on its own authority. As the destruction of a Pakistan Navy Atlantique maritime reconnaissance aircraft by two IAF fighters in August 1999 illustrated, the shooting down of this overflight could have escalated tensions.[55]

Almost a month later, U.S. president George Bush sent Deputy National Security Adviser Robert Gates to urge restraint on India and Pakistan. After traveling to Moscow, Gates arrived in Islamabad on 20 May 1990 and met with President Ghulam Ishaque Khan and Pakistan army chief General Mirza Aslam Beg, who had just concluded Zarb-i-Momin. Gates made the following points: Washington had war-gamed every possible Indo-Pakistani confrontation and Pakistan was the loser every time; in the event of a war, Islamabad should not expect any support from Washington; and Pakistan must refrain from supporting terrorism in the Indian part of Kashmir.[56] Gates carried the same message to the Indian leaders: India must avoid

51. Author's interview with Colonel John Sandrock, former air attaché, U.S. Embassy (New Delhi), Washington, D.C., 18 November 1994. Sandrock was at the embassy during the 1990 crisis.

52. "Conflict Prevention," ed. Krepon and Faruqee, 13–19.

53. Deshmukh, "Spring 1990 Crisis," 38.

54. Author's interview with senior IAF official, January 1995.

55. The Pakistani aircraft reportedly had crossed the international border three times and allegedly was "spying" over Indian airspace. See Air Commodore Jasjit Singh, "Atlantique Mission had to be Cleared at the Highest Level", Indian Express, 12 August 1999; and "Atlantique Intruded Thrice, Turned Hostile," Indian Express, 14 August 1999.

56. Seymour M. Hersh, "On the Nuclear Edge," New Yorker, 29 March 1993, 67–68; "Conflict Prevention," ed. Krepon and Faruqee, 8–9; J. Burns, "US Urges Pakistan to Settle Feud with India over Kashmir," New York Times, 21 May 1990.

provoking Pakistan. Although India might win a war, the long-term costs would exceed any short-term benefits.[57] There was another reason for the Gates mission: to reduce the possibility of a nuclear war breaking out between India and Pakistan. Gates asserted this himself: "The intelligence community was not predicting an immediate nuclear war. But they were predicting a series of clashes that would lead to a conventional war that they believed would inevitably go nuclear."[58] Although some reports indicate that a nuclear attack from Pakistan was imminent, this threat has been downplayed by almost everyone involved in the crisis, including the U.S. State Department, the U.S. ambassadors to India and Pakistan, the military attachés posted there, and Indians and Pakistanis who were in a position either to convey or to receive this threat.[59] The principal secretary to the prime minister, B. G. Deshmukh, who was present at the meeting with Gates in New Delhi, has stated that "at no time was there any mention by Gates about the threatened use by Pakistan of any nuclear weapon."[60] What, then, was the source of this perception if Pakistan's leaders saw little threat of nuclear war? The Pakistani military did in fact carry out some activities that suggested preparations for a nuclear strike, possibly to provoke Washington's intervention to resolve the crisis. Such action would be consistent with the Pakistani policy of seeking external assistance in disputes with India as a means to achieve balance against a more powerful neighbor.[61]

One Indian analyst, however, has characterized the events of May 1990 as a "crisis along the Islamabad-Pakistan axis wherein Pakistan . . . bucked U.S. cautionary advice and crashed though the amber light of nuclear ambiguity."[62] According to this interpretation, General Beg gave the order to assemble nuclear devices during the crisis. This allegation is corroborated by U.S. officials, including U.S. ambassador to Pakistan Robert Oakley.[63]

Although evidence of a nuclear threat from Pakistan during the 1990 crisis is inconclusive, India took several measures to deal with nuclear-armed Pakistan. One measure was the restraint shown by India in shelving its hot-pursuit policy. While there is no concrete evidence as to why the policy was

57. Hagerty, "Nuclear Deterrence in South Asia," 101.

58. Quoted in Christopher Andrew, For the President's Eyes Only: Secret Intelligence and the American Presidency from Washington to Bush (London: HarperCollins, 1995), 516.

59. See Hersh, "On the Nuclear Edge," 56–73; "Conflict Prevention," ed. Krepon and Faruqee, 43–46; and Andrew, For the President's Eyes Only, 516–17.

60. Deshmukh, "Spring 1990 Crisis," 38. The estimate that nuclear war was imminent also was denied by then–Indian foreign secretary Muchkund Dubey in an interview with the author, New Delhi, March 1995.

61. Hagerty, "Nuclear Deterrence in South Asia," 104.

62. C. Uday Bhaskar, "The May 1990 Nuclear Crisis: An Indian Perspective," Studies in Conflict and Terrorism 20 (1997): 321.

63. Mitchell Reiss, Bridled Ambition: Why Countries Constrain Their Nuclear Capabilities (Washington, D.C.: Woodrow Wilson Center Press, 1995), 188.

abandoned, realist theory provides the most likely answer: the desire to prevent the situation from escalating into general war, which could have brought about nuclear retaliation. Another measure was to provide some transparency and reassurance to the other side by allowing the U.S. military attachés to survey and report on troop deployment.

Even before the 1990 crisis, V. P. Singh's government established the so-called core group, composed of the foreign secretary, the defense secretary, the home secretary, the three intelligence chiefs, the three service chiefs, a joint secretary from the prime minister's office, and the finance secretary. The atomic bureaucracy participated when invited. The core group ensured close intragovernmental cooperation, which was evident during the 1990 crisis. It anticipated the Strategic Core Group (SCG) of the National Security Council (NSC), which was constituted on 24 August 1990, after the Indo-Pakistani crisis had been resolved. The council was to make medium and long-term assessments of the internal and geostrategic environment that would serve as a guide for shaping government policy.[64] The SCG was composed of the cabinet secretary as chairman and representatives of the three services and the ministries concerned. The NSC was designed to assess long-term threats, while the SCG was responsible for the more immediate responses. Although the NSC ceased to exist after the fall of the National Front government, the current BJP government has resurrected it.

Various appointments and policies announced by the Indian government in early 1990 also shaped India's nuclear doctrine. Raja Rammana, the head of the scientific group that conducted the 1974 test, was made minister of state for defense, suggesting that India had given higher priority to its nuclear weapons and missile-development programs.[65] In February 1990, Prime Minister V. P. Singh said, "India would have to review its peaceful nuclear policy if Pakistan employed its nuclear power for military purposes."[66] In April, Prime Minister Singh referred to Pakistan's nuclear capability and said, "Confronted with a nuclear threat, I think we will have to take a second look at our own policy . . . I think we will have no option but to match it."[67] This opinion was reinforced by Rammana, who stated in the Rajya Sabha in May 1990 that India would rise to meet the challenge should Pakistan use its nuclear weapon capability first.[68]

64. "Statement on the Constitution of the National Security Council," New Delhi, 24 August 1990, *V. P. Singh: Selected Speeches and Writings, 1989–90,* MIB, GOI (New Delhi: GOI 1993), 69.
65. "Iyengar, Rammana Appointments Open Bomb Speculation in India," *Nucleonics Week,* 22 February 1990.
66. "Kashmir: Echoes of War," *Economist,* 27 January 1990.
67. *IX Lok Sabha Proceedings,* MOD, Demand for Grants, 1990–91, 9 April 1990, columns 483–85.
68. Quoted in K. Subrahmanyam, "Nuclear Force Design," in Bharat Karnad, ed., *Future Imperilled: India's Security in the 1990s and Beyond,* (New Delhi: Viking, 1994) 188.

Finally, India made a nuclear no-first-use pledge in the nonpapers exchanged with Pakistan in January 1994. The nonpaper on confidence-building measures makes a "proposal for entering into an agreement undertaking that neither side will be the first to use or threaten to use its nuclear capability against the other."[69] This statement implied a second-strike capability. Although it does not indicate whether the Indian response would be conventional or nuclear, the nonpaper covered both these options. Hence Indian nuclear concerns about Pakistan following the 1990 crisis led to the creation of a new institutional framework for developing a no-first-use policy and a second-strike capability.

To the outside observer, these developments might appear to be tentative measures for integrating nuclear planning into the broader arenas of foreign and defense policy, but for Indian leaders, many of whom have voiced strong opposition to *any* formal consideration of nuclear doctrine, these changes were significant. In response to the three nuclear crises of the 1980s, India's military doctrine shifted from a purely conventional deterrent to one that incorporated nuclear weapons. While the conventional deterrent was based on a doctrine of offensive defense, which implied a strategy of preventive war, nuclear deterrence was based on a doctrine of no first use and second-strike retaliation. Conventional deterrence was not abandoned. Instead, it was buttressed by nuclear deterrence, without the actual deployment of nuclear weapons. This policy emerged from a consensus among political, technical, and military actors. The effort to integrate nuclear weapons and strategy into India's existing conventional capability was only partially successful, however, because of the difference in the perceptions of politicians, scientists, and the military and their varying responses to the nuclear crises. The realist response to Pakistan's development of nuclear weapons was mitigated by the perceptions and actions of Indian politicians and scientists.

Kargil: Testing the New Nuclear Relationship

In the spring of 1999 about a thousand officers and men of Pakistan's Northern Light Infantry crossed the LOC into India in the Kargil sector and threatened not only Highway 1A—the lifeline beween Kashmir and Ladakh—but also the Indian hold on Siachen.[70] The Indian army spotted these intrusions in early May. The seriousness of the intrusion became clear

69. See Rakesh Sood, "Implementing Confidence Building Measures—India and Her Neighbours," paper presented at the Ninth Regional Disarmament Meeting in the Asia-Pacific Region, Kathmandu, 24–26 February 1997, 7.

70. *Pakistan Army's Misadventure in Kargil,* published by the Army Liaison Cell, Army Headquarters, New Delhi, 8.

when two reconnaissance patrols were reported missing and Pakistani artillery scored direct hits on the ammunition dump at Kargil. On 26 May, the IAF launched air strikes to dislodge the well-entrenched intruders on the Indian sides of the LOC. They lost two aircraft to shoulder-fired surface-to-air-missiles.[71] On 31 May, just over a year after he declared India a nuclear weapon state, Vajpayee described the situation as "warlike," and both the Indian and Pakistan armed forces went on full alert.[72] The Indian navy in particular established an offensive posture along the Makran coast of Pakistan.[73] As India continued the air and ground campaign in Kargil (without crossing the LOC), it suffered heavy losses trying to regain the heights, and contemplated crossing the LOC. While several officials called for action, a minority asked for restraint.[74]

Throughout this period both the Indian and the Pakistani prime minister remained in contact over the telephone. For instance, Vajpayee called Pakistani prime minister Nawaz Sharif on 24 May (two days before the air strikes were launched) and warned him that "all possible steps" would be taken to clear the intruders from Kargil. Similarly, Sharif called Vajpayee on 28 May and offered to send the Pakistani foreign minister for talks. Sharif again called Vajpayee on 13 June, a day after the talks between the foreign ministers deadlocked, to resume the dialogue.[75]

The two prime ministers also had established a back-channel of communication through former Pakistani foreign secretary Niaz A. Naik and R. K. Mishra, an Indian publisher with close ties to Vajpayee. They both shuttled between New Delhi and Islamabad during the Kargil crisis. This back-channel was established between the two prime ministers' offices soon after the Lahore Declaration in February 1999 to discuss a number of bilateral issues, including Kashmir.[76] While there is some indication that the Indian ministry of external affairs was involved, there is no evidence to suggest that

71. Gurmeet Kanwal, "Pakistan's Military Defeat in Kargil," in Jasjit Singh, ed., *Kargil 1999: Pakistan's Fourth War For Kashmir* (New Delhi: Knowledge World, 1999).

72. "Soldier's Hour," *India Today*, 26 July 1999, 23.

73. C. Uday Bhaskar, "The Maritime Dimension," *Economic Times*, 21 July 1999.

74. Lt. Gen. (Ret.) V. R. Raghavan, "Crossing LOC Not an End in Itself," *Hindustan Times*, 29 June 1999.

75. See "Dial-A-PM", *India Today*, 28 June 1999; and "Kargil Calender," *India Today*, 26 July 1999.

76. Vajpayee and Sharif signed the Lahore Declaration on 21 February 1999, following a high-profile bus trip made by Vajpayee from Delhi to Lahore. The Declaration called for the "resolution of all outstanding issues, including Jammu and Kashmir." This was the first time that India had agreed to put Kashmir on the agenda. A Memorandum of Understanding, also signed by the Indian and Pakistani foreign secretaries, reiterated the importance of a resolution to Jammu and Kashmir and called for measures to reduce the risk of accidental or unauthorized use of nuclear weapons. This memorandum highlighted the need to implement "existing Confidence Building Measures" and upgrade communication links between the two directors general of military operations. See http://www.indiamonitor.com/lahore.htm.

the same was true in Pakistan. In fact, the Pakistan army might deliberately have been kept out of this process. This back-channel was particularly useful for ensuring communication between the two prime ministers during the early days of Kargil, although it was not designed for this purpose. It apparently was shut down around 29 June, when Islamabad publicly distanced itself from the Naik mission to India.

Despite these informal exchanges, Sharif warned during a visit to the front line on June 21 that, "there will be more Kargil-like situations" in the future.[77] A few days later the Pakistan Prime Minister threatened to use the "ultimate weapon," and warned of "irreparable losses" if India crossed the LOC, issuing the clearest nuclear threat up to that point in the Indo-Pakistan conflict.[78] None of the Indian leaders issued a counterthreat. Defense Minister Fernandes merely cautioned that Sharif's threat should "not be taken casually" and hoped that international pressure would deter Pakistan from using its nuclear weapons in war.[79] Home Minister Lal Krishna Advani, who in May 1998 had confronted Pakistan with hot pursuit and a tacit nuclear threat, reiterated the government's intention not to cross the LOC because this approach "has given the country decided advantages."[80] India's decision not to escalate had more to do with the success of international pressure on Pakistan than with Sharif's nuclear threat.

This pressure, led primarily by the United States, was evident in U.S. president Bill Clinton's admonitions by telephone to Sharif, the G-8 communiqué, and the visit of General Anthony Zinni, commander-in-chief of the U.S. Central Command to Islamabad for a face-to-face meeting with General Musharraf. These efforts forced an increasingly isolated Pakistan to look for a way out of the Kargil crisis.[81]

Following Sharif's visit to Washington in early July and the decision to withdraw unilaterally, a meeting was held between the Indian director general of military operations (DGMO) and Pakistan's director of military operations (DMO) near Amritsar on 11 July 1999. The Pakistani DMO agreed that the Pakistani withdrawal would be completed by first light on 16 July 1999.[82] Small groups of Pakistani intruders remained, but they were evicted by 25 July 1999. On 26 July, the Indian DGMO declared at a press conference that all Pakistani intruders had been evicted from the Kargil district, bringing the longest Indo-Pakistan military confrontation to an end. [83]

---

77. "Sharif Warns of More Kargil-like Situtation, Urges Dialogue," *Deccan Herald*, 21 June 1999.
78. "Nuclear Blackmail?" *Hindustan Times*, 26 June 1999.
79. "Pak Nuke Threat not to be Taken Casually: Fernandes," *Hindustan Times*, 30 June 1999.
80. "Intruders will be evicted by winter: Advani," *Hindustan Times*, 30 June 1999.
81. W.P.S. Sidhu, "The U.S. and Kargil", *The Hindu*, 15 July 1999.
82. Indian Army Headquarters Press Release, 11 July 1999. Also see "Lull after Storm as Pak Troops Start Withdrawing," *Economic Times*, 13 July 1999.
83. "Last Three Pockets of Intrusion Vacated," *Hindustan Times*, 27 July 1999.

Like the previous three crises, the Kargil crisis, too, had its genesis in the nuclear equation and Pakistani interest in testing the limits of this relation. Although the Pakistani plan to intrude across the LOC in Kargil was at least several years old, its implementation at this juncture reveals that Islamabad may have been emboldened by its newly demonstrated nuclear status. For India, the Kargil incident reinforced New Delhi's existing posture of dealing with threats by using its conventional forces. New Delhi also is likely to build up its conventional military capabilities, particularly in the Kargil region, to deter conventional and nuclear conflict. The draft Indian nuclear doctrine, released after the Kargil crisis, made only a passing reference to the border situation. National Security Adviser Brijesh Mishra stated, "The recent operations in Kargil have demonstrated, our system and the political leadership, believe in great responsibility and restraint, as you would expect from the largest democracy in the world," revealing that the declaratory doctrine remains distinct from the ground realities. [84]

For both India and Pakistan, the Kargil episode proved that although the risk of escalation remains, it also is possible to have a limited conventional engagement only if both sides are not willing to escalate to full-scale war. This may explain why Sharif declared at the height of the confrontation that "there will be more Kargils."[85] While the Kargil confrontation was the most significant crisis between the two nuclear weapon states, both Islamabad and New Delhi learned to signal each other, manage the crisis, and prevent dangerous escalation. Democracy in Pakistan, however, became the victim of this success when Prime Minister Sharif was ousted in a coup led by General Musharraf in October 1999, primarily because of disagreements over the handling of the Kargil conflict.

INDIA'S POLITICAL LEADERSHIP:
USING NUCLEAR WEAPONS FOR POPULARITY

Realist theory predicts that Indian political leaders would support measures to deploy nuclear weapons and delegate use of nuclear authority to maximize the state's security. In reality, however, Indian leaders, including Rajiv Gandhi (who ordered weaponization), V. P. Singh (who created some operational structure), and even Vajpayee (who declared India a nuclear weapon state), did the bare minimum to operationalize the nuclear option.

---

84. Opening Remarks by National Security Adviser Brijesh Mishra at the release of the Draft Indian Nuclear Doctrine, 17 August 1999, http://www.meadev.gov.in/govt/opstm-indnucld .htm.

85. "Sharif Warns of More Kargil-like Situations, Urges Dialogue," *Deccan Herald,* 21 June 1999.

There are several possible explanations for this behavior. Realists would argue that Indian leaders might have been keen to weaponize, deploy, and delegate nuclear command and control to the military but lacked the technology to implement these plans. Organizational theory, by contrast, would suggest that Indian leaders might have remained unwilling to weaponize fully because this would have entailed delegating control over the nuclear arsenal to the military, whom they wanted to keep out of nuclear decision making. Neocultural theory would suggest that nuclear weapons are seen by political leaders essentially as a way to enhance their domestic standing and their nation's international status. As a corollary, they would consider nuclear weapons useless except in response to the most extreme threats and are therefore reluctant either to talk about their use in military terms or to create a serious nuclear deterrent force.

While each of these propositions has some explanatory value, the best explanation for the behavior of Indian political leaders is provided by neocultural theory, which argues that doctrines reflect domestic political and military culture and that political leaders shape military policy to maximize their own domestic political interests. This could explain why attempts are made to convert every incremental development in the Indian nuclear weapons capability into popular support for political objectives.[86] Thus a factor behind Prime Minister Indira Gandhi's decision to give the green light for the 1974 peaceful nuclear explosion was domestic politics. Despite the dramatic victory against Pakistan in 1971, Gandhi's party witnessed a drop in its popularity in the 1972 general elections. Thus the nuclear test was used to bolster her position by representing it as a major achievement for India, which in turn was identified with the ruling Congress party. Opinion polls taken a month after the test revealed that the decision to test had overwhelming popular support. A staggering 91 percent of the adult literate population had heard about the test and 90 percent of those polled felt "personally proud of this achievement."[87]

In the 1980s, Indira Gandhi linked the separatist movements in India to conventional war and Pakistan's nuclear capability. In July 1983, she warned that the country had to be cautious because Pakistan was strengthening its nuclear installations and sealing its borders. It was because of

86. For the role of nuclear weapons in domestic politics, see Perkovich, *India's Ambiguous Bomb;* Lavoy, "Learning to Live with the Bomb"; Sidhu, "The Development of an Indian Nuclear Doctrine"; Scott D. Sagan, "Why Do States Build Nuclear Weapons? Three Models in Search of a Bomb," *International Security* 21 (Winter 1996–97): 54–86.

87. See "Public Opinion on India's Nuclear Device," *Monthly Public Opinion Surveys* 19 (June 1974): Blue Supplement, III–IV, cited in Sagan, "Why Do States Build Nuclear Weapons?" 68. Opinion polls conducted soon after the May 1998 tests reflected similar support for Vajpayee's decision. See, for instance, "Solid Support," *India Today,* 25 May 1998, http://www.india-today.com/itoday/25051998/poll.html, in which 87 percent of the respondents approved of the testing and 86 percent supported weaponization.

these developments, she said, that she had been calling for all political parties to join together and fight separatist and divisive forces.[88] Gandhi hoped to use India's expanding conventional military apparatus and its growing nuclear and missile capabilities as symbols to awe a domestic audience, especially when the state was threatened by separatist movements in Assam, Punjab, and later Kashmir. Rajiv Gandhi's government ran a series of television advertisements leading up to the 1989 elections acclaiming India as a responsible regional peacekeeper and a great nation capable of manufacturing the Agni missile and building nuclear power plants.[89]

If governments with clear majorities used strategic military achievements to strengthen their domestic political standing, it has been even more important for the current spate of minority governments in India to use these symbols of prestige to improve their domestic position and to support what Peter Lavoy has described as "nuclear nationalism."[90] In a telling incident, politicians accompanying then–defense minister Sharad Pawar to witness the second Agni test on 29 May 1992 asked the missile scientists to declare the test a success for domestic political consumption even though it had failed. This test was later described as "partially successful" rather than a failure.[91]

After the series of tests in May 1998, Home Minister Advani felt compelled to issue a nuclear threat to Pakistan. Although China is cited as the primary motivation behind India's nuclear weapon program, it is irrelevant to most Indians, who consider Pakistan to be the more significant threat. Thus, for the right wing of the BJP, which Advani represents, the best way to translate the nuclear weapons advantage into political gain is to take a strong stand against Pakistan.[92] The minority BJP government also used images from the May 1998 tests for its posters in the by-election of Pokhran constituency, while the timing of the release of the draft nuclear doctrine is seen as a "poll-eve gimmick" by commentators.[93]

Similarly, nuclear nationalism is evident in the actions of Indian leaders at the international level. For instance, international treaties and regimes that impinge on India's domestic politics have to be challenged. Here the Indian experience reveals an interesting interaction between the realist and neocultural arguments. While realists view doctrine as a rational response to external threats, this approach yields to other interpretations if international threats impinge directly or indirectly on domestic politics. The

88. *BBC Summary of World Broadcasts (SWB)/Far East (FE)/*7388/B4, 18 July 1983.

89. *Times of India,* 22 July 1989.

90. Peter R. Lavoy, "Nuclear Arms Control in South Asia," in *Arms Control towards the 21st. Century,* ed. Jeffrey A. Larsen and Gregory J. Rattray (Boulder: Lynne Rienner, 1996), 280.

91. Author's interview with senior missile scientists involved in the second Agni test, February 1997.

92. I am grateful to Ashutosh Varshney for this insight.

93. Achin Vanaik, "The Draft Nuclear Doctrine," *Hindu,* 4 September 1999.

crossover of external pressure into domestic politics was evident during the Comprehensive Test Ban Treaty (CTBT) negotiations. Both the P. V. Narasimha Rao and H. D. Deve Gowda governments showed unwavering support for India's strategic enclave (and opposition to the CTBT) when the opposition parties warned them that signing the CTBT would compromise national security. The pressure exerted by the impending entry into force of the CTBT in 1999 also influenced the May 1998 tests. Although India has vehemently opposed the CTBT and did not sign it, the perception was that after 1999 the door to enhancing India's nuclear capability would be closed, a highly unpopular situation as far as domestic politics is concerned. Former prime minister Inder Kumar Gujral, a nuclear dove who held office just before the present BJP government came to power, admitted that had he continued in office until September 1999, "the pressure [to test] would have been difficult to resist."[94]

Indian leaders support the right to bear nuclear arms for political reasons, but they are reluctant to think about how to use these weapons except when absolutely necessary. In fact, the term "deterrence" was officially used for the first time only in 1988 by then–defense minister Pant, primarily to converse with other countries who use this term to describe their nuclear policies. When the leadership eventually talked about how it might actually employ nuclear weapons in the 1990s, it spoke in terms of a no-first-use doctrine. Indian leaders apparently believe that a minimum deterrence capability is essential to counter the growing nuclearization of the region. In light of the Brasstacks experience, in which the military nearly forced a preventive war onto the political leaders, there was great hesitation both to deploy nuclear forces and to delegate command and control to the military. Even during the 1980s, Indian leaders resisted the temptation to deploy a nuclear deterrent force.

This attitude might change if a BJP government continues in power. Foreign minister and senior party ideologue Jaswant Singh laments the "lack of resolve to finish off the enemy when the opportunity arose" and calls for political leaders to think strategically and create military doctrines.[95] Prime Minister Vajpayee was the first leader to declare that nuclear weapons would be used for self-defense before he made a qualified no-first-use offer.[96] Despite the position of the present BJP leadership, the traditional reluctance of Indian politicians to think about the use and deployment of nuclear weapons meant that these issues were left to the nuclear technocrats and the armed forces.

94. Private conversation with former prime minister Inder Kumar Gujral at an Asia Society luncheon on 8 July 1998.
95. Singh, "What Constitutes National Security?" 6–7.
96. "Nuclear Weapons Only for Self-Defence, Says PM," *Hindu*, 15 May 1998.

NUCLEAR AND MILITARY TECHNOCRATS:
"STRENGTH RESPECTS STRENGTH"

Realist theory predicts that a state would want to create reliable nuclear weapons and delivery systems to reduce its insecurity from the threat posed by nuclear-armed adversaries. Not only have India's technocrats been reluctant to acknowledge the threat posed particularly by Pakistan's nuclear weapon capability but they also have refused to link their own leisurely paced weaponization to any particular external nuclear threat. In October 1983, for example, Indian Atomic Energy Commission (AEC) chairman Homi Sethna discounted Pakistan's nuclear capability.[97] Indian atomic scientists generally scoffed at the Pakistani nuclear weapons capability as late as 1995. Rammana, revealing his reservations, said, "For a long time I was not at all convinced of their capability . . . they may have produced one, maybe two at the most. But I don't think that they were capable of more than that. In fact, even now I am not convinced."[98] Indian nuclear scientists regard nuclear weapons and missiles as symbols of prestige. Nuclear weapons are touted as evidence of the nation's technical prowess and scientific competence, especially when compared with the low level of development in other sectors of the economy. According to one account, "In a country where the bullock cart still constitutes a principal mode of transportation, India's space program stands out as a dramatic achievement."[99] These technical achievements help to elevate India to the level of the world's leading developed nations. Following the maiden flight of the Agni missile, journalists noted with pride India's entry into the "exclusive" missile club of half a dozen countries.[100]

Pride in the nuclear and missile programs is enhanced because these capabilities were developed despite concerted efforts, through various technology control regimes, to prevent India from acquiring technology. Development of missile technology challenges the exclusive nature of the missile club and the technology control regimes, which India considers to be discriminatory. When asked why India should build nuclear-capable missiles, A. P. J. Abdul Kalam, chief of the Defense Research and Development Organization (DRDO), rarely cites security concerns but instead repeats his favorite mantra: "strength respects strength." In fact, one of the official mandates for defense research is "to develop critical components, technologies . . . and to reduce the vulnerability of major programmes

97. See *Indian Express*, 6 October 1983.
98. Author's interview with former AEC chairman Raja Rammana, Bangalore, 17 March 1995.
99. First Lieutenant Jerrold F. Elkin and Captain Brian Fredricks, "Military Implications of India's Space Program," *Air University Review* 34 (May-June 1983): 56.
100. Tushar Bhatt and S. Srinivasan, "Trail-Blazing with Agni," *Telegraph*, 28 May 1989; Dilip Bobb with Amarnath Menon, "Chariots of Fire," *India Today*, 15 June 1989.

[such as missiles] . . . from various embargoes/denial regimes, instituted by advanced countries."[101]

The scientists were willing to build alliances with the armed forces to ensure that the projects were supported both politically and financially. This situation is epitomized by the Prithvi missile, which was designed and built by the DRDO without any clear military requirement for the weapon.[102] When the Prithvi was successfully test-flown, the services were asked to write a formal requirement that fitted the Prithvi's specifications. This document was essential to ensure that funding for the missile program continued and that the missile would be put into production. But the technocrats are reluctant to give the military too much authority because it would erode their own position in the bureaucratic hierarchy. The dilemma for the technologists is to obtain military support for various programs, including the nuclear weapons program, while retaining overall control and allowing the least possible delegation of authority to the military. Organizational theory is useful to explain the DRDO's and AEC's attempts to protect their parochial organizational interests, while neocultural theory best describes the quest of the Indian technocrats to acquire technology that others are trying to deny them and that they regard as symbols of prestige.

INDIAN ARMED FORCES: ADAPTING THE CONVENTIONAL FOR THE NUCLEAR

Throughout the 1980s, the Indian armed forces tried to create doctrines and military formations that would meet both conventional and nuclear threats with existing hardware.[103] When he commanded the College of Combat at Mhow during the early 1980s, General Sundarji commissioned a series of essays to examine nuclear issues from a military perspective.[104] Given the known nuclear capabilities of China and the potential nuclear capability of Pakistan, the authors concluded, India's conventional deterrence was bound to erode and would not be able to counter a nuclear-armed ad-

---

101. *MOD Annual Report, 1996–97* (New Delhi: GOI, 1997), 55.

102. See A. P. J. Abdul Kalam with Arun Tiwari, *Wings of Fire* (Hyderabad: Universities Press, 1999), 114.

103. The U.S. Army attempted the same in the 1950s when it set up the Pentomic divisions to fight a nuclear and conventional war. General Sundarji, who had attended the military college at Fort Leavenworth in the United States in 1967, drew the inspiration for his Reinforced Armoured Plains Infantry Mechanized Division from the Pentomic divisions (author's interview with General Sundarji).

104. Lieutenant General K. Sundarji, "Effects of Nuclear Asymmetry on Conventional Deterrence," *Combat Paper*, No. 1 (Mhow, April 1981), and "Nuclear Weapons in Third World Context," *Combat Paper*, No. 2 (Mhow, August 1981).

versary.[105] The essays called for introducing nuclear weapons into the Indian military, suggesting that once India had acquired a minimal nuclear force, deterrence would be ensured.[106] While these essays do not reveal what would happen if deterrence failed, there is some evidence that these issues were examined at the classified level.

Nuclear doctrines were not seen as separate from conventional doctrines but as an adjunct to them. The Indian army began to acquire equipment with nuclear, biological, and chemical defense capabilities and to incorporate a doctrine of denial based on an ability to disperse and concentrate quickly. Although this ability was a by-product of the Reinforced Armoured Plains Infantry Mechanised Division (RAPID) formations, built around the new doctrines based on mobility and mechanization, it provided a modicum of protection in a nuclear scenario and may have enhanced the ability to operate in an environment contaminated by nuclear fallout. RAPID doctrine and formations were tested in Exercise Brasstacks.

Like the army, the IAF also followed a two-pronged strategy concerning nuclear weapons. One was a strategy of conventional military operations against nuclear weapons sites, which corresponded to the weapon option policy.[107] This approach was refined and elaborated, particularly to target nuclear installations, during the 1983–84 crisis. Partly as a response to Exercise Brasstacks and partly as a response to their own internal goals, the Pakistanis appear to have weaponized their nuclear capability during or soon after the 1987 crisis. Therefore, a preventive attack on Pakistan's nuclear installations could no longer guarantee that Pakistan would be denied nuclear weapons. This led to a reevaluation of the Indian doctrine, which changed to target the nuclear delivery aircraft rather than the nuclear installations.[108] Eric Arnett considered the IAF's emphasis on planning for a conventional war an "indication that Indian military planners do not take the Pakistani nuclear capability seriously," whereas evidence shows that India's doctrine does take this capability seriously.[109] More recently, however, Arnett has conceded that the IAF's offensive counter-air capability,

---

105. General Sundarji wrote: "There were only three contributors (out of about 50) who felt that nuclear weapon asymmetry would not degrade conventional deterrence to the extent that producing a nuclear deterrent was called for" ("Effects of Nuclear Asymmetry," 2).

106. Sundarji, "Nuclear Weapons in Third World Context," 1.

107. Singh, "Air Strategy and Force Levels," 79.

108. Eric Arnett, "Conventional Arms Transfer and Nuclear Stability in South Asia," in *Nuclear Weapons and Arms Control in South Asia after the Test Ban*, ed. Arnett (Oxford: Oxford University Press, 1998), 76–84.

109. Eric Arnett, "Nuclear Stability and Arms Sales to India: Implications for U.S. Policy," *Arms Control Today* 27 (August 1997): 8.

based on state-of-the-art precision-guided munitions, is designed to deny the Pakistan air force a nuclear weapons delivery system.[110]

To facilitate the induction of nuclear weapons, the IAF sought the creation of a strategic air command (SAC) under which aircraft (the Jaguar), missiles (Agni and Prithvi), and strategic reconnaissance and intelligence collection systems could be integrated to maximize effectiveness.[111] Calls for creation of a SAC increased after the launch of the Prithvi and Agni missiles in February 1988 and May 1989, respectively. While the proposal to create a SAC remained on paper, there were reports that by mid-1989 six squadrons of nuclear-delivery aircraft were operational.[112] In the aftermath of the May 1998 nuclear tests, officials confirmed that India had built an aircraft-deliverable nuclear weapon in 1988.[113] Beyond this, there is little information on exactly how the nuclear weapon delivery mission is integrated with the other IAF missions.

Another indication of the IAF's preparedness to deliver nuclear weapons was the decision to adopt the Prithvi missile. With a throw weight of one ton, this missile potentially could be armed with a nuclear weapon. The fact that these missiles, which would provide a substantial preemptive capability, have not been deployed close to the border suggests that they may be held in reserve for a second strike.

While the army and the IAF made doctrinal and operational changes to deal with Pakistan's nuclear capability, the Indian navy has attempted to carve out a sea denial role for itself, particularly with respect to the nonlittoral nuclear forces in the region. This doctrine dates back to the 1971 USS *Enterprise* episode.[114] Although the precise objective of the United States in deploying Task Force 74 is still a matter of debate, the Indians regard this intrusion as a form of gunboat diplomacy.

Subsequent Indian naval doctrine candidly spoke of "raising the cost of intervention" but did not elaborate how it would achieve this objective.[115] This concern was revived in the late 1970s and early 1980s, when the United

110. Arnett, "Conventional Arms Transfer," 75.

111. See Air Commodore Jasjit Singh, "The Strategic Deterrent Option," *Strategic Analysis* 13 (September 1989): 601. Former air chief marshal S. K. Mehra also endorsed this view in an interview with the author, January 1995.

112. "Indian Fixed-Wing Nuclear Delivery 'A Reality,' " *Defense and Foreign Affairs Weekly,* 3–9 October 1989, 2.

113. Chengappa, "Bomb Makers," 31; John F. Burns, "India, Eye on China, Insists It Will Develop Nuclear Deterrent," *New York Times,* 7 July 1998, A7.

114. In the middle of the 1971 Indo-Pakistani war the U.S. president sent the USS *Enterprise*–led Seventh Fleet, designated Task Force 74, to the Bay of Bengal. The force reached the bay on 13 December, five days before the war ended, and remained 1,760 kilometers from Dhakha until January 1972, when it set sail for the Pacific.

115. K. Subrahmanyam coined this phase in *Our National Security,* Monograph 3 (London: Economic and Scientific Research Foundation, 1972), xxi.

States declared its intent to set up a separate Indian Ocean command and a rapid deployment force (RDF). Senior U.S. naval officers argued that the "goal of the RDF was not only to stop Soviet infiltration or invasion, but also any kind of instability that might prove dangerous to U.S. interests in the area."[116] This plan was regarded as particularly ominous by the Indian navy in view of the expansion in its area of interest following the Law of the Sea conference and the delineation of a 200-nautical-mile (about 360 kilometers) exclusive economic zone. As a result, one strand of Indian naval strategy was planned exclusively to counter any potential superpower intervention in the region.

A nuclear-powered submarine equipped with nuclear missiles is the ideal weapon to counter a nuclear-armed naval task force. Even a nuclear-powered submarine armed with conventional missiles would pose a serious threat to an opposing task force. Indian officials decided to construct nuclear-powered submarines because of their ability to remain submerged for long periods of time compared to conventional submarines. One such submarine operating in the Indian Ocean would give India a sea denial capability. According to India's former navy chief, Admiral J. G. Nadkarni, this would enable India "to pose a dangerously high level of threat to them [non-littoral naval forces]."[117] Nadkarni also insisted that the navy's nuclear submarine program, called the Advanced Technology Vessel (ATV), could not be confined to propulsion but had to be developed in tandem with nuclear weapons.[118] This point of view was shared by another naval chief, Admiral Vishnu Bhagwat, who asserted that a submarine-based, second-strike nuclear capability is central to the doctrine of no first use of nuclear weapons.[119]

Other senior naval officers also pointed to the danger posed by the nuclear-armed submarines of extraregional navies, which in many ways was a greater threat than the surface components. For instance, Admiral S. N. Kohli declared that "India cannot be content to have nuclear submarines of other powers prowling round the Indian Ocean and not be able to deter them in any way. The presence of an Indian attack submarine would make

116. Inaugural address by Admiral S. N. Kohli at the International Seminar on the Indian Ocean, organized by the University of Allahabad, 12 February 1983, 8. See also Admiral A. K. Chatterji, "American Military Presence in the Indian Ocean," *Sainik Samachar*, 25 January 1981, 6–11.

117. Admiral J. G. Nadkarni, "Foreign and Defence Policies for India in the 1990s," in *The Indian Ocean and Its Islands*, ed. S. Chandra, B. Arunachalam, and V. Suryanarayan (New Delhi: Sage, 1993), 50.

118. Author's interview with former chief of naval staff Admiral J. G. Nadkarni, March 1995. See also M. K. Roy, *War in the Indian Ocean* (New Delhi: Lancers, 1995), 115.

119. Atul Aneja, "Submarine-Based N-Capability Vital," *Hindu*, 2 October 1998.

Waheguru Pal Singh Sidhu

them think twice before undertaking such a deployment."[120] Preventing
other navies from treating the Indian Ocean as their own lake was possibly
the logic behind the lease of a Charlie-I class submarine (named INS
Chakra) from the Soviet Union in the late 1980s and the navy's own ATV
project. To that extent, the navy has a deterrence doctrine that is now in
search of an appropriate weapons platform.

Whose Finger Is on the Nuclear Trigger?

Political leaders and nuclear technocrats have been reluctant to include
the armed forces in either the decision making about or the development of
nuclear weapons. During preparations for the 1974 test, the army dug the
shaft and the IAF ferried personnel, but neither was informed about the
purpose of the exercise. In contrast, DRDO scientists were actively involved
with preparing the 1974 device and providing the conventional explosive
used to detonate it.[121] Thus the armed forces were kept uninformed about
the state of India's nuclear weaponization.[122] This situation has continued
since the May 1998 tests. The nuclear technocrats have retained the weapons in their hands and have not allowed the armed forces to integrate the
weapons into their force structures.[123]

The technocrats are unwilling to include the armed forces in the nuclear
planning process for several reasons. First, technologists developed nuclear
weapons as symbols of technological prowess, rather than for use on the battlefield. Senior nuclear and missile scientists who discount the growing evidence of Pakistan's nuclear weapons capability nonetheless have argued in
favor of India going overtly nuclear to symbolize its status as a great nation.

Second, tensions between political leaders and the military, evident in
the conduct of military operations in three of India's wars, also appear to
have affected nuclear weapons command and control arrangements. In
fact, one of the major achievements cited by civilian scientists is that they

120. Tai Ming Cheung, "Command of the Seas," *Far Eastern Economic Review*, 27 July 1989, 16.
121. Author's interviews with DRDO and AEC scientists, New Delhi, Mumbai, and Bangalore, April 1997.
122. In a talk titled "Nuclear Policy in India" at the United Services Institute of India on 4
November 1992, Raja Rammana narrated a story to a primarily military audience about how
the U.S. military had not been informed by the scientific community as to the number of nuclear devices the country possessed, implying that the Indian armed forces must remain uninformed, too. See Stephen P. Rosen, *Societies and Military Power: India and Its Armies* (Ithaca: Cornell University Press, 1996), 251–52.
123. Raj Chengappa, "Worrying over Broken Arrows," *India Today*, 13 July 1998; Manoj Joshi,
"Atomic Age Warfare," *India Today*, 20 July 1998.

[154]

won the struggle to retain control of the nuclear weapons capability. Although the civilian scientists do not elaborate exactly when and how this struggle was won, it probably occurred during the crises of the 1980s.

The small role played by the military in India's nuclear program has created peculiar problems for command and control, particularly pertaining to the release of nuclear weapons into the hands of the military. According to Stephen Rosen, the "problem of doctrine for nuclear weapons use has been handled by civilians by writing a set of detailed instructions on how to obtain access to nuclear weapons and how to employ them." In the words of V. S. Arunachalam, the former chief of DRDO, "If New Delhi goes up in a mushroom cloud, a certain theater commander will go to a safe, open his book, and begin reading at page one, paragraph one, and will act step by step on the basis of what he reads."[124] This plan simply lacks credibility.

More realistically, India may initially embrace a nondeployed and nonactivated deterrence. This would entail not only keeping the warhead and delivery systems separated but maintaining divided control over these components of the nuclear arsenal. Specifically, while the army and the air force will be responsible for the delivery system—either a Prithvi missile or an aircraft—the nuclear warhead itself will be kept by a separate organization. The DRDO is the organization likely to retain possession of the nuclear warheads, given its proximity to the nuclear scientists and its seniority over the armed forces. Only when the key decision makers are convinced that a crisis could lead to a nuclear attack would the order be given to release nuclear warheads. This order would be conveyed from a national command post outside New Delhi though a series of codes sent over several communication channels to assure its authenticity.[125]

Although this rudimentary arrangement could alleviate the need for a multilayered and sophisticated command and control system and might be adequate for a crisis that develops over a few days or even weeks, it would not be effective in the case of an out-of-the-blue preemptive nuclear first strike. Moreover, while such a plan may work with respect to Pakistan, a doctrine to counter the Chinese threat remains undeveloped.

Will India's current divided control arrangement and the no-first-use commitments continue, or are they likely to change over time? This plan is likely to continue if the nuclear threat remains at the present level, if the operational role of the military is confined to the conventional battlefield and if the political leaders' supremacy over the military and technocrats remains intact. A shift in any of these variables, however, could lead to a new arrangement.

124. Rosen, *Societies and Military Power*, 252.
125. Chengappa, "Worrying over Broken Arrows."

Realist, organizational, and neocultural theories support this contention. Realist theory predicts that if the security threats to India increased either through a high-alert deployment posture for Pakistan's nuclear arsenal, through a greater level of nuclear and missile cooperation between Pakistan and China, or from the erosion of China's own no-first-use guarantee, India might be compelled to enhance its nuclear alert posture. This would entail an overt deployment posture and a greater level of nuclear predelegation to the military so as to avoid losing nuclear retaliatory capability in the case of a decapitating first strike.

Organizational theory predicts that the military will attempt to have a greater say in the operational aspect of the nuclear arsenal and will exert pressure for predelegation. In India, according to one assessment, if the military is included in the decision-making process, the nuclear deterrence posture will become more overt.[126] This also might occur if the technocrats, who now control the nuclear arsenal, believe that they would advance their own parochial interests by building alliances with the military. This was the case with the missile program after the initial development and tests, when the DRDO had to get the military (the ultimate customers) on board to advance the program further. This is likely to be the case in the efforts to develop a sea-based deterrence capability. In fact, the history of the ATV project shows that the AEC/DRDO project progressed slowly because of the Indian navy's objections.[127]

Neocultural theory predicts that a politically weak government increasingly dependent on the military to maintain stability both domestically and regionally, or a highly nationalistic government with a strategic culture similar to that of the military, might favor giving the military a greater role in security decision making or might allow it greater autonomy in its own operations. The former trend was evident in the 1980s during the tenures of Indira and Rajiv Gandhi, when, according to Stephen Cohen, "for several reasons, Mrs. Gandhi (and her son and successor, Rajiv Gandhi) acceded to service pressures after 1981 for more and better equipment, improved pay and working conditions, and even some of their more adventurous military

126. Shekhar Gupta, "India Redefines its Role," *Adelphi Paper* 293 (London: Oxford University Press for IISS, 1995), 46.

127. Three articles provide a fascinating account of this tussle. See B. K. Subbarao, "Re-Orientation of DAE Needed to Counter Pakistani Threat," *Hindu*, 22 November 1994. In response, former AEC chairman Srinivasan wrote another article stating the official position of the program and in many ways corroborating Commodore Subbarao's story. See M. R. Srinivasan, "The Nuclear Submarine Project," *Hindu*, 8 December 1994. Commodore Subbarao then responded with an even lengthier article challenging many of Srinivasan's assertions and providing even more details of the project: B. K. Subbarao, "DAE: Beneath the Veil of Secrecy . . .," *Hindu*, 14 February 1995.

advice."[128] The latter trend is apparent in the similarity between the strategic culture propounded by the highly organized and semimilitarized component of the ruling BJP, the Rashtriya Swayamsewak Sangh, or National Volunteer Force, and the Indian military. It is no coincidence that several senior retired military officers have joined the BJP.

India developed a de facto doctrine of deterrence from one based purely on a conventional capability to one that is buttressed with nuclear weapons in the 1980s—*without* deploying nuclear weapons. The doctrine is based on the premise that India would first use its conventional capability to counter military threats from either China or Pakistan. If these countries threatened or launched a nuclear attack, however, India would respond with its own nuclear weapons in a second strike.

This doctrine evolved in the absence of clear instructions from political leaders regarding India's nuclear arsenal and against the backdrop of a series of nuclear crises between India and Pakistan in the 1980s. Consequently, like most professional militaries, the Indian military took the initiative in the early 1980s to develop options to deal with a nuclear scenario. These options included plans for a conventional preventive war that would target the adversary's nuclear weapon capability.

India's own nuclear weapon capability, which was in place by the late 1980s, was not, however, fully integrated into conventional war plans because civilian leaders and nuclear technocrats opposed giving control of nuclear weapons to the armed forces. The resultant no-first-use doctrine reflects these command and control arrangements.

Despite the absence of a fully weaponized nuclear arsenal, the foundation of a rudimentary second-strike doctrine and related command and control system was laid. This system was one of divided control, in which civilians had absolute control over the nuclear arsenal and the military was in possession of the delivery systems. In the future, however, the divided control arrangement could change to one in which the possession and the right to use nuclear weapons is delegated to the military. If the military were to get operational control of nuclear weapons, India's nuclear doctrine also might become more preemptive.

---

128. Stephen P. Cohen, *The Indian Army: Its Contribution to the Development of a Nation* (Delhi: Oxford University Press, 1990), 208.

[6]

Pakistan's Nuclear Use Doctrine and Command and Control

ZAFAR IQBAL CHEEMA

Since the late 1980s, Pakistan has pursued a doctrine of minimum nuclear deterrence and conventional defense to balance India's nuclear and conventional forces. Pakistan has resisted strong international pressures over the last three decades so it could acquire the small nuclear force it now possesses to support this doctrine. The nuclear tests it carried out on 28 and 30 May 1998 indicate the determination with which numerous Pakistani political and military leaders have pursued this goal. The decision to respond promptly to the nuclear tests that India had carried out earlier in that month demonstrated Pakistan's ability to cope with complex technological and strategic issues pertaining to nuclear weapons development. The 1998 tests have enhanced the credibility of Pakistan's nuclear deterrent against Indian political coercion or military invasion.

South Asia is considered the world's most likely nuclear flash point. Several reasons are offered for the possible breakdown of nuclear deterrence between India and Pakistan. In the 1980s, the inexperienced leaders and crisis-prone nature of India and Pakistan were identified as potential sources of trouble.[1] Today, the absence of a credible nuclear doctrine along with nuclear command and control problems alarm observers. Are these fears legitimate or do they originate from the cultural biases of the Western strategic community? Does a lack of technological sophistication adversely affect the performance of command and control systems and the stability of nuclear deterrence? What is the likelihood that one of the recurrent crises between India and Pakistan will escalate? Is it possible that miscalculations,

---

1. *Nuclear Weapons and South Asian Security*, Report of the Carnegie Task Force on Non-Proliferation and South Asian Security (Washington, D.C.: Carnegie Endowment for International Peace, 1988), 2–44.

accidents, or false alarms might unleash a nuclear war on the Indian subcontinent?

Pakistan did not have a nuclear declaratory, deployment, or employment doctrine before May 1998. But in the wake of the 1998 nuclear tests, Pakistan has been formulating such plans. Its decisions to assemble a small nuclear force rapidly, to diversify weapons by using designs that rely on both uranium and plutonium, to develop comprehensive missile programs, and to take steps to miniaturize nuclear warheads suggest the outline of an emerging nuclear doctrine.[2] Similarly, the decisions of Pakistani leaders to address an asymmetric strategic balance with India, to ward off crises that threaten their national security, and to neutralize prospective nuclear blackmail by invoking nuclear weapons and missile capabilities further suggest the formulation of a nuclear doctrine. Public declarations about the doctrine need to be differentiated from its operational and functional dimensions.

On one level, Pakistan's development of a nuclear deterrent is consistent with realist theory: when the conventional military balance in South Asia began to shift in India's favor after the 1971 Bangladesh war, Pakistani officials began to think about acquiring nuclear weapons; when India exploded a nuclear device in 1974, Pakistan's bomb program began in earnest; and when India tested five nuclear weapons in May 1998, Pakistan detonated six nuclear explosions on two days, 28 and 30 May. Five of Pakistan's tests were in response to India's 1998 test series, while the sixth was to match India's 1974 explosion. The reactions of Pakistani political and military leaders to changes in the regional security environment have been rapid, reasoned, and exactly in keeping with realist expectations.

Two other aspects of Pakistan's strategic behavior are less well explained by realism. First, although they possessed a nuclear bomb–making capability at least ten years before the 1998 nuclear tests, Pakistani officials began a serious effort to devise a nuclear use doctrine and develop a secure command and control system only *after* the tests. While this delay is not strongly at odds with realist expectations, realism does not offer a full explanation. Other factors, such as deliberate ambiguity about the nature of its nuclear weapons program and the organizational cultures of other governmental groups, must be examined to explain why Pakistan is only now beginning to fashion its decade-old nuclear weapons capability into a credible and secure deterrent.

Pakistan's low-intensity conflict with India over Kashmir, of which Kargil is the most recent example, is another matter that is not readily explained by realism. Realist logic dictates that the military forces of nuclear-armed states will treat each other with extreme caution if they cannot avoid

2. "Pakistan Working on Miniaturized N-Warheads," *Nation* (Islamabad), 16 April 1998, 9.

each other altogether.[3] In contrast, Pakistani troops and Pakistan-supported guerrillas were engaged in risky military actions in Kashmir during the Kargil conflict in summer 1999, although the dispute has been simmering since 1989.[4] Instead of resisting the use of force because of a fear of nuclear escalation, Pakistani officials appear to have calculated that the fear of nuclear war would dissuade India from escalating the conflict, thereby permitting Pakistan to make political, if not territorial, gains. This pattern of behavior, which is described as the "stability-instability paradox," is not predicted by realism.[5]

In May 1999, one year after the nuclear tests, the belief that a nuclear standoff permits offensive conventional operations to take place without fear of escalation was put to the test. Indian army units in Kashmir were surprised to discover that significant numbers of armed forces had crossed the Line of Control (LOC) separating Pakistani and Indian-controlled territory near Kargil and were threatening to cut off the main supply road to Siachin Glacier and Ladakh in northern Kashmir. Throughout the ensuing conflict, Pakistani government officials insisted that these units were independent local mujadeen freedom fighters without ties to the Pakistani military.[6] Severe fighting ensued until July 1999: two Indian MiG aircraft were shot down inside the Pakistani side of the LOC, an Indian military helicopter was destroyed by a Stinger missile, and an estimated one thousand soldiers were killed in combat.[7] The Pakistani armed forces were ordered to be prepared for an Indian military attack outside of the Kargil area: "There is almost a red alert situation," a military source told the Pakistani press on 25 June, "though we still believe that there is no chance of the Kargil conflict leading to a full-fledged war between the two sides."[8] On 4 July, however, the crisis ended when Pakistani prime minister Nawaz Sharif flew to Washington and "recommended" that the freedom fighters withdraw after receiving a pledge that the U.S. president would take an active interest in

3. See Kenneth N. Waltz, "More May Be Better," in Scott D. Sagan and Kenneth N. Waltz, *The Spread of Nuclear Weapons: A Debate* (New York: Norton, 1995).

4. See Dexter Filkins, "Pakistani Admits Troops Are Fighting Indians in Kashmir," *Los Angeles Times*, 17 June 1999.

5. Waltz acknowledges that "war can be fought in the face of deterrent threats," but he insists that "the higher the stakes and the closer a country moves toward winning them the more surely the country invites retaliation and risks its own destruction" ("More May Be Better," 5). For background on the stability-instability paradox and new nuclear states, see Peter R. Lavoy, "The Strategic Consequences of Nuclear Proliferation," *Security Studies* 4 (Summer 1995): 739–40.

6. Ardeshir Cowasjee, "Lessons Learnt?" *Dawn* Weekly Wire Service, 17 July 1999.

7. Sumantra Bose, "Kashmir: Sources of Conflict, Dimensions of Peace," *Survival* 41 (Autumn 1999): 150.

8. Ihtasham ul Haque, "Peace Linked to Kashmir Solution," *Dawn* Weekly Wire Service, 26 June 1999.

resolving the Kashmir crisis in the future. One of the reasons for his sudden trip to Washington, Sharif told the press on 6 July, "was his fear that India was getting ready to launch a full-scale military operation against Pakistan," which could lead to a nuclear clash between India and Pakistan.[9] After the crisis ended, the Kargil operation was widely seen as having been a risky undertaking.

PAKISTAN'S NUCLEAR POLICY

Until the May 1998 nuclear tests, Pakistan had pursued a policy of deliberate ambiguity in its development of nuclear weapons. In the absence of conventional security alternatives and nuclear security guarantees, nuclear weapons were viewed as a necessary counter to a perceived threat from India. Pakistan initially imported and then indigenized nuclear-related technologies to achieve self-sufficiency in nuclear weapons production. Openness would have undermined these efforts; Pakistan would have been isolated and subject to international sanctions if found in violation of various nuclear and missile control regimes such as the Non-Proliferation Treaty (NPT), the Nuclear Suppliers Group, and the Missile Technology Control Regime. Finally, Pakistan did not want to jeopardize its relations with the United States while Soviet troops were fighting in Afghanistan. When Pakistani scientists accomplished uranium enrichment in 1987 and acquired critical elements of a nuclear weapons capability, Pakistan's leaders began to hint that they possessed a nuclear capability. They described this capability as peaceful but convertible into a weapon if the country's national security were threatened. Following the May 1998 tests, this ambiguous position yielded to a more explicit deterrent posture.

Zulfiqar Ali Bhutto, who first served as foreign minister under President Ayub Khan's regime in the mid-1960s and then as president and prime minister from 1972 to 1977, is generally recognized as the political architect of Pakistan's nuclear weapons program. As foreign minister, Bhutto urged Ayub Khan to develop nuclear weapons, advice the president overruled. The Pakistan Atomic Energy Commission, headed by I. H. Usmani, steered Ayub away from the nuclear option.[10]

Bhutto made the issue public in 1965 when he stated that Pakistan would acquire nuclear weapons because of the threat India's nuclear program posed to Pakistan's national security: "If India developed an atomic bomb,

---

9. "U.S. Involvement Essential: PM," *Dawn* Weekly Wire Service, 10 July 1999.
10. See Ashok Kapur, *Pakistan's Nuclear Development* (London: Croom Helm, 1987), 24–28; and Zafar Iqbal Cheema, "Pakistan's Nuclear Policy under Z. A. Bhutto and Zia-Ul-Haq: An Assessment," *Strategic Studies* 15 (Summer 1992): 5–20.

we too will develop one even if we have to eat grass or leaves or to remain hungry, because there is no conventional alternative to the atomic bomb."[11] Bhutto's statement was widely endorsed by Pakistani elites, and the press also called for the development of nuclear weapons.[12] In *The Myth of Independence*, written after the 1965 India-Pakistan war, Bhutto stated that the acquisition of nuclear weapons was imperative because an arms embargo by the United States after the war had undermined the country's conventional military capability.[13] As neocultural theory predicts, however, Bhutto used the slogan "eat grass to make the bomb" as a vehicle for domestic political gains after he left Ayub Khan's government and formed the Pakistan People's Party.[14] Bhutto's personal ambitions became the first manifestation of an evolutionary process that led to Pakistan's nuclear doctrine of minimum deterrence.

Pakistan's nuclear program was launched in the mid-1970s by the civilian government of Z. A. Bhutto; the military had little interest in the program except for some ancillary roles it was assigned. Military interest increased, however, after General Zia-Ul-Haq came to power in 1977. He synchronized Pakistan's pursuit of nuclear weapons with the U.S. effort to modernize Pakistan's conventional forces during the Afghan conflict. Zia was the author of Pakistan's policy of nuclear ambiguity. He thought that Bhutto's open talk of developing nuclear weapons was "irresponsible" and the reason for Pakistan's increasing international isolation.[15] In contrast, Zia remained silent about the rationale for developing a nuclear deterrent and denied that Pakistan was pursuing such a capability.

Even when Pakistan's security situation deteriorated after the Soviet invasion of Afghanistan in 1979, Zia maintained a policy of calculated nuclear ambiguity. While negotiating economic and military aid packages with the United States, he refrained from providing verifiable assurances that Pakistan would not produce nuclear weapons. Zia and Abdul Qadeer Khan began to hint about Pakistan's nuclear weapons capability in 1987, once Pakistan had succeeded in processing highly enriched uranium and had acquired other elements of a nuclear infrastructure.[16] Khan at times was direct about this new capability: "America knows it. What the CIA has been

11. Z. A. Bhutto, *Awakening the People* (Rawalpindi: Pakistan Publications, 1970), 21; Kausar Niazi, *Aur Line Cut Gaee* (And the line was cut) (in Urdu) (Lahore: Jang Publications, 1987), 77.
12. "We Must Make the Bomb," *Dawn* (Karachi), 30 September 1965; "Pakistan Should Also Make A-Bomb," *Dawn*, 20 October 1965.
13. Z. A. Bhutto, *The Myth of Independence* (Karachi: Oxford University Press, 1969).
14. Cheema, "Pakistan's Nuclear Policy."
15. Ibid.
16. Kuldip Nayar, "Pakistan Can Make an A-Bomb: Says Pakistan's Dr. Strangelove," *Observer* (London), 1 March 1987; "Knocking at the Nuclear Door," interview with General Zia-Ul-Haq, *Time*, 30 April 1987.

saying about our possessing the bomb is correct and so is the speculation of some foreign newspapers."[17] In an interview with *Time* magazine, Zia confirmed that Pakistan could develop nuclear weapons: "You can write today that Pakistan can build a [nuclear] bomb whenever it wishes." He hastened to add that Pakistan had no intention of making nuclear weapons.[18] Subsequent Pakistani leaders kept their nuclear intentions ambiguous until the May 1998 nuclear tests.

On becoming prime minister in December 1988, Benazir Bhutto pledged her opposition to nuclear weapons but refused to sign the NPT.[19] The crucial question, however, was not her willingness to stop pursuing a nuclear weapons program but her ability to influence nuclear decision making in Islamabad. She did not control the Nuclear Weapons Program Coordination Committee chaired by President Ghulam Ishaque Khan.[20] After her dismissal as prime minister, she revealed that she had not been in charge of Pakistan's nuclear program and that during the 1990 Kashmir crisis, Pakistan had crossed the "Red Line" without her knowledge.[21] She never clarified what she meant by crossing the Red Line. She probably meant either that Pakistan had started to enrich uranium to a weapons-grade level after briefly halting enrichment in 1989–90 or that it had assembled a nuclear device to deter India from going to war over Kashmir.

President Ishaque Khan (1988–93) pursued Zia's policy of ambiguity in letter and spirit. Soon after Benazir Bhutto assumed power in January 1989, Khan chaired a meeting attended by Chief of Army Staff General Mirza Aslam Beg, Prime Minister Bhutto, and three other "very responsible persons" to consider crucial aspects of Pakistan's nuclear policy. Beg later noted that in view of "the global scenario, the regional security, and the pressing needs of economic aid, it was decided that only in the first phase, i.e., the stage of uranium enrichment, Pakistan should temporarily put a 'restraint' on its efforts, or so to say, a policy of restraint was adopted."[22] Research continued on the remaining elements of weapons production: preparation of the device, integrated system testing, and construction of delivery systems. The goal was to gain greater competence so that "at the time of emergency, the nation would be able to cope with the situation."[23]

17. Nayar, "Pakistan Can Make an A-Bomb."

18. "Knocking at the Nuclear Door."

19. *Nuclear Proliferation in South Asia: Containing the Threat,* staff report to U.S. Senate, Committee on Foreign Relations, (Washington, D.C.: U.S.Government Printing Office, 1988), 17.

20. "Pakistan's Atomic Bomb," *Foreign Report,* 12 (January 1989): 2.

21. Seymour Hersh, "On the Nuclear Edge," *New Yorker,* 29 March 1993, 68–73. The authenticity of the Hersh report has been questioned.

22. General (Ret.) Mirza Aslam Beg, *Development and Security: Thoughts and Reflections* (Rawalpindi: FRIENDS, 1994), 178.

23. Ibid., 166, 178.

"Taking the overall situational imperatives and the national interest into perspective," Beg writes, "all the members unanimously reached the assessment that Pakistan had acquired the requisite nuclear capability vitally needed for its security and that it has significantly added to its defensive strength by achieving a credible deterrence."[24]

By the time Nawaz Sharif became prime minister in 1990, a consensus existed among Pakistani elites to retain their nuclear capability. In his first address to the National Assembly on 7 November 1990, Sharif echoed the establishment line that Pakistan's nuclear program was meant for peaceful purposes but had a built-in security option.[25] He reiterated this position until the end of his government in 1993. In 1994, while leader of the opposition, Sharif stated publicly that Pakistan possessed the atomic bomb.[26] In her second tenure as prime minister (1993–96), Benazir Bhutto often stated that Pakistan's nuclear program was intended for peaceful purposes but could be converted to military uses if national security were threatened. She reiterated this policy during a 1994 television interview: "We have neither detonated one, nor have we got nuclear weapons; we have the capability and the capacity to do it, but since we believe in nonproliferation, we would rather not do so unless there was a threat that was so severe that it left us no other option."[27] Even after Sharif took over as prime minister for a second time in 1997, there was no change in Pakistan's declaratory nuclear policy until the Indian nuclear tests on 11 and 13 May 1998.

The Indian tests generated immense pressure in Pakistan to demonstrate its nuclear might. This pressure was increased by the belligerent statements senior Indian leaders made immediately following the tests. Indian home minister L. K. Advani called on Pakistan to roll back its "anti-India" policy and, more specifically, its support for the Kashmiri struggle for independence. He also announced a "pro-active Kashmir policy," which ominously threatened hot-pursuit military raids into Pakistan's part of Kashmir, to teach Islamabad a lesson.[28] Pakistani officials were increasingly concerned about the threat posed by rising Hindu fundamentalism and became more determined to respond in kind to the Indian nuclear tests. The dynamics of domestic politics also influenced the quick decision to test.

The United States strongly urged Pakistan not to opt for tit-for-tat nuclear tests and promised substantial economic and military assistance—lifting the

---

24. Ibid., 177–78.
25. *Dawn*, 8 November 1990.
26. Jeffrey R. Smith and Thomas P. Lippman, "Pakistan Reactor That May Yield Large Quantities of Plutonium," *Washington Post*, 8 April 1995.
27. S. Hidayat Hussain, "Command and Control of Nuclear Weapons in Pakistan," *Swords and Ploughshares* 9 (Fall 1994): 11–14.
28. *News* (Rawalpindi), 14 May 1998, 1.

Pressler Amendment that stopped economic and military aid, finally making good on an old agreement to provide sixty F-16s, delivering major new weapon systems—if Islamabad refrained from testing a nuclear device. Pakistan rejected the package, apparently because it failed to provide an assurance of continuous military support against India.[29] Besides talking to the Americans, Pakistan foreign secretary Shamshad Ahmad went on an emergency visit to China before the tests.[30] In the wake of these exchanges, Pakistan's cabinet unanimously approved the nuclear tests.[31] As realism would predict, Pakistan reacted to India's newly disclosed nuclear capability and its increasingly assertive rhetoric by testing its own nuclear devices.

PAKISTAN'S NUCLEAR WEAPONS CAPABILITY

The Pakistan Atomic Energy Commission (PAEC), established in 1955, initially demonstrated little interest in developing nuclear weapons. Despite an intragovernmental debate on the matter in the 1960s, there was little political or technological movement in this direction until after Pakistan's military defeat and dismemberment in 1971 by India and the Indian nuclear explosion in 1974.[32] In the mid-1970s, Z. A. Bhutto took the first step toward the development of a nuclear weapons capability by establishing the uranium enrichment plant at Kahuta. The plant went into operation in 1987.[33] There are different estimates of Kahuta's enriched uranium output capacity. David Albright suggests that Pakistan could have produced 130–220 kilograms of weapons-grade uranium by 1993.[34] A Pakistani study estimates that Kahuta has produced 200 kilograms of 90 percent enriched uranium and that in addition to this highly enriched uranium (HEU), Pakistan might have accumulated 6 to 22 tons of low enriched (3–5 percent) uranium, which it could convert into HEU in less than one year.[35] Pakistan's fissile material capacity seems enough for two to three nuclear weapons per year. The stockpile would enable it to produce twenty-five to forty nuclear weapons, enough for a small minimum deterrent force, by 1999.[36] In April 1995 Pakistan also completed a 40-megawatt "safeguards-

29. *News*, 27 June 1998, 12.
30. *Nation*, 21 May 1998, 1.
31. *Nation*, 29 May 1998, 1.
32. Bhutto, *Myth of Independence*; Nayyar, "Pakistan Can Make an A-Bomb."
33. Nayar, "Pakistan Can Make an A-bomb."
34. David Albright et al., *World Inventory Of Plutonium and Highly Enriched Uranium* (Oxford: Oxford University Press and SIPRI, 1993), 161.
35. A. H. Nayyar, A. H. Toor, and Zia Mian, "Fissile Material Production Potential in South Asia," *Science and Global Security* 6 (1997): 189–203.
36. These figures range between lower and higher estimates. For a more detailed and precise estimate, see M. Zafar Iqbal Cheema, "Indian Nuclear Strategy" (Ph.D. dissertation, Department of War Studies, King's College, London University, 1991), appendixes 1 to 10.

free" reactor near Khushab in Punjab, with a plutonium production capacity of 9–12 kilograms per year.[37] Pakistani officials, however, deny that they can use material from the Khushab plant because they lack the capability to reprocess reactor-grade plutonium for use in a weapon.

Pakistan had the capability to manufacture and assemble nuclear devices before its nuclear tests in 1998. General Zia claimed in 1987 that Pakistan could make nuclear weapons: "Pakistan has the capability of building the Bomb whenever it wishes. Once you have acquired the technology, you can do whatever you like."[38] Pakistan's foreign secretary admitted in a February 1992 interview with the *Washington Post* that Pakistan could produce weapons-grade uranium and weapons cores and assemble a nuclear device.[39] Pakistan claims to have carried out five nuclear tests on 28 May and a sixth on 30 May 1998. These tests verified three main areas of weaponization: low-yield detonations, high-yield fission, and boosted fission.[40] According to Khan, Pakistan used "ready-to-fire nuclear warheads" and not experimental devices for its May 1998 tests.[41] There is no indication that Pakistan has deployed a nuclear force for crisis and conflict situations, although it apparently is working to develop this capability.

NUCLEAR DELIVERY SYSTEMS

The U.S.-supplied F-16 is the Pakistani aircraft most likely to be used for nuclear delivery missions. Pakistan procured forty F-16 aircraft, optimized for a fighter-bomber role, in the early 1980s, under a limited force modernization program undertaken with the United States in the wake of the Soviet military intervention in Afghanistan. The United States took special care not to provide Pakistan with any equipment that would facilitate nuclear delivery missions, especially the electrical mechanisms necessary for safe maintenance, transportation and delivery of nuclear weapons by F-16s.[42] Pakistan probably modified the F-16s to prepare them for nuclear delivery. A 1989 *Foreign Report* article suggested that Pakistan had designed a bomb to be carried beneath the wings of an F-16 and indicated that weapons-delivery flight training was being carried out. The bomb design had undergone a series of wind-tunnel tests and programmed in-flight computer system testing to determine the correct flight path for a nuclear

37. Smith and Lippman, "Pakistan Reactor."
38. "Knocking at the Nuclear Door."
39. *Washington Post,* 7 February 1992.
40. *News,* 29, 31 May 1998, 1; *Nation,* 29, 31 May 1998, 1.
41. "Ready-to-Fire N-Warheads Used," *Nation,* 29 May 1998, 1.
42. *Weapons Proliferation in the New World Order,* hearing before the U.S. Senate, Committee on Government Affairs, 102d Cong., 2d sess., 15 January 1992, 20–25.

bomb run.[43] Pakistan currently has about thirty-four nuclear-capable F-16 aircraft in its inventory.[44] Most Indian military establishments and nuclear facilities can be targeted with the F-16s.

On 25 April 1989, Pakistan successfully test-fired its first short-range ballistic missile, the Hatf-1. This missile has a 1,500-kilogram liftoff weight and carries a 500-kilogram payload. Pakistan also has test-fired Hatf-2, a two-stage version of Hatf-1, which has a 2,500-kilogram liftoff weight and a 500-kilogram payload.[45] Hatf-1 and Hatf-2 have a range of 80 and 300 kilometers respectively and are for battlefield use.[46] In July 1997 Pakistan test-fired Hatf-3, a missile with a liftoff weight of 5,500 kilogram, a 500-kilogram payload, and a range of 800 kilometers.[47] Hatf-3 can strike important strategic installations and military targets in most of western and central India. Research and development for the Hatf missile series, including development of a highly accurate guidance system, was undertaken at the Khan Research Laboratories in Kahuta.[48] In addition, Pakistan apparently has acquired a small number of Chinese short-range M-11 tactical missiles with a range of 300 kilometers.[49]

Pakistan test-fired Ghauri, an intermediate range ballistic missile, on 6 April 1998. Ghauri is a three-stage rocket with a 700-kilogram payload, a 1,500-kilometer range, and the capability to carry nuclear warheads.[50] Equipped with the latest guidance technology, Ghauri (also called Hatf-5) will be able to hit all major Indian cities, nuclear facilities, and strategic installations. It also can engage India's naval bases in the east with its optimal range of 2,200 kilometers. The missile is named after an Afghan ruler, Sahab-ud-din Ghauri, who invaded India and defeated the famous Indian maharaja, Prithvi Raj, around 1206 A.D.—a fact that underlines Pakistan's view of Ghauri as its response to India's Prithvi missile.[51] Ghauri is important to Pakistan's maintenance of a credible deterrent capability against India. Shaheen-I, Pakistan's recently test-fired missile, with a range of 1,000 to 1,100 kilometers, terminal guidance, and solid fuel system, possesses a rapid reaction capability. It would significantly enhance Pakistan's strategic and political position vis-à-vis India. Pakistan's choice of medium and

43. "Pakistan's Atomic Bomb," *Foreign Report*, 12 January 1989, 1.
44. *Military Balance, 1997–98* (London: International Institute for Strategic Studies [IISS], 1997), 160.
45. *News*, 9 January 1992, 1.
46. "Pakistan in Missile Build Claim," *Jane's Defense Weekly*, 18 February 1989.
47. "Pakistan Confirms Hatf-III Test-Fire," *Nation*, 4 July 1997, 1–7.
48. "Pakistan Develops Missiles," *Flight International*, 15 April 1989.
49. Hersh, "On the Nuclear Edge," 64–70.
50. *News*, 7 April 1998.
51. "BJP Concerned over Pak Ghauri missile," *Nation*, 7 January 1998, 14.

intermediate range missiles (e.g., Hatf-3, Ghauri, and Shaheen) provides it with a diversity of nuclear force deployment options.

Pakistan may already have acquired the technology to miniaturize nuclear warheads for missile-based delivery systems and to develop boosted weapons. Some observers believe that further testing would have to be undertaken before Pakistan could deploy missiles using these technologies.[52] Other observers believe that Pakistan can already produce warheads compact enough to be carried by Hatf-3 and the Chinese M-11 missiles.[53]

A realist, action-reaction syndrome drives the nuclear weapons and missile programs of both India and Pakistan. Each side accuses the other of initiating the missile race. Pakistanis allege that India began the missile race by deploying Prithvi-II close to its border in Jullundur.[54] The Indian armed forces reportedly have asked for one hundred of these missiles to make "Pakistan's entire territory vulnerable to its lethal attack."[55] The deployment of Prithvi and the development of Agni accelerated Pakistan's quest for the Ghauri and Shaheen missiles.

EXPLAINING PAKISTAN'S NUCLEAR AND MISSILE DEVELOPMENT

In the aftermath of its 1971 partition, Pakistan's perception that India wished to dismember it further was enhanced by India's growing conventional military strength. U.S. arms embargoes weakened its ability to mount a conventional military defense against India and added to Pakistanis' sense of vulnerability. The 1974 Indian nuclear explosion intensified Pakistani perceptions of a threat and generated an impetus to develop nuclear weapons. Prime Minister Bhutto called the Indian nuclear test a fateful development: "A more grave and serious event has not taken place in the history of Pakistan. The explosion has introduced a qualitative change in the situation between the two countries."[56] The lack of nuclear security guarantees from China or the United States accentuated these fears. Pakistan's foreign secretary under Bhutto, Agha Shahi, emphasized at the June 1974 Geneva Disarmament Conference: "The road has been thrown open for the emergence of a seventh and eighth nuclear power."[57]

52. "Pakistan Working on Miniaturized N-Warheads," *Nation*, 16 April 1998.
53. Hersh, "On the Nuclear Edge," 55–73.
54. *Missile Proliferation: Survey of Emerging Missile Forces* (Washington, D.C.: Congressional Research Service, 1988), CRS-71–72.
55. *International Herald Tribune*, 26–27 November 1998, 5.
56. See Z. A. Bhutto's statement in the National Assembly of Pakistan on 7 June 1974, in *Pakistan Times* (Rawalpindi), 8 June 1974, 1.
57. The full text of Shahi's statement is in *Financial Times* (London), 13 June 1974.

The growing disparity between Indian and Pakistani conventional military capabilities forced Islamabad to cling more tenaciously than ever to its nuclear weapons. Pakistani policy is influenced by the belief that nuclear weapons are the only way to preserve a broad strategic equilibrium with India, to neutralize Indian nuclear threats or blackmail, and to counter India's large conventional forces. Pakistan's strategic nuclear objective is to deter India from further dismembering Pakistan, not to pursue any wider international power and status. Pakistan, therefore, could be seen as the poster case of defensive realism.

The end of the Cold War has not alleviated Pakistan's security concerns. Pakistan's insecurity originates from the experience of India's recurrent use of force to resolve disputes with its neighbors, beginning with its forcible occupation of the princely states of Hyderabad, Junagadh, and Kashmir in 1947 and the Portuguese colony of Goa in 1961 and especially the Indo-Pakistani conflicts of 1965 and 1970–71. Pakistanis believe that India's perception of itself as a great power and the British legacy of forward defense influence India's regional security policy. They further believe that India aims to limit Pakistan's military acquisitions and growth for an adequate conventional defense despite the fact that India has been one of the largest recipients of arms transfers in the Third World. Russian military supplies of sophisticated weapon systems such as Su-30 aircraft provide India with a marked conventional military edge.[58]

The Pakistani strategic and scientific communities agree that nuclear deterrence is the best way to ensure peace with India. On three occasions in the past—in winter 1986–87, spring 1990, and May 1999—the threat of another Indo-Pakistani war loomed. As W. P. S. Sidhu describes in the previous chapter, in 1986–87 India concentrated one-quarter of a million troops about 20 miles from Pakistan's southern border in Sind. This military exercise, code-named Brasstacks, raised Pakistani fears that India wanted to exploit Pakistan's risk of a two-front war against both India and Soviet forces located in Afghanistan. According to Pakistani military analysts, Brasstacks not only involved an Indian military buildup unprecedented since 1947 but also posed a direct threat to Pakistan's territorial integrity. Some Indian scholars believed that the exercises were intended to stop Pakistan from interfering in the Sikh insurgency in India's province of East Punjab by threatening retaliation against Pakistan's "trouble spot" in Sind. Others thought that the exercises were designed to test how well Pakistan responded to a looming two-front war.[59]

58. *Military Balance*, 160.
59. Zafar Iqbal Cheema, "Report of the Study Tour of India and Pakistan," 25 June–24 July 1988, manuscript, 23–25.

Pakistani troops took up positions in the north that were interpreted as threatening by India, and many observers believe that Pakistan made veiled nuclear threats to defuse the crisis. Khan apparently communicated the nuclear threat to India: "Nobody can undo Pakistan or take us for granted. We are here to stay and let me be clear that we shall use the bomb if our existence is threatened." Some experts doubt whether Khan's ultimatum was conveyed to India during the Brasstacks exercise, and by 28 January 1987 the crisis has passed. Phase IV of the exercises (Brasstacks-IV, February–March 1987) was still under way, however, at the time of Khan's interview.[60] It is possible that General Zia and his close military associates sought to compensate for Pakistan's strategic and military disadvantages in a two-front war by pointing out that they would use nuclear weapons.[61]

Nuclear weapons also might have played a part in defusing the crisis that arose in spring 1990. This crisis was rooted in an unprecedented and largely indigenous Kashmiri struggle for independence from India that erupted in 1989. India alleged that Pakistan was supporting the struggle in Kashmir and deployed its strike corps along the border near Rajasthan in the south while taking up defensive positions in the north, as it had done during the Brasstacks exercises. Indian prime minister V. P. Singh warned that Pakistan "cannot get away with taking Kashmir without war," and members of the Indian parliament stated that if a war took place, Pakistan would cease to exist. Fearing an Indian attack to deflect pressure from Kashmir, Pakistan invoked its nuclear weapons capability to ward off the Indian threat.[62] According to a U.S. official, Beg, then chief of staff of the Pakistan army, and his colleagues thought that "the only way for the Pakistanis to deal with the Indians is to be able to take out New Delhi. There's no way that sending ten F-16s with conventional bombs is going to do it. Only the nukes could strike back." According to Hersh, Beg authorized the technicians at Kahuta to assemble nuclear weapons, to evacuate Kahuta, and to transport nuclear weapons from their storage facility to the nearby air base in Baluchistan in response to the threat of Indian air strikes.[63] When Pakistan prepositioned F-16s on full alert, ready to launch on command, the message that Pakistan would use nuclear weapons if a war took place was clearly conveyed to India.[64]

60. For a detailed account of the Brasstacks crisis, see *Brasstacks and Beyond: Perception and Management of Crisis in South Asia*, ACDIS Research Report (Urbana: Program in Arms Control, Disarmament, and International Security, University of Illinois at Urbana-Champaign, 1995), 30.
61. Author's interview with Kuldip Nayar, New Delhi, 16 July 1988.
62. Hersh, *On the Nuclear Edge*, 64.
63. Ibid., 62.
64. Ibid., 65.

Threats of nuclear use occurred for a third time on the subcontinent during the Kargil conflict. In early May 1999, the Indian army confronted Kashmiri militants backed by Pakistani army units that had occupied about eight kilometers of Indian territory near the LOC in the Kargil hills of northern Kashmir. This infiltration was unusually large and took place in extremely rugged terrain.[65] Fighting continued throughout May and June, with heavy military and financial losses on both sides. Indian leaders considered attacking more accessible spots along the LOC and Pakistan's border, a move that would have expanded the conflict. Pakistan threatened the use of nuclear weapons if India carried out such attacks.[66] In the end, India exercised restraint and the conflict remained localized. Following a 4 July 1999 U.S.-Pakistan summit meeting in Washington, D.C., the Nawaz regime was persuaded to withdraw the militants across the LOC by late July 1999. Even though the two sides avoided nuclear war, the Kargil incident was the first time that overt nuclear threats were made during open hostilities between India and Pakistan.

COMMAND, CONTROL, AND COMMUNICATIONS SYSTEMS

Little information is available about Pakistan's nuclear command and control, but the lack of records documenting such systems does not mean that orderly plans do no exist or are unavailable to senior policymakers. Activities related to Pakistan's nuclear weapons program are closely guarded secrets. Analysts such as Babar Sattar draw liberal inferences when they suggest that this absence of information reflects disagreement among policymakers and disarray in command and control procedures.[67] The opaque character of nuclear activities in South Asia might explain why command and control issues have received little public attention. States that do not admit to having nuclear weapons do not discuss their plans, procedures, and command structures for engaging in nuclear war.

There is no evidence to suggest that Pakistan has developed specialized nuclear command, control, communication, and intelligence systems. Pakistani officials have, however, recognized many of the demands inherent in maintaining effective command and control for nuclear deterrent forces. Beg stated some time ago that, "given the tension, mutual mistrust and suspicion

65. Hilary Synnott, *The Causes and Consequences of South Asia's Nuclear Tests*, Adelphi Paper 332 (London: Oxford University Press for the IISS, 1999), 35.
66. Adrian Levy and Sumit Das, "Nuclear Alert Sounded in Pakistan," *Sunday Times*, 30 May 1999.
67. Babar Sattar, "The Non-Proliferation Regime and Pakistan." Manuscript.

between India and Pakistan, it is dangerously tempting for each to launch an attack before being attacked which could escalate to a nuclear level. Such a possibility demands the setting up of elaborate command, control and communication structures as was done by the U.S. and U.S.S.R. during the Cold War."[68] He also noted that the Pakistani military was willing to subordinate itself to political authority when it came to using nuclear weapons: "The question as to 'who shall push the nuclear button,' is only hypothetical. In the context of Pakistan, as in all democratic polities, it is always the 'popular will' vested in the legislature which shall be the final presser of the button, but that eventuality shall never come."[69] He is implying that because of Pakistan's parliamentary system, the prime minister would have final authority on the use of nuclear weapons. Organization theory suggests, however, that the continuing strong influence of the Pakistan armed forces, especially the army, in the development of a nuclear doctrine may lead to demands for predelegation of authority from the prime minister to employ nuclear weapons during crisis or wartime situations.

Several parties might be involved in the process of authorizing the use of nuclear weapons, according to Shafqat Ali Khan: "Main actors involved are, the government (the President and the Prime Minister), the Armed Forces (the Army, the Air Force, and the Chairman JCSC); the Ministry of Foreign Affairs and the nuclear bureaucracy (the PAEC and the KRL). The nature of interaction among these actors is not clear, but in all probability it is a highly symbiotic relationship."[70] Beg revealed, however, that a National Nuclear Command Authority (NNCA) was established by Z. A. Bhutto, who, as chief executive, also chaired the authority. The NNCA worked to institutionalize policymaking, define Pakistan's nuclear force structure, and determine the alert posture of Pakistan's nuclear forces. Once a political decision was taken, the army chief of staff executed the order "within the limits of the NNCA."[71] But apart from Beg's account, no other public information is available on the NNCA.

To achieve its strategic objective of maintaining a credible deterrent against an Indian first strike, Pakistan requires only a modest command and control system. Several factors will shape the evolution of this system. First, reliance on existing command and control systems, combined with the basic state of weaponization, probably prevents Pakistan from installing sophisticated safety features that might be found in more advanced

68. Beg, *Development and Security,* 156–57.
69. Ibid., 171.
70. Shafqat Ali Khan, "Pakistan," *Nuclear Weapons after the Comprehensive Test Ban,* ed. Eric Arnett (New York: Oxford University Press, 1996), 75.
71. "NNCA Responsible for Safeguarding Nuclear Program, Says Beg," *News,* 2 June 1998.

arsenals: permissive action links, electronic monitoring and environmental sensing devices to stop unauthorized use or detonation, "safe" nuclear warheads, and hardening against electromagnetic pulse. Development of dedicated command and control technologies and associated infrastructure is not, however, beyond Pakistan's technological capability. In the meantime, Pakistan will continue to rely on the existing command and control systems originally developed for conventional military purposes.

Second, under Pakistan's constitution before the military takeover on 12 October 1999, the Defense Council (DC) and Defense Committee of the Cabinet (DCC) are designated to formulate and manage Pakistan's defense policy; they have not, however, played a decisive role in strategic nuclear decision making. Chaired by the prime minister, the Defense Council includes the ministers of defense, foreign affairs, finance, interior, states and frontier regions, information and broadcasting, communications and production; the secretaries of defense, finance, and foreign affairs; the chairman of the Joint Chiefs of Staff Committee (JCSC), and the chiefs of the three armed forces. Also chaired by the prime minister, the Defense Committee of the Cabinet consists of the ministers of defense, foreign affairs, and finance; the secretaries of defense, finance, and foreign affairs; the chairman of the JCSC and the chiefs of the three services.[72] The DC is a policy planning body while the DCC is its executive organ. The regular involvement of the DC and DCC in decisions about nuclear command and control is unlikely, even though both bodies might be asked to ratify the overall thrust of Pakistani nuclear weapons policy. For example, the DCC endorsed the prime minister's decision to conduct the May 1998 nuclear tests, and it also debated whether Pakistan should sign the CTBT in the aftermath of the May tests. [73] It deliberated following the recent announcement of an Indian nuclear doctrine and, in response, endorsed a minimum deterrent strategy. Since the introduction of the eighth amendment to the 1997 constitution, the prime minister is at the top of the nuclear decision-making hierarchy with the armed forces and the nuclear bureaucracy, in descending order, holding varying degrees of control and responsibility.[74]

Although the 12 October 1999 military coup in Pakistan has led to obvious changes in command and control at top echelons, it has produced little change in nuclear readiness and operational strategy. The Pakistani military has been an important player in nuclear policy since General Zia's

---

72. *White Paper on Higher Defense Organization* (Islamabad: Ministry of Defense, Government of Pakistan, 1976).

73. *Nation*, 8 September 1998, 1.

74. Ayesha Siddiga-Agha, "Ad Hocracy, Decision-Making and Pakistan's Arms Production and Nuclear Projects," *Indian Defense Review*, July 1996, 25–26.

regime in the late 1970s. The Defense Council and the Defense Committee of the Cabinet during Nawaz Sharif's second tenure (1997–99) were involved in defense policymaking, but their role remained confined to endorsing rather than to making crucial decisions, espcially in the nuclear field. After the May 1998 nuclear tests, authority to use nuclear weapons rested with the prime minister. The situation has changed following the October 1999 takeover in which General Pervez Musharraf replaced the prime minister as Pakistan's chief executive. Musharraf already occupied two key positions: chief of army staff and chairman of the Joints Chiefs of Staff Committee, and has now assumed the powers of the prime minister. He has constituted a National Security Council to deal with important national issues, replacing the defunct DCC. The highest military decisionmaking institution dealing with command and control of nuclear weapons continues to be the Joint Chiefs of Staff Committee, consisting of the three service chiefs.

Third, because of the strong role Pakistan's armed forces played in decisions about national security policy and conventional military strategy, they probably will also play a leading role in devising and managing the procedures that control Pakistan's nuclear weapons. Pakistan's military influences nuclear policy through both formal and informal channels. General Headquarters and perhaps even corps commanders would be involved in the decision to use nuclear weapons. The Pakistani air force probably would play an important planning role as long as the country continues to rely on aircraft to deliver nuclear weapons. Eventually, the navy could play a more important role in nuclear war planning if Pakistan developed a sea-based delivery system to augment its second-strike capability or to respond to India's planned "Sagarika" SLBM.

Fourth, and most important, because of the growing involvement of all three of the armed services in operational and command and control matters, the Joint Staff Headquarters (JS HQ) appears to be the most likely forum for dealing with nuclear command and control issues. The JS HQ was established in the early 1970s to ensure coordination of command, control, and communications among the three armed forces and to be the civil-military liaison for strategic decision making. The organizational procedures adopted at the JS HQ institute collective decision making by both civilian and military leaders in peace and war. Political, strategic, and military representatives and issues come together in the JCSC to shape Pakistan's strategic policies.[75] The only significant player not represented in the JS HQ is the nuclear bureaucracy (e.g., Khan Research Laboratories and Pakistan Atomic Energy Commission), which probably will be included after the

75. *White Paper on Higher Defense Organization.*

formation of a Strategic Command Authority to deal specifically with nuclear command and control.

Fifth, because of the relatively small size of its nuclear forces, Pakistan probably would construct a highly centralized command and control system that predelegates a minimum amount of authority to commanders of operational forces. Because of the short distances and times involved, Pakistan would emphasize developing surveillance and intelligence systems to supply early warning in peacetime. If nuclear-armed missiles eventually were deployed in a survivable mode, they would reduce the vulnerability of Pakistan's small nuclear arsenal and increase the credibility of deterrence.[76] The possibility of accidental or unauthorized use can never be ruled out, but the high degree of professionalism in the Pakistani armed forces mitigates this risk to some degree.

PAKISTAN'S NUCLEAR DOCTRINE

Pakistan has not formally announced a nuclear doctrine. In practice, however, it is pursuing a doctrine of minimum deterrence and conventional defense. Pakistan's plans to miniaturize nuclear warheads, develop several types of ballistic missiles, assemble a small nuclear force, and address the asymmetric strategic equilibrium with India by relying on nuclear weapons, suggest the outline of an emerging nuclear doctrine. Other objectives of Pakistan's nuclear policies are to maintain territorial integrity and political sovereignty vis-à-vis India. Pakistan's foreign minister Abdul Sattar declared in November 1999, "Minimum nuclear deterrence will remain the guiding principle of our nuclear strategy." He stated that as India enlarges its nuclear arsenal, "Pakistan will have to maintain, preserve and upgrade its capability in order to ensure survivability and credibility of the deterrent."[77] Pakistan's strategic policy emphasizes deterrence rather than war fighting.

Pakistan views India's nuclear doctrine as offensive and provocative, and a threat to regional and global stability.[78] Although the draft doctrine was not officially approved by the Indian government, Pakistani observers generally believe that the Indian government will embrace it almost in its entirety. Responding to the draft Indian nuclear doctrine in August 1999, the Defense Committee of the Cabinet during Nawaz Sharif's administration stated that future development of Pakistan's nuclear weapons program will be "determined solely by the requirement of our minimum de-

---

76. Scott D. Sagan, "The Perils of Proliferation," *International Security* 18 (Spring 1994): 90–92.
77. "Pakistan to Upgrade Nuclear Deterrent," *Dawn*, 25 November 1999.
78. "Pakistan Says Indian Nuclear Plan Threatens Global Stability," *News*, 26 August 1999.

terrent capability, which is now an indispensable part of our security doc-trine."[79]

The dangerous aspect of the draft Indian doctrine is that it relies upon "the maintenance of highly effective conventional capabilities not just to raise the threshold of conventional military conflict, but to deal with the threat of use of nuclear weapons by an adversary."[80] This is a preemptive threat that undermines nuclear crisis stability. Conventional preemptive strikes against an adversary's nuclear forces might lead to a nuclear ex-change. India's draft nuclear policy apparently is a war-fighting doctrine.[81]

Statements emanating from New Delhi have generated further uncer-tainties about the stability of nuclear deterrence. Indian Defense Minister George Fernandes declared on 5 January 2000 at a seminar on "Challenges of Limited War" organized by the Institute of Defense Studies and Analy-ses that Pakistan's possession of nuclear weapons does not rule out the pos-sibility of a limited conventional war.[82] The theme was reiterated by Indian army chief General V. P. Malik, who stated that despite Pakistan's nuclear weapons capability, India would cross the LOC in hot pursuit of Kashmiri militants.[83]

Pakistani officials have not stated explicitly whether nuclear weapons would be used to deter a conventional military attack by India, to overcome early setbacks in a conventional war, to counteract an emerging strategic disadvantage, or as weapons of last resort. Pakistan's rejection of India's suggested bilateral "no-nuclear-first-use" pledge suggests, however, that nuclear weapons are integral to its defense and deterrent doctrine. Pak-istani officials believe that acceptance of a "no-first-use" pledge would un-dermine the credibility of Pakistan's deterrence against Indian attack. Pak-istani leaders also have no faith in the credibility of India's no-first-use pledge, which they consider to be more declaratory posturing than an ac-tual policy. They believe there is no way to verify an Indian no-first-use pledge.

Since its partition in 1971, Pakistan has attempted to increase its strategic self-sufficiency by introducing new weapon systems, diversifying arms ac-quisitions, developing an indigenous arms industry, and building nuclear weapons and ballistic missiles. Even though Pakistan's nuclear infrastruc-ture is smaller than that of India, it contains all the elements of a viable nu-clear force and constitutes a credible minimum deterrent. Despite India's

79. Ibid.
80. "Draft Report of the National Security Advisory Board on Indian Nuclear Doctrine," (New Delhi: Government of India, 17 August 1999).
81. Rodney W. Jones, "Pakistan's Nuclear Posture," *Dawn*, 14 September 1999.
82. Afzal Mahmud, "India's Aggressive Posture," *Dawn*, 31 January 2000.
83. Ibid.

conventional superiority, the nuclear balance greatly reduces India's ability to achieve a quick and cheap victory over Pakistan.[84] "Although India . . . appears to possess formidable military capabilities," notes Ashley Tellis, "a more detailed analysis suggests that its combat power is insufficient to overwhelm Pakistan within the constraints of a short war."[85]

In time, Pakistani officials will specify the contingencies warranting nuclear retaliation. The first contingency would be to deter a large-scale conventional war with India. The implementation of India's Army 2000 Plan, aimed at splitting Pakistan in the vicinity of the Bahawalpur-Multan sector, or a repeat of the Brasstacks exercises might compel Pakistan to consider the use of nuclear weapons. Any operation premised on deep penetration of Pakistan's territory by Indian forces or large-scale attacks threatening to destroy Pakistan's territorial integrity would likely force consideration of the use of nuclear weapons. The second contingency warranting the employment of nuclear weapons by Pakistan would be to deter Indian nuclear threats or coercion. The nuclear factor is widely believed to be the key element for conflict management in South Asia.[86] Although the exact role nuclear weapons played in ending the 1986–87 and 1990 crises is unclear, there is general recognition that nuclear weapons have influenced strategic decision making by imposing restraint on the usually bellicose behavior of India and Pakistan. A third cause for use would be to deter India from using chemical weapons. India has officially declared a significant stockpile of chemical weapons, after signing the Chemical Weapons Convention as a non-chemical-weapon state.

Pakistan's political and military leaders are increasingly mindful of the need to maintain a constant vigil to ward off preemptive air or missile attacks by India either to decapitate Pakistan's command and control systems or to destroy its nuclear forces. Rumors circulated in May 1998, for instance, that India, in collaboration with Israel, attempted to carry out preemptive air strikes to destroy Pakistan's nuclear facilities. A Ministry of Foreign Affairs spokesman stated that the Pakistani government had evidence that Israeli F-16s were operating at India's Srinagar air base, from which air strikes could be launched against Pakistan's nuclear infrastructure, especially Kahuta.[87] It was reported that Pakistan deployed Ghauri missiles at unidentified sites to retaliate in the event of strikes against its nuclear

84. For a detailed numerical comparison of Indian and Pakistani armed forces, see *Military Balance*, 153–54, 159–60.

85. Ashley J. Tellis, *Stability in South Asia*, Documented Briefing (Santa Monica: RAND, 1997), viii.

86. Devin Hagerty, "Nuclear Deterrence in South Asia: The 1990 Indo-Pakistan Crisis," *International Security* 20 (Winter 1995): 79–114.

87. "Indian Preemptive Threat," *Nation*, 28 May 1998, 1.

installations.[88] One report even suggested that some of the Ghauri missiles were equipped with nuclear warheads, but there is little evidence to substantiate this report. The missiles apparently were moved out of Khan Research Laboratories in the morning when unusual Indian air activity was observed.[89] The missile deployment suggests that Islamabad would interpret India's preemptive strikes as an act of war and respond appropriately.[90]

The proximity of potential combatants, little early warning time, and a lack of strategic depth might induce Pakistan to alert its nuclear forces to prevent their destruction if a crisis develops. The situation injects an element of instability in the deterrent relationship between India and Pakistan. Pakistan, however, has long faced this kind of threat. In December 1982, U.S. intelligence apparently detected that India had developed contingency plans to launch preemptive strikes against Pakistani nuclear installations, particularly Kahuta. General Zia signaled that such an attack by India would prompt Pakistan to retaliate with all available means, possibly including air strikes by Pakistani F-16s against Indian nuclear facilities and air bases.[91] Press accounts about the possibility of Indian preemptive air strikes against Kahuta surfaced again after a 1984 CIA briefing to U.S. senators. According to these reports, Indian military planners believed the only way to stop Pakistan's nuclear weapons program was to destroy its nuclear infrastructure.[92] Fear of Pakistani retaliation, as Sidhu suggests in the previous chapter, averted this danger.

India might not be the only country in South Asia that perceives a possible need to launch preventive or preemptive strikes against an opponent's nuclear infrastructure. Pakistan's political and military leaders might opt for preemption rather than be the victims of an Indian preemptive attack. A successful first strike or even decapitation attack, however, is a formidable challenge for any would-be attacker: it requires simultaneous precision strikes against a variety of targets, and any failure risks immediate nuclear retaliation.[93] Several factors weigh heavily against the inclusion of preemptive strikes in the nuclear doctrines of either India or Pakistan: an inability to carry out precision air strikes, especially at long ranges, and a lack of the requisite weapons to cover all potential counterforce targets. By default, countervalue targets (i.e., population centers) become the likely nuclear targets in the region.

88. *News*, 28 May 1998, 1.

89. "Redefining Nuclear Order," *Nation*, 9 September 1998, 5.

90. "Indian Preemptive Threat," *Nation*, 28 May 1998, 1.

91. Milton R. Benjamin, "India Said to Eye Raid—Pakistani A-Plants, *Washington Post*, 20 December 1982.

92. *Nucleonics Week* 25 (20 September 1998): 4.

93. See Peter D. Feaver, "Command and Control in Emerging Nuclear Nations," *International Security* 17 (Winter 1992–93): 161–81.

Nuclear Force Structure

The size of Pakistan's nuclear arsenal will be determined by the availability of fissile material, the number and types of available delivery systems, decisions about nuclear employment doctrine (i.e., the adoption of a counterforce or countervalue strategy), and the size of the Indian nuclear arsenal. Likely targets for nuclear weapons might include four to five major cities, several key military-industrial complexes, vital communication centers, important strategic air bases, and battlefield targets such as command headquarters, strike corps, and strategic reserves. This adds up to about twenty-five targets in India that Pakistan's nuclear forces would cover. Allowances also would have to be made for the failure of some weapons and delivery vehicles to reach their targets because of technical failures, enemy defenses, and destruction of a proportion of the force in the event of a preemptive enemy strike. Assuming a 50 percent attrition rate, a sufficient Pakistani nuclear force might be roughly fifty deliverable warheads. Because targets such as large cities and industrial areas may require the use of more than one weapon, the Pakistani force could reach about seventy-five deliverable warheads.

These estimates suggest that Pakistani nuclear planners are likely to build an arsenal of forty-five to sixty nuclear warheads. This number would constitute a credible minimum deterrent against India for the next five years. Pakistan, however, has a large stockpile of low-enriched uranium that can be converted into weapons-grade material in a relatively short period of time. This stockpile increases the potential choices available to Pakistan's leaders. Pakistan probably will have the capability to produce seventy-five to one hundred weapons of various yields, suitable for engaging countervalue or counterforce targets, over the next ten years. This force would include an adequate second-strike capability against even the most extreme contingencies Pakistan is likely to face.

Pakistan's targeting strategy will evolve along with its nuclear systems toward a mix of counterforce and countervalue targets. Neither Pakistan nor India has access to the sophisticated C³I systems that provide the intelligence and accurate surveillance needed completely to destroy counterforce targets in a first strike. General Vijai K. Nair's assessment is that "both Pakistan and India have antiquated command, control and communication systems whose assurance levels are dangerously low. Besides the obsolescence factor, these systems do not incorporate survivable facilities to ride out a nuclear exchange."[94] This assessment, however, is a bit outdated.

94. Brig. Vijai K. Nair, *Nuclear India* (New Delhi: Lancer International, 1992), 57, 170–71.

The use of tactical nuclear weapons on the battlefield would raise new problems of intelligence gathering and assessment, making it difficult for India or Pakistan to control the course of a future conflict. Any likely threat or use of tactical nuclear weapons by India risks nuclear escalation by Pakistan. Each side would then strive to manage escalation. Pakistan eventually would have two targeting choices: either to respond rapidly against Indian counterforce targets or to deter Indian use of tactical weapons by threatening to destroy Indian population centers. Pakistan would have only a short time to respond to an imminent nuclear threat because of India's close proximity and Pakistan's lack of strategic depth. The fear of an Indian first strike against its nuclear weapons and command and control systems might force Pakistan to use nuclear weapons early in a conflict or, in the words of General K. Sundarji, "Pakistan must decide whether to use them or lose them."[95] Under these circumstances, an officially declared nuclear doctrine that states explicitly when Pakistan would use nuclear weapons to safeguard its security would help to deter any Indian adventurism.

Deterrence operates between India and Pakistan because each country's nuclear weapons can inflict unacceptable damage on the other. As India and Pakistan hold each other's cities hostage, the risk of annihilation of tens of thousands of civilians makes their countervalue deterrence stable. In addition, they are in the process of building second-strike capabilities into their nuclear arsenals.

Pakistan's nuclear arsenal has reduced the prospect that India will use force to solve regional problems, which had been a recurrent obstacle in relations between India and Pakistan since their independence. A robust nuclear deterrent not only safeguards Pakistan's sovereignty and territorial integrity against external threats but also strengthens its ability to resist Indian efforts to dominate the region. Pakistan's nuclear weapons enhance its foreign policy leverage vis-à-vis India and its other neighbors.

India and Pakistan have now tested nuclear weapons. India also has announced a draft nuclear doctrine that probably will serve as the basis of its official nuclear policy. Pakistani leaders have made explicit statements about how they intend to use nuclear weapons, which suggest the outlines of an emerging nuclear doctrine. Nuclear deterrence, however, is a dynamic relationship that requires constant vigilance to detect and counteract destabilizing developments. The latest Indo-Pakistani conflicts and crises have brought them to the brink of nuclear war. Mutual restraint imposed by fear of nuclear devastation and facilitated by U.S. mediation has helped

95. General K. Sundarji, *Blind Men of Hindustan: Indo-Pakistan Nuclear War* (New Delhi: UBS Publishers, 1993), 215–16.

avert catastrophe. The recent conflict in Kargil, however, indicates that nuclear deterrence on the subcontinent is precarious.

The possibility of an accidental or unauthorized use of nuclear weapons cannot be ruled out. India and Pakistan's geographic proximity only allows for about five minutes' warning time following a ballistic missile launch. Time constraints create a serious impediment to rational deliberation and compel India and Pakistan to adopt launch-on-warning policies. Problems of early warning undermine the emergence of stable nuclear deterrence in the region.

What if deterrence were to fail? A nuclear war could result in complete economic collapse in India and Pakistan. Widespread destruction of communication and government infrastructure could cause political disintegration in both countries. The human suffering created by nuclear war would be horrific, impeding recovery and the revival of civil society.

The prospect of nuclear war makes it imperative for India and Pakistan to find political solutions to the conflicts that are fuelling a regional arms race. In the meantime, both sides must exercise restraint and explore arms control and confidence building measures to create a stable deterrent situation in South Asia.

[7]

The Democratic People's Republic of Korea and Unconventional Weapons

JOSEPH S. BERMUDEZ JR.

During the past forty-five years, the Democratic People's Republic of Korea (DPRK) has worked hard to produce chemical, biological, and nuclear weapons and delivery systems. It has done so following its national philosophy of *Juche* (self-sufficiency), overcoming severe resource constraints and determined international opposition. Why has the DPRK developed such weaponry and what are its plans for using this arsenal? This chapter makes three central arguments. First, the DPRK came into being at the end of World War II when chemical, biological, and nuclear weapons were employed in East Asia. This formative experience, coupled with U.S. nuclear threats during the Korean War, has both provided the North Korean leaders with strong motives to develop unconventional weapons and encouraged a belief that their use is appropriate under a variety of strategic circumstances. Second, the DPRK leaders believe that their unconventional weapons can serve as a strong deterrent against a potential attack by the United States and the Republic of Korea (ROK) and provide a shield behind which DPRK offensive actions against the ROK could proceed with less risk of U.S. escalation. Third, the DPRK has devoted significant resources to the development of missile capabilities and has developed covert special forces operations as an alternative means to deliver chemical, biological, and nuclear weapons if necessary. The DPRK leadership gives every indication that it is highly reluctant to "negotiate away" its unconventional arsenal in peacetime and that it is highly willing to use these weapons in war.

In terms of the theories outlined in Chapter 1, the DPRK case provides strong support for the importance of strategic culture and other societal-level factors in determining doctrine and command systems. Realism predicts that states will use unconventional weapons primarily to deter other states from attacking them. DPRK leaders certainly have such deterrent goals in mind, but the development and nature of their more offensive military options are better understood in the context of the unique historical experience and myths promoted by the leaders of this isolated country. Organization theory is the least useful approach to explain emerging DPRK doctrine and control procedures, primarily because the Korean Workers' Party (KWP) has maintained very tight control over any independent thinking and operations inside the DPRK military.

Because DPRK officials view the rest of the world through a thick historical lens, a historical approach should be taken when analyzing the regime's policies. This chapter begins by describing DPRK leaders' motivations for developing chemical, biological, and nuclear weapons. It then explores the potential use of these weapons by the DPRK through a survey of the weapons arsenal, delivery systems, strategic thought, command and control, targeting, and safety policy.

MOTIVATIONS

A primary motivation for the DPRK to develop nuclear, biological, and chemical weapons is to ensure national survival by deterring potential South Korean or American aggression. For DPRK leaders, however, deterring the United States also creates the opportunity to reunify Korea by force and under their terms.[1] These motivations for acquiring nuclear, biological, and chemical weapons cannot be understood without appreciating the role played by Kim Il-song, who was the leader of the DPRK for forty-six years until his death in 1995. During this period, real power in the DPRK rested in the hands of a small group of men who had fought as partisans with Kim Il-song against the Japanese during World War II. They viewed Japan not only as a neighbor and important trading partner but also as the nation that occupied Korea and brutally oppressed the Korean people. DPRK leaders never have concealed their belief that the United States is their principal enemy and the ROK is America's puppet. These leaders maintain that the United States interfered in an internal dispute (i.e., the Fatherland Liberation or Korean War) and threatened to use nuclear weapons during that conflict. Since that time, the claim goes, the United States has prevented the unification of Korea and threatened the existence of the DPRK with nuclear weapons. They also contend that the United States controls the United Nations and directs world opinion against the DPRK. DPRK leaders view U.S.

1. Author's interview with North Korean officials.

actions in Vietnam, Grenada, Panama, Iraq, and Somalia as analogous to their own situation: the United States acts like a bully "kicking the door in" by interfering in other countries' internal affairs.[2]

Pre-World War II to 1953

To understand North Korean motivations for acquiring unconventional weapons, it is necessary to explore the period before World War II. During the late 1930s, the Japanese military developed a small chemical and biological warfare capability and used it against the Chinese. Later on in the war, the Japanese also conducted chemical and biological weapons experiments on Allied prisoners of war, Russians, and Chinese civilians.[3] At that time, Kim Il-song and other future North Korean leaders were young peasant guerrillas who were sporadically fighting the Japanese, first with the Communist Chinese and later with the Soviet army. These young men were influenced by what they learned about these chemical and biological operations.[4] As news about the events at Hiroshima and Nagasaki spread throughout the world, nuclear weapons came to be viewed as the ultimate "doomsday" weapon, a perception that was reinforced by Koreans who had been in Hiroshima and Nagasaki at the time of the bombing.[5]

The Korean People's Army (KPA) was established in 1948. When the Soviet Union and the KWP of North Korea created the P'yongyang Institute and the Central Security School to train officers for the KPA and the Ministry of Internal Affairs, both schools offered courses in chemical defense. Taught by Soviet advisers using Soviet manuals, these courses described the technical characteristics of chemical and biological warfare and addressed the effects of nuclear weapons on the battlefield.[6] By the time of the Fatherland Liberation War, the KPA had established a chemical warfare element in the General Staff Department and trained a small number of dedicated chemical officers.

During the war, fears of nuclear, biological, and chemical weapons were dramatically reinforced by two events. First, both the DPRK and People's Republic of China (PRC) suffered repeated, and to them unexplained, outbreaks of infectious diseases such as small pox, influenza, dengue fever,

2. Wording used by North Korean officials in interviews with author, on condition of anonymity.

3. Peter Williams and David Wallace, *Unit 731: Japan's Secret Biological Warfare in World War II* (New York: Free Press, 1989), 45; Sheldon H. Harris, *Factories of Death: Japanese Biological Warfare, 1932–45, and the American Cover-Up* (New York: Routledge, 1994), 67–73.

4. I interviewed several subjects at various locations from 1988 to 1998, on condition that all information would be used anonymously.

5. Peter Hayes, *Pacific Powderkeg* (Lexington, Mass.: Lexington Books, 1991), 241–46.

6. U.S. Army, *ATIS Enemy Documents: Korean Operations*, Issue No. 16, GHQ, FEC, MIS, GS, 1–26.

and cholera that caused numerous civilian and military casualties. Chinese and North Korean leaders, with Soviet assistance, used these outbreaks to fabricate evidence of U.S. use of biological weapons. This fabricated evidence was accepted as true by middle-level leaders and average soldiers and citizens.[7] Second, North Korean fears of nuclear attack were exacerbated by repeated U.S. threats to use nuclear weapons against KPA and Chinese units in Korea and, if necessary, against the PRC proper to end the war. These threats struck a raw nerve because the leaders of both nations remembered the bombing of Hiroshima and Nagasaki, and neither the PRC nor the DPRK could withstand a nuclear attack or respond in kind. These threats were instrumental in bringing about the 1953 armistice agreement. Since then, a nuclear inferiority complex has pervaded DPRK strategic thinking and foreign policy, leading DPRK leaders to spend their lives and their nation's resources to make sure that they never again experience this type of coercion.[8]

1954–1969

Since the Fatherland Liberation War, the continued U.S. presence on the Korean peninsula and the inclusion of the ROK under the U.S. nuclear umbrella have contributed to peace. To DPRK leaders, the U.S. presence reinforced the belief that the DPRK had little choice but to comply with the 1953 Armistice Agreement or face devastation from nuclear attack. In the immediate postwar years, the DPRK possessed no unconventional weapons or the capabilities to produce them. DPRK leaders came to believe that possession of such weapons would serve as a powerful deterrent to United States/ROK aggression or blackmail.

Tensions increased on the Korean peninsula in the 1960s as the DPRK undertook increasingly aggressive moves against the ROK. Kim Il-song consolidated his power in 1961 by appointing his supporters to all important positions in the government and the KWP. Most were active or retired generals, collectively known as the "partisan generals." This consolidation of power allowed the military to dominate DPRK foreign policy. The partisan generals initiated a broad military reorganization and modernization program to transform the KPA from a prenuclear Soviet-style organization into

7. Kathryn Weathersby, "Deceiving the Deceivers: Moscow, Beijing, Pyongyang, and the Allegations of Bacteriological Weapons Use in Korea," *Cold War International History Project Bulletin* 11 (Winter 1998): 176–84; Milton Leitenberg, "New Russian Evidence on the Korean Biological Warfare Allegations: Background and Analysis," *Cold War International History Project Bulletin* 11 (Winter 1998): 185–99.

8. Rosemary Foot, *The Wrong War: American Policy and the Dimensions of the Korean Conflict, 1850–1953* (Ithaca: Cornell University Press, 1985); Robert A. Pape, *Bombing to Win: Air Power and Coercion in War* (Ithaca: Cornell University Press, 1996), 137–73.

a modern fighting force capable of quickly capturing the entire ROK. A major aspect of this program was the development of chemical and biological weapons.

The creation of an extensive network of underground facilities for the military and key civilian industries dates to the Fatherland Liberation War. But for practical and economic reasons, this policy was abandoned during the immediate postwar years.[9] It was not until the early 1960s that Kim Il-song renewed construction of underground facilities under the military doctrine known as the Four Military Lines, to reduce DPRK nuclear vulnerability. He announced: "The entire nation must be made into a fortress. We do not have an atomic bomb. Therefore, we must dig ourselves into the ground to protect against the threat of atomic bombs."[10] By the late 1970s, the DPRK had become the most heavily fortified nation in the world. This construction doctrine has complicated foreign intelligence collection because many critical activities are carried out belowground, beyond the reach of "national technical means."

The Soviet Union provided a 2-megawatt IRT-2000 research reactor to the DPRK in 1965 while the first steps were being taken by the DPRK to establish a nuclear capability. Progress was slow in all the weapons programs because of limitations in personnel, industrial resources, and technology. The chemical industry had just recovered from the Fatherland Liberation War, and the state of nuclear and biological research was rudimentary.

Pilot production of chemical weapons also began in the late 1960s. The KPA developed an embryonic offensive chemical weapons capability, while the biological warfare program began basic research (possibly into the wartime diseases that affected the KPA).[11] Kim Il-song and the partisan generals apparently viewed chemical weapons as the "poor man's atomic bomb." They believed that these weapons could be used both to deter U.S. aggression and to strike the ROK and Japan. These beliefs helped encourage the DPRK to initiate an aggressive policy of subversion against the ROK during the late 1960s. This policy, termed "revolution in the South," produced the January 1968 attempt to assassinate ROK president Park Chung Hee at the presidential residence (the so-called Blue House) in Seoul, the seizure of the USS *Pueblo* that same month, and the April 1969 downing of a U.S. Navy EC-121M.[12] The recklessness of the partisan gener-

9. U.S. Army, "Capabilities of the Munitions Industry of North Korea," declassified Intelligence Staff Study, Project 9050, 15 June 1955, 5–6.

10. So Yong-ha, "Capacity for Nuclear Weapons Development," *Hoguk*, July 1989, 119–22; quoted in FBIS-EAS-89–148, 3 August 1989, 23–26.

11. Interview data.

12. Joseph S. Bermudez Jr., *North Korean Special Forces—2nd Edition* (Annapolis: U.S. Naval Institute Press, 1997); interview data; Defense Intelligence Agency, *North Korean Armed Forces Handbook (U)*, January 1971, 119–46; John G. Hubbell and David Reed, "Mission: To Murder a

als, the unexpectedly aggressive nature of the U.S. response, and the real possibility of an accidental war with the United States had a sobering effect on Kim Il-song.[13] He purged the partisan generals and terminated the aggressive phase of the revolution in the South.

The era of the partisan generals demonstrated that the DPRK's military leaders, poorly educated and unskilled in diplomacy, were unqualified to formulate and implement foreign policy. They were woefully naive and inept at managing international crises. This created a perilous situation in which miscalculation by either North Korean or American leaders, combined with the poor state of communications between the two nations and a rudimentary KPA chain of command, could easily have resulted in an inadvertent or accidental war.[14]

Kim and his new colleagues realized that their chemical and biological weapons capabilities could not deter a U.S. nuclear threat. The partisan generals' evaluation of these weapons as a deterrent was based on the assumption that the United States knew of the KPA offensive chemical and biological weapons capability. At this time, however, Americans were unaware of any significant unconventional weapons development. Moreover, even if U.S. intelligence analysts had been aware of this capability, they probably estimated that the DPRK would be deterred from employing chemical or biological weapons by the threat of either a response in kind or nuclear escalation. This fundamental failing in the effort to develop accurate estimates of each other's behavior repeatedly has plagued United States–DPRK relations.

1970–1989

When the United States announced in 1971 that it was reducing its presence in the ROK, the government in Seoul decided to initiate a covert nuclear weapons program to deter DPRK aggression.[15] Fear of aggression

---

President," *Reader's Digest*, July 1968, 142–47; "North Korea on Alert for Any Retaliation," *New York Times*, 16 April 1969, 8; William Beechem, "Nixon Declares United States Will Protect Planes Off Korea," *New York Times*, 19 April 1969, 1.

13. Dae-sook Suh, *Kim Il Sung: The North Korean Leader* (New York: Columbia University Press, 1988), 239.

14. Scott D. Sagan, "Mutual Security Interests in the Asian-Pacific Region: Exercises, Accidents, and Crisis Management," in *The Transformation of the Asian Pacific Region: Prospects for the 1990s* (Palo Alto, Calif.: Center for International Security and Cooperation, Stanford University, and the Institute of Far Eastern Studies, Soviet Academy of Sciences, 1991), 211–48; and Suh, *Kim Il Sung*, 211–48.

15. U.S. House of Representatives, *Investigation of Korean-American Relations*, Subcommittee on International Organizations, Committee on International Relations, 95th Cong., 2d sess., 80; Alden D. Pierce, "Morning Calm, Nuclear Sunset: South Korea's Nuclear Option" (Master's thesis, Naval Postgraduate School, Monterey, Calif., 1998), 39–45.

was reinforced in 1974, when the DPRK conducted its third assassination attempt against ROK president Park Chung Hee.[16] That year, the United States confirmed the existence of the ROK covert nuclear weapons program. The United States subsequently pressured the ROK to abandon its nuclear program in return for increased military and political assistance. Secretary of Defense James R. Schlesinger announced in 1975 that the ROK was under the United States nuclear umbrella: "If circumstances were to require the use of tactical nuclear weapons . . . I think that would be carefully considered . . . I do not think it would be wise to test [U.S.] reactions."[17] U.S. threats and revelations about the ROK covert nuclear weapons program precipitated the decision by DPRK leaders to transform their nuclear research program into a weapons program.

As a result of the continued U.S. nuclear threat and suspicions about the existence of an ROK nuclear weapons program, chemical and biological weapons probably reached their lowest value for deterrence and battlefield operations for the DPRK regime in the mid-1970s. During the 1980s, however, DPRK leaders took renewed interest in chemical and biological weapons because of a series of Ministry of People's Armed Forces (MPAF) studies of chemical weapons operations during and after the Iran-Iraq War. The KPA decided that these weapons were useful because of their demonstrated effectiveness on a modern battlefield and because worldwide public opinion had been desensitized to the use of chemical weapons by widespread Iraqi and Iranian employment of them.[18] The eroding military superiority of the KPA over the ROK also encouraged a doctrine of first use of chemical weapons in any war with the ROK or the United States. KPA leaders probably remained reluctant to employ biological weapons on the Korean peninsula because of their own vulnerability but viewed the use of biological weapons against Japanese and American interests outside the Korean peninsula to be more acceptable for several reasons. An attack outside Korea would not directly affect the DPRK but would clearly demonstrate the military prowess of the KPA. A biological attack also would serve as a warning that further conflict with the DPRK would be extraordinarily costly to the United States and Japan.

16. Interview data; "Chongryon, P'yongyang's Advance Guard in Japan," in *Some Facts about North Korea* (Seoul: Naewoe Press, 1984), 90–93; Richard Halloran, "Seoul President Escapes Assassin," *New York Times*, 15 August 1974, 1; Richard Halloran, "Assassin's Bullet Kills Mrs. Park," *New York Times*, 16 August 1974, 1.

17. For background, see Jack Anderson and Les Whitten, "U.S. Pullout Leaves Asia in Ferment," *Washington Post*, 9 July 1975, C23; Joseph Kraft, "Korean Lessons," *Washington Post*, 26 June 1975, A23; and "Schlesinger Warns N. Korea U.S. May Use Nuclear Arms," *St. Louis Post Dispatch*, 21 June 1975.

18. Interview data. It is believed that DPRK assistance was critical to Iran's development of a chemical and biological weapons capability at that time.

DPRK officials view nuclear weapons as a primary means to ensure national survival because they believe that only nuclear weapons could deter a U.S. nuclear attack. These officials also might believe that under certain circumstances nuclear weapons could deter other aggression short of nuclear war. In one scenario, if the DPRK were to use chemical weapons during a conventional war with the ROK, the United States might escalate and respond with nuclear weapons. If, however, the DPRK could threaten to answer in kind to nuclear retaliation, the United States would be less inclined to use nuclear weapons in response to the DPRK's first use of chemical weapons on the Korean peninsula.

In the early 1990s, concerns that the DPRK was nearing the nuclear weapons threshold precipitated an international crisis with the United States. President Bill Clinton declared in July 1993, "It is pointless for them [the DPRK] to try to develop nuclear weapons because if they ever use them, it would mean the end of their country."[19] Four months later, Clinton stated that "North Korea cannot be allowed to develop a nuclear bomb."[20] By 1994, U.S. Defense Department officials estimated that the DPRK might possess one or two nuclear weapons.[21]

The October 1994 signing of the Agreed Framework between the United States and the DPRK occurred just as the DPRK had built or was about to build nuclear weapons. This agreement resulted in the suspension or severe curtailment of plutonium production.[22] There is reason to believe, however, that it has not led to the suspension of the entire nuclear weapons program. Although the agreement gave DPRK leaders a diplomatic victory, they might have lost a significant deterrent to future U.S. nuclear threats and an expanded American military presence on the Korean peninsula. The Agreed Framework therefore has forced the DPRK to rely more heavily on its chemical, biological, and ballistic missile programs for deterrence.[23]

19. Ruth Marcus, "Clinton Threatens Annihilation If N. Korea Uses Nuclear Arms," *Washington Post*, 12 July 1993; Helen Thomas, "Clinton Issues Strong Warning to North Korea," United Press International, 11 July 1993.

20. "Clinton-TV Text," Associated Press, 7 November 1993.

21. Office of Naval Intelligence, *DNI Posture Statement*, Washington, D.C., 1994; Barbara Starr, "No Dongs May Soon Be Nuclear, Warns USN," *Jane's Defense Weekly*, 18 June 1994, 1; "U.S. Pentagon Comments on North Korea," United Press International, 3 April 1994.

22. Department of State, "Agreed Framework between the United States of America and the Democratic People's Republic of Korea," Washington, D.C.: U.S. Government Printing Office, 26 October 1994; "More Reports on U.S.-DPRK Accord in Geneva," *Yonhap*, 21 October 1994, quoted in FBIS-EAS-94–205, 21 October 1994.

23. Interview data; Cmdr. Scott Shuman, U.S. Navy, "Countering the Korean Nuclear Threat," U.S. Naval Institute, *Proceedings*, July 1994, 63–64; Paul Bracken, *North Korea: Warning and Assessment*, testimony prepared for U.S. House of Representatives Armed Services Committee, Hearing on the Situation on the Korean Peninsula, 103d Congress, Second Session, 24 March 1994.

Joseph S. Bermudez Jr.

Chemical weapons apparently are seen as operational-level weapons, whereas biological weapons are seen as strategic-level weapons with limited utility. Four events shaped this perception: Operation Desert Storm; the United States–DPRK Agreed Framework; the 1995 Aum Shinrikyo cult sarin attack on the Tokyo subways; and the death of Kim Il-song and the resulting transition of power in the DPRK leadership. The KPA Institute for Military Sciences and the Strategy Research Institute conducted extensive "lessons learned" studies of Operation Desert Storm and concluded that the threat of chemical weapons, especially when used in conjunction with ballistic missiles, can have a significant effect on how the United States conducts military operations. Members of the institute apparently also have concluded that the remarkable sensitivity of the Japanese population to the Aum Shinrikyo cult sarin attack has increased the deterrent value of the DPRK chemical arsenal.[24]

The DPRK continued its ballistic missile programs during the early 1990s. The No-dong 1 became operational in 1993, and development began on two new ballistic missile systems: the Taep'o-dong 1 and Taep'o-dong 2, with estimated ranges of 2,500 kilometers and 6,000 kilometers respectively. The Taep'o-dong 1 missile threatens almost all U.S. facilities (e.g., Guam) in East Asia and the Taep'o-dong 2 has the potential to strike directly at the United States. If armed with a nuclear warhead, it will provide the DPRK with what it has long sought: a way to inflict significant societal damage on the United States at a level comparable to the destruction suffered by the DPRK during the Fatherland Liberation War. The 1998 launch of the three-stage Taep'o-dong 1 SLV signals the future strength of North Korea's missile threat.

U.S. deterrent threats have contributed to the maintenance of peace on the Korean peninsula, but they also have encouraged DPRK leaders to believe that they must possess nuclear, chemical, and biological weapons to counter U.S. nuclear threats.[25] The 1994 statements by Kang Myong Do, a defector and son-in-law of then DPRK prime minister Kang Song-san, provide insight into this conviction: "North Korea's nuclear development is not intended as a bargaining chip as seen by the Western world, but for the maintenance of its system under the circumstances in which it is faced with economic difficulties and a situation following the collapse of Eastern Europe. . . . There is a firm belief that the only way to sustain the Kim Chong-il system is to have nuclear capabilities."[26] Kim Chong-il, Kim Il-song's son

24. Interview data.

25. Paul Shin, "Korea-Defection," Associated Press, 13 September 1991.

26. "North Korean Defectors 27 July News Conference," *Choson Ilbo*, 28 July 1994, 3–4, quoted in FBIS-EAS-94-145, 28 July 1994, 59–63; James Sterngold, "Defector Says North Korea Has 5 A-Bombs and May Make More," *New York Times*, 28 July 1994, A7.

and successor, has maintained this line of thought. According to defectors, he believes that if the KPA is weak, the state's survival will be in jeopardy and that "only when our military force is strong, can we take the initiative in a contact or dialogue with the United States or South Korea."[27]

CHEMICAL, BIOLOGICAL, AND NUCLEAR WEAPONS CAPABILITIES

The DPRK can employ a variety of chemical and biological weapons throughout the Korean peninsula. It also possesses the ability to use these weapons worldwide using unconventional delivery methods. The 8 to 13 kilograms of weapons-grade plutonium that the DPRK is estimated to have extracted before signing the 1994 Agreed Framework could be enough for one to three nuclear weapons. The DPRK could employ these weapons throughout the Korean peninsula and possibly against Japan.

Chemical agents reported to be in the KPA inventory include adamsite (DM), chloroacetophenone (CN), chlorobenzyliidene malononitrile (CS), hydrogen cyanide (AC), mustard family (H or HD), phosgene (CG and CX), sarin (GB), soman (GD), tabun (GA), and V-agents (VM and VX). Because of North Korea's limited ability to produce or acquire certain precursors, the KPA chemical program is based primarily on mustard, sarin, and the V-agents. The DPRK has an annual chemical agent production potential of 4,500 tons in peacetime and 12,000 tons in wartime. Current estimates suggest that it possesses a stockpile of 2,500 to 5,000 tons of chemical agents.[28]

Defensive biological warfare has received considerable attention in the DPRK since the Fatherland Liberation War. Offensive biological warfare, however, has not received similar emphasis, probably because the DPRK has a limited biotechnology capability and realizes that once such weapons are employed, control over them on the Korean peninsula is problematic. The KPA also calculates that biological weapons can potentially be more detrimental to the KPA than to the ROK or United States because of the DPRK's limited biomedical capabilities. DPRK biological weapons research has focused on several strains of bacteria: anthrax (*Bacillus anthracis*), botulism (*Clostridium botulinum*), cholera (*Vibrio cholera 01*), hemorrhagic fever (probably the Korean strain), plague (*Yersinia pestis*), smallpox (*Variola*), ty-

---

27. "Defector to ROK on Kim Chong-il's Control of DPRK Military," *Win*, June 1996, 161–67, quoted in FBIS-EAS-96–197.

28. Interview data; Joseph S. Bermudez Jr., "Inside North Korea's CW Infrastructure," *Jane's Intelligence Review* 8 (August 1996): 378–82; "Military Estimates DPRK Chemical Arms Stocks," *Seoul Sinmun*, 15 April 1995, cited in FBIS-EAS-95–073; and "North Said to Own 1,000 Tons of Chemical Weapons," *Yonhap*, 21 March 1995, cited in FBIS-EAS-95–054.IIR 1 771 0085 86 [Declassified].

Joseph S. Bermudez Jr.

phoid (*Salmonella typhi*), and yellow fever. There is no indication that the DPRK uses genetic engineering or advanced biotechnology to develop these bacteria. It would be prudent to assume that the DPRK possesses a stockpile of biological weapons.[29]

The DPRK now possesses all the requisite technologies, personnel, and infrastructure to produce nuclear weapons comparable to at least first-generation U.S. nuclear weapons.[30] Estimates of the DPRK nuclear weapons inventory are based on its likely weapons design technology and the quantity of weapons-grade plutonium it possesses. The U.S. Department of Energy reported in January 1994 that depending on the technology used, as little as 4 kilograms of plutonium would be sufficient to produce a nuclear weapon.[31] With 8 to 13 kilograms of weapons-grade plutonium, the DPRK could have one to three nuclear weapons. If the fuel from the May–June 1994 refueling of the 5-MW(e) reactor is reprocessed, it will provide enough plutonium to manufacture four to five additional nuclear weapons.[32] Based on KPA doctrine and operations, availability of delivery systems, and availability of fissile material, the KPA probably planned to make ten to twenty nuclear weapons in the 30- to 60-kiloton range by the year 2000, for use as an operational force, with a small reserve.[33]

DPRK leaders face many technical and strategic trade-offs in developing a nuclear weapons inventory. One trade-off relates to the amount of fissile material available. DPRK officials must decide whether to develop a few large-yield weapons or more numerous lower-yield weapons. This trade-

29. Interview data; Office of the Secretary of Defense, *Proliferation: Threat and Response* (Washington, D.C.: U.S. Government Printing Office, 1997), 4–8; "Status of Public Health—Democratic People's Republic of Korea, April 1997," *Morbidity and Mortality Weekly Report* 46 (20 June 1997): 561; "North Korea Capable of Fighting War Single-Handedly for 3–4 Months," *Seoul Sinmun*, 30 December 1998, 22–23; John H. Cushman Jr., "U.S. Cites Increase in Biological Arms," *New York Times*, 4 May 1988, A9.

30. Interview data; Office of the Secretary of Defense, *Proliferation;* Joseph S. Bermudez Jr., "Military-Technical Observations of the DPRK Nuclear Program," Center for National and Strategic Studies, Los Alamos National Laboratory, Los Alamos, New Mexico, 1994; U.S. Congress, Office of Technology Assessment, *Technologies Underlying Weapons of Mass Destruction*, OTA-BP-ISC-115 (Washington, D.C.: U.S. Government Printing Office, 1993).

31. U.S. Government Accounting Office, *Nuclear Nonproliferation: Implications of the U.S./North Korean Agreement on Nuclear Issues*, GAO/RCED/NSIAD-97-8, October 1996, 3.

32. Interview data; U.S. Government Accounting Office, *Nuclear Nonproliferation: Implementation of the U.S./North Korean Agreement on Nuclear Issues*, GAO/RCED/NSIAD-97–165, June 1997; U.S. Government Accounting Office, *Nuclear Nonproliferation: Implications, Treaty on Nonproliferation of Nuclear Weapons, Problems of Extension* (Moscow: Russian Federation Foreign Intelligence Service, 1995), 1–73, cited in JPRS-TAC-95–009-L; David Albright, "North Korean Plutonium Production," Institute for Science and International Security (ISIS), Washington, D.C., 24 June 1994.

33. Interview data. These figures are similar to those found in statements by the DPRK defector Kang Myong Do, "North Korean Defectors," 3–4; Sterngold, "Defector Says North Korea Has 5 A-Bombs," A7.

off is exacerbated by the fact that the accuracy of their ballistic missiles is relatively poor, requiring larger warheads for each missile.

DPRK nuclear weapons designers probably have focused on three basic areas: a rudimentary nuclear explosive device; a free-fall aircraft-deliverable weapon; and a ballistic missile warhead. A workable nuclear warhead for the No-dong 1 or Taep'o dong 1–2 will require significant design sophistication. Until this is achieved, the DPRK will depend on aircraft or unconventional means to deliver nuclear weapons.

The DPRK could deliver nuclear, biological, or chemical weapons with artillery, rocket artillery, aircraft, cruise missiles and unmanned aerial vehicles, ballistic missiles, and unconventional systems. The primary tactical means to deliver chemical and biological weapons would be rocket artillery and aircraft.[34] At the strategic level, ballistic missiles and unconventional systems would be used. The DPRK's increasing ability to produce cruise missiles and unmanned aerial vehicles provides an additional way to deliver small quantities of chemical or biological weapons.[35] Ballistic missiles are North Korea's system of choice for the strategic delivery of nuclear weapons.[36]

The DPRK possesses one of the world's largest special operations forces and has demonstrated its ability to employ small units throughout the world by using its merchant fleet as a covert means of transportation. In regional contingencies, the DPRK could employ its fleet of patrol, coastal, and midget submarines to land special operations personnel and to release chemical or biological agents. Another unconventional mode of delivery for biological and chemical weapons is by balloon, a method the DPRK has used for over twenty years to disseminate propaganda to the ROK and Japan. Given these activities, the DPRK probably has explored the use of unconventional methods and its special operations forces to deliver unconventional weapons.[37]

Strategic Thought

The DPRK views its unconventional arsenal primarily as a means of deterrence, believing that as long as it is able to "inflict pain" on the United States, the ROK, and Japan, the United States will be deterred from attacking the

34. Interview data; ROK Ministry of National Defense, *Defense White Paper*, various editions from 1993 to present; Randy Jolly, "PACAF Power," *World Airpower Journal* 14 (Autumn/Fall 1993): 138–47; John Lake, "Mikoyan MiG-23/27 'Flogger' " *World Airpower Journal* 8 (Spring 1992): 40–85; John Lake, "Mikoyan MiG-29 'Fulcrum' " *World Airpower Journal* 4 (Winter 1990/91): 44–91.

35. Interview data.

36. Ibid.

37. *North Korean Special Forces—2nd Edition*; Joseph S. Bermudez Jr., *Terrorism: The North Korean Connection* (New York: Taylor and Francis, 1990), 74–76, 139–41.

DPRK. In 1998 Hwang Chang-yop, the most senior DPRK official ever to defect, described the way the DPRK might use nuclear weapons: "For one thing, they will use them [nuclear weapons] if South Korea starts a war. For another, they intend to devastate Japan to prevent the United States from participating. Would it still participate, even after Japan is devastated? That is how they think."[38]

By implication, the greater North Korea's chemical, biological, and nuclear capabilities and the farther it can project them (i.e., by building long-range ballistic missiles or by using unconventional means of delivery), the greater their deterrent value. In both private and public conversations, DPRK officials express apprehension about the U.S. nuclear threat. They acknowledge that they could not win a nuclear war with the United States. They also reluctantly admit that they probably could not survive a high-intensity conventional war with the United States. They are quick to point out, however, that any war between the United States and the DPRK would be "extremely bloody." They also state that they are willing to fight to the end and that "the United States might win such a war, killing half our people, but it would not win the minds of the people."[39] Because they cannot win a war against the United States and the ROK, DPRK officials have developed a strategy to inflict as much pain as possible on the United States and its allies.

During the 1990s, DPRK leaders also developed a secondary view of their unconventional arsenal: using chemical weapons against U.S. facilities within the ROK, while maintaining the ability to strike at Japan, would provide significant military benefits and not incur a U.S. nuclear response. Consequently, the KPA has developed a policy of operational "first use" of chemical weapons against strategic targets (e.g., airfields, command and control centers, ports, missile batteries) in the ROK at the onset of any DPRK-initiated conflict on the Korean peninsula. This first-use chemical doctrine is part of a larger KPA grand strategy that calls for a "one-blow, nonstop" attack to capture the entire Korean peninsula before the United States and the world can react. North Korean leaders believe that several developments suggest that the time has arrived for this first-use strategy: the world has been desensitized by the use of chemical weapons in the Middle East, and the United States cannot respond in kind.

Command and Control

At first glance, North Korea's command and control system for nuclear, biological, and chemical weapons appears cumbersome and conflict-prone

38. "Defector Hwang Chang-yop Interviewed," *Sindong-A*, July 1998, 328–345, quoted in FBIS-EAS-98-191.
39. Wording of DPRK officials in interviews with author.

because of overlapping areas of responsibility among the KWP, government, and the Ministry of People's Armed Forces. The command and control system is, however, rudimentary.[40] The reason for this paradox is the nature of the DPRK hierarchy, in which a single person can hold numerous high-ranking positions in the KWP, MPAF, and the government. The DPRK's command and control of nuclear, biological, and chemical weapons is more familial than technical or professional. This familial structure is reinforced by the promotion system in the MPAF: all promotions must be approved by the KWP and MPAF, while those at brigade level and above must also be approved by Kim Chong-il. This proclivity for tight centralized control makes it unlikely that DPRK leaders have delegated wide-ranging operational launch authority to subordinates. The possible exception to this rule might be a scenario in which local commanders have been given specific wartime instructions to use chemical, biological, or nuclear weapons under certain conditions (e.g., a nuclear attack on the DPRK, loss of command authority for a specified period of time, or confirmed American or South Korean use of chemical weapons). Since chemical weapons are stored at army and corps-level depots, MPAF rules of engagement might allow corps commanders to use chemical weapons without prior permission from the national command authority under specific conditions (e.g., if there is an unexplained loss of communication with the national command authority during a national emergency).

Decision-Making Process

There is a common misperception that during his more than forty years as leader of the DPRK, Kim Il-song ruled with absolute control and was virtually impervious to the desires and concerns of his government or people. Although he certainly ran the show, Kim shared power with a small, tightly knit circle of people, most of whom shared a common history reaching back to the days of the "anti-Japanese partisan struggle" during the 1930s and 1940s.[41] This group functions as a consensus-building and filtering mechanism in the DPRK leadership, the effectiveness of which has varied over time. Neither Kim Chong-il nor Kim Il-song could use nuclear, chemical, or biological weapons, initiate a war or pursue a policy that directly threatened national survival without first gaining the consensus of this coterie.

40. Interview data; Joseph S. Bermudez Jr., "North Korea's Nuclear Infrastructure," *Jane's Intelligence Review* 6 (February 1994): 74–79. This is a simplified explanation of the DPRK nuclear, biological, and chemical weapons chain of command, several subordinate organizations of which are not mentioned.

41. The average age of a DPRK vice president is seventy-eight, politburo member seventy-five, and military leader seventy-two.

Joseph S. Bermudez Jr.

Since the death of Kim Il-song in July 1994, a series of dramatic changes has occurred in the DPRK leadership. Most of these changes were initiated by Kim Chong-il as he consolidated his power. Kim has sought the support of the KPA by promoting 664 generals and granting the military greater privileges. It remains to be seen how this transition, which is similar to the partisan generals period of the 1960s, will affect North Korean command and control procedures. The naval skirmishes in the Yellow Sea in July 1999 and the threat of a Taep'o-dong missile test in August 1999, however, suggest that military leaders are exerting more influence over military and foreign affairs, which itself increases the possibility that miscalculation or misunderstanding could lead to an accidental war. [42]

Like the NBC command and control structure, the decision-making process for the employment of unconventional weapons appears to be rudimentary, familial, and with few internal checks and balances. This process proceeds through four event-driven phases. An event, or series of events, occurs and is analyzed by the appropriate departments of the KWP Central Committee and the National Defense Commission. These analyses then are passed to the leadership with a recommendation. If a consensus is reached that unconventional weapons are to be used, an order will be issued to the MPAF and the State Security Department. In the case of nuclear or biological weapons or special warheads for ballistic missiles, the MPAF Security Command would coordinate with the State Security Department to provide the weapons.[43] Under extreme conditions, however, the familial instincts of the DPRK inner circle could always lead them to take matters into their own hands and give the order to use unconventional weapons without outside consultation.

DPRK Targeting Strategy

The DPRK probably would use chemical weapons under three circumstances: a United States/ROK attack against the DPRK; a DPRK decision to launch a war of reunification; or if DPRK leaders believe that their demise is imminent. DPRK leaders view chemical weapons as operational assets and plan to use them against the following target categories: U.S. facilities and personnel in South Korea, ROK cities and military facilities, U.S. military facilities in Japan and East Asia, Japan, and U.S. assets worldwide. Primary

42. Interview data; Shuman, "Countering the Korean Nuclear Threat," 63–64; Bracken, *North Korea;* Paul Bracken, "Nuclear Weapons and State Survival in North Korea," *Survival,* 35 (Autumn 1993): 137–53.
43. Whether an actual military order would need to be issued to the MPAF and the State Security Department is debatable because the heads of these two ministries are members of the decision-making group.

targets for chemical strikes against U.S./ROK military facilities would include front-line troops, Chinhae Navy Base, Kunsan Air Base, Osan Air Base, Inch'on, Pusan, and Yongsan. Attacks on front-line troops would be conducted primarily by rocket artillery and aircraft. Targets deeper within the ROK would be reached using aircraft and Hwasong missiles. Chemical weapon attacks against U.S. bases in Japan and East Asia (e.g., Guam) most likely would be carried out with No-dong 1 or Taep'o-dong ballistic missiles.[44] Attacks against U.S. assets worldwide would require unconventional methods of delivery.

While DPRK leaders view biological weapons as strategic assets, they probably are concerned about the unpredictable nature of these weapons and the DPRK's own vulnerability to any disease unleashed on the Korean peninsula. Likely biological weapons targets would therefore be limited by the need to inflict the maximum amount of emotional and political destruction or disruption on the United States, the ROK, and Japan. If the DPRK decided to use biological weapons, it probably would do so several days or weeks in advance of a conventional military attack, to degrade critical U.S./ROK personnel (e.g., pilots, senior officers), overload U.S./ROK medical systems, and spread panic among the civilian population. It also could use biological weapons as a terror weapon, or as a weapon of last resort, against the Japanese or U.S. mainlands. The DPRK likely would use its special operations forces to deliver biological weapons. It is also assumed that the DPRK would prefer to employ such weapons on foreign soil rather than on the Korean peninsula. In the event of a U.S./ROK invasion, however, there is little doubt that the DPRK also would use them on its own soil.

While the DPRK is unlikely to use nuclear weapons except in the direst situations, there are several scenarios that could lead to nuclear threats or to the unconsidered use of nuclear weapons. An example of such a scenario would be a U.S./ROK Osirak-type raid on the DPRK nuclear infrastructure. In the past, both sides have perceived the likelihood of such a raid in opposite terms. American leaders viewed it as a low priority, while the DPRK leadership considered a preventive strike to be a likely U.S. response to the discovery of the DPRK's nuclear infrastructure.[45] If such a raid were to occur, the DPRK would be likely to respond with both conventional ballistic missile attacks against ROK nuclear facilities and limited attacks along the demilitarized zone. The risk of a DPRK nuclear response in this

---

44. "Says Long-Range Missile Bases Built," KBS-1, 24 August 1993, cited in FBIS-EAS-93–162, 24 August 1993, 23; "N. Korea Ready to Attack U.S. Bases—Defector," Reuters, 24 August 1993.

45. "U.S. Pentagon Comments on North Korea," United Press International, 3 April 1994; Jim Abrams, "Korea-Aspin," Associated Press, 13 December 1993.

situation is high, especially following any military or diplomatic misstep or misperception that exacerbates the crisis.

If the DPRK conducts an Indian/Pakistani–style nuclear test during a period of elevated tensions, this should be viewed as a sign of extreme danger. A test might indicate that DPRK leaders believe they are being backed into a corner and are about to employ nuclear weapons. Ultimately, if the DPRK is able to produce an inventory of ten to twenty nuclear weapons, it is likely to use them first on the battlefield and then follow approximately the same targeting strategy described for its chemical and biological weapons. Such attacks would require approximately seven to ten nuclear warheads in the 30- to 60-kiloton range. Nuclear strikes against U.S. bases in Japan and East Asia probably would be carried out by No-dong 1 or Taep'o dong 1–2 ballistic missiles and require an additional three to seven nuclear warheads. Attacks against U.S. assets worldwide, at the present time, would call for unconventional means of delivery.

The DPRK might use nuclear or biological weapons in an asynchronous manner, employing a different strategic time frame than would other countries.[46] In most countries, policymakers believe that retaliation should quickly follow an attack. DPRK leaders, however, could plan to retaliate weeks, or even months, after an initial attack on their territory. An asynchronous plan of attack provides the advantages of surprise and an opportunity to deliver covertly nuclear or biological attacks, even following the defeat of DPRK forces on the battlefield. This delayed attack option would reduce incentives to predelegate authority to field commanders to use nuclear or biological weapons in the face of an imminent or unfolding attack.

SURVIVABILITY AND READINESS

The survivability of North Korea's unconventional arsenal is enhanced by the closed and secretive nature of DPRK society and the policy of Four Military Lines, which calls for selectively "hardening" segments of the military and industrial infrastructure. Both conditions have hampered the collection of intelligence on the status and locations of the DPRK programs and forces. Even when they are identified, secrecy and hardening make them difficult to neutralize.

The survivability and readiness of DPRK chemical, biological, and potential nuclear forces are facilitated by the fact that these forces are deployed in fortified bunker complexes throughout the country and typically near the

46. Testimony by Defense Intelligence Agency director General Patrick M. Hughes, "Global Threats and Challenges: The Decades Ahead," Statement for U.S. Senate, Select Committee on Intelligence, 28 January 1998.

systems that will deliver them. The DPRK also is developing mobile missile systems, including transporter-erector-launchers and even mobile-erector-launchers. DPRK leaders have created a ballistic missile force that is at least twice the size of the one that Iraq possessed during Operation Desert Storm. They recognize that these actions pose a significant targeting problem for the United States, especially if their missiles are moved among fortified locations. To launch an attack, a TEL or MEL would move out of its bunker, travel a short distance to a presurveyed launch site, launch, and then return to a bunker (not necessarily the one it started from).

Despite a high degree of survivability, several factors call into question the readiness of DPRK unconventional weapons. Foremost among these are quality control and the financial resources of both the production program and the KPA. To ensure the operational readiness of ballistic missiles, the missiles have to be manufactured to consistent standards and then maintained. According to anecdotal information, ballistic missile workmanship and quality control in the DPRK are uneven. Proper maintenance of ballistic missiles requires training and supplies, both of which are in short supply in the KPA. The storage of missile systems in non-climate-controlled tunnels and bunkers also increases maintenance requirements. Similar questions concerning quality control and maintenance exist in the chemical and biological weapons programs. By contrast, because of their critical importance, it is probable that the quality control and operational readiness of North Korean nuclear weapons are as high as the existing state of the art in North Korea will allow.

Safety and Security

The DPRK is the most closed and security conscious society in the world. Through a host of overlapping organizations and security agencies, the DPRK regime maintains absolute control over all its citizens and soldiers and the information to which they have access. Therefore, nuclear, biological, and chemical weapon activities are organically secure and do not exhibit the telltale security measures apparent in Western or Third World countries (e.g., extensive multilayered barrier fences and fortified guard bunkers). In the DPRK, simple roadblocks, fences, and internal security forces are sufficient to ensure security.

There apparently is a division of responsibility for the security of unconventional weapons in the DPRK. All nuclear and biological weapons, as well as special warheads for ballistic missiles, are under the protection of the State Security Department and Political Security Bureau. Chemical weapons are under the control of the MPAF and are stored at special munitions depots down to corps, and possibly division, level. Their security is provided by KPA troops.

Joseph S. Bermudez Jr.

Given the real possibility of political collapse in the DPRK, concerns about whether the security surrounding unconventional weapons might disintegrate are well founded. If the collapse is "soft," existing unconventional weapons might be destroyed or quietly handed over to the new government. If the collapse is "hard," unconventional weapons might be used against the ROK, Japan, or the United States in a last gesture of defiance, sold abroad to a "rogue" nation, or used by renegades or criminals as bargaining chips against a new government. If instability is as likely following the demise of long dictatorships as some suggest, North Korea's unconventional weapons could endanger regional security in some very nontraditional ways.[47]

Development of Unconventional Weapons Doctrine

Since the 1960s, KPA troops have trained for defensive operations in a war in which the United States used nuclear, chemical, or biological weapons. Today, this training is relatively extensive and involves realistic exercises twice a year.

Little is known about the development of an NBC doctrine in North Korea. Such a doctrine would likely borrow from PRC and Soviet doctrine and would be modified to fit the unique requirements of the Korean peninsula. The KPA General Staff's Nuclear-Chemical Defense Bureau (which is responsible for nuclear, biological, and chemical warfare matters) is known to study U.S. nuclear warfare doctrine. These studies may have influenced the KPA's development of an offensive nuclear war doctrine. Along with the Nuclear-Chemical Defense Bureau, the Research Institute for Military Sciences and the Strategy Research Institute would play critical roles in the development of doctrine.[48]

It is unlikely that North Korean political and military leaders debate, in the Western sense of the term, offensive nuclear, biological, and chemical weapons use doctrines. It would appear that the work of the Research Institute for Military Sciences and the Strategy Research Institute, along with input from the appropriate MPAF bureaus, is accepted by the leadership.

There appears to be a dichotomy of thought in the DPRK concerning unconventional weapons. Low and middle-level military and civilian special-

47. Richard K. Betts and Samuel P. Huntington, "Dead Dictators and Rioting Mobs: Does the Demise of Authoritarian Rulers Lead to Political Instability?" *International Security* 10 (Winter 1985–1986): 112–46.
48. Interview data; "Weekly Assesses DPRK Nuclear War Preparations," *Chugan Choson* 30 June 1994, 26–28, cited in FBIS-EAS-94-126, 30 June 1994, 38; "North Missile Sites Said Along PRC Border," *Yonhap*, 8 April 1994, cited in FBIS-EAS-94-068, 8 April 1994, 33; "Says Long-Range Missile Bases Built."

ists have a realistic understanding of the military, technical, and practical aspects of employing nuclear, chemical, and biological weapons. The leadership, however, apparently attributes to these weapons far greater political, physical, and military effectiveness than is justified.[49]

Although much about the Democratic People's Republic of Korea's unconventional weapons arsenal is unknown, what is known is alarming. During the past forty-five years, the DPRK has developed such weapons with determination. It possesses the ability to use these capabilities throughout the Korean peninsula, East Asia, and, to a lesser degree, the world.

These nuclear, biological, and chemical capabilities are managed by a leadership that views such weapons as necessary for national survival. This perception has its origins in the Japanese use of chemical and biological weapons and the U.S. nuclear bombing of Japan during World War II. This perception has been further reinforced by North Korea's years of confrontation with the United States and the ROK and the lessons it has learned from various conflicts in the Third World. Although often viewed as "irrational," "illogical," or simply "crazy" by Western standards, North Korean leaders have acted in a rational manner given their experiences.

The DPRK has developed a strategic doctrine that includes the operational "first use" of chemical weapons and ballistic missiles in a war of reunification. Underlying this motivation is a KPA grand strategy calling for a "one-blow, nonstop attack" to capture the entire Korean peninsula before the United States and the world can react; a fanatical distrust of both the ROK and U.S. governments; and the belief that the ROK and the United States possess, and are willing to employ, nuclear weapons against the DPRK. Although North Korean leaders are unlikely to initiate a war using nuclear weapons, they believe the Americans and their South Korean partners are highly likely to use nuclear weapons on the Korean peninsula. U.S. officials and military leaders, by contrast, apparently believe that the North Korean regime is highly unstable and willing to do anything to preserve its deteriorating political, economic, and military position. These disparate perceptions increase the likelihood that the Korean peninsula will be the next location for the use of nuclear, chemical, or biological weapons.

49. Interview data; "Hwang's Nuke Statement—Issue with Korea and U.S.," *Choson Ilbo*, 23 April 1997; "NK Capable of Scorching Korea with Nuclear, Chemical Weapons: Hwang," *Korea Times*, 22 April 1997; "N. Korea Could Hit South with Nuclear Weapons—Report," Reuters, 22 April 1997.

[8]

Terrorist Motivations and Unconventional Weapons

JESSICA STERN

Will terrorists use weapons of mass destruction? Debate about this question tends to be conducted in extremes. Optimists suggest that terrorists "want a lot of people watching not a lot of people dead," that they prefer "patient harassment" to large-scale murder and are unlikely to turn to unconventional weapons.[1] But such optimism ignores the fact that terrorism is not a static phenomenon. Although change tends to be evolutionary rather than revolutionary, new modes of terrorism have emerged with regularity over the years. By contrast, pessimists suggest that because of the growing availability of unconventional weapons, acts of macro terror resulting in hundreds of thousands or millions of deaths are all but inevitable.[2] Proponents of this view exaggerate the threat. Using chemical, biological, or nuclear weapons to create mass casualties would require more than just having the materials or agents in hand. The terrorists would need to detonate or disseminate the weapons, which presents technical and organizational obstacles that few groups would be able to surmount.[3] And relatively few terrorists would want to kill millions of people, even if they could.

This chapter takes the middle ground in this debate, arguing that the risk of unconventional terrorism is growing. Some terrorists do want a lot of people dead or injured, and they are increasingly considering unconventional weapons with this goal in mind.[4] And some terrorists are likely to be

1. Brian Michael Jenkins, "International Terrorism: A New Mode of Conflict," in *International Terrorism and World Security*, ed. David Carlton and Carolo Schaerf (London: Croom Helm, 1975), 15. On terrorists' purported aim to harass, see Kenneth Waltz, "Waltz Responds to Sagan," in Scott D. Sagan and Kenneth Waltz, *The Spread of Nuclear Weapons: A Debate* (New York: Norton, 1995), 94–96.

2. Proponents of this new school include James Woolsey, Joseph Nye, and Richard Danzig.

3. R. Danzig and P. B. Berkowsky, "Why Should We Be Concerned about Biological Warfare?" *Journal of the American Medical Association* 278 (6 August 1997): 431–32.

attracted to high-technology weapons, not to kill large numbers but to get more people's attention. Chemical, biological, and radiological weapons evoke dread out of proportion to their lethality, making them suited for theatrical acts of violence calculated to attract attention. Attacks using unconventional weapons, however, are likely to remain uncommon. This is especially the case for attacks intended to create mass casualties, which would require a level of technological and organizational skill possessed by few terrorist groups. The pessimists are right that it makes sense to prepare for attacks resulting in mass casualties, but governments should do so with the understanding that they are buying insurance for a low-probability event. Governments should pay more attention to more likely kinds of attacks, which would kill tens or hundreds rather than millions. Such attacks could involve the use of low-technology dissemination devices to poison food, livestock, agricultural products, unprotected sources of water, enclosed areas such as buildings or subway cars, or small open areas.

Candidates for employing these weapons are found at the intersection of three subsets: terrorists who want to use the weapons despite formidable political costs, terrorists who are able to acquire or produce them, and terrorists who have the ability to deliver or disseminate them covertly. This chapter shows that the area created by the intersection of these sets is small but growing, especially for low-technology attacks such as disseminating chemical or biological agents in an enclosed space. Such attacks would not kill millions, but their effects still could be devastating.

The chapter begins by discussing the Aum Shinrikyo cult, a terrorist group that overcame the technical, organizational, and political obstacles to using unconventional weapons. Despite its substantial intellectual, financial, and technological resources, however, the cult failed to carry out the kind of macro terror attacks its leader had envisaged. Both the cult's successes and its failures are instructive. It failed to acquire nuclear weapons. It also failed to disseminate biological agents over large areas. But it succeeded in carrying out chemical attacks using crude equipment for dispersing gases. While the pessimists often describe the cult's Tokyo subway attack as a watershed event in the history of terrorism, it actually constitutes an evolutionary change from earlier terrorist attacks.

---

4. Director of Central Intelligence George Tenet warned that a growing number of groups are looking into the feasibility of using chemical, biological, and radiological weapons (Statement by Acting Director of Central Intelligence George J. Tenet before U.S. Senate, Select Committee on Intelligence, "Hearing on Current and Projected National Security Threats to the United States," 105th Congress, 1st Session, 5 February 1997). Prior to the Oklahoma City bombing, the FBI typically encountered around a dozen incidents annually involving threats, boasts, or actual attempts to acquire or use unconventional weapons. Now the FBI is handling around a hundred such cases per year (Author's interview with Robert Blitzer, FBI, 26 January 1998).

Next the chapter turns to a more general discussion of terrorists' motivations. Three theoretical approaches applied elsewhere in this book to explain state behavior—the rational actor approach, organizational theory, and the notion of strategic culture—provide insight into the kinds of terrorist groups most likely to consider the use of unconventional weapons. Some terrorists might want to use these weapons in mass-destruction mode, others might carry out low-technology attacks such as contaminating foods or pharmaceuticals, while others might use them to assassinate individuals. Technical and organizational obstacles for the various types of attacks also are explored.

HOW HAVE TERRORISTS USED UNCONVENTIONAL WEAPONS?

Terrorists, like most states, have used unconventional weapons only rarely and on a small scale. Although the available data are incomplete, the trend is clear: most terrorists use conventional weapons, not unconventional ones. From 1968 to 1980, the CIA recorded twenty-two incidents around the world in which "exotic pollutants," including chemical, biological, and radiological materials, were used. The incidents accounted for less than one-half of 1 percent of all international terrorist incidents during that period, and none of the twenty-two incidents involved weapons per se.[5] Of more than eight thousand international incidents recorded in the RAND-St. Andrews Chronology of International Terrorist Incidents, fewer than sixty involved terrorists plotting, threatening, or actually using nuclear, chemical, biological, or radiological agents.[6] Terrorists have never used nuclear devices, although Aum Shinrikyo tried to acquire them.[7]

As a rule, terrorists tend to be conservative and stick to proven tactics. Occasionally they develop new techniques or technologies, sometimes creating new norms. Until the 1960s, assassination predominated as a terrorist tactic. In the late 1960s, terrorists crossed a moral threshold: they began to launch random attacks, killing innocent people. Hostage-taking became popular by the early 1970s. Hijacking planes and attacking embassies emerged as a tactic in the late 1970s, and by the early 1980s there had been a rash of similar attacks.[8] A norm of sparing women and children began to

5. Joseph Pilat, "World Watch: Striking Back at Urban Terrorism," in *NBC Defense and Technology International* (June 1986), 18.

6. Bruce Hoffman, "Viewpoint: Terrorism and WMD: Some Preliminary Hypotheses," *Nonproliferation Review* 4 (Spring 1997): 45–52.

7. John Deutch, Statement for the Record before the Permanent Subcommittee on Investigations of the Senate Committee on Governmental Affairs, 20 March 1996, 7.

8. I thank Martha Crenshaw for this insight. For more detail, see Manus I. Midlarsky, Martha Crenshaw, and Fumihiko Yoshida, "Why Violence Spreads: The Contagion of International Terrorism," *International Studies Quarterly* 24 (June, 1980): 262–98; "Rejoinder to 'Observations on Why Violence Spreads,'" ibid., 306–10.

erode in the mid-1980s. For example, in 1989 the Provisional Irish Republic Army (PIRA) assassinated the German wife of a British soldier. In that same year, PIRA murdered a British soldier and his child.[9] In 1984, the Rajneeshee cult poisoned salad bars in Oregon, making 750 people ill. Their goal was to influence local elections. In 1985, Sikh terrorists began blowing up airplanes, killing 363 people on an Air India jet. The ad hoc group of terrorists responsible for the World Trade Center bombing broke through other barriers. They attacked Americans inside the United States, which foreign terrorist groups had rarely tried before. They were not trying to influence policy but to exact revenge by killing 250,000 Americans—far more victims than had ever been targeted before.[10]

Aum Shinrikyo

The Aum Shinrikyo cult broke another taboo: using or attempting to use or acquire nuclear, chemical, and biological weapons to kill large numbers of people. No political or moral constraints held the cult back. It was able to produce chemical weapons, although the sarin used in the Tokyo attack was made in haste and was impure. The Tokyo subway attack would have been far more deadly had the cult used a purer form of sarin and a more sophisticated dissemination device. It was not able to meet the difficult challenge of disseminating biological agents effectively, a constraint likely to hold many groups back if the goal is to create mass casualties. Nor did the cult succeed in acquiring nuclear weapons.

Asahara's Motivations.   Shoko Asahara, the leader of the cult, was born on the southern Japanese island of Kyushu. Like many Japanese in the 1980s, Asahara developed an interest in spirituality. He traveled to India, where he perfected his meditation technique, learning, he asserted, to levitate. He also claimed to have learned to pass unencumbered through solid walls, to intuit people's thoughts, and to chart their past lives.

In 1984, Asahara formed a company called Aum, Inc. The company produced health drinks and ran yoga schools. In 1986, *Twilight Zone,* a Japanese new age journal, ran pictures of Asahara apparently suspended in midair in the lotus posture. Attendance at his yoga schools rose, and with the profits Asahara was able to open schools throughout Japan.

Soon afterward Asahara claimed to have heard a message from God while meditating, telling him that he had been chosen to lead God's army.

9. U.S. Department of State, *Patterns of Global Terrorism, 1989* (Washington, D.C.: U.S. Government Printing Office, 1990), 51–52.

10. Secret Service agent Brian Parr testified at Ramzi Yousef's hearing that Yousef confessed he intended to kill 250,000 Americans. See Gail Appleson, "Prosecutor: Yousef Aimed to Kill Thousands," Reuters, 2 November 1997.

At about the same time Asahara met a historian who predicted that Armageddon would come by the year 2000. Only a small group would survive, the historian told Asahara, and the leader of that group would emerge in Japan. Asahara put two and two together: he was to be the leader of that group. Asahara began planning for the apocalypse. He changed the name of his company to Aum Shinrikyo (Aum Supreme Truth) and expanded his empire throughout the globe.[11]

Asahara chose Shiva the Destroyer as the principal deity for Aum Supreme Truth; he also emphasized the Judeo-Christian notion of Armageddon. At a seminar in 1987, Asahara made his first prediction: between 1999 and 2003 nuclear war would break out. There were fewer than fifteen years to prepare, Asahara warned. Nuclear war could be averted, but only if Aum opened a branch in every country on earth. Those who were spiritually enlightened—the members of the Aum cult—would survive even a nuclear holocaust.

Capital, Labor, and Technology. As Asahara's spiritual prowess grew, he found new ways to assist in his students' spiritual development while expanding revenues. Students were encouraged to cut off all ties with the outside world and to hand over all their assets as a way to improve their spiritual development. He opened a compound near Mount Fuji, which would ultimately include a hospital and laboratories where research on unconventional weapons would be carried out. Over time, the cult became rich, with $1.4 billion in assets. This level of resources could have funded a national nuclear effort: for example, South Africa's quest to obtain a nuclear weapon cost that government some $200 million.

Many of those attracted to Asahara's promise of spiritual enlightenment were scientists, medical doctors, and engineers from Japan's top schools. One was Seiichi Endo, who had been trained at Kyoto University and was working at the university's Viral Research Center. Another was Hideo Murai, an astrophysicist who became Asahara's "engineer of the apocalypse."[12] A surprising number of highly educated young people were enthralled by Aum's dramatic claims to supernatural power, its vision of an apocalyptic future, and its esoteric spiritualism.[13]

Asahara used Russia as a supermarket for acquiring military equipment and training. He also sought recruits among Russia's scientific elite. Minister of Defense Pavel Grachev apparently paved the way for three groups of

11. David E. Kaplan and Andrew Marshall, *The Cult at the End of the World* (New York: Crown, 1996).
12. Ibid., 28.
13. Ibid.

Aum Shinrikyo cult members each to spend three days with military units in the Taman and Kantemirov Divisions, where they were trained to use military equipment for a fee.[14] The cult allegedly received substantial assistance from Oleg Lobov, then head of President Boris Yeltsin's Security Council.[15]

The Decision to Use Unconventional Weapons. Asahara was convinced that the CIA planned to use unconventional weapons against Japan. He believed that the apocalypse would come sometime in the 1990s and that the cult would need every available weapon to survive. He was sure that he had been selected to rule the superhuman race that would survive Armageddon, and he wanted to hasten the process by instigating a war between Japan and the United States. Japanese authorities also were closing in on the cult, and Asahara planned to use chemical and biological agents as an assassination tool.[16] Asahara further believed that high technology would give him an edge over aliens, to whom he attributed "levels of consciousness" higher than that of human beings.[17]

Asahara put his scientists to work on developing high-technology weapons, repeatedly sending his deputy to Russia to purchase weapons and scientific assistance. The cult bought a Russian Mi-17 combat helicopter, allegedly for disseminating chemical or biological agents over populated areas.[18] The group also was actively trying to purchase Russian nuclear warheads, according to the CIA.[19]

These efforts soon led to attempts to use the weapons. Asahara directed a series of attacks with biological agents. In April 1990, cult members carried out attacks against the Japanese Diet, the Imperial Palace, American naval bases at Yokosuka and Yokohama, and elsewhere in the city of Tokyo using three trucks outfitted to spray botulinum toxin. No botulinum was detected during these attacks, and no one was reported to have become ill. In July 1993 the cult tried to disseminate anthrax at several sites, including areas near the Imperial Palace and the Diet. Once again, there was no observable effect.[20]

14. "Prosecutors Investigate Lobov's Links to Religious Sect," FBIS-SOV-97-144, 24 May 1997, translated from Moscow Interfax; "Lobov Faces Questions over Investigation of Japanese Sect," FBIS-SV-97-084, 25 April 1997, translated from Moscow Interfax.
15. "Prosecutors Investigate Lobov's Links."
16. Staff Report, U.S. Senate, *Hearings on Global Proliferation of Weapons of Mass Destruction,* Permanent Subcommittee on Investigations, 104th Congress, 1st Session, 1 November 1995; Kaplan and Marshall, *Cult.*
17. Kaplan and Marshall, *Cult,* 66.
18. Staff Report, U.S. Senate, *Hearings on Global Proliferation.*
19. John Deutch, Statement for the Record.
20. William Broad, "How Japan Germ Terror Alerted World," *New York Times,* 26 May 1998.

Cult members also tried spreading anthrax from the roof of their headquarters building. This technique also failed, but it created a terrible smell. It smelled like burning flesh, one resident told the press. When inspectors went to the Aum building, they were told that the smell was from a mix of soybean oil and perfume—Chanel Number 5—which the cult was burning to purify the building.[21]

Aum had intended to kill hundreds or even thousands of people in these biological attacks, but all of them failed because the strain grown by the scientists was nonlethal, the dissemination technique failed, or both. The relative ease of growing biological agents has led some experts to conclude that biological weapons are easy to make. But a terrorist would have to overcome several hurdles: acquiring the appropriate strain, growing it, and disseminating it as a respirable aerosol. Cultures can be acquired from a variety of sources, including nature and, reportedly, former Soviet laboratories trying to make ends meet.[22] If a terrorist group managed to acquire the right strain, replicating it would be the easiest step. But disseminating it over large open areas—the only way to carry out macro terror attacks using biological agents—would present formidable challenges. Microorganisms can be disseminated in two forms: as liquid slurries or as dry powders. Producing liquid slurries is relatively easy, but disseminating but them as respirable infectious aerosols is not. Dry powders can be disseminated more easily. But high-quality powders require development involving skilled personnel and sophisticated equipment unlikely to be available to many terrorist groups. Disseminating biological agents inside an enclosed space would be easier to accomplish, although in most cases the number of people exposed to the agent would be limited.

Chemical terrorism, by contrast, is far easier to carry out, largely because chemical agents are volatile (meaning that some of the agent will spontaneously form a poisonous gas). Not surprisingly, the cult was more successful in its attempts to use chemical agents. Aum purchased property in the resort town of Matsumoto to establish a branch office there. But when the original owner of the land learned the true identity of the purchaser, he tried to invalidate the sale. Soon after Asahara's lawyer informed him that the three judges apparently were preparing to rule against him, Asahara decided to murder the judges with poison gas. The three judges survived the attack when the wind changed direction, but the poison spread over the

21. Kaplan and Marshall, *Cult*, 96; CIA, "The Chemical, Biological and Radiological Terrorist Threat from Non-State Actors," paper presented at Aspen Strategy Group conference "The Proliferation Threat of Weapons of Mass Destruction and U.S. Security Interests," Aspen, Colorado, 10–15 August 1996.
22. Al Jenter, "Elements Loyal to Bin Laden Acquire Biological Agents 'Through the Mail,' " *Jane's Intelligence Review* 11 (August 1999), 5.

town. By the morning after the attack, seven people had died, and two hundred were ill.[23] Dogs lay dead in the streets, and fish floated dead in a nearby pond. Doctors investigating the incident noted that victims had markedly reduced levels of acetylcholinesterase (an enzyme necessary for proper functioning of the nervous system), a sign that the victims had been exposed to toxic organophosphate-based insecticides or nerve agents. But even after traces of sarin, a nerve agent, were found in the pond, authorities did not suspect terrorism. No terrorist group had claimed responsibility, and the idea that terrorists could be responsible for such a heinous crime seemed too far-fetched. Instead, authorities hypothesized that a farmer who had been making his own pesticides had made sarin accidentally.[24]

Nine months later, on 20 March 1995, the cult struck again. By this time the police were closing in on the group, and cult scientists had to work fast. Asahara believed that an attack on the Tokyo subway would divert attention away from the cult's facilities, which the police were planning to raid.[25] The terrorists placed hastily made poison-filled pouches on five subway cars and then punctured the pouches with umbrellas specially fitted with needles in their tips.[26] Sarin is volatile; soon after the pouches had been punctured, poisonous fumes filled the cars. Despite the hastily planned, crude technique, twelve people died in the incident, and several hundred were injured. Although more than five thousand people went to hospitals after the incident, a large fraction of them apparently were traumatized but physically unharmed.[27] Two subsequent attacks failed, in part because police were on the lookout for suspicious packages. On 5 May 1995, cult members left bags—one containing sodium cyanide and the other sulfuric acid—in the Shinjuku station in Tokyo, with the intention of disseminating cyanide gas in the station. And on 4 July 1995, similar improvised chemical devices were found in rest rooms in four stations.[28]

23. A total of six hundred eventually became ill. See John F. Quinn, "Terrorism Comes to Tokyo: The Aum Shinri Kyo Incident," paper presented at the Association of Former Intelligence Officers, 1996 Annual Convention, Fair Oaks Marriott Hotel, Falls Church, Virginia, 25 October 1996.

24. Leonard Cole, *The Eleventh Plague* (New York: W. H. Freeman, 1996), 151–52.

25. David Kaplan, "Aum Supreme Truth," paper presented at the workshop "Motivations and Patterns of Behavior Associated with Chemical and Biological Terrorism," Monterey Institute Washington Office, Washington, D.C., 23 June 1998, 10.

26. Jonathan Tucker, "Chemical/Biological Terrorism: Coping with a New Threat," *Politics and the Life Sciences* 15 (September 1996): 167–84; Ron Purver, "The Threat of Chemical/Biological Terrorism," *Commentary* 60 (August 1995), http://www.csis-crs.gc.ca/eng/comment/com60e.html.

27. Summary based on Kaplan and Marshall, *Cult*, 237–52. See also Staff Report, U.S. Senate, *Hearings on Global Proliferation*. Also based on author's interviews with John Sopko; Quinn, "Terrorism Comes to Tokyo."

28. CIA, "Chemical, Biological and Radiological Terrorist Threat."

The Aum Shinrikyo cult intended to kill thousands. The group had built up a large chemical weapons production capacity and was working on plans for disseminating chemical and biological agents over a major Japanese city. Cult members had hidden a bottle containing an ounce of VX—enough to kill about fifteen thousand people—which was recovered by the Tokyo police in September 1996.[29] They had amassed hundreds of tons of chemicals used in the production of sarin—reportedly to make enough sarin to kill millions of people.[30] Police found a large amount of *Clostridium botulinum*, together with 160 barrels of the media required for growing the bacteria.[31] Members of the cult visited Zaire on the pretext of providing medical assistance to victims of Ebola, with the actual objective of finding a sample of the virus to culture as a warfare agent.[32] The cult was cooperating with Russian Mafia groups, North Korea, and, indirectly, Iran, in smuggling nuclear materials and conventional munitions out of Russia through Ukraine.[33] The group also was plotting a chemical attack in the United States.[34]

Senator Sam Nunn held a hearing on Aum Shinrikyo in November 1995. The senator's staff testified that at the time the Tokyo attack was carried out, Aum Shinrikyo had some fifty thousand members, thirty thousand of whom were Russians. The Aum had offices in Bonn, Sri Lanka, New York, and Moscow, as well as in several Japanese cities. U.S. officials admitted that despite the alarming range of Aum Shinrikyo's activities, it was not on the "radar screen" of the U.S. intelligence community.[35]

Despite Asahara's arrest and imprisonment in May 1995, Aum Shinrikyo is still thriving in Russia.[36] A large group of Aum supporters reportedly remains employed at Krasnoyarsk-29. Smaller groups are employed at other nuclear facilities throughout Russia and the former Soviet Union.[37] The cult is also resurfacing in Japan, selling computers and other high-technology goods.[38]

29. "Tokyo Police Find Bottle of a Cult's Deadly Gas," *New York Times,* 13 December 1996, 15.
30. Nicholas Kristof, "Tokyo Suspect in Gas Attack Erupts in Court," *New York Times,* 8 November 1996, 14.
31. Cole, *Eleventh Plague,* 155.
32. Staff Report, U.S. Senate, *Hearings on Global Proliferation.*
33. After Asahara was arrested, North Korea may have moved its nuclear smuggling base of operations to Tumen, China, making use of a North Korean organized criminal ring to smuggle nuclear-related equipment as well as nuclear materials (E-mail communication with Ed Evanhoe, former CIA agent stationed in Japan, 5 November 1996).
34. Nicholas D. Kristof, "Japanese Cult Said to Have Planned Nerve-Gas Attacks in U.S.," *New York Times,* 23 March 1997, 14.
35. Staff Report, U.S. Senate, *Hearings on Global Proliferation.*
36. "Prosecutors Investigate Lobov's Links."
37. E-mail communication with Ed Evanhoe, 5 November 1996.
38. Interview with anonymous Japanese reporter, 16 April 1998.

TERRORISTS' MOTIVATIONS TO USE UNCONVENTIONAL WEAPONS:
THREE MODELS

Contrary to popular perception, Shoko Asahara was procedurally rational in the sense that he was maximizing his objectives. His goals may not have been substantively rational, but he was a "rational actor." He believed that by carrying out mass murder he would help to bring on Armageddon, hastening the day when he would emerge as the leader of a new race. Asahara also had "cultural" reasons for wanting to use chemical, nuclear, or biological weapons. The core myth for millenarian movements can influence whether the group turns violent: Aum's core myth was a violent deity called Shiva the Destroyer. Asahara was interested in technology, in part because he believed it would give him an edge over aliens, and he seems to have been fascinated by the Nazi use of nerve agents. Aum Shinrikyo also had command over vast financial and human resources. Asahara recruited scientists, including those working in Russian military facilities, and he found allies in the Japanese and Russian governments willing to assist him achieve his goals by supplying Aum with weapons and training. These assets allowed Aum to pursue chemical or biological weapons, but Asahara did not succeed in using them to achieve mass destruction. What insights do the three perspectives on terrorist motivation explored here—the rational actor model, organizational theory, and strategic culture—offer into the motivations and behavior of the Aum cult and other terrorist organizations?

Rational Actor Model

Rational models assume that groups and bureaucracies make decisions as unitary actors. Actors are presumed to maximize expected benefits relative to costs. Most proponents of the rational approach assume that states optimize security and that similar strategic situations will produce similar decisions about unconventional weapons. Culture, organizational styles, previous interactions, and domestic pressures all are essentially irrelevant; actors are assumed to rely on estimates of costs and benefits to guide their actions.

The rational actor model implies that terrorist groups will pursue violence only when it enhances their long-term goals. The model suggests that terrorists who hope to influence policy (rather than to destroy the government outright or kill for its own sake) are unlikely to resort to mass destruction, although they might use these weapons to commit acts of economic sabotage or to kill small numbers of people.

The assumption of procedural rationality suggests that the terrorist is maximizing an objective function. It does *not* necessarily imply substantive rationality. When Thomas Schelling wryly observes that "despite the high ratio of damage and grief to the resources required for a terrorist act, terrorism has proved to be a remarkably ineffectual means to accomplishing anything," he is assuming that terrorists have substantively rational objectives.[39] They may in fact be pursuing chaos, or they may be pursuing organizational or personal objectives that have nothing to do with their purported goals.[40] The terrorist who believes that social chaos is an end in itself or that by creating such chaos he can hasten the Messiah's return can be just as rational in his strategy as the secular terrorist fighting for ethnic autonomy or social reform. These religious terrorists are not using violence to persuade an audience of the righteousness of their cause: their audience is God and the members of their own group. They may not even take credit for their terrorist acts.

Getting People to Watch. Unconventional weapons could serve specific objectives for which conventional weapons are less well suited. Terrorists could use a chemical weapon, for instance, to attract more attention than they would otherwise gain with attacks using conventional weapons. Studies of perceived risk show that there is an inexact correlation between scientists' assessment of risk and the level of fear invoked by risky technologies and activities.[41] Radioactive, chemical, and biological poisons are mysterious, unfamiliar, indiscriminate, uncontrollable, inequitable, and invisible, all characteristics associated with heightened fear. The horror of these weapons enhances their military effectiveness and their terrorizing potential. While all terrorists aim to frighten, some might be especially attracted to the idea of weapons that, used in the right way, would have more bark than bite. [42] Terrorists might turn to unconventional weapons because they believe that the press is paying them insufficient attention or that governments are decreasingly receptive to their demands.

Economic Terrorism. Unlike conventional weapons, radiological, chemical, and biological agents could be used to destroy crops, poison foods, or

39. Thomas Schelling, "What Purposes Can 'International Terrorism' Serve?" in *Violence, Terrorism, and Justice*, ed. R. G. Frey and Christopher W. Morris (Cambridge: Cambridge University Press, 1991), 20–21; Sun-Ki Chai, "An Organizational Economics Theory of Antigovernment Violence," *Comparative Politics* 26 (October 1993): 99–110.

40. Schelling concedes that terrorists might sometimes hope to attract attention and air grievances, but he focuses on these objectives only as an "an intermediate means toward political objectives." He explicitly excludes religious cults from his discussion ("What Purposes," 20).

41. See, for example, Paul Slovic, Baruch Fischoff, and Sarah Lichtenstein, "Facts and Fears: Understanding Perceived Risk," in *Societal Risk Assessment: How Safe Is Safe Enough?*, ed. Richard Schwing and Walter Albers (New York: Plenum Press, 1980), 181–216.

42. This section reflects Chapter 3 in Jessica Stern, *The Ultimate Terrorists* (Cambridge, Mass.: Harvard University Press, 1999).

contaminate pharmaceuticals. They also could be used to kill livestock. Terrorists might use these agents to attack corporations perceived to be icons of the target country, for example, by contaminating batches of Coca-Cola. By claiming to contaminate products, terrorists could use these agents to force the government to recall foods or pharmaceuticals.

Several cases of economic terrorism have been reported in the press. One of the best-known cases involving chemical agents occurred in 1989, when an unidentified person, presumed to be Chilean, called the U.S. embassy in Santiago claiming that he had poisoned fruit destined for the United States and Japan. The caller explained that because a series of bombings and assassinations had done nothing to improve the lot of Chile's lower classes, he believed it was necessary to involve other countries and employ a new technique.[43] The Food and Drug Administration conducted an exhaustive search and discovered two grapes containing a small amount of cyanide, although the quantity was insufficient to cause illness or injury. The Chilean fruit industry claimed that the incident cost Chile $333 million.[44] In 1991, the Chilean government joined forces with Chilean fruit growers and exporters to sue the United States for damages totaling $466 million.[45] Although no one was bodily harmed, the incident was immensely costly for all parties involved. In a similar case in January 1986, the Australian, British, Canadian, and U.S. embassies in Colombo, Sri Lanka, received letters purporting to be from a Tamil guerrilla group warning that tea destined for export had been poisoned with potassium cyanide.[46]

Terrorists could force a government to engage in a costly cleanup operation by using radiological agents or anthrax spores. Such weapons would kill city residents, but the terrorists could warn authorities in advance if imposing costs on the target population were their only goal. Unlike conventional weapons, anthrax and radiological agents could persist in soil or structures for many years.

The Department of Energy's (DOE) Nuclear Emergency Search Team estimates that a small improvised nuclear device (with a 6.2-pound aerosolized mass of plutonium) that fizzled (i.e., its chemical detonators exploded but failed to produce a nuclear reaction) would nonetheless contaminate a seventy-three-square-mile area, costing many billions of dollars to clean up.[47] Another DOE study found that if ten kilograms of plutonium

43. Bill Brigg and Verne Modeland, "The Cyanide Scare: A Tale of Two Grapes," *FDA Consumer,* July–August 1989, 7.

44. *Los Angeles Times,* 3 October 1990.

45. "Chilean Government and Fruit Producers and Exporters Demand $466 Million in Damages from the U.S.," *Chronicle of Latin American Affairs,* 29 August 1991: http://ladb.unm.edu.

46. *New York Times,* 5 January 1986, 5.

47. "NEST Consequence Report, Containment and Effects," internal Department of Energy memorandum, January 1997.

Jessica Stern

were accidentally dispersed in a fire, the cost of cleaning up the surrounding area would be around $3 billion. If that same 10 kilograms of plutonium were disseminated with an explosive device, the cost of cleanup would rise to $200 billion.[48]

Thus even under the assumptions of *substantive* rationality, terrorists wanting to inflict economic or psychological pain might be drawn to chemical, biological, or radiological agents. For many economic attack scenarios, nuclear, biological, or chemical weapons would be more efficient than conventional weapons.

Millenarianism.   Millenarians believe that the present age is corrupt and that a new age will dawn after a cleansing apocalypse. Only a lucky few (usually envisaged to be selected on the basis of adherence to doctrine or ritual) will survive the end time and experience paradise.[49] Many evangelical Protestants believe in a doctrine of rapture: that the saved will be lifted off the earth to escape the apocalypse that will precede the Second Coming of Christ. But some millenarians believe that the saved will have to endure the seven years of violence and struggle of the apocalypse, and they want to be prepared.[50] Asahara told his followers that in the coming conflict between good and evil they would have to be able to fight with every available weapon.[51] A similar belief system explains the Christian Identity movement's attraction to survivalism.

"Premillennial tension" is alleged to have brought about new age thinking and vague fears among many people.[52] Thousands of "millennial madness cults" have emerged, according to the Christian Research Institute, which tracks religious sects.[53] Although many of the leading figures in prophecy, including those who do not subscribe to the Judeo-Christian tradition, have prognosticated that the world will end around the year 2000, they do not agree on the exact day. "Some have opted for the 1990s, others for 1999, yet others for 2000 or 2001; to be on the safe side, some give a

48. The cost of cleaning up after an accidental detonation releasing 10 kilograms of plutonium in a mixed urban-rural setting would be $80 billion in 1994 dollars. See Douglas R. Stephens et al., "Probabilistic Cost-Benefit Analysis of Enhanced Safety Features for Strategic Nuclear Weapons at a Representative Location" (Livermore, Calif.: Lawrence Livermore National Laboratory, 1994, UCRL-JC-115269).

49. Millenarian doctrines are generally religiously based, but some are not. See Jean E. Rosenfeld, "Pai Marire: Peace and Violence in a New Zealand Millenarian Tradition," *Terrorism and Political Violence* 7 (Autumn 1995): 83.

50. "End Times Jitters," interview with Michael Barkun, *Klanwatch Intelligence Report*, Summer 1997, 17.

51. FBIS-SOV-97-09, 6 May 1997, from Moscow *Trud*, 6 May 1997, 1–2.

52. Ibid.

53. " 'Millennial Madness' Said to Drive Fringe Groups," *Washington Times*, 29 March 1997, 3.

[214]

vaguer, later date," Walter Laqueur observes.[54] Others are betting that the world will end by 2030.[55] Nor is there consensus on the exact circumstances or location of the apocalypse. Some predict floods, conflagrations, epidemics like AIDS, or exotic, emerging diseases; others predict that wars or nuclear terrorism will bring about the end of the world.[56]

Some millenarians believe that they can assist God in speeding up the process leading to the Messiah's appearance by taking vengeance against perceived sinners. A member of a millenarian group known as the Covenant, Sword, and the Arm of the Lord described his group's thinking about the timing of the apocalypse: "The original timetable was up to God, but God could use us in creating Armageddon—that if we stepped out [by killing sinners] things might be hurried along. You get tired of waiting for what you think God is planning," he explained.[57] He and fellow members of the Covenant group were convicted of bombing a gas pipeline, a church whose membership included homosexuals, and a synagogue. The cult had acquired 30 gallons of cyanide in order to poison municipal water supplies, but members were arrested before carrying out their plot.[58]

Macro Terror to Exact Revenge and Create Chaos. Politically motivated terrorists who desire to change societies rather than destroy them would presumably avoid killing very large numbers of people.[59] But some terrorists want to destroy the government. William Pierce, leader of the neo-Nazi organization National Alliance, aims to initiate a worldwide race war and establish an Aryan state. "We are in a war for the survival of our race," he explains, "that ultimately we cannot win . . . except by killing our enemies. . . . It's a case of either we destroy them or they will destroy us, with no chance for compromise or armistice."[60] Ramzi Yousef, mastermind of the World Trade Center bombing, claimed he was retaliating for U.S. aid to Israel. He held the Israeli army responsible for the murder, torture, and imprisonment of Muslims and for killing his own friends and relatives.[61] "I support

54. Walter Laqueur, "Fin-de-siècle: Once More with Feeling," *Journal of Contemporary History* 31 (January 1996): 40.

55. Author's interview with Pastor Robert Miller, a leading Identity Christian cleric, 21 April 1988.

56. Ibid.

57. Author's interview with Kerry Noble, 2 March 1998.

58. It is unlikely that the plan would have worked because city reservoirs tend to be large and dilution would have rendered the cyanide essentially harmless. Noble claimed that the group had not yet identified an appropriate city.

59. The nature of the constituency is a key variable here. If the terrorists' constituents see the targeted group as subhuman, or if terrorists have no clear constituency, political constraints against macro terrorism are less likely to bind.

60. Quotes from *Klanwatch Intelligence Report,* May 1996, 6–8.

61. Appleson, "Prosecutor."

terrorism as long as it is used against the United States and Israel. You are more than terrorists. You are butchers, liars, and hypocrites. . . . You keep talking about terrorism to the media, but behind closed doors you support terrorism," he claimed at his trial.[62]

Yousef and the ad hoc group of radical Islamic extremists with whom he worked intended to bring the World Trade Center buildings down.[63] They hoped to kill 250,000 Americans, Yousef confessed.[64] Had the buildings collapsed as the terrorists intended, the FBI estimates that some 50,000 people would have died, but the terrorists made a minor error in their placement of the bomb. Nonetheless, the structural integrity of one of the twin towers and of the adjoining Vista Hotel was in jeopardy. They would have collapsed—perhaps within days of the bombing—had the buildings not been reinforced with steel supports, according to the FBI.[65] Investigators reportedly found a cache of sodium cyanide in the bombers' warehouse. Some experts, including the sentencing judge, are convinced that cyanide was used in the bomb but that it burned instead of vaporizing.[66] If Yousef had succeeded in disseminating cyanide, hundreds or thousands of people could have been poisoned.

Overcoming Countermeasures. Terrorists sometimes innovate because government countermeasures force them to find new vulnerabilities. When governments implemented security measures to protect embassies and prevent hijacking, terrorists were forced to contrive new techniques. Metal detectors made it harder to bring guns onto planes, so rather than hijacking aircraft, terrorists began blowing up planes with plastic explosives. Concrete barriers at U.S. embassies and government buildings made driving bombs onto the site more difficult. Now terrorists use more powerful explosives, detonating them outside the perimeter. Terrorists could turn to

62. Gail Appleson, "Bomb Mastermind Gets Life in US Prison," Reuters, 9 January 1997.
63. Ramzi Ahmed Yousef, convicted mastermind of the World Trade Center plot, told an FBI agent that lack of equipment (and not political or moral qualms) prevented him from destroying the World Trade Center towers (Benjamin Weiser, "Trial Begins for Chief Suspect in Trade Center Blast," *New York Times*, 4 August 1997, 16).
64. Appleson, "Prosecutor."
65. *Terrorism in the United States* (Washington, D.C.: U.S. Department of Justice, 1993). Six people died in the World Trade Center bombing, and over a thousand were injured. The incident was extremely costly for insurers: by late March 1993, they had paid out $510 million ("World Trade Center Insurers Have Paid $510 Million So Far," *Washington Post*, 30 March 1993, 12). Not all engineers accept the FBI's assessment of the imminence of collapse.
66. In his sentencing statement, Judge Kevin Duffy claimed, "You had sodium cyanide around, and I'm sure it was in the bomb. Thank God the sodium cyanide burned instead of vaporizing" ("Sentencing statement of Judge Kevin Duffy, trial judge of World Trade Bombing case," included in the appendix to *Global Proliferation of Weapons of Mass Destruction*, Hearings Before the Permanent Subcommittee on Investigations of the Committee on Governmental Affairs, U.S. Senate, pt. 3, 104th Congress, 2nd Session, 27 March 1997, 276. See also *Terrorism in the United States*, 25.

chemical, biological, or radiological agents because they would not be picked up by the detectors now in use at many government buildings and at airports.

The Constituency for Terrorism.   Terrorists are influenced by the need to appeal to their existing and potential constituency. Religious and secular terrorists have different constituencies. Politically motivated terrorists usually see themselves as acting on behalf of an aggrieved group that is demanding greater autonomy, a separate homeland, or greater rights. The Irish Republican Army, for example, is likely to be strongly influenced by the need to raise funds in the United States. But religious terrorists believe that their violent actions are dictated by a divine authority. The government is often believed to be working at cross-purposes with the divine: secular rulers and the laws they uphold are therefore utterly illegitimate. In such cases, acts of extreme violence are not only justified, they are required of true believers.[67] The constituency for religious terrorism includes God and the other members of the organization; there is no outside "audience." Often religious terrorists do not claim credit for their attacks because their goal is to create fear rather than to persuade the government to alter its policies. Because there are no political constraints against acts of extreme violence, members' tolerance for violence becomes the binding constraint. Terrorist groups or individuals (e.g., disgruntled workers) seeking revenge are also particularly dangerous. Like religious terrorists, they are unconstrained by political costs because they are not seeking to change policies.

Organizational Theory

Organizational theorists observe that bureaucracies are made up of self-interested and competitive subunits whose choices are guided by the interests of their unit rather than the organization as a whole. The implication is that officials will support projects that expand their domain or budget—even if the projects or policies in question are counter to overall organizational interests.

Organization theory also asserts that there are inherent limits on the ability of organizations to make rational calculations and to coordinate action. Bureaucracies are assumed to operate within bounded or limited rationality. They conduct myopic searches based on inherent biases, recent experiences, or current responsibilities; they plan incrementally rather than taking the long view. They tend to focus on immediate tasks rather than long-term objectives, and they use standard operating procedures rather

67. Author's interview with Kerry Noble, 2 March 1998.

than searching for the best approach to get the job done.[68] Over time, organizations begin to confuse ends with means. They focus on surrogate measures of progress rather than their actual objectives, eventually losing sight entirely of their long-term goals in a form of "goal displacement."[69] In short, the theory assumes that bureaucracies are not unitary actors and that competition among subunits can lead to suboptimal outcomes from the perspective of the overall organization.

This model predicts that the survival of the terrorist group—rather than any particular political objective—would become the group's primary raison d'être. Groups could turn to unconventional weapons to advance immediate organizational interests (group survival) rather than long-term political objectives. Conversely, in cases where unconventional weapons could advance their long-term objectives, terrorists might nonetheless avoid these weapons because of individual members' fears or biases. Contrary to the assertions of the rational actor model, this model predicts that leaders of large groups may not necessarily control tactical or even doctrinal decisions. Instead, outcomes could depend on competition among factions, members' recent experiences, or a tendency to employ standard operating procedures. Small organizations also are likely to be influenced by group dynamics.

Group Dynamics and Attitude toward Risk. Experiments carried out by psychologists suggest that under certain circumstances, groups can be more likely to take risks than can individuals.[70] Group dynamics also can lead members to develop unrealistically optimistic views of the group's invulnerability, a presumption of the group's morality, and pressure to conform.[71] Group dynamics presumably would exert a particularly powerful influence when people operate outside the law and are forced to go underground because members then rely exclusively on each other. In interviews with Argentine guerrillas, Maria Moyano-Rasmussen found that although the guerrillas initially were pursuing political objectives (fighting military rule), they continued operating even after the country's return to constitutional rule. Over time, they became militarized and increasingly violent,

68. Scott D. Sagan, "The Perils of Proliferation: Organization Theory, Deterrence Theory, and the Spread of Nuclear Weapons," *International Security* 18 (Spring 1994): 66–107.

69. I thank Scott Sagan for suggesting this point.

70. For discussion, see Jack S. Levy, "Prospect Theory, Rational Choice, and International Relations," *International Studies Quarterly* 41 (1997):103.

71. Irving Janis, *Victims of Groupthink* (Boston: Houghton Mifflin, 1972); Jerrold Post, "Terrorist Psycho-Logic," in *Origins of Terrorism: Psychologys, Ideologies, Theologies, States of Mind*, ed. Walter Reich (New York: Cambridge University Press, 1990).

pursuing violence apparently for its own sake.[72] Donatella della Porta's interviews with left-wing militants show that as these organizations cut off all ties with outsiders, commitment to the cause becomes self-generating, and risk-taking increases.[73]

Problems with Command and Control. Over time terrorist organizations tend to recruit operatives to do their "dirty work" who are moved to commit violence for exogenous reasons unrelated to the group's purported objectives. A 1987 study of Italian terrorist organizations shows that over time, terrorists tended to recruit younger, less politically experienced, and more marginally committed members. This finding applies to both right- and left-wing organizations.[74] Sometimes leaders serving jail sentences recruit the ordinary criminals they meet there to use in terrorist operations upon their release.[75]

Sometimes followers' weaker commitment to the purported objectives of the group leads them to commit extreme acts of violence that the leader does not countenance. Followers who are less interested in the long-term goals of the movement (and more interested in violence for its own sake) would presumably be less worried about generating a public opinion backlash against the group. For example, in April 1997, four members of a Texas-based chapter of the Ku Klux Klan were caught planning to blow up a natural gas refinery. Their purpose was to divert attention from an armored car robbery. The four planned to use the money to finance future terrorist operations. The "imperial wizard" of the chapter was so apprehensive about the plan that he turned the four in to the FBI several days before they intended to carry out the attack.[76]

Individual operatives can have their own reasons for turning to terrorist violence unrelated to the group's purported goals. "Individuals are drawn to terrorism in order to commit terrorist violence," Jerrold Post argues.

---

72. Maria Moyano-Rasmussen, "Going Underground in Argentina: A Look at the Founders of a Guerrilla Movement," in *Social Movements and Violence: Participation in Underground Organizations,* ed. Donatella della Porta (Greenwich, Conn.: JAI Press, 1992), 105–29.

73. See della Porta's review of the literature on these points, "Research on Individual Motivations in Underground Political Organizations," in *Social Movements and Violence,"* ed. della Porta, 3–28.

74. Leonard Weinberg and William Eubank, "Recruitment of Italian Political Terrorists," in *Multidimensional Terrorism,* ed. Martin Slann and Bernard Schecterman (Boulder: Lynne Reinner, 1987); Nachman Tal, "Islamic Terrorism in Egypt: Challenge and Response," Jaffee Center for Strategic Studies, *Strategic Assessment* 1 (April 1998): 8.

75. Author's interview with Jordanian and Israeli officials, July–August 1999.

76. David E. Kaplan and Mike Tharp, "Terrorism Threats at Home," *US News and World Report,* 29 December 1997, 22–27.

They feel "psychologically compelled" to commit violent acts, and the political objectives they espouse are only a rationalization.[77] Although psychiatrists have found no particular terrorist pathology, some believe that many terrorists have had a difficult childhood producing narcissistic wounds, resulting in a proclivity toward "splitting," that is, projecting the hated parts of the self onto the outside world. According to this line of reasoning, the desire to destroy the establishment is driven by the terrorist's search for identity. By striking out at the enemy, the terrorist hopes to destroy the enemy within.[78] This dynamic could result in operatives taking unauthorized vengeance against society for their own reasons unrelated to the group's cause; such acts are equivalent to military officers making politically unauthorized use of their weapons.

Sometimes followers may be less willing to commit extreme acts of violence than their leaders. Shoko Asahara tried to supplement his power to persuade by brainwashing his recruits. But in at least one case, his brainwashing efforts failed. In March 1995, a member of Aum Shinrikyo who was struck by a guilty conscience neglected to arm a device intended to disseminate botulinum toxin on the Tokyo subway.[79]

Terrorists use other command and control techniques. One system is to recruit mentally unbalanced youths to carry out suicide missions.[80] Another technique is to force operatives to conduct suicidal missions against their will. For example, Israeli police captured a sixteen-year-old who was about to carry out a suicide bombing. The boy claimed he had no desire to kill himself—for Allah or anyone else—but that the Shiite militia had compelled him to carry out their orders by threatening his family. In other cases, leaders have tricked operatives into carrying out suicide attacks by telling them there were escape routes that did not in fact exist.[81] The problem with these techniques—recruiting mentally unbalanced youths, brainwashing recruits, and threatening operatives' families—is that there is no guarantee that the technique will work. Commandos can feign willingness to carry out the mission and in the end refuse to carry it out. Mental illness could have unforeseen effects. While some depressed operatives may follow instructions in carrying out suicide missions, others could carry out unsanctioned acts of violence, possibly including attacks resulting in mass casualties.

77. Post, "Terrorist Psycho-Logic," 25.
78. Ibid., 25–40.
79. Kaplan and Marshall, *Cult*, 235–36.
80. Ariel Merari, "The Readiness to Kill and Die: Suicidal Terrorism in the Middle East," in *Origins of Terrorism*, ed., Reich, 205.
81. Thomas Friedman, "Boy Says Lebanese Recruited Him as a Car Bomber," *New York Times*, 14 April 1985, 1, cited in Walter Reich, "Understanding Terrorist Behavior," in *Origins of Terrorism*, ed., Reich, 271.

Strategic Culture

Strategic culture theories assert that actors make decisions based on cultural and historical experiences. The national interest is conceived through a lens that both simplifies and distorts reality. Alastair Iain Johnston explains that analogies, metaphors, and precedents are invoked to guide choice and filter perceptions of the adversary's behavior. [82] Strategic culture implies that behavior is not fully responsive to the behavior of others but is influenced by internal dynamics. [83]

This approach suggests that rather than rationally calculating costs and benefits, terrorist groups are influenced by myths, metaphors, and history. Some terrorists could be attracted to plagues because they want to mimic the avenging God of the Old Testament. Others may choose sarin or cyanide because of the Nazi connection to these weapons. Still others may find unconventional weapons appealing because they seem scientific and sophisticated.

Core Myths for Millenarian Groups. Groups that model themselves on an avenging angel or vindictive God (such as Christ with a sword, Phineas, or Asahara's deity Shiva the Destroyer) are more likely to lash out than those whose core myth is the suffering Messiah. Millenarian organizations operating during periods when apocalyptic fears are generally aroused are more likely to be susceptible to becoming violent. Some millenarian movements turn their violence against themselves. For example, the group Heaven's Gate, based in a suburb of San Diego, California, was inspired by the appearance of the Hale-Bopp comet in 1997 to commit mass suicide. Thirty-nine cult members "shed their containers" in the hope that their spirits could board a spaceship cult members believed was hiding in the comet's tail.

An Avenging God as Model and Metaphor. Terrorists hoping to create an aura of divine retribution might be attracted to biological agents. The fifth plague used by God to punish the Pharaoh in the story of Exodus was murrain, which is a group of cattle diseases that includes anthrax. In Samuel 5, God turns against the Philistines with a "very great destruction" by killing them with a pestilence that produced "emerods" in their secret parts. Medical historians consider these "emerods" to be a symptom of bubonic plague.[84] Some terrorists might believe they are emulating God by employing these agents.

82. Alastair Iain Johnston, "Thinking about Strategic Culture," *International Security* 19 (Spring 1995): 32–64.
83. Ibid., 34.
84. Hans Zinsser, *Rats, Lice and History* (Boston: Little, Brown, 1963), 110.

The core myth for the Christian Identity movement and for National Patriots is the story of Phineas, who took the law into his own hands by boldly murdering a tribal chief, together with his foreign-born concubine, for flouting a proscription against intermarriage. God rewarded Phineas for "purifying" the community by averting a devastating plague.[85] Christian Patriots take this passage as a directive to make "atonement" for America's sins and "balance the scales of justice" by committing acts of violence.[86] Interestingly, the Zealots-Sicarri, Jewish terrorists active in the first century A.D., also were motivated to follow in Phineas's footsteps.[87] Modern followers of Phineas might try to use poisons or plagues to mimic God.

The Aura of Science. Terrorists find technology appealing for a variety of reasons. Some terrorists might want to impress their target audience with high technology. William Pierce, who studied physics at Cal Tech, is interested in high-technology weapons. In his novel *The Turner Diaries*, right-wing extremists use nuclear, chemical, biological, and radiological weapons to take over the world. Pierce believes he can attract more intelligent recruits to his neo-Nazi organization National Alliance over the Internet than over the radio or through leaflets. He is also explicitly targeting military personnel for recruitment, presumably because they have access to higher-technology weapons than those available on the street.[88]

Constraints on Terrorists' Use of Unconventional Weapons

Candidates for using unconventional weapons successfully represent the intersection of three sets: groups that want to use these weapons despite formidable political risks, groups that are both technically proficient and capable of acquiring the weapons or raw materials, and groups whose organizational structure enables them to deliver or disseminate the weapons covertly. The number of groups capable of meeting these criteria is likely to be small, especially for operations in which these weapons are used to kill large numbers of people.

Fortunately, there is likely to be a negative correlation between psychological motivation to commit extremely violent acts and technical prowess. Experts claim that schizophrenics and sociopaths may *want* to commit acts

85. Num. 25:11.
86. "Terrorists in the Name of God and Race," *Klanwatch Intelligence Report*, August 1996, 1–4.
87. David C. Rapoport, "Fear and Trembling: Terrorism in Three Religious Traditions," *American Political Science Review* 78 (September 1984): 658–677.
88. Author's interview with William Pierce, 22 April 1997.

of mass destruction, but they are probably the least likely to succeed.[89] Schizophrenics often have difficulty functioning in groups, which would be necessary for large-scale open-air dissemination of chemical, biological, or radiological agents or for producing a jerry-rigged nuclear device.

State-sponsored terrorists are the most likely to overcome technical obstacles, but the sponsoring state would presumably weigh the risk of massive retaliation. Nonetheless, several particularly violent state-sponsored incidents in recent years make clear that it would be imprudent to rely exclusively on traditional deterrence against state-sponsored acts of terrorism employing chemical, nuclear, or biological weapons: some delivery systems have no return address.[90]

Technical Obstacles

With the end of the Cold War and the breakup of the Soviet Union, unconventional weapons and their components have become easier to acquire. The black market is now offering nuclear materials, guidance systems, and other components of nuclear weapons. Law enforcement authorities have seized hundreds of caches of stolen nuclear materials, most of which are nonfissile, radioactive sources that could be used in radiation dispersal devices. South African biological weapons scientists have been caught offering their expertise to Libya,[91] and fears are widespread that underpaid Russian weapons experts might provide biological weapons expertise and materials to Iran.[92] Technical constraints will no longer prevent terrorists from engaging in low-technology incidents like disseminating chemical, biological, or radiological agents on a plane or a train. But chemical, biological, and radiological agents are still significantly harder to acquire and use than fertilizer bombs, for example, so terrorists would need to be strongly motivated to get them.

89. B. J. Berkowitz et al., *Superviolence: The Civil Threat of Mass Destruction Weapons* (Santa Barbara: ADCON Corporation, 1972), 3–9, 4–4.

90. Some of the more violent state-sponsored attacks include the 1988 attack on Pan Am 103, for which two Libyan intelligence operatives were indicted, and Hezbollah's 1983 attacks on the United States embassy and the United States Marine barracks in Lebanon (Statement of Louis J. Freeh, director of the U.S. Federal Bureau of Investigation, before U.S. Senate, Appropriations Committee, 13 May 1997).

91. James Adams, "Gadaffi Lures South Africa's Top Germ Warfare Scientists," *Sunday Times*, 26 February 1995; Paul Taylor, "Toxic S. African Arms Raise Concern; US Wants Assurance '80s Program Is Dead," *Washington Post*, 28 February 1995.

92. James Adams, "The Dangerous New World of Chemical and Biological Weapons," in *Terrorism with Chemical and Biological Weapons*, ed., Brad Roberts, (Alexandria, Va.: Chemical and Biological Arms Control Institute, 1997), 23–42.

Chemical and Biological Terrorism. Terrorists could acquire chemical and biological agents from state sponsors or they could steal them from national stockpiles. Thefts of chemical weapons in Albania and Russia make clear that some national stockpiles are vulnerable. Although international treaties bar production and use of chemical and biological weapons, several countries listed by the State Department as supporters of terrorism also are believed to possess chemical weapons and at least some biological weapons capability.

Terrorists also could try to make chemical or biological warfare agents, possibly with the assistance of former government scientists or widely disseminated poison manuals. College-trained chemists and biologists could produce chemical or biological agents, though they might have trouble disseminating them (especially biological agents, which are not volatile) in the open air.

Many types of attacks could be contemplated. Several countries have developed anti-crop and anti-livestock agents, which would be easier to use then antipersonnel agents. Poisoning prepared foods or pharmaceuticals would be significantly easier than disseminating chemical or biological agents in air. Crude food poisons, like salmonella and shigella, are relatively easy to produce and disseminate. Using chemical and biological agents to assassinate individuals would be easier than carrying out mass-casualty attacks. Terrorists might also try to disseminate industrial or agricultural poisons. The tragic accident at Bhopal, India, in December 1984, illustrates the lethal potential of toxic industrial chemicals: Indian officials estimate that more than seven thousand people died from exposure to the methyl isocyanate that had leaked in the accident.[93] As a rule, however, toxicity is negatively correlated with the ease of acquiring or producing chemical substances. Because agricultural chemicals are less toxic than nerve agents, a much larger quantity would be required to inflict a large number of casualties.

Many terrorists are capable of using commonly available industrial or agricultural chemicals, or even warfare agents, to contaminate prepared foods, livestock, or crops. Some also would be capable of disseminating these poisons in an enclosed space like a building, a plane, or a train. But few would be capable of mounting the most deadly attacks, like disseminating biological agents over large open areas. State-sponsored groups are most capable of overcoming technical barriers to mass-casualty attacks, but the sponsor would presumably weigh the risk of retaliation before supporting this type of terrorist attack.

93. John-Thor Dahlburg, "Bhopal Marks 10th Anniversary of Gas Disaster," *Los Angeles Times*, 4 December 1994, 1.

Radiological Terrorism and Nuclear Terrorism. Nonfissile radioactive isotopes are available from a variety of sources. Hospitals use radioactive sources for sterilizing medical equipment; industry uses them for pest control, sterilization, and measuring movement of gases, water, and silt. Radioactive isotopes also are used in well logging (water, oil, and gas wells) and weld and structural inspections. High-level wastes from nuclear reactors contain—in addition to plutonium—several nonfissile radioactive isotopes. Terrorists might try to spread radioactive material by creating a crude bomb or by attacking a nuclear power plant. Spreading radioactive material is probably feasible for many terrorists, but it would not be very deadly.

Only the most sophisticated terrorist group is likely to consider manufacturing its own nuclear weapon. For these groups, the binding constraint probably will be acquiring fissile material (highly enriched uranium or plutonium), which is much more highly protected than nonfissile radioactive sources. The Non-Proliferation Treaty allows export of fissile materials only for peaceful purposes and requires importing states to submit to monitoring by the International Atomic Energy Agency. But a spate of nuclear smuggling incidents indicates that fissile materials could be available on the black market. While most nuclear smuggling incidents have involved radioactive isotopes that could not be used to make a bomb, a dozen or so have involved weapons-usable fissile materials, according to the DOE.[94]

In the unlikely (but not impossible) event that terrorists buy or steal a sufficient quantity of fissile material, a key question is whether they could fashion a detonatable nuclear device, with or without state sponsorship. A group of nuclear weapons designers was commissioned in 1987 to consider this possibility. They concluded that building a crude nuclear device, assuming that a terrorist group had sufficient quantities of fissile material in hand, is "within reach of terrorists having sufficient resources to recruit a team of three or four technically qualified specialists" with expertise in "several quite distinct areas [including] the physical, chemical and metallurgical properties of the various materials to be used . . . technology concerning high explosives . . . electric circuitry; and others."[95] The designers concluded that terrorists might even be able to detonate plutonium oxide powder without actually making a bomb, although such an operation would be extremely dangerous and would require "tens of kilograms" of material. This possibility makes the new availability of nuclear material and the paucity of paid work for weapon scientists troubling.

94. U.S. Department of Energy, *Monthly Status Report on Illicit Trafficking of Nuclear Materials,* October 1997.
95. Paul Leventhal and Yonah Alexander, *Preventing Nuclear Terrorism* (Lexington, Mass.: Lexington Books, 1987), 9, 58.

The South African nuclear program, closed down in 1989 and revealed by President F. W. de Klerk in 1993, provides some insight into how easily a sophisticated terrorist group could acquire a gun-assembly device covertly if it had fissile materials in hand. Waldo Stumpf (the head of South Africa's Atomic Energy Corporation) estimated in 1994 that the entire project, including enriching the uranium, cost $20 million per annum, or about $200 million over the lifetime of the program.[96] Costs would have been significantly lower had South Africa been able to purchase the highly enriched uranium. Thus if a terrorist group had highly enriched uranium in hand, the cost of producing the bomb could be minimized. In the early 1980s, forty people were involved in South Africa's nuclear weapons program, but only twenty were actually making the weapons.[97]

The number of people actually involved in making the weapons—twenty—is shockingly small, but it is significantly more than the "three or four highly trained specialists" that the Nuclear Task Force envisaged. Nonetheless, the South African case shows that some established terrorist groups (for example, Hezbollah) have the requisite capital, although that by no means implies that they have the motivation or the capability to acquire the requisite expertise and equipment.

Terrorists might try to steal or buy a bomb ready-made. This would be more difficult than stealing conventional or chemical weapons. But the status of Russia's nuclear security system is problematic. Inventory systems are antiquated. Custodians are dispirited, underpaid, and underfed. Warheads, especially while in transit, could be vulnerable to theft or sabotage. The strains in Russia's nuclear security system are particularly disquieting because of the increasingly chaotic nature of Russian society.[98]

Obstacles to Covert Delivery

Successfully employing unconventional weapons would entail specific organizational requirements. The group would need technically trained members, who also would need to know how to acquire weapons or components (on the black market, from state sponsors, or through co-opted

96. Waldo Stumpf, "South Africa's Nuclear Weapons Programme," in Kathleen C. Bailey, *Weapons of Mass Destruction: Costs versus Benefits* (New Delhi: Manohar, 1994), 75. These figures assume 1994 exchange rates (presumably in 1994 dollars).

97. By 1989, when the program was shut down, the workforce had risen to three hundred people, half of whom were directly involved in weapons work. See David Albright, "South Africa's Secret Nuclear Weapons," ISIS Report, May 1994. I was able to confirm in general terms these approximate figures in interviews with U.S. government officials who had interviewed South African nuclear specialists.

98. National Security Concept Paper quoted in David Hoffman, "Russia Draws Bleak Picture of Its Security," *Washington Post*, 25 December 1997.

government or military officials). The group would have to be organized to evade law enforcement and intelligence officials. The group's location and its ability to recruit law enforcement officials (like Aum Shinrikyo and the Branch Davidians) also would affect its ability to evade detection. And the group would need to maintain cohesion while planning to escalate to more lethal tactics. Preventing defections would require that operatives be convinced that using unconventional weapons for the group's purpose is not immoral. This conviction could come about through racial or religious prejudice against the intended victims or possibly through brainwashing. The more charismatic the leader and the greater the ability to impose discipline, the more likelihood of success.

Two group structures are likely to be especially difficult to penetrate: ad hoc groups and small "phantom cells." Groups that come together on an ad hoc basis to carry out a single operation, such as the group responsible for the World Trade Center bombing, would be hard to penetrate because they exist for a limited period of time. Two militant Palestinians were arrested in 1997 just before their crude, homemade bombs were set to detonate on the New York subway system. An informant told police about the imminent attack, which could have killed thousands. Police breathed a sigh of relief when it was determined that the two men were not part of a larger Hamas conspiracy. But as Steven Emerson observes, "The self-activation of individual bombs and terrorists, indoctrinated in the propaganda disseminated by radical Muslim organizations, is far more difficult to prevent than organized acts of strategically premeditated murder."[99]

The Aryan Nations umbrella organization is urging neo-Nazis and Christian Patriots to form phantom cells of fewer than twelve members. Followers are urged not to communicate directly with the leadership of the movement so as to avoid detection by law enforcement officials.[100] Technically trained extremists operating in small groups or as individuals would be incapable of using nuclear weapons or employing chemical or biological agents in sophisticated mass-casualty attacks, but large groups would not be required for low-technology operations, which could still be quite deadly.

The conventional wisdom that rational terrorists would avoid using unconventional weapons is wrong. Although terrorism with nuclear, chemical, or biological weapons is likely to remain uncommon, a small but growing number of terrorists could attempt to use these weapons in the belief

---

99. Steven Emerson, "Foreign Terrorists in America: Five Years after the World Trade Center Bombing," testimony before U.S. Senate, Judiciary Subcommittee on Terrorism, Technology, and Government Information, 24 February 1998.

100. "Leaderless Resistance, an Essay by L. R. Beam," http://www.crusader.org/texts/bt/bt04.html.

that doing so would advance their goals. The most likely candidates are apocalyptic and extreme right-wing groups, who view secular rulers and the law they uphold as illegitimate. They are unconstrained by fear of government or public backlash. Often they consider their victims subhuman because they are outside the group's religion or race.

Religious groups may have substantively irrational goals, but they are still "rational actors" maximizing a set of objectives. Secular terrorists want to change government policies, a mission familiar to terrorism experts. But religious groups often want to destroy the government outright, making mass murder potentially rational. Some of these groups may also have "cultural" reasons for pursuing unconventional weapons. They may desire to mimic an avenging God, to imitate Hitler, to display scientific prowess, or to emulate other states or terrorists.

Organizational pressures also could induce some groups to commit extreme acts of violence. Followers tend to be more interested in violence for its own sake than in the group's purported goals, making them less inhibited by moral or political constraints than are leaders. Leaders may have difficulty designing command and control procedures that work.

Few terrorists would be capable of overcoming the technical and organizational obstacles to using unconventional weapons. The Aum Shinrikyo cult is an example of such an outlier group. Shoko Asahara, motivated by millenarian ideas, was convinced that an apocalypse was imminent. He believed he was fighting a total war against the forces of evil. No constituency (beyond his followers and the divine) held his violent tendencies in check. And he had substantial technical and financial capital at his disposal. Nonetheless, the cult's most successful attack was a low-technology attempt to disseminate impure sarin. The attack would have been far more lethal had the cult used a more sophisticated dissemination device. Disseminating a chemical agent in an enclosed space and contaminating food are probably the least challenging ways to use these weapons and are likely to remain the most common form of terrorism involving unconventional weapons.

The emergence of ad hoc groups of religious extremists, who recruit technically trained commandos from around the world, and the growth of American right-wing extremism are particularly troubling developments. Some right-wing groups are aware of the technical barriers to disseminating biological agents over broad areas and are seeking to hire experts. Hezbollah and other foreign religious groups now operating in the United States are alleged to be looking into chemical weapons. The millennium could induce some millenarians to turn violent.

These developments make clear that governments cannot afford to rely on the conventional wisdom about the likelihood that terrorists will employ chemical, biological, or nuclear weapons. Although the most likely type of unconventional terrorism involves the use of crude devices to deliver impure chemical agents or industrial poisons, governments need to be prepared for more serious acts of violence involving these weapons.

There is much that can be done to reduce the likelihood of chemical, biological, or radiological terrorism. But the only way to prevent it would be to implement far greater police control than the United States has ever known. The cure, in other words, could be worse than the disease. Therefore, it is essential to strengthen programs for managing consequences by broadening training for "first responders," the police and firefighters likely to be on the scene in the event of an attack. Other essential remedies include developing and deploying new pharmaceuticals; strengthening international monitoring of disease in humans, animals, and plants; improving detectors for chemical, biological, and radioactive materials; deploying detectors more broadly; and strengthening laws related to possession of chemical and biological agents. These actions could alter groups' calculations about the utility of unconventional weapon attacks. And they could greatly reduce the number of lives lost if attacks nonetheless occur.

[9]

Conclusions: Planning the Unthinkable

LEWIS A. DUNN, PETER R. LAVOY,

AND SCOTT D. SAGAN

Revelations in the aftermath of the 1991 Gulf War about Iraq's pursuit of nuclear, biological, and chemical arms focused unprecedented attention on the proliferation of these highly destructive weapons. Throughout the 1990s, officials in many countries began to worry more about the consequences of proliferation. These fears were underscored by moments of high risk: the threat of war over North Korea's pursuit of nuclear weapons; the confrontation between the international community and Iraq over the elimination of its nuclear, biological, and chemical weapons; the development of nuclear reactor and ballistic missile programs in Iran; the use of chemical and biological agents by the Aum Shinrikyo cult; and the crisis in Kashmir that followed the detonation of nuclear explosives by India and Pakistan.

This volume breaks new ground in the effort to understand the risks of proliferation. Scholars and policy analysts have long focused on nuclear proliferation, not on the full spectrum of nuclear, biological, and chemical proliferation.[1] Moreover, this literature has focused primarily on the development of theory. Scholars have developed alternative theories about whether nuclear proliferation would lead to stable deterrence or result in dangerous crises and nuclear accidents, but efforts to test these theories were limited by the severe lack of empirical information on proliferators'

---

1. For exceptions, see Steve Fetter, "Ballistic Missiles and Weapons of Mass Destruction," *International Security* 16 (Summer 1991): 5–42; Richard K. Betts, "The New Threat of Mass Destruction," *Foreign Affairs* 77 (January–February 1998): 26–41; Richard A. Falkenrath, Robert D. Newman, and Bradley Thayer, *America's Achilles' Heel: Nuclear, Biological and Chemical Terrorism and Covert Attack* (Cambridge, Mass.: MIT Press, 1998); and Lewis A. Dunn, "On Proliferation Watch," *Nonproliferation Review* 5 (Spring–Summer 1998): 59–77.

plans and policies.[2] This limitation was unfortunate but not surprising, given the novelty of the subject matter and the secrecy with which new proliferators covered their intentions. The authors of case studies in this volume, however, have performed the important and difficult task of looking behind these veils of secrecy to determine how the new military powers are planning to use and control their new nuclear, biological, and chemical weapons.

This chapter distills the insights contained in the country-specific chapters and offers our conclusions about the meaning of these findings. It first discusses military doctrine, summarizing the findings of the case studies and highlighting cross-country patterns. We next focus on the different patterns of military decision making and command and control systems. The causes of these patterns are then explored by using the three main theoretical frameworks or lenses—organization, neorealist, and strategic culture theory—outlined in Chapter 1. Finally, we offer suggestions for further scholarly analysis and discuss the policy implications of this study.

Two important themes should be noted from the start. First, there is considerable diversity in the ways in which new proliferators have thought about chemical, biological, and nuclear weapons. Indeed, the diversity in their thinking about doctrine and command and control led us to conclude that the now popular term *weapons of mass destruction* (WMD) is misleading and can have a harmful effect on the way analysts and policymakers address the proliferation puzzle. We therefore refer specifically to nuclear, biological, and chemical arms. There are important differences among these three weapons categories (and significant distinctions within them), especially in their potential lethality and destructiveness. Nuclear weapons remain unmatched in their ability to wreak vast and immediate damage. By contrast, chemical weapons are far less potentially destructive; protection and defensive measures can greatly reduce their impact on the battlefield against well-trained troops. Biological weapons fall somewhere in between. Like nuclear weapons, biological weapons threaten great destruction to unprotected military forces and civilian populations and can be thousands of times more lethal than the most deadly chemical agents. These technical differences have been recognized before. The previous chapters, however, are novel in demonstrating how the leaders of states and nonstate groups understand these distinctions and adjust their doctrines accordingly.

2. See Scott D. Sagan and Kenneth N. Waltz, *The Spread of Nuclear Weapons: A Debate* (New York: Norton, 1995); Lewis Dunn, *Containing Nuclear Proliferation*, Adelphi Paper 263 (London: International Institute for Strategic Studies, 1991); Peter R. Lavoy, "The Strategic Consequences of Nuclear Proliferation," *Security Studies* 4 (Summer 1995): 695–753.

Lewis A. Dunn, Peter R. Lavoy, and Scott D. Sagan

Second, we have also rejected the use of the common term "rogue states" because it, too, obscures reality. Although it is important not to ignore or condone the offensive ambitions of some states and their disregard for international norms and legal commitments, describing them as rogues leads many observers to conclude that the leaders of such states are irrational. For example, the rogue state label blurs the extent to which leaders such as Iraq's Saddam Hussein and North Korea's Kim Chong-il pursue carefully calculated stratagems for threatening or using nuclear, biological, or chemical weapons to achieve their political and military ambitions. The rogue label also can result in underestimating the potential to deter these states from using nuclear, biological, or chemical weapons.

One final caveat is required. The case studies draw on limited information and address a set of moving targets. Military doctrines and command and control procedures for nuclear, biological, and chemical weapons are matters that few states or nonstate groups are willing to discuss openly. These matters also are still subject to internal deliberation and change. In some states, moreover, sharp contrasts can be discerned among the views of political leaders, the technical establishment, and the armed forces. Our conclusions therefore will be subject to change as future proliferators' policies change. The evidence and frameworks presented here, however, will still offer a sound place to start in understanding future developments.

DIVERSITY OF MILITARY DOCTRINES

Our case studies reveal a diversity of emerging doctrines for the threatened or actual use of nuclear, biological, or chemical arms. In contrast to neorealist predictions, which emphasize that deterrence is the only reasonable strategy among states armed with nuclear, chemical, or biological weapons, several countries clearly view these weapons as facilitating expansive regional political and military ambitions. In other countries, nuclear weapons appear more valuable to serve domestic and international political purposes rather than to enhance military security.

At one end of the "usability" spectrum, the political-military elite in the Democratic People's Republic of Korea (DPRK) views chemical weapons as a vital force multiplier, if not the key to implementing its overall doctrine of a "one-blow, nonstop" military offensive against the Republic of Korea (ROK). For North Korea's leaders, moreover, biological and nuclear weapons serve as a shield behind which offensive military operations can be implemented. Their programs appear to be designed to deter a U.S. nuclear response to the large-scale use of chemical weapons and to blackmail potential coalition partners from supporting South Korea in resisting a North Korea attack.

Similarly, a mix of using chemical (and possibly biological) weapons in pursuit of war-fighting advantages and deterrence of outside intervention appears to be the basic strategy of Saddam Hussein's Iraq. For nonstate groups motivated by extremist religious or political objectives, such as Japan's Aum Shinrikyo cult, unconventional weapons are also attractive instruments for killing mass numbers of people or creating social chaos.

Toward the other end of the spectrum, Pakistani leaders may view nuclear weapons primarily as a means to deter Indian conventional attacks. Pakistan's 1999 military initiative in Kashmir, however, shows that some of its leaders also are tempted to use nuclear capabilities as a shield to permit more offensive conventional operations. The Iranian regime is likewise a mixed case. Political authorities in Teheran may view their chemical weapons and future nuclear option primarily in deterrent terms, but the Islamic Revolutionary Guard Corps apparently has developed more offensive plans, at least for the use of chemical weapons.

Israel's political leaders are the clearest example of statesmen who view nuclear arms as weapons of last resort. As Avner Cohen argues, Israeli leaders, at least through the 1973 Yom Kippur War, were extremely reluctant to develop operational plans for the wartime use, or even testing, of nuclear weapons. Finally, for the leaders in New Delhi, nuclear weapons are symbols of India's claim to global status and equality with China. India's politicians—both Indira Gandhi's Congress Party at the time of the first nuclear test in 1974 and the Bharatiya Janata Party of Atal Vajpayee at the time of the 1998 tests—also have viewed demonstrations of India's nuclear weapons capability as a way to enhance their domestic political standing. Given these goals, it is not surprising that Indian official nuclear use doctrine has been developed in only the most preliminary manner.

Normative concerns appear to have constrained the willingness of both Israeli and Indian elites to discuss and resolve details of nuclear doctrine and use. Political leaders who ordered the creation of Israel's nuclear infrastructure were forced in crises to start to plan for the use of nuclear weapons, only to find the exercise unpalatable, even abhorrent. Thinking about the use of nuclear weapons among India's political leaders has been constrained by their pledge of no first use of nuclear weapons, which is a legacy of India's Gandhian principles and self-ascribed claim to moral leadership on nuclear issues. How far these influences would hold in a future crisis, however, is hard to assess.

With few exceptions, neither chemical nor biological weapons policies have been subject to the same normative constraints. Jonathan Tucker and Timothy McCarthy show that Iraq's robust chemical and biological weapons programs have had payoffs for Saddam's domestic political position, his military capabilities, and his leadership in some corners of the Arab world. In Iran, the decision to acquire, and ultimately use, chemical

Lewis A. Dunn, Peter R. Lavoy, and Scott D. Sagan

weapons reflected military necessity in the face of repeated Iraqi use of chemical weapons in the Iran-Iraq War. As Gregory Giles shows, normative constraints were influential only initially, when the Ayatollah Khomeini originally opposed the production and use of chemical weapons on the grounds that such weapons were inconsistent with Islamic values and teachings.

Deterrence and Blackmail

In many countries, nuclear, biological, or chemical weapons are viewed as instruments of deterrence. But these countries differ significantly in their answers to the question, *What is to be deterred and by what threats?* Several states have a doctrine to use nuclear, biological, or chemical weapons as instruments of blackmail to support aggressive military strategies and political ambitions.

All these military doctrines could be labeled as a kind of deterrence doctrine but only if one recognizes that deterrence can take on more offensive forms and is not always intended to protect the status quo. Different countries plan to use their new unconventional weapons capabilities to deter overwhelming conventional attacks; nuclear or chemical attack or blackmail; preventive conventional strikes to disrupt their pursuit of nuclear weapons; outside military intervention in regional conflicts; and nuclear retaliation for the first use of chemical or biological weapons. Many different types of retaliatory threats also are evident: the threat of retaliation in kind for use of nuclear, biological, or chemical weapons (e.g., Iranian use of chemical weapons to retaliate against Iraqi chemical attacks); the threat of retaliation with one type of unconventional weaponry in response to use of another (e.g., Iraqi use of chemical or biological weapons in response to Israeli nuclear use or DPRK use of chemical or biological weapons in response to U.S. nuclear use); threats of nuclear first use in response to overwhelming conventional attack (Pakistan's nuclear use in response to Indian conventional attacks); and the threat to use unconventional weapons in response to preventive attacks on other unconventional weapons development programs (e.g., Iraqi or Iranian use of chemical or biological weapons in response to Israeli conventional preventive action against their nuclear, biological, or chemical weapons production or storage facilities).

Western writings tend to view deterrence as a defensive doctrine to preserve the territorial status quo and prevent military attack.[3] But the case

---

3. For an important exception that emphasizes the difficulties involved in differentiating offensive and defensive threats, see Richard K. Betts, *Nuclear Blackmail and Nuclear Balance* (Washington, D.C.: Brookings Institution, 1987).

studies show that many new actors plan to use unconventional deterrents both to support the status quo and to change it. The most clear-cut cases are Iraq and the DPRK, whose leaders view chemical and biological weapons as a shield behind which to pursue aggression against neighbors. W. P. S. Sidhu also notes, however, that some Indian officials similarly believe that India's nuclear weapons arsenal permits "hot pursuit" of Kashmiri rebels into Pakistani territory. Zafar Iqbal Cheema also relates that some Pakistani officials believe that their country's growing stockpile of nuclear weapons creates new opportunities for military or paramilitary operations to loosen India's hold over Kashmir and that these officials implemented that theory, with disastrous results, in the 1999 Kargil crisis.

It is difficult to offer generalizations, however, about whether, to what extent, and in what detail the political and military decision makers in these countries have thought through the operational requirements of deterrence. Political leaders in India and Pakistan, for example, stress their commitments to minimum deterrence postures, but, at least in the former, only a rudimentary doctrine has been developed. In contrast, the leadership of the DPRK appears to have decided that deterring the United States requires a capability to strike not only the Republic of Korea, Japan, and U.S. bases in the Pacific but also the American homeland. The leaders of several countries, including Iraq, Iran, and the DPRK, also appear to have given considerable thought to the problem of how to communicate their resolve to use various weapons and delivery systems. This has resulted in explicit declaratory policy pronouncements (e.g., by Saddam Hussein) as well as the use of military exercises (e.g., Iran) and missile test firings (e.g., the DPRK) to convey a willingness to use nuclear, biological, and chemical weapons.

With regard to the narrow issue of targeting doctrines, several different policies appear to have been adopted. Retaliation against cities, apparently with biological weapons or nuclear weapons, clearly is contemplated by North Korea and Iraq—in both cases reflecting the belief that this threat would be the most effective means to inflict pain on the United States and its coalition partners. Iraq, however, also launched Scud missiles against Israel's Dimona nuclear reactor and a suspected Israeli missile base—more traditional counterforce targets—during the 1991 Gulf War. In contrast, Iran's posture to deter Iraq's use of chemical weapons appears to rely on symmetrical uses against Iraqi battlefield formations. Indeed, during the Iran-Iraq War, Iran probably sought to avoid targeting Iraqi population centers with chemical weapons because it feared that to do so would result in Iraqi chemical attacks on Iranian cities. In a future war in South Asia, an Indian conventional military breakthrough is possible and Pakistan initially might target Indian battlefield forces with tactical nuclear weapons, but then could escalate to attack Indian cities if battlefield use failed to deter further Indian advances.

[235]

Lewis A. Dunn, Peter R. Lavoy, and Scott D. Sagan

What role counterforce plays in the doctrine and thinking of the new nuclear-armed countries is open to debate. There is no explicit evidence that any of them is contemplating pursuit of a nuclear counterforce targeting doctrine or plans to use nuclear weapons in a preventive strike to block a neighbor from acquiring nuclear, chemical, or biological weapons. The Indian military, however, did explore the possibility of using conventional weapon attacks to stop Pakistan's acquisition of nuclear weapons. Israel also used conventional attacks in 1981 to set back Iraq's nuclear weapons program.

Use in Offensive Military Operations

Several countries see biological and chemical weapons in more traditional terms as a way to enhance offensive military operations. Much like the Soviet Union in the Cold War era, Iraq and the DPRK regard the use of chemical and biological weapons as a force multiplier to support offensive operations. As Joseph Bermudez notes, a key element of the DPRK doctrine for a "one-blow, nonstop" military attack on South Korea has been the first use of chemical weapons to strike air bases, airports, key communications nodes, logistics, personnel, and urban areas. Pyongyang's war plans also might call for the offensive use of biological weapons, though concerns about the possible health effects on its own forces and citizens, as well as the greater fear of a U.S. nuclear response, could dissuade it from employing its biological arsenal. Offensive use of both chemical and biological weapons against comparable sets of targets likely figures in Iraqi military doctrine as well. Both the DPRK and Iraq probably would employ covert and overt means of delivery.

In a somewhat different vein, Iran's IRGC appears to have offensive war plans to use chemical weapons against U.S. naval forces in the Persian Gulf. The presumed Iranian objective would be to harass U.S. forces and impede their access throughout the Gulf. The use of chemical and biological weapons as weapons of mass disruption can clearly be part of an offensive strategy for nonstate groups as well. The Aum Shinrikyo cult released sarin, anthrax, and botulinum toxin to disrupt Japanese society and government so that it might take power in the ensuing chaos. As Jessica Stern notes, the Aum cult may serve as a model for some other terrorist groups who hold similar goals and similar disregard for the lives of potential victims.

By contrast, less evidence can be found of thinking about the battlefield use of nuclear weapons to support offensive military operations—at least for now. But were the DPRK to acquire greater numbers of nuclear weapons—from the one or two it might now possess—that country could well consider nuclear use on the battlefield to support offensive military operations. As states acquire larger nuclear arsenals, they may be tempted to integrate them as a tactical asset into their existing conventional force structures and war plans. Similarly, the lack of experience with terrorist use of nuclear weapons may be more the result of lack of access than lack of interest in such weaponry.

The Doctrinal Development Process

It is clear from our case studies that doctrinal preferences vary considerably among different players. India is an interesting case in point. While the civilian political elite sees nuclear weapons primarily as symbols of international prestige and tools of domestic politics, the atomic energy and civilian defense establishments envision the development and testing of those weapons as legitimizing their large budgets and demonstrating India's technical prowess. To the Indian army, nuclear weapons serve primarily as a deterrent to Pakistani nuclear use against Indian forces or cities and possibly to future Chinese aggression. The views of the Indian navy and air force are similar to those of the army but also reflect unique service biases. The August 1999 "Draft Report" on Indian nuclear doctrine tried to please all of these interests by calling for a triad of aircraft, mobile land-based missiles, and sea-based delivery systems. But when Indian nuclear doctrine is more fully developed, as budgetary limits are confronted and if military crises emerge, these contrasting political and bureaucratic preferences could produce severe tensions.

Giles's analysis of Iran's chemical weapons doctrine also reveals that different domestic groups hold different perceptions and preferences. Iran's civilian leaders and high-ranking officers in its regular military appear to think of chemical weapons as a deterrent to Iraqi use of chemical weapons in a future conflict. The IRGC, however, seems to be preparing to use chemical weapons to impede U.S. naval operations in the Gulf. As Iran expands its biological weapons program and possibly acquires nuclear weapons, similar problems with coordination among Iranian military organizations are likely to emerge.

Doctrinal learning and evolution in these states can unfold partly in response to new information about opponents' changing capabilities and plans. Instances of doctrinal evolution, however, raise the question of whether countries that recently have acquired nuclear, biological, or chemical weapons will develop relatively complex or very simple military doctrines. The answer may vary depending on the country and its domestic political characteristics and on whether nuclear, chemical, or biological weapons are involved. Two general patterns of behavior are likely. On the one hand, some states, such as Iran, Iraq, and the DPRK, have detailed plans to employ biological and chemical weapons and potentially nuclear weapons. On the other hand, another group of states, including India and Israel (at least before 1973) and possibly Pakistan, appears not to have worked out all the details of operational doctrines for its nuclear forces.

Iraq, Iran, and the DPRK have implemented fairly well-thought-out and militarily demanding operational doctrines for the use of chemical weapons. Iraqi deterrence doctrine has shown an appreciation for the need to ensure a survivable reserve force and to communicate the existence of these capabilities, the resolve to use them, and the apparent delegation of command authority in case decapitation occurs. In pursuing a chemical deterrent capability vis-à-vis Iraq, Iran appears to have mastered the operational details to use such weapons effectively on the battlefield. Somewhat differently, Iranian chemical weapons exercises show a fairly sophisticated signaling capability. There is also some evidence that during the Iran-Iraq War the most senior Iranian officials, including the Ayatollah Khomeini, were sensitive to the need not to strike Iraqi populations with chemical weapons lest that result in Iraqi chemical weapons strikes on Iranian cities.

In contrast, the apparent belief of India's civilian political leaders that nuclear weapons are essentially political status symbols and bargaining chips has meant that Indian leaders focused only on the technical requirements for stable nuclear deterrence with Pakistan after the basic decision to develop an arsenal was made. As Sidhu notes, civilian distrust of the military and the impact of normative taboos have served to reinforce the reluctance of these politicians to address complex operational matters. Operational planning has been left to the nuclear establishment and to informal activities on the part of the Indian armed services. Cohen's chapter indicates that this pattern also characterizes Israel's nuclear experience. If Israeli political leaders had confronted a true "last resort" scenario in 1973, their reluctance to contemplate in advance how nuclear weapons might be used to avert national catastrophe could well have resulted in an employment of nuclear weapons that might come too late to improve a deteriorating battlefield situation.

The limits on the information available in all these cases suggest that great caution be used in making judgments about whether and how key doctrinal matters have been addressed. This is an area of great political and military sensitivity. Considerable doctrinal development, therefore, might well be under way in some of these countries, unbeknownst to outside observers. Or such developments could be taking place in relative isolation among certain players but not others, for example, among the weapons designers or among senior military officers. At the same time, the lack of available information could indicate that little thought is being given to critical questions concerning the risks of chemical or biological weapons use, the requirements of stable deterrence, or the problems of command and control.

Whether more thinking about the unthinkable is good and less thinking is bad, however, is an open question. Many Americans are inclined to believe that more thinking about unconventional weapons is likely to result in greater restraint, a lessened likelihood of accidental or unintentional use, and greater stability. But it could be the case that more thinking will lead in some instances to a greater ability and willingness to employ these weapons effectively for offensive purposes, to arms racing based on exaggerated fears and requirements, and to less, rather than more, stability. The relationship between doctrinal complexity and stability clearly will need further analysis as more evidence comes to light about the evolving doctrines and control structures of emerging military powers.

THE MISLEADING WEAPONS OF MASS DESTRUCTION LABEL

While most discussions of weapons proliferation treat nuclear, biological, and chemical arms together as weapons of mass destruction the case studies suggest that this label is misleading. Significant differences clearly exist in the thinking and planning of these countries regarding the use of nuclear, biological, and chemical weaponry. Nearly all of these new military powers regard chemical weapons as the most usable of the so-called weapons of mass destruction, especially with regard to use on the battlefield to gain tactical military advantage. At the other end of the spectrum, nuclear weapons are viewed as the least usable in war. This may partly be due to the strength of mutual nuclear deterrence, but the cases also suggest that the global taboo against nuclear weapons use has affected doctrinal thinking (and certainly discussions of doctrinal matters), at least in India and Israel. The limited evidence that emerges from our case studies suggests that thinking about the use of biological weapons, like the destructive potential of the weaponry, stands somewhere between that on chemical weapons and nuclear weapons. On the whole, biological weapons are perceived as more risky to use for tactical advantage than chemical weaponry, less valuable than nuclear weaponry as a political symbol or bargaining chip, but potentially attractive as a strategic deterrent for countries lacking a nuclear arsenal.

The WMD label that scholars and policymakers often place on all three kinds of unconventional weaponry obscures these important differences between chemical, biological, and nuclear weapons, differences that actors in proliferant states perceive. Treating all unconventional weapons as part of a single WMD category discourages the rigorous military and technical analysis that would make it more possible to prepare for the full set of potential threats. Ignoring the differences between these weapons, for example, can encourage analysts to ignore how adversaries might use biological or chemical weapons in ways that fall below the threshold at which they would fear a nuclear response. This could lead to overconfidence in the strength of nuclear weapons as a deterrent to the use of chemical and biological weapons. Use of the WMD label also could encourage potential proliferators to acquire the more easily and cheaply developed weaponry—chemical and biological weapons—in the belief that they can deter even the strongest nuclear or conventional military power. This danger can be witnessed when leaders in proliferant nations refer to chemical and biological weapons as "poor man's atomic bombs." For example, in 1995, Hojiat o-Eslam Akbar Hashemi-Rafsanjani, then Speaker of the Iranian parliament, was explicit in this regard: "Chemical and biological weapons are poor man's atomic bombs and can easily be produced. We should at least consider them for our defense. Although the use of such weapons is inhuman, the [Iran-Iraq] war taught us that international laws are only drops of ink on paper."[4]

In short, for both analytic and policy reasons, the "weapons of mass destruction" label should be abandoned. The label obscures reality more than it helps us see clearly. And it may encourage some states to make that reality even more dangerous.

MILITARY DECISION MAKING AND COMMAND AND CONTROL

Any decision to use nuclear, chemical, or biological weapons would be a difficult one. Across the case studies, two quite different patterns of decision making appear likely to shape that choice—one highly personalistic, the other only somewhat less so. The role of the military in the decision-making process also varies, in terms of both acquisition and operations. So do the relationships among political leaders, scientists and technical authorities, and military and paramilitary organizations. These command and control procedures mirror the broader political and institutional processes in particular countries. The exceptions noted—for example, Saddam Hussein's readiness to delegate authority to use chemical weapons during the Iran-Iraq War and apparently more limited authority over biological weapons during the Gulf War—were produced by military necessity overriding political considerations.

---

4. *Mideast Mirror*, 31 January 1995, 10.

The Processes of Decision Making

Two broad patterns of decision making appear likely to shape future decisions about the threat or use of nuclear, chemical, or biological weapons. At one extreme, some leaders will make crucial military decisions on their own, limited by weak checks and balances and in some instances by no identifiable constraints at all. At the other extreme, some leaders are constrained by their decision-making system and would need considerable internal support, if not a strong consensus among political and military elites, to use unconventional weapons.

The first extreme is seen in the highly personalized Iraqi decision making about chemical and biological weapons and missile policies. In Iraq, power to order use of chemical and biological weapons essentially rests with a single "supreme leader," who is able to impose his will on all elements of the political, technical, intelligence, and military establishments. Advice on whether and how to use these weapons probably would be sought only from a handful of advisers, most of whom have close personal, family, or tribal ties with the supreme leader and few of whom gain authority from their professional expertise or bureaucratic standing. This highly centralized decision-making pattern also characterized the DPRK under Kim Il-song, and eventually could come to characterize the DPRK under Kim Chong-il. Another example is Shoko Asahara, who planned and directed the Aum Shinrikyo cult's chemical and biological attacks almost entirely on his own.

By contrast, in Israel, India, Pakistan, and Iran, the highest leader—whether political, military, or religious—might have the personal authority only to veto decisions to threaten or use nuclear, chemical, or biological weapons and in some instances might not even be the first among equals. In each case, these leaders would need to consult closely with other individuals representing influential political groupings and key technical, bureaucratic, and military institutions. At least in the democracies, even that claim to a veto authority depends ultimately on the legitimacy provided by electoral success and popular or parliamentary support.

For instance, Ayatollah Khomeini, in his role as the supreme religious authority, initially vetoed proposals from the Iranian political and defense leadership that Iran acquire chemical weapons in response to Iraq's use of these weapons. Similarly, Israel's prime minister, Golda Meir, made the final decision not to raise the matter of possible nuclear use in the war cabinet during the 1973 Yom Kippur War. Had she chosen to raise the issue, the decision on whether, how, and when to demonstrate Israel's nuclear capability would have been a collective one. Pakistan is a mixed case. During periods of military rule, there are few checks and balances on nuclear decision making. If there is a civilian government, (as existed before the October 1999 coup and may exist again in the future), then the ultimate decision for the first use of nuclear weapons likely would also be taken by some combination of the president, the prime minister, and the chief of the army staff in consultation with the separate corps commanders.

The role of the military ranges widely in use decisions and in other choices about the development and deployment of nuclear, chemical, and biological weapons. In Israel, at least before 1973, and in India up until now, the military has been virtually excluded from the nuclear decision-making process, both in peacetime and in crisis or conflict. Moreover, in neither of these countries did the professional military have a major influence over the decisions involved in developing nuclear weapons. The Iraqi armed forces also have had little influence over strategic decisions.

By contrast, there is extensive military involvement in Pakistan, Iran, and the DPRK, both in fundamental policy formulation and on more operational matters. In Pakistan, even during periods of civilian rule military leaders must be considered as the first among equals in nuclear decision making. As Cheema notes, however, after the October 1999 coup, the military government no longer required even nominal civilian approval of its decisions. Not only the regular military in Iran but also the IRGC are powerful participants in military decision making; both control missiles and chemical weapons. Finally, the tradition of overlapping organizations in the DPRK, where some individuals serve simultaneously in the Korean Peoples' Army, in the Korean Workers' Party, and in the government, blurs the distinction between military and nonmilitary participation in planning the unthinkable.

Command and Control Procedures and Processes

Information remains highly limited concerning the procedures and processes for the command and control of nuclear, chemical, and biological weapons in the cases we consider.[5] The information that does exist, however, suggests a strong preference for assertive, centralized command and control in most of these countries. Maintenance of central control has drawn little on technical measures and mirrored instead the patterns of control and authority characteristic of the broader political-social milieu.

Iraq and Iran rely heavily on parallel security structures and the infusion of political control personnel to ensure central control. The use of special

5. For earlier studies of this issue, see Peter D. Feaver, "Command and Control in Emerging Nuclear Powers," *International Security* 17 (Winter 1992–93): 160–87; Gregory F. Giles, "Safeguarding the Undeclared Nuclear Arsenals," *Washington Quarterly* 16 (Spring 1993): 173–86.

units for physical control of chemical weapons in Iraq, as well as the special role of the IRGC in guarding Iran's chemical munitions, is consistent with the reliance on such units to control domestic political opponents in both societies. Similarly, it appears that familial ties are an important component for ensuring control over North Korea's chemical weapons stockpile, as is the reliance on DPRK security agencies. In contrast, the bedrock of command and control in Israel and India is the perpetuation of long-ingrained habits of military deference to civilian authority. In these countries, it appears that warheads for unconventional weapons are not co-located with delivery vehicles in peacetime, again providing a means of assertive control.

In several cases, however, there are signs of some possible loosening of the principle of assertive, centralized control, at least over the battlefield use of chemical weapons and possibly also over biological weapons used in retaliation for nuclear attack. For instance, Iran's Revolutionary Guards appear not only to serve as instruments of control for the wider regime but also to have the potential to act independently should they so choose. In effect, this dual control created a new form of decentralized control. During the later stages of the Iran-Iraq War, Saddam Hussein predelegated the authorization to use chemical weapons. Comparable authority for the battlefield use of chemical weapons, once a basic decision to use such weapons has been made, also might be delegated to the Iranian military command and to lower-level DPRK commanders.

The evidence that during the 1991 Gulf War Saddam Hussein apparently authorized the use of biological weapons in response to a nuclear attack on Baghdad raises the most far-reaching example of a tempering of central control in response to military exigency. During and after the war, various Iraqi officials claimed that Saddam had delegated such authority to military commanders. McCarthy and Tucker provide strong evidence to be skeptical about Saddam Hussein's claim that he personally had ordered *all* military commanders to launch chemical and biological weapons at Tel Aviv in retaliation against a possible U.S. or Israeli nuclear strike against Baghdad. Still, their evidence suggests that the leader or leaders of a select unit of Iraqi special forces did hold predelegated authority to use hidden biological weapons if Saddam Hussein were killed in a nuclear strike. This suggests that when extreme conditions arise—including fears of a nuclear first strike or attacks directed at the leadership itself—even a strong preference for central control could be overtaken by other practical considerations.

The Iranian and Iraqi cases thus raise important issues about how to think about command and control problems in new states that possess nuclear, chemical, or biological weapons. The intellectual framework developed during the Cold War in the United States conceived of the command and control problem as a trade-off between reducing the risks of unauthorized use

Lewis A. Dunn, Peter R. Lavoy, and Scott D. Sagan

(if the system was too decentralized) and reducing the risk of a failure of deterrence through nuclear decapitation (if the system was too centralized). In many new proliferant states, however, the command and control problem is even more complicated. Leaders there are concerned not only about unauthorized use and decapitation but also about whether granting predelegated authority to use strategic weapons would be seen internally to signal who will be chosen in a future leadership succession. In addition, the heads of unpopular regimes may also worry about whether commanders in charge of the weapons would actually use them even in retribution for a decapitation attack on the national capital. These factors should encourage leaders to give delegated authority to use unconventional weapons only to a highly restricted set of loyal subordinates. How leaders deal with the predelegation issue in future crises will likely depend therefore on the strength of these political considerations as well as on the nature and credibility of the military decapitation threat facing the leadership.

There is an important lesson here for U.S. policy. A leader's decision to predelegate the capability and authority to use chemical or biological weapons inevitably raises the risk of unauthorized use by a lower-level commander and the danger of a mistaken "retaliation" after a false warning of an attack. Two incidents from the 1991 Gulf War illustrate the point. On 28 January 1991, the United States bombed a large ammunition bunker outside of Basrah. The resulting explosion was so large that both the Russians (using their infrared satellite monitors) and the Israelis (who were receiving downlinks from the U.S. satellites) contacted Washington to ask if U.S. forces had just detonated a nuclear weapon. On 7 February 1991, when the United States used a "Daisy Cutter" BLU-82 bomb, an SAS British commando behind the lines saw the explosion, which was so large that he announced on an open (unclassified) radio, "Sir, the blokes have just nuked Kuwait."[6]

Such incidents raise perplexing questions about U.S. military targeting practices: should the U.S. military plan attacks against an adversary's command, control, and communication capabilities, even in the midst of war? The problem also highlights one risk of the U.S. "calculated ambiguity" policy of threatening nuclear retaliation in response to biological or chemical weapons use.[7] Do such U.S. threats increase incentives for other leaders

6. Eliot A. Cohen, *Gulf War Air Power Survey*, Vol. 2, pt. 1, (Washington, D.C.: U.S. Government Printing Office, 1993) 281; "A Psy-Ops Bonanza in the Desert," ITV News Bureau, Ltd., 18 April 1991; Douglas Waller, "Secret Warriors," *Newsweek*, 19 June 1991, 24.

7. For further analysis see Scott D. Sagan, "The Commitment Trap: Why the United States Should Not Use Nuclear Threats to Deter Biological and Chemical Weapons Attacks," *International Security* 24 (Spring 2000): 85–115.

to predelegate biological or chemical weapons use authority and, if so, is the net effect of U.S. policy to raise or lower the probability that chemical or biological weapons will be used against U.S. military forces or allies? Finally, the danger of predelegation raises profound questions about future U.S. or coalition war aims against any enemy armed with chemical, biological, or nuclear weapons. On the one hand, there will be strong incentives to overthrow any such regime that attacks its neighbors. On the other hand, if U.S. or coalition war aims include the overthrow of a hostile regime, this could encourage predelegation and spasm use of such chemical, biological, and nuclear weapons as the final revenge by political leaders or military commanders who have little left to lose.

THE THEORIES EVALUATED

Chapter 1 of this book presents three alternative theories that seek to explain why and how actors develop specific types of military doctrines and command and control systems. Organization theory identifies a set of parochial military interests and biases that lead senior officers to favor offensive doctrines, preventive wars, preemptive strikes, decisive counterforce options, and delegative command systems. It also focuses attention on the special interests of the players inside weapons laboratories and scientific institutions that promote the development of increasingly advanced weapons systems. Organization theorists argue that such biases should exist in virtually all professional militaries and weapons laboratories and that these interests are likely to have strong direct or indirect effects on the development of military doctrine and command and control systems.

Realism, in contrast, focuses on the military threats to a state's national security or its more expansive national ambitions. Realists assume that actors respond with relatively high degrees of rationality to such threats and develop the doctrines and command systems best suited to counter them. Dissimilar states in similar strategic situations, therefore, should develop similar doctrines and command structures.

Finally, theories emphasizing the importance of strategic culture predict a different set of outcomes. Many cultural theorists look inside the state and argue that civilians primarily pursue domestic political ends, rather than defense and foreign policy goals. They also argue that political leaders and military officers are strongly influenced by cultural norms about what are appropriate and legitimate means to use to achieve their goals. For strategic culture theorists, political and military leaders in different states are likely to be constrained in their thinking and behavior by religious beliefs, myths and memories of their nation's historical experiences, and the degree to which they believe in emerging taboos concerning the uses of unconventional weaponry.

In short, organization theorists would predict that military officers are perfectly willing to think about the unthinkable; after all, that is their job. Parochial interests and biases of the professional military and their supporters in weapons laboratories should have a significant influence over the war plans and command systems that states develop with new strategic arsenals. Realists would predict that the highest political authorities in the state would be forced by international threats to think long and hard about the unthinkable, however reluctant they initially might be to do so. The military plans and command structures of the state should reflect reasonable choices considering the stark options available to political and military leaders facing serious threats.

Strategic culture theory suggests that when the moral or cultural norms in a state envision unconventional weapons or their use as unthinkable, doctrines and command systems will be constrained. For states or nonstate actors that lack such norms, planning for the use of such weapons could be a normal, perhaps even desirable, part of security policy. The use of chemical, biological, or nuclear weapons should be easier to contemplate and order by state leaders—such as those in Iran and the DPRK—who believe that grave injustices involving unconventional weapons have been inflicted upon their countries in past wars and crises.

How well do these theories fare against the evidence discovered in the case studies? Before each theory is addressed, two points about the nature of theory building and testing are in order. First, it is important to recognize that these three theories can predict similar outcomes and therefore can be tested or evaluated only through empirical observations about actual behavior *and* its apparent causes. In this sense, our theories have served as lenses for the case study authors: they have encouraged scholars to focus on different parts of a complex reality, examining whether the specific factors that were predicted to be important and the outcomes that were expected to flow from such factors actually exist in each case.

Second, although these theories best can be seen as competitive or alternative explanations for doctrinal and command system developments, scholars and policymakers should not assume that one theory necessarily offers the best explanation for all cases. Indeed, while our examination of how actors are planning the unthinkable does suggest that one general theoretical approach—realism—is more powerful than the others, we also find that significant exceptions do exist. The existence of these exceptions—international cases that are "outliers" in a statistical sense—is important and should be analyzed in depth, not ignored.

This finding has important implications for theory and policy. For theory, it suggests that multicausality exists in this issue area: most states develop doctrines and command systems as rational, or at least reasoned, responses to major international threats, but others do not.[8] For policymakers, this finding is both a reminder and a warning. It is a reminder that not all new military powers will behave in the same ways and adopt policies for the same reasons. It is a warning that any single undifferentiated policy that seeks to address or counter all unconventional weapons proliferation threats is unlikely to succeed.

Organization Theory: Past Constraints and Emerging Problems

At first glance, organization theory fares poorly in the case studies: military doctrines and command systems do not reflect the parochial interests and organizational biases of the professional military. This finding, however, is best understood as pointing to a necessary underlying condition that must be present for organization theory to explain doctrinal developments. Military biases and parochial organizational interests appear in most cases—as the theory predicts—but these biases were not highly influential in determining doctrinal and command and control outcomes. In three of the case studies—India, Iraq, and Israel—the military largely has been cut out of national decision-making circles concerning the potential uses and control of chemical, nuclear, and biological weapons. Political authorities in these states have been highly sensitive to problems of military influence and have tried to minimize it, at least during peacetime, by refusing to delegate responsibility for planning weapons doctrine, much less providing direct control of the weapons themselves.

There are important exceptions to this central observation. The professional military in Iran, having had its senior leadership expelled or executed after the revolution, has been docile. The IRGC, however, has fought hard to maintain its own stockpile of chemical weapons, has created its own offensive plans to use them against U.S. and coalition forces, and appears to have developed an autonomous ability to employ these weapons. From an organizational theory perspective, this is not surprising; from an international security perspective, however, it is disturbing.

The Pakistani decision-making process displays particularly troubling qualities in light of organization theory. Although full details about the May 1999 Pakistani decision to support the incursion of irregular armed forces across the Line of Control into the Kargil area are not known, the Pakistani military apparently planned and trained for the operation in the

8. By multicausality we mean the condition in which the same outcome is produced by more than one basic causal force, like a disease that has two very different etiologies. It does not refer to the normal condition in social science in which a complex variety of factors influences outcomes.

belief, following the logic of what has been called the "stability/instability paradox," that the nuclear balance between India and Pakistan permitted more offensive actions to take place with impunity in Kashmir. Indeed, even at the height of the fighting in Kargil, the Pakistani army leaders insisted that "there is no chance of the Kargil conflict leading to a full-fledged war between the two sides."[9] Reports from both India and Pakistan have suggested that Prime Minister Nawaz Sharif approved in general of the plan to cross the Line of Control but was not fully briefed on its operational details or its military implications.[10] His later statement that he recommended the pull-out of the "insurgents" from Kargil because of "his fear that India was getting ready to launch a full-scale military operation against Pakistan" certainly provides a clear contrast to the confident military assessment of the risks involved.[11]

This interpretation of the Kargil crisis as a test of the "stability/instability" paradox raises two points about civil-military relations and decision making concerning unconventional weapons. First, it suggests that professional military officers may be more likely than civilians to believe that "stable" deterrence at one level of unconventional weaponry still permits conventional attacks to take place without significant fear of escalation. This tendency could be due to either organizational biases in favor of offensive operations or to the organizational proclivity for incremental planning, which focuses attention away from the effects of current actions on contingencies covered "under the next plan." If such factors lead to military overconfidence in the ability to control escalation, it would produce an important caveat to the general argument that military officers support only decisive operations. Senior U.S. military officers, for example, all supported a conventional attack on Cuba in October 1962, telling President Kennedy that the Soviet Union would not dare counterattack in Berlin because of U.S. nuclear forces.[12] Similarly, the Pakistani military's advice to the civilian-led government that there was "no chance" of a full-fledged war with India during the Kargil crisis may reflect overconfidence in the ability of nuclear weapons to deter the Indians from attacking outside the Kargil area. Second, this interpretation also raises concerns about whether nuclear learning about the need for caution will take place after serious crises. Some observers might learn from Kargil that fears of escalation are present and powerful and therefore con-

9. Ihtasham ul Haque, "Peace Linked to Kashmir Solution," *Dawn Weekly Wire Service*, 26 June 1999.

10. See, for example, Ayaz Amir, "What Is the Political Leadership Up To?" *Dawn Weekly Wire Service*, 3 July 1999; Jason Burke, "In the Land of the Enemy," *India Today*, 12 July 1999.

11. "U.S. Involvement Essential: PM," *Dawn Weekly Wire Service*, 10 July 1999.

12. Ernest May and Philip Zelikow, *The Kennedy Tapes* (Cambridge, Mass.: Harvard University Press, 1997), 174–86.

strain the initiator of the crisis, not just the defender. Other observers might conclude, however, that weak-willed civilians backed down when they need not have made concessions. Reports that the senior officers in the Pakistani army opposed the withdrawal of the forces from Kargil and blamed the government for an unnecessary retreat do not auger well for nuclear learning preventing future crises. "People in the Army thought we were close to settling the 1971 score with India," one Pakistani officer reported after the Kargil crisis. "Before the orders for retreat came, everyone from an ordinary officer to a General officer was convinced that within the next six weeks, at least three divisions of the Indian Army would surrender or abandon the territory up to the Siachen Glacier."[13]

A subtle form of military influence also occurred in the events of May 1998 leading up to the Pakistani nuclear tests. Whatever chance there was that Prime Minister Sharif would decide not to test in response to the Indian nuclear explosions was eliminated by a false intelligence report of an imminent preventive military strike by India and Israel, which some observers believe was deliberately disseminated by Pakistani military intelligence officers who favored a test, to force the government's hand.[14] This kind of organizational behavior, a deliberate effort to manufacture a "war scare" by an out-of-control intelligence agency, raises questions about who would be in control of strategic and tactical warning information, not just the weapons themselves, in future crises or wars.

It is troubling to speculate on how such problems of intelligence and civil-military relations could influence potential uses of Pakistani nuclear weapons in a war. Given the lack of institutional checks on the power of the military in Pakistan, it is not clear whether a Pakistani prime minister or president could prevent a battlefield use, or even a larger strategic strike, if senior military leaders were convinced (even though the prime minister and president were not) that the use of nuclear weapons was required to maintain the security of the state. It also is not clear that the information on which such convictions were built would be based on objective facts or biased assessments. When a member of the military heads the Pakistani government, a situation that existed in the aftermath of the October 1999 coup, these problems will be exacerbated. Without a civilian prime minister, there will be fewer counterbalances against military biases or influence from the intelligence services in making strategic decisions.

13. Karam Khan, "COAS Trying to Eliminate 'Disquiet' among Army Ranks over Kargil Issue," News Intelligence Unit, http://www.pakdef.com/army/news8.html.

14. Barbara Crossette, "Pakistan Says India Uses False Threats to Justify Nuclear Arms," *New York Times*, 8 July 1998, A3; Anjum Niaz, "Pakistan Is Probably a Stronger Country Than Most Pakistanis Think'—U.S. Ambassador," *Dawn Magazine*, 19 July 1998.

The final example of powerful military biases is India. While it is true that Indian civilian authorities have refused to delegate control of the emerging nuclear arsenal to the military, it is because of this deep civilian lack of trust in the military that the armed services have had to plan the unthinkable on their own. The push for conventional counterforce options against Pakistani nuclear delivery systems in the 1990s, the development of preventive war studies in the early 1980s, the budgetary pressures present in the late 1990s to construct a triad of navy, army, and air force nuclear weapons, and the not so hidden military pressures for preventive strikes against Pakistan during the 1987 Brasstacks crisis all are signs that military interests and biases continue to influence nuclear decision making even in peacetime, when nuclear weapons themselves are kept firmly in civilian hands.

These examples highlight an important insight about organizational behavior. When senior political authorities act to ensure that military officers or weapons scientists do not autonomously determine weapons employment doctrine or command structures, the biases and parochial interests of such important organizational actors do not vanish. They lie dormant within the political system and can emerge later, in surprising ways, to influence weapons policy choices.

A key theoretical issue, about which we lack adequate evidence, is whether such organizational biases grow stronger during crises, when there is insufficient time for detailed civilian intervention in all aspects of operational plans and command systems, or whether civilian leaders will be able to assert or maintain tight control under pressure. Similar questions arise over the ability of political leaders to prevent military authorities from working directly with weapons development program managers to circumvent civilian authority, especially during crises. Realists are certainly right to argue that political authorities have strong incentives to maintain very strict control over unconventional weapons and ballistic missiles. The evidence cited above, however, should heighten concerns about the ability of central civilian authorities to maintain discipline over their military organizations and scientific establishments in future crises.

Realism: Rational Rogues, Reluctant Realists, and Outliers?

Realism fares the best among our theories. This is an important finding because realism was subject to a barrage of intellectual assaults in the 1990s and is not as dominant a paradigm as it was in earlier periods.[15] Our evidence, however, supports a traditional or "classical" version of realist the-

15. Ethan Kapstein, "Is Realism Dead?" *International Organization* 49 (Autumn 1995): 751–74.

ory, rather than the more structural "neorealism" developed by Kenneth Waltz and other scholars.[16]

Neorealism's assumption that states are best seen as rational, unitary actors that pursue defensive security above all other goals led Waltz and other neorealists to hold a "status-quo bias" and to argue that the spread of nuclear weapons would lead to a series of stabilizing, "countervalue" deterrent doctrines.[17] In contrast, classical realist theory assumed revisionist states exist that have strong interests in overturning the status quo, which logically would encourage the development of more offensive military doctrines. A form of realist theory that explains why some international actors pursue more ambitious goals than just their own security, narrowly defined, is necessary to explain the diversity of military doctrines we find to operate among new military powers and nonstate groups.

Our case studies nevertheless reveal strong elements of "rational" calculation behind the military doctrine in the states involved. State leaders—whether in democracies such as India and Israel, or dictatorships such as Iraq or North Korea, or mixed regimes as in Pakistan and Iran—appear to have developed the outlines of a military use doctrine with nuclear, chemical, or biological weapons to maximize the chances of achieving their goals.[18] Some of these states might well harbor ambitions that make them appear to be "rogues" in the eyes of Western policymakers, but their development of military doctrines to pursue such goals suggests that they are better regarded as rational actors rather than as either "crazy states" or "undeterrable" adversaries.[19]

---

16. See Kenneth N. Waltz, "Realist Thought and Neorealist Theory," *Journal of International Affairs* 44 (Spring 1990): 21–37; and Stephen M. Walt, *The Origins of Alliances* (Ithaca: Cornell University Press, 1987). On neoclassical realism, see Fareed Zakaria, "Realism and Domestic Politics: A Review Essay," *International Security* 17 (Summer 1992): 177–98; Randall Schweller, "Neorealism's Status Quo Bias: What Security Dilemma?" *Security Studies* 5 (Spring 1996): 90–121; Gideon Rose, "Neoclassical Realism and Theories of Foreign Policy," *World Politics* 51 (October 1998): 144–72; Jack Snyder, *Myths of Empire: Domestic Politics and International Ambition* (Ithaca: Cornell University Press, 1991).

17. See Waltz, "More May Be Better," in Sagan and Waltz, *Spread of Nuclear Weapons.*

18. Scholars must guard against assuming that they know the goals of state leaders because they can observe the behavior of these states. Our case study authors were sensitive to this issue and therefore have tried to assess the authenticity of statements such as Saddam Hussein's claims to desire leadership in the Arab world, Iran's stated security concerns about Israel (and unstated fears of Iraq), or North Korea's calls for unification. Our authors assess the doctrines against these goals rather than using the doctrines to provide an understanding of "revealed preferences."

19. See Yehezkel Dror, *Crazy States: A Counter-Conventional Strategic Problem* (Lexington, Mass.: Heath Lexington, 1971); Michael T. Klare, *Rogue States and Nuclear Outlaws: America's Search for a New Foreign Policy* (New York: Hill and Wang, 1995); Anthony Lake, "Confronting Backlash States," *Foreign Affairs* 73 (March–April 1994): 45–55; and Robert S. Litwak, *Rogue States and U.S. Foreign Policy* (Washington, D.C.: Woodrow Wilson Press, 2000).

This realist view also helps to explain Iran's development and use of chemical weapons in the 1980s and its pursuit of nuclear and biological weapons today. Although the Islamic leaders considered chemical weapons to be morally repugnant, they reluctantly accepted them into the Iranian arsenal after repeated Iraqi chemical attacks proved effective on the battlefield. Similarly, although some strategic elites in Teheran remain opposed to the development of nuclear weapons on both moral and strategic grounds, their reservations are likely to diminish in the future if Iraq's unconventional weapons threat to Iran reemerges.[20]

Empirical evidence also supports realism's prediction that state leaders will be forced to adopt some form of decentralized command and control system, for the sake of deterrence, if they face a serious risk of a decapitation attack from one or more adversaries. Although strategic culture theory would predict, for example, that Saddam Hussein would never predelegate the authority to use chemical or biological weapons to other Iraqi officials, the evidence suggests that he did, at least in a highly restricted manner. Other case studies, such as Cohen's examination of Israeli nuclear policymaking, suggest that leaders can reasonably refuse to delegate authority when they face only conventional threats, or even biological weapons threats, that do not pose serious risks of decapitation strikes.

There are, however, important exceptions. Critical aspects of the military doctrines and command and control systems of India, Iran, and Iraq do not fit easily into the realist paradigm. From a realist perspective, it is difficult to reconcile the Indian government's claim that it needs nuclear weapons to deter China (which has both conventional and nuclear superiority over India) with its simultaneous declaration that it will follow a strict policy of no first use of nuclear weapons. The logical disconnect between these two Indian government positions could suggest either that Indian leaders are highly constrained by a nuclear version of Ghandian principles of nonaggression or that their basic nuclear weapons policy is designed for purposes other than enhancing military security vis-à-vis China. Neither of these explanations, however, fits neatly into the central realist paradigm. The only explanation of this aspect of Indian nuclear doctrine that is compatible with realist expectations is that New Delhi's no-first-use declaration is a propaganda device targeted at Pakistan, which itself must rely on a policy of first nuclear use against India.

The unusual Indian approach to nuclear doctrine also is reflected in its emerging command and control systems. The Indian government remains

---

20. Peter Jones, "Iran's Threat Perceptions and Arms Control Policies," *Nonproliferation Review* 6 (Fall 1998): 39–55; Sharam Chubin, "Does Iran Want Nuclear Weapons?" *Survival* 37 (Spring 1995): 86–104.

committed to a highly assertive nuclear command and control system and refuses to place warheads on delivery systems or permit direct military involvement in nuclear command and control systems. Although this policy could maximize the safety and security of India's emerging nuclear weapons arsenal, it is not what a realist would expect, given the vulnerability of Indian territory to potential attacks from China, the stated future nuclear rival, and from Pakistan, the traditional security concern. We leave it to the reader to decide whether such a condition is reassuring or alarming or both. The policy may also be subject to rapid change: Indian command and control procedures could be altered by a reluctant New Delhi government if confronted by more threatening Pakistani or Chinese nuclear weapons deployments.

Iran also presents some puzzles for realist theory. The problem with realism in this case is less with its assumption of rationality or reasoned decisionmaking than with its *unitary actor* assumption. Unlike the other states and even the nonstate actors analyzed in this book, there is no single chemical weapons doctrine or command system in Iran. Instead, the divided responsibilities and bureaucratic power struggles between the Iranian military and the Islamic Revolutionary Guards Corps has produced a patchwork chemical warfare doctrine, with the IRGC possibly planning on its own for the first use of chemical weapons against U.S. naval forces in the Persian Gulf and the regular army planning for more defensive uses of chemical weapons. Similar lack of integration is seen in Iranian nuclear and chemical arms control policy. In April 1998, the leader of the IRGC openly criticized the Teheran government for signing the Non-Proliferation Treaty and the Chemical Weapons Convention: "Will we be able to protect the Islamic Republic from International Zionism by signing conventions to ban proliferation of chemical and atomic weapons?"[21]

Finally, realists would have no difficulty in understanding why Iraq would want unconventional weapons: Baghdad suffered disastrous defeats in the Iran-Iraq and Persian Gulf Wars and has been subjected to intrusive UNSCOM inspections and periodic U.S. and British bombing attacks since 1991. Furthermore, leaders in Baghdad must be concerned about the future of the Iranian nuclear weapons program. Indeed, the fact that the current Islamic regime in Teheran *and* the Shah's regime maintained covert nuclear weapons programs both provides another piece of evidence supporting realism and serves as a reminder that even a post-Saddam Iraq might wish to keep a nuclear option open over the long term. Yet other important aspects of Iraqi policy are more puzzling from a realist perspective. Realism does not explain why Iraq would feel compelled to try to share its chemical

21. As quoted in Jones, "Iran's Threat Perceptions," 41.

weapons capability with other Arabs, as it did in 1990. Realism does not easily explain why Iraq would continue its resistance to UN inspections in the mid-1990s rather than trying to get a "clean bill of health," having the sanctions lifted, and then starting weapons development programs anew. Realism does not easily explain why Iraqi weapons designers would place a concrete warhead on top of a Scud missile, given that the accuracy of the missile would not permit a direct hit on Israel's Dimona reactor, the intended target. And realism would not easily explain why Iraq started the two major wars under Saddam's rule that ended in military defeat and resulted in international isolation, domestic instability, and the weakening of the Iraqi state. Ironically, the problem with realism in this case may be precisely because Iraqi decision making resembles realists' common "unitary actor" assumption. As Tim McCarthy and Jonathan Tucker note, one needs to understand that Saddam Hussein's personal wishes are always implemented, even if they are based on questionable assumptions. And one needs to understand Saddam's personal ambitions, not just Iraqi security concerns, to understand the persistent offensive thrust of much of Iraqi policy.

Strategic Culture

Despite the fact that strategic culture arguments are in vogue both in policy circles and in the academic literature, our case studies provide less evidence to support such theories.[22] Most of the new military powers and non-state actors have developed employment doctrines with chemical, biological, and nuclear weapons that are designed to maximize their national or group security interests, as they envision them. It is tempting for scholars and policymakers to interpret any behavior that differs from their own as somehow a product of a "bizarre" strategic culture. The common assumption is that "we are rational, they are constrained by culture." Most of our case studies, however, find that once one understands the key strategic goals of the key actors, analysts can fairly accurately predict doctrines and command systems without having to delve deeply into broader cultural influences.[23]

22. Michael Moodie, *Chemical and Biological Weapons: Will Deterrence Work?* (Alexandria, Va.: Chemical and Biological Arms Control Institute, 1998), 31, 65; Stephen Peter Rosen, *Societies and Military Power: India and Its Armies* (Ithaca: Cornell University Press, 1996); Peter J. Katzenstein, ed., *The Culture of National Security: Norms and Identity in World Politics* (New York: Columbia University Press, 1996); Michael C. Desch, "Culture Clash: Assessing the Importance of Ideas in Security Studies," *International Security* 23 (Summer 1998): 141–70.

23. For an example of how strategic culture approaches help explain the strategic goals that motivate weapons development programs, see Peter R. Lavoy, "Nuclear Myths and the Causes of Nuclear Proliferation," *Security Studies* 2 (Spring–Summer 1993): 192–212.

As is the case with organization theory, strategic culture approaches might be most helpful in explaining anomalies that cannot be understood by realist arguments. Such anomalies can both encourage and discourage the use of unconventional weapons. On the one hand, for example, any state in a strategic condition similar to that of the DPRK—an isolated state hoping for reunification with a stronger hostile neighbor that is defended by a nuclear superpower—would be interested in developing chemical or nuclear weapons. But the possibility that many North Koreans believe that the United States used biological weapons against them during the Korean War—a belief that started as wartime propaganda but may have become embedded in strategic culture and reified in the rigid socialization of DPRK elites—could help explain the virulence of their desire for such weapons today. On the other hand, the reluctance of Israeli leaders "to think the unthinkable" in severe crises has become part of Israeli strategic culture, encouraged by the policy of "nuclear opacity."

Whether these specific cultural constraints and pressures will continue to have strong effects in the future is not clear. The leaders of the DPRK could come to hold more reasonable (and historically more accurate) beliefs about the Korean War experience.[24] Or the Iraqi threat could force Israeli leaders to plan the unthinkable in more detail, as the Tel Aviv government contemplates the use of more explicit nuclear threats to deter Iraq's biological weapons.[25]

The central lesson is that a state's strategic culture is shaped by its historical experience of military threats, but its behavior is also influenced by the magnitude and nature of the military threats it will confront in the future. As the cases of Iran and Israel remind us, cultural constraints can influence military doctrine, but they also can be overcome by extreme conditions of military necessity. Efforts to reduce the threats that leaders feel to their state's security, through arms control regimes and diplomatic initiatives, thus not only influence incentives to acquire specific kinds of weaponry. Such efforts can also encourage the strength and longevity of normative constraints even by states that have chemical, biological, or nuclear weapons by reducing the likelihood that conditions of extreme emergency, when military necessity rules, will emerge.

24. See Kathryn Weathersby, "Deceiving the Deceivers: Moscow, Beijing, Pyongyang, and the Allegations of Bacteriological Weapons Use in Korea," and Milton Leitenberg, "New Russian Evidence on the Korean War Biological Warfare Allegations," both in *Cold War International History Bulletin* (Winter 1998): 176–99.

25. See Shai Feldman, "Israeli Deterrence and the Gulf War," in *War in the Gulf: Implications for Israel*, ed. J. Alpher (Jerusalem: Jerusalem Post Press, 1992), 184–208.

CONCLUSIONS

For scholars and researchers, this book provides a set of questions and hypotheses to guide future analysis. Scholars should feel challenged to use our approach to provide more fine-grained analysis as new evidence emerges about the countries included in this volume, as well as to apply the ideas to emerging military powers and nonstate organizations not examined here, including, for example, South Africa, South Korea, China, and Islamic terrorist organizations. In addition, we hope this study will spark further debate and research on the conditions in which organizational biases and cultural norms influence both strategic thought and actual state behavior.

Scholars and policymakers alike also should be warned that unconventional weapons programs and doctrines often change—and not always for the better. On the one hand, conditions, perceptions, and personalities can change in such a fundamental way that existing nuclear, biological, and chemical weapons policies lose their attractiveness. Witness the decisions taken by Brazil, Argentina, and South Africa to abandon their nuclear weapons programs in the 1990s or the United States to terminate its biological and chemical warfare efforts many years earlier. On the other hand, circumstances can arise that make unconventional weapons more appealing. In this respect, Israel, Iran, and India appear to be much more comfortable with their own unconventional weapons programs today than they were in previous years.

Our case studies make clear the diversity of doctrines being developed by these countries. Some states developed nuclear (and possibly biological) weapons as instruments of last resort; that is, they would be employed only to prevent catastrophic military defeat threatening total national destruction. Another set of countries developed chemical, biological, and nuclear weapons to serve expansionist purposes; "deterrence" for them is a means of blackmailing neighbors and preventing intervention by outsiders. And nonstate groups that are driven by extreme religious or political aims might employ nuclear, biological, or chemical weapons simply to kill people and wreak havoc. In these rare cases, in which violence is its own reward and death is expected, even welcomed, deterrence is not a relevant concept.

At the same time, our case studies strongly suggest that references to rogue states can be dangerous and misleading. The expansionist or offensive objectives of these countries are at odds with established international norms and law. But even law-breaking states are not necessarily crazy states or unable to calculate costs and gains; rather, their cost-benefit calculations can sometimes lead them to challenge the existing international or regional political and legal order and to take aggressive actions to undermine it. As such, these states should be considered potentially deterrable, rather than clearly undeterrable. This should be an important consideration when U.S. policymakers, and others, make defense plans to deal with states that recently have acquired nuclear, biological, and chemical weapons.

In the final analysis, a central lesson of the research presented here should be the need for a mixture of humility and caution. A strong dose of humility is necessary: the diversity of the doctrines and command systems emerging in the new world disorder means that scholars and policymakers will not be able to predict, with accuracy, all the conditions and kinds of failure modes that will occur. Caution is equally necessary because the consequences of failure are so tragic. Reasonable people can and will disagree, in the coming decade, about the relative roles that missile defense and deterrence doctrines should play in efforts to cope with new proliferation threats. But they should agree that our ability to devise strong deterrents and appropriate responses should deterrence fail will be aided by more realistic and detailed appraisals of the threats we face. The decision of a future U.S. president about how to respond to a nuclear, chemical, or biological weapons attack somewhere in the world will be a monumental one. The appropriate response is more likely to be chosen if American leaders have been encouraged to contemplate the full set of options for retaliation and the long-term consequences of each well in advance of the day of decision. In short, future American political and military leaders must also think about the unthinkable: how best to respond to the next use of chemical, biological, or nuclear weapons.

Contributors

Joseph S. Bermudez Jr. is a consultant to *Jane's Intelligence Review*.

Zafar Iqbal Cheema is Professor and Chairman of the Department of Defense and Strategic Studies, Quaid-i-Azam University, Islamabad, Pakistan.

Avner Cohen is a Senior Research Fellow at the National Security Archive at George Washington University.

Lewis A. Dunn is a Corporate Vice President and Manager of the Weapons Proliferation and Strategic Planning Operation of Science Applications International Corporation. He is also a former Assistant Director of the U.S. Arms Control and Disarmament Agency and served as Ambassador to the 1985 Nuclear Non-Proliferation Treaty Review Conference.

Gregory F. Giles is an Assistant Vice President of Science Applications International Corporation and Manager of its Weapons Proliferation Analysis Division.

Peter R. Lavoy is Director for Counterproliferation Policy in the Office of the Assistant Secretary of Defense for Strategy and Threat Reduction and Assistant Professor of National Security Affairs at the Naval Postgraduate School in Monterey, California.

Timothy V. McCarthy is a Senior Analyst at the Center for Nonproliferation Studies at the Monterey Institute of International Studies. He served as a weapon inspector for the UN Special Commission on Iraq (UNSCOM).

Scott D. Sagan is Co-Director of the Center for International Security and Cooperation and Associate Professor of Political Science at Stanford University.

Waheguru Pal Singh Sidhu is the MacArthur Fellow at the Centre for International Studies and a Senior Associate Member of St. Anthony's College, Oxford University.

Jessica Stern is a Senior Fellow at the Belfer Center for Science and International Affairs, Harvard University, and an Adjunct Fellow at the Council on Foreign Relations.

Jonathan B. Tucker directs the Chemical and Biological Weapons Nonproliferation Project at the Center for Nonproliferation Studies of the Monterey Institute of International Studies.

James J. Wirtz is Associate Professor in the Department of National Security Affairs at the Naval Postgraduate School in Monterey, California.

Index

Index

Index

Index

McCarthy, Timothy, 233, 243, 254
McNamara, Robert S., 21
Mehra, S. K., 152
Meir, Golda, 117–18, 121–23, 241
Menon, Amarnath, 149
Menon, Comdr. K. R., 133
Merari, Ariel, 220
Meshkini, Ayatollah, 83
Meyer, Steven M., 44
Mian, Zia, 165
Midlarsky, Manus I., 204
Millenarian movements, 211, 214–15, 221–22
Miller, Robert, 215
Miller, Steven, 13
Millis, Walter, 41
Mirror-imaging, 17
Mishra, Brijesh, 145
Mishra, R. K., 143
Missiles
    Al-Abbas, 55
    Agni, 133, 137, 147, 149, 152, 168
    Ghauri, 167–68, 177–78
    Hatf-1, 167
    Hatf-2, 167
    Hatf-3, 167–68
    Hatf-5, 167
    Al-Hussein, 52, 54–55, 66, 70–72, 74–75
    Jericho, 117–18
    M-11, 167–68
    No-dong 1, 190, 193, 197
    Prithvi, 133, 150, 152, 155, 167
    Sagarika, 174
    Scud, 7, 82, 89–90, 93, 119, 122, 254
    Scud-B, 54–55, 70
    Shaheen-1, 167–68
    Shehab-3, 86, 90
    Silkworm, 86
    Stinger, 160
    Taep'o-dong 1, 190, 193, 196–98
    Taep'o-dong 2, 190, 193, 196–98
Missile Technology Control Regime (MTCR), 2, 161
Mitrokhin, Igor, 70
Mlyn, Eric, 11
Mobile erector-launchers (MELs), 70–71, 75, 199
Modeland, Verne, 213
Moodie, Michael, 254
Moon, John Ellis van Courtland, 34
Moran, Daniel, 8
Moravesik, Andrew, 24
Morris, Christopher W., 212
Moyano-Rasmussen, Maria, 218, 219
Mueller, John, 11, 34
Murai, Hideo, 206

Murphy, Richard, 58
Musharraf, Gen. Pervez, 144–45, 174
Mutual assured destruction (MAD), 11, 29–30
The Myth of Independence (Bhutto), 162
Myth of uniqueness, 17

Nadkarni, Adm. J. G., 153
Nagasaki, 6, 184–85
Naik, Niaz N., 143
Nair, Gen. Vijai K., 179
Nasser, Gamal Abdul, 111, 114, 116
National Alliance, 215
National Security Council (NSC)
    of Pakistan, 174
    U.S., 28, 112
Nayar, Kuldip, 135, 136, 162, 163, 165, 170
Ne'eman, Yuval, 109, 118–20
Neff, Donald, 112
Nehru, Jawaharlal, 132
Neocultural theory. *See* Strategic culture theory
Neorealism. *See* Realist theory
Netanyahu, Benjamin, 122
Newman, Robert D., 230
Niaz, Anjum, 249
Nitze, Paul, 26
Nixon, Richard, 152
Noble, Kerry, 215, 217
Non-Proliferation Treaty (NPT), 2, 6, 85, 161, 163, 225, 253
North Korea. *See* Democratic People's Republic of Korea
NSC-68, 19
Nuclear ambiguity, 111, 159, 161, 163. *See also* Nuclear weapons: opaque nuclear posture
Nuclear disarmament, 127
Nuclear nationalism, 147
Nuclear revolution, 11
Nuclear Suppliers Group, 161
Nuclear war fighting, 127, 176
Nuclear weapons, 6, 231
    alerts of, 113–14, 117–19, 170
    as national insurance policy, 109
    as national safety valve, 109
    nonintroduction pledge, 104, 115
    opaque nuclear posture, 104, 105–8, 121, 123, 171, 255
    research, development, and production of, 105–8, 110, 129, 131–32, 137, 149–50, 161–66, 179, 192–93, 225–26
    "retaliation only" posture, 128
    taboo against use of, 11, 34–35, 116, 120, 122–24, 239

[267]

Index

Cornell Studies in Security Affairs

edited by Robert J. Art Robert Jervis *and* Stephen M. Walt